JEWISH PARTICIPATION IN THE FIRE SERVICE
IN THE SECOND WORLD WAR : LAST VOICES

Also by Martin Sugarman

Fighting Back: British Jewry's Military Contribution in the Second World War

Under the Heel of Bushido: Last Voices of the Jewish POWs of the Japanese in the Second World War

We Will Remember Them: A Record of the Jews Who Died in the Armed Forces of the Crown from 1939 (with Henry Morris)

Jews in the Merchant Navy in WW2 – Last Voices

Bletchley Park: the Jewish Contribution
(with and published by Michael A Kushner)

Jewish Participation in the Fire Service in the Second World War

Last Voices

MARTIN SUGARMAN

VALLENTINE MITCHELL
LONDON • CHICAGO

First published in paper in 2023 by Vallentine Mitchell

Catalyst House,	814 N. Franklin Street,
720 Centennial Court, Centennial Park,	Chicago, Illinois
Elstree WD6 3SY, UK	60610 USA

www.vmbooks.com

First published in paper by Vallentine Mitchell in 2023
Copyright © 2016 Martin Sugarman
First published in cloth in 2016

British Library Cataloguing in Publication Data:
An entry can be found on request

ISBN 978 1 803710310 (paper)
ISBN 978 1 910383087 (ebook)

Library of Congress Cataloging in Publication Data
An entry can be found on request

All rights reserved. No part of this publication may be reproduced in any form or by any means, electronic, mechanical, photocopying, reading or otherwise, without the prior permission of Vallentine Mitchell & Co. Ltd.

I dedicate this book to my Jewish history mentor,
Sir Martin Gilbert, to whom we all owe so much.
1936–2015

And to all those Jewish members of the Fire Service and other Auxiliary Civil Defence Services, and all those of all faiths and none, who gave their lives in defence of the UK in the Second World War

לח כִּי עֲנַן יְהוָה עַל-הַמִּשְׁכָּן, יוֹמָם, וְאֵשׁ, תִּהְיֶה לַיְלָה בּוֹ--לְעֵינֵי כָל-בֵּית-יִשְׂרָאֵל, בְּכָל-מַסְעֵיהֶם. {ש}

'For the cloud of the Lord was upon the tabernacle by day, and there was fire therein by night, in the sight of all the house of Israel, throughout all their journeys.'

Exodus XL 38

'The Fire Service were the forgotten front line fighters ... heroes with grimey faces.'

Winston Churchill

Contents

List of Plates	ix
Dedications	xvii
Forewords and Messages	xviii
Prologue by Martin Sugarman	xxvi
Acknowledgements	xxviii
List of Abbreviations	xxxi
Introduction by Stephanie Maltman and Martin Sugarman	1
Roll of Honour	13

THE TESTIMONIES

1.	Bergit Braach	45
2.	Sam Chauveau	47
3.	Leonard Clements	55
4.	Harry Errington/Ehrengott, GC	57
5.	Sidney Gabriel	67
6.	Hyman Gilbert	69
7.	Joe Gilbert	71
8.	Manny Gold	73
9.	Samuel Guttenberg/Godfrey	77
10.	Sidney Hart/Hartz	83
11.	Martin Hichberger	85
12.	Renee Hurst née Gordon	87
13.	Margaret 'Peggy' Jacobs née Joseph, BEM	89
14.	Eric Kaufmann	93
15.	Sylvia Kay(e)	95
16.	Jack Krisman	97

17.	Noel Landau, BEM	101
18.	Leslie Leveson	105
19.	Ben Levinson	107
20.	Albert 'Bert' Levy	109
21.	Renee Malin née Titton	113
22.	Leonard Marks	115
23.	Hyman Mesnick	117
24.	Marie Morris née Garcia	125
25.	Ruth Myers née Carne	127
26.	Andrew Nunes Nabarro, GM	129
27.	Abraham 'Alf' Nathan	131
28.	Morris Nathan	133
29.	Rudolf Peierls	135
30.	Charles Poulsen/Paulsen	137
31.	Lou Sherman	149
32.	Reuben Wilner	153

Short Stories	157
Epilogue by Charles Poulsen	181
Record of Honour	185
The Parliamentary Documents	321
Some of those who Served	325
Appendix 1: A Note on Other Fire Units	387
Appendix 2: Aspects of Anti-Semitism	389
Appendix 3: Attitudes to Aliens	393
Addendum	395
Selected Bibliography	399
Index	401

Plates

1. Grave of Firewatcher Eric Aron.
2. Grave of Fireman Solomon Belinsky.
3. Fire Brigade Registration Card of George Leslie Cohen.
4. *Jewish Chronicle* article describing the death of George Leslie Cohen.
5. Fire Brigade Registration Card of Jacob Woolf Corby.
6. Israel Deutch, AFS.
7. Grave of Israel Deutch.
8. Fireman Hyman Feldman.
9. Grave of Firewatcher Philip Freeman.
10. Advert in *The Jewish Telegraph* (May 2013), seeking information about the family of Philip Freeman of Leeds.
11. The Gevelb cousins.
12. The war memorial at the corner of High Street and Cline Avenue, Shanklin, Isle of Wight.
13. *Jewish Chronicle*, 12 March 1943, reporting the death of David Cohen and Harry Glantzspigel.
14. The tribute from Harry Glantzspigel's Fire Brigade comrades at Marlow Road Cemetery.
15. The original grave register entry for G.E. Goldsmith.
16. Fireman Barnet Greenberg.
17. Copy of Barnet Greenberg's Fire Brigade enrolment form.
18. One of Barnet Greenberg's referee letters.
19. Letter of condolence sent by the Deputy Chief Fire Officer to Barnet Greenberg's mother in June 1941.
20. Grave of Fireman Joseph Greenberg.
21. Grave of Firewatcher Nat Greenberg.
22. Firewatcher Jacob Heiser.
23. Fireman David Lattner.
24. Memorial for Fireman David Lattner.
25. Certificate of Disposal (of a body) of Jewish Firewatcher Samuel Levy of Bristol.
26. Grave of Firewatcher Hetty Lewin.

27. The 2003 unveiling of the plaque in memory of Fireman Abraham Lewis.
28. Abraham Lewis.
29. Abraham Lewis and Hyman Benstock.
30. Talia Fox with the Star of David poppy wreath she laid in memory of her great grandfather Abraham Lewis/Bookatz, , at the Fire Brigade memorial in September 2008.
31. Memorial to Samuel Libbert.
32. *JC* article about the death of Samuel Libbert.
33. Memorial to Samuel Libbert.
34. Grave of Alexander Paul.
35. Grave of Fireman Pizer Pearl.
36. Grave of Fireman Manuel Rabinowitz.
37. The forlorn marker in place of the disintegrated headstone of Firewatcher Max Randal.
38. Memorial to Fireman Alexander Schooler.
39. Fireman Alexander Schooler.
40. Grave of Helen Sussman.
41. Firewoman Bergit Braach, later Forchhammer.
42. Firewoman Bergit Braach, later Forchhammer.
43. Station Commander Sam Chauveau.
44. Sam Chauveau in 1996 unveiling the Fireman Memorial at the Stock Exchange Building in the City of London.
45. The Sam Chauveau Room at the London Fire Brigade Museum in Southwark.
46. Leonard Clements.
47. Harry Errington/Ehrengott GC.
48. Harry Errington on the AJEX Parade in the 1990s with his GC.
49. Harry Errington at the Soho Fire Station on his 90th birthday in 2000.
50. Grave of Harry Errington.
51. The entire squad of the Rathbone Place sub-station.
52. The site of Jackson and Allum garage at 7–9 Rathbone Street, W1, as it looks in 2015.
53. Harry Errington at his 90th birthday party at Soho Fire Station in 2000.
54. Harry Errington's George Cross citation in the *London Gazette*, 5 August 1941.
55. Fireman Manny Gold.
56. Fireman Manny Gold, Standing left.
57. Fireman Manny Gold, at Royal Academy.
58. Fireman Sam Guttenberg aka Godfrey.
59. Station Officer Sidney Hart/Hartz, 3rd left, sitting.

60. Station Officer Sidney Hart Hartz.
61. Fireman Heinz Martin Hichberger.
62. Firewoman Margaret 'Peggy' Jacobs, BEM.
63. Eric Kaufman.
64. Eric Kaufman.
65. Jack Noah Krisman.
66. Fire Station Commandant Noel Landau, BEM.
67. Fire Station Commandant Noel Landau.
68. *JC* article about Noel Landau and photo.
69. Leading Fireman Leslie Leveson's Fireman and Civil Defence card issued in 1939.
70. Leading Fireman Leslie Leveson.
71. Firewoman Renee Titton.
72. Renee Titton.
73. Renee Titton.
74. Leonard Jonas Marks
75. Firewoman Maria Garcia later Morris.
76. Firewoman Ruth Carne.
77. Firewoman Ruth Carne as the then married Mrs Myers.
78. Leading Fireman Andrew Nunes Nabarro, George Medal, Portsmouth; painting by Bernard Hailstone.
79. Nabarro's photo and mention in *The War Illustrated*, 10 October 1941.
80. Abraham 'Alf' Nathan.
81. Professor Rudolf Peierls.
82. Charles Poulsen.
83. Fireman (Sir) Lou Sherman.
84. Reuben Wilner.
85. Frederick Abdela.
86. Firewatcher Richard Abraham.
87. Leonard Eliezer Abrahams.
88. Max Abrahams.
89. Fireman David Adams.
90. Alfred Adler.
91. Alfred Adler.
92. Harold (Harry) Barnett.
93. Hyman Benstock.
94. Charles Berg and Fireman Lewis Orinsky aka Ormsby.
95. Nathan Bernard Berg.
96. Firewatcher Dr Walter Berlin.
97. Woolf Bernstein.
98. Woolf Bernstein.
99. Leon Blumenkehl.

100. Leon Blumenkehl's Fire Brigade Union Card.
101. Leon Blumenkehl's Certificate of Service with the NFS.
102. Nathan Borenstein aka Renn.
103. Firewoman Doris Bluston.
104. *JC* article describing Fireman Solomon Bogush's Commendation for Gallantry.
105. Arnold Brewer.
106. Firewatcher Irmgard Broniatowski, née Fruchtzweig.
107. Gustav Bunzl.
108. Gustav Bunzl.
109. Rare copy of an apologetic letter to Gustav Bunzl from his Acting Station Officer in Cheltenham.
110. Jack Clifford aka Jacob Cohen.
111. Fireman Harry Cohen.
112. Henry/Isidore Cohen, later Henry Coe.
113. Henry/Isidore Cohen.
114. Henry/Isidore Cohen.
115. Fireman Henry/Isidore Cohen talking to Churchill during the Blitz in the film *1940; A Reminiscience*.
116. Fireman Lew Cohen.
117. Mendel Cohen.
118. Sgt Tony Copitch.
119. Jack Cramer.
120. Fireman Harry Denton.
121. Fireman Alec Deutch.
122. Firewoman Sylvia Dloogatz/Douglas, later Kaye, Northampton AFS.
123. Sylvia Dooglatz.
124. Sylvia Dooglatz.
125. Sylvia Dooglatz.
126. Despatch Rider Firewoman Renee Donn aka Glambotsky.
127. Renee Donn.
128. Renee Donn.
129. David Louis Ellis.
130. David Ellis.
131. David Ellis.
132. Sidney Enlander.
133. Philip Evans aka Even.
134. Steffi Fabian, later Elias.
135. Steffi Fabian's German membership card of the Hamburg Jewish Cultural Society.
136. The Kindertransport identity document for refugee and later Firewatcher, Daniel Falkson.
137. Firewatcher Hans Nathan Feld.

138. Rae and Larry Feldman.
139. Firewoman Betty/Betsy Fine aka Rubens.
140. Fireman Max Fox and his five serving brothers.
141. Fireman Clarence Colman 'Frank' Franklin.
142. Louis Franks.
143. Firewoman Libby Frumkin/Sacks.
144. Firewoman Zelda Gatoff, Newcastle.
145. Barnett 'Benny' Glass.
146. Alfred Bernard Gold.
147. Samuel Goldberg.
148. Barnett 'Barney' Grant.
149. Firewoman Gertie 'Gerry' Grant.
150. Fireman Philip Grossman.
151. Lawrence Isaac Halon.
152. *JC* article about the double BEM awards to Harris and Davis in early 1941.
153. Section Officer Fireman Harry Harris BEM.
154. Firewoman H. Harris, London.
155. Section Leader Oscar Edward Harris.
156. Mick 'Michael Isaac' Hart.
157. Henry 'Harry' Hart.
158. Firewatcher Georg Heim with grandson John Francken.
159. William Heiser/Hayes.
160. Philip Jacobs AFS.
161. Fireman Arthur Wolfe Joseph.
162. Leslie Kalisky.
163. Izzy 'George' Kaufman.
164. Nathaniel Kaufman.
165. Adolphus 'Alf' Kay.
166. Joe Kerbel.
167. Eva Evans later Klopstock.
168. Eva Evans.
169. Jack Jacob Korn.
170. Fireman Phillip 'Philli' Kruyer.
171. Firewoman and telephonist Nita Krotosky/Greene.
172. Benjamin Lakumsky-Isaac, later Lakum.
173. Samuel Lang in Hull.
174. Samuel Lang.
175. Fireman Myer 'Mick' Levy.
176. Fireman David Lipman's various Fire Brigade documents.
177. Barney and David Lipman.
178. Sketch of West Hampstead Fire Sub-Station by Jewish Firewoman artist, Julia Lowenthal.
179. Fireman Joshua Manches.

180. Fireman A. Marks.
181. Judith Marks aka Shaw.
182. Fireman Solomon Marks.
183. Fireman Bernard Martin.
184. Fireman Leslie Martin.
185. Fireman Leslie Miller.
186. Fireman Louis Moont with wife Joyce.
187. Louis Moont.
188. Louis Moont.
189. Manuel Nadell.
190. Edward Natali.
191. The Nissenthal family 1942–43.
192. Lewis Nyman.
193. Jack Oliver.
194. Simon Ososky/Osbourne.
195. Eric Palmer.
196. Phyllis Peters.
197. Firewoman Hazel Pearl.
198. Alexander 'Sunny' Pinner.
199. Manfred Plaut.
200. Jack Pollins.
201/202 Jack Pollins, Bushell, Hyman Benstock and S. Temple, with signed back of photograph
203. Myer Pollins.
204. Myer Pollins and Michael Kay.
205. Firewatcher Peter Prager.
206. Jack Press.
207. Barney Prever aka Brifor.
208. Barney Prever.
209. Discharge through injury/illness certificate of 199939 Driver/Fireman Jack Press aka Meyer Isaac Prachzker.
210. Doris Rath later Moritz.
211. Driver/Fireman Morris Rosenberg.
212. Jewish Firefighter Michelle Kent and her grandfather, Second World War Fireman Joseph Sack.
213. Firewoman Clare Elizabeth Salaman.
214. Fireman Michael Sampson with brother Julius.
215. Solomon Samuel.
216. Siblings Bert Segal AFS, Beulah Segal AFS and then WAAF; and Robin (Bob) Segal AFS to Army.
217. Louis Serota.
218. Philip Shalet, first left in back row.
219. David Shank.

220. First World War medals of Moshe Shertasky aka Sherrick.
221. Jack (Jacob) Joseph Shiman.
222. Jack Silver.
223. Reuben Sloan.
224. Noah (Norman) Simmons.
225. Esther Spiro, later Black.
226. Esther Spiro.
227. Fire Guard Phil Solomon aka Akivah 'Keeva' Patronovski with his son Leo.
228. City Alderman and Fire Guard organizer Woolf Solomon BEM.
229. Sylvia Spicker.
230. Isaac Speck.
231. Firewoman Eva Charlotte Sternheim aka Sternham.
232 Philip Maurice Stone with his wife.
233. Philip Maurice Stone.
234. Fireman Albert Tisman.
235. London Fireman Reuben Waxman.
236. Reuben Waxman.
237. Michael Visokle aka West.
238. Fireman brothers Nathan and Morris Weinstein.
239. Fireman Leslie Wilson.
240. David Winston.
241. Moses 'Michael' Zetter.
242. Derrick David Zimmerman.
243. Moses 'Michael' Zetter.
244. Fireguards, many Jewish, at the factory of David Matz in Manchester.
245. Tyson Street station, Manchester: Solly Lieberman, Mendel Wander and Louis Parretsky aka Parry.
246. Morris Goldstone and Arthur Geller.
247. Morris Goldstone.
248. Sonny Goodman.
249. Judd Goldberg.
250. Queen's Road sub-station, Manchester: Leslie Peters, Moe Waxman and Solly Guise.
251. Judd Goldberg.
252. Queen's Road sub-station 1940: Leslie Peters and Solly Guise.
253. Harold Basil Glaskie.
254. Whitechapel Fire Station Commercial Rd, E1.
255. The Jewish Fire Brigade at the Fohrenwald DP camp, Germany 1945–46.
256. Jewish members of the various Civil Defence branches at the Great Synagogue Duke Street.

257. Hendon Fire station with Phyllis Miller, Enid Harris/Perez, Olga Charnie and Dianne Leapman.
258. Firewoman Enid Harris said this Fireman at Hendon station was Jewish but could not recall his name.
259. A reunion of Jewish Firewomen at Sinclair House in Redbridge, on 13 January 2008.
260. Sylvia Dorff/Beer.
261. *Ilford Recorder*, 17 January 2008, about the reunion of Firewomen.

Dedications

The author wishes to sincerely thank The John S. Cohen Foundation for their generous support, without which the publication of this book would not have been possible; and remembering their relative, Fireman Israel Meyer Noble, who was wounded in action during the Second World War.

Also, David Glass, remembering Fireman Ben (Barnett) Glass

The author also sincerely thanks the following individual donors, who gave generously in the name of their relatives who were Jewish personnel in the Fire Service in the Second World War:

Elizabeth Aram, remembering Gustav Bunzl
Alan and Shirley Brown, remembering Jack Silver and David Latner
Bernard Chaplin, remembering Sidney Chaplin and Jacob Cohen/Clifford
Carl Goldberg, remembering Julius Goldberg
Dr Anthony Joseph, remembering Arthur Wolfe Joseph
Alan Klein, remembering Sidney Klein
Robert Landau, remembering Noel Landau, BEM
Michael Leaver, on behalf of The Firefighters Memorial Trust and The Worshipful Company of Firefighters
Georgina Marks and Derek Marks, remembering Jonas Leonard Marks
Barbara Newman and Sylvia Powell, remembering Morris Rosenberg
Esther and Richard Savinson, OBE, remembering Solomon Samuel
Dr Philip Wander and Daniel Wander, remembering Mendel Wander

Foreword by Richard Overy

It is a remarkable fact that the sacrifices made by the civilian population of Britain's cities during the Second World War under the hail of enemy bombs has never been fully acknowledged among the many national memorials to servicemen and servicewomen, even to the animals used in war. Yet the millions of men, women, boys and girls who volunteered to help Britain's civil defence effort ran exceptional risks and faced extraordinary hazards as they fought on the home front against the grim effects of city-bombing.

Perhaps the most challenging and dangerous of those occupations was the work of the fire services. The regular firemen, organized in local brigades, were too few to cope with the expected bombing if war broke out and their work was supplemented by an Auxiliary Fire Service set up in 1938. From 5,000 full-time firemen in 1937 the fire services expanded to 225,000 by the height of the Blitz in 1940, of whom 193,000 were volunteers in the AFS. This vast army of civilian volunteers knew the dangers they faced, but they fought with a remarkable bravery against the devastating fires, often under fire from the hail of high-explosive and incendiary bombs. Without them, the consequences of the bombing in lost lives and burned out buildings would have been very much greater than it was.

This book is a fitting tribute to one section of the British population that volunteered in large numbers for the fire service, both full-time and as part-timers. The Jewish firefighters were over-represented in the fire service of the capital, and played their part in other blitzed cities as well. In London they came forward to protect the districts they lived in in the East End – one of the main targets of German bombers – and in the north-west boroughs. They suffered more than their share of casualties as well, with 32 dead firefighters in London. Others were invalided out of the service or spent months recovering from horrific injuries or from pneumonia contracted in soaking uniforms on freezing winter nights.

The testimonies and stories reproduced here show that the construction of a 'Blitz spirit' was not a straightforward one. Jewish volunteers were subject to casual anti-Semitism from their non-Jewish colleagues, and sometimes overt hostility from those regular firemen who supported Oswald Mosley's Blackshirts. Before the Blitz started, there was often hostility from the wider public to the idea that men were sheltering from military service by opting for fire-fighting. Jewish men and women faced a double jeopardy in the fire service: not only did they face the dangers from German bombs, but they faced anti-Semitic prejudice from a public that was supposed to be fighting against Hitler's anti-Semitic Germany. The same hostility was shown to pacifists who joined the fire service as conscientious objectors. But once the bombing began, it was evident to the public that the firemen and firewomen were not shirkers at all but undertook the most arduous job there was to do on the home front. Whether Jews, 'aliens' or pacifists, prejudice slowly evaporated in the common endeavor of civil defence.

Many of the descriptions from the survivors make clear just how difficult the work of a fireman was. Holding a heavy hose that threatened all the time to tear away from your grip, surrounded by falling masonry and the crackling flames, listening out for the noise of a bomb descending close by, it is difficult to imagine a more dangerous environment. All the time the firemen coped with exhaustion, soaking wet uniforms, short of food and hot drinks, sometimes short of decent uniforms, and seldom allowed the full time off they were supposed to get. The testimonies here show examples of supreme bravery, but all of those who took part over the four years during which bombs (and later on V1s and V2s) fell on British cities displayed exceptional courage and endurance. It is clear from these accounts that the experience was remembered afterwards with the intensity it deserved.

There has long been a view of Britain's war effort as a 'People's War' in which a democratic society was tested as a whole and not just on the battlefield. There is a fundamental truth in this. The men and women whose stories make up this volume were ordinary people who would never have expected in their civilian lives to find themselves one day manning hoses or emergency telephones or fire tenders under a hail of bombs, or dragging bodies, alive and dead, from flaming buildings. The Jewish firefighters were defending their homes and districts from a regime bent on the destruction of European Jewry and they were doing so as ordinary citizens with a strong sense of community. Fighting back was difficult in the context of German-occupied Europe, but for the Jews who volunteered to combat the bombs, there was a way of fighting back. Despite the initial obstacles of prejudice and distrust, the Jewish firefighters were also fighting for a more democratic and tolerant Britain.

Richard Overy,
Professor of History, University of Exeter

Foreword by Colin Shindler

The firefighters of Irish heritage during the 9/11 attack on New York were lauded for their courage and resilience. The tragedy drew public attention to the Irish tradition of serving in the New York City Fire Department – to save the lives of others at the risk of their own. It was important to commemorate their action and sacrifice in September 2001.

These men and women were the descendants of immigrants who had fled the potato famine of the 1840s – the Great Hunger – and crossed the ocean in search of a better life. Many found it – as did their Jewish brothers and sisters – in New York. The firefighters of 2001 acted as they did because they were defending their city and helping their fellow citizens.

Over three quarters of a century ago, another community of immigrants rallied to the defence of their city. The Jews of London's East End knew that Hitler's bombs were not only directed at them and their families but at their city and at their neighbours. They served in disproportionate numbers in the broad civil defence movement – and often as firefighters and firewatchers. From the Battle of Britain through the Blitz to the dropping of V1s and V2s in 1944–45, the Jews of Whitechapel and Aldgate confronted the Nazis who had vowed to ignite London and break the will of the people.

British Jews understood only too well the threat of an imminent German invasion, following the retreat from Dunkirk and the onset of the Battle of Britain. The conflict between two major European powers was being transformed into a war of survival for the Jews.

Heydrich's appointee, Dr. Franz Six, was charged with the creation of six *einsatzgruppen* to be located in London, Manchester, Birmingham, Bristol, and Liverpool to deal with the Jews of England and Wales and one unit either in Edinburgh or in Glasgow, responsible for the Jews of Scotland. A *Jewish Chronicle* editorial summed up the fear and the determination of British Jews during the summer of 1940.

At this critical hour for mankind, let every Jew and Jewess utter a solemn vow that, come what may and whatever the trials in store, they will stand body and soul by Britain, giving all that they have, never despairing, determined that so far as they can achieve it, the crowning disaster of a desolate world under the heel of a cruel and remorseless master shall not be.

The rush to fight Hitler on the Home Front by putting out fires and rescuing the survivors from their destroyed homes was therefore central and not peripheral. It was more than a sudden responsibility. Older Jews – many of whom had immigrated from Russia and Poland – had watched the zeppelins over London during the First World War and bore witness to the destruction that they wreaked. The age of air travel had spawned the war against civilians.

Older Jews who were unable to join the armed forces therefore volunteered for the Fire Service where they could make a contribution to defeating Nazism. Some worked down the (Petticoat) Lane on the stalls, others had their businesses in the area.

According to the 1931 census, 330,000 Jews lived in Britain – of whom about a third lived in London's East End. The rise of homegrown fascism under the leadership of Oswald Mosley persuaded many Jews to join the Communist party because it was viewed as activist and determined to stand up to the acolytes of Hitler. Their Jewishness was often defined by a rejection of anglicisation and assimilation. They did not warm to the luminaries of Anglo-Jewry such as Sir Basil Henriques and Lord Bearstead who advised them to become 'Englishmen of the Jewish persuasion'. Following the battle of Cable Street in 1936, the East End of London became a bastion of the Communist Party of Great Britain (CPGB). Indeed it is estimated that approximately ten percent of Britons who fought in the international brigades in Spain were Jewish, yet Jews were only just over one half of one per cent of the population. The hypnotic embrace of Communism was broken by the Molotov–Ribbentrop pact, but for those who remained in the CPGB, many joined the Fire Service once Hitler had turned against Stalin and invaded the USSR in 1941.

Yet the Fire Service was also a microcosm of British society – and it also reflected anti-Semitism within Britain. The struggle against Hitler was not perceived generally as a struggle against anti-Semitism but primarily as one for the security of the country and the freedom of its people. As Chamberlain, himself, remarked after *Kristallnacht*: 'No doubt the Jews aren't a lovable people: I don't care about them myself, but that is not sufficient to explain the pogrom'. Some in the Fire Service found a scapegoat in 'foreign Jews' due to the unemployment, hunger and injustices of the 1930s. Others – particularly those who had seen service in the armed forces – had never met a Jew before and their views were coloured by historic stereotypes. Yet the struggle against

Nazism and the common suffering – Hitler's bombs did not distinguish between Jew and non-Jew – bridged the gap.

The firefighters of the Second World War were regarded as neither civilians nor members of the armed forces – and their story, unlike their present-day Irish-American counterparts, has been marginalised and with the passage of time forgotten. The Jewish contribution to their remarkable persistence in standing up to Hitler has also been lost in the mists of time. This book by Martin Sugarman therefore reclaims them for the twenty-first century reader. It documents their bravery and their stories during the Second World War. It reclaims those who perished from the anonymity of the grave and restores them to their rightful place in history.

It is clear that for the author of this work, this is a labour of love. The dedication is all too apparent. This book is therefore above all an act of remembrance.

These Jewish firefighters of yesterday understood the evil of the times and they acted. They did not stand aside. They did not become bystanders.

The *mishnaic* sage, Hanina ben Dosa, perceived such motivation and such determination two thousand years ago:

When one's deeds are even greater than one's knowledge, the knowledge is effective

But when one's knowledge is greater than one's deeds, the knowledge is futile

Colin Shindler
Emeritus Professor, SOAS University of London
London, September 2015

LONDON FIRE BRIGADE

An important part of the ethos of the London Fire Brigade is that its firefighters should reflect the communities they serve. So it is a great pleasure to read these compelling stories of the Jewish men and women of the Fire Brigade in London, chiefly during the Blitz, but also in towns and cities across the country throughout the war.

These are the true histories of British people in the thick of it, drawn from their local communities and going about their business in the most trying conditions. Martin Sugarman's research has been long and thorough, and the characters he mentions come alive in these pages, in engaging stories and telling photographs. Like many other Britons, they were doing a dangerous and necessary job, often under terrific bombardment. But perhaps they, more than most, had reason to recognise the deadly threat of the fascist armies across the sea.

I thank them all.

Ron Dobson
London Fire Commissioner

GREATER MANCHESTER
FIRE AND RESCUE SERVICE

I feel very honoured to have been asked to write a foreword to this important book for all kinds of reasons.

Firstly, it celebrates the courage of a lot of people – 'heroes with grimy faces' as Churchill described them, people whose self-sacrifice and bravery saved countless lives and made an enormous impact on the people of this country during some of its darkest hours.

I was born in 1960, well after the war but as a young child I still remember my parents and grandparents talking about the Blitz as if it were just yesterday, which to them it was - but to me seemed such a long time ago.

Importantly, the book celebrates and offers accounts of not just any group of people - or indeed any group of firefighters. Rather, its focus is on Jewish firefighters (firemen and firewomen) who came from all walks of life from nuclear physicists to bakers; and not only had to face the same dangers that other firefighters faced but also had to contend with fascism and anti-Semitism as well as sexism, issues that strike at the very heart of our values as a society.

It's both remarkable and inspirational that Martin Sugarman outlines tale after tale in a matter of fact - sometimes even 'humorous' – way that just covers the sensitivity almost as if it was merely an incidental dimension to the stories and didn't matter too much. But, of course it matters a lot and it adds another important layer to the history of the Fire and Rescue Service in the UK.

Such records form a truly vital component in organisational memory, because as the world moves forward to face its new threats from terrorism we must never forget some of these lessons from the past. And for all the speed of technology feels like massive change happens in just a few years, societies take a lot longer to evolve. So, we really do need reminders like Martin's stories here, to illustrate how key values such as tolerance and fairness, and courage and bravery transcend faiths and culture and that as a society - and a fire and rescue community - we really are at our best when we put boundaries aside and face our challenges together. But, as the book illustrates, we can't take that for granted

Well done Martin for such an extensive and stimulating account.

Steve McGuirk, former CFO & CEO
Greater Manchester Fire Service
CBE, QFSM, DL, MA, Ba Hons, BSC, FIFireE

Prologue

The material used in this book has been gathered over many years, from many sources, by the author and kept mostly in the Archives of the Jewish Military Museum now based at the Jewish Museum in Camden. Those who have helped I have named in the Acknowledgements or in the text, though I wish to pay especial tribute to Stephanie Maltman whose knowledge and guidance have been invaluable and whose devotion to the story of the Jewish Fire Service personnel has been both zealous and second to none.

Naturally and inevitably, when the 'call' went out for information, not everyone in the Jewish community would have seen it, try though I did to spread the word far and wide. And of course by the time I started my work on this topic, so many of the Firemen and Women, who were in most cases in their 30s when war began, had passed away. But nevertheless the research is presented here, gaps and all, as a tribute to the courage and tenacity of the Jews who served in the Fire Brigade in Britain and even abroad, in the Second World War, and as yet another example of the part played by the Anglo-Jewish community, out of proportion to our numbers in the general population, in the Civil Defence (CD) of Britain during those terrible, dark days. Indeed, my own father when on leave from Army service in the UK during the Blitz, before he went overseas, gave personal testimony to me of the many incidents he and other soldiers were sent to, in order to assist Firemen and CD workers to rescue the injured and retrieve the dead from horrific bombings and fires in London; the carnage he saw was forever imprinted on his memory.

Finally, to anticipate a question that many readers may ask, here is why I wrote this book:

> Another volunteer in east London only narrowly escaped a fight with a soldier who shouted about 'windy Yids' through the railings at the firemen, many of whom were Jewish, as they drilled in the station yard. In May 1940 the same fireman was actually asked to leave a Soho restaurant because he was in uniform, the manager

only reluctantly agreeing that he could stay. Six months later during the Blitz, still in uniform, he was given the best table, waited on by the manager personally and given his meal 'on the house' as 'nothing can be too good for a London Fireman'. [Quoted in Longmate, *How We Lived Then*, p.97; taken from an eye-witness story in *The Bells Go Down*]

If anyone reading this has further photographs of family and friends who served, and stories and anecdotes, then in the eternal hope that this publication may one day be updated, please contact me at AJEX with further details. I should add that all the photographic and text information herein has been used with the permission of the families and archives concerned.

Martin Sugarman
Hackney 2015

Prologue to Updated Edition

I am delighted to have the chance to see this book go into an updated edition in the capable hands of Vallentine Mitchell, my publisher. The subject appears to have struck a chord with the general public as well as the Jewish community and my original appeal for any omitted names, both in writing and at several talks I have given with my colleague Stephanie Maltman, resulted in us being able to add a large number of new names to both the Roll and Record of Honour especially.

I would like to dedicate this edition to my wonderful family – my wife Jane, children Gideon, Joel and Leah and grandchildren Lauryn and Lylah Sugarman, Eliora and Eila Sugarman and Polly, Mia and Benjamin Pyman. And of course to the amazing Jewish men and women who served in the Fire Service in WW2 in our nation's hour of need.

Martin Sugarman,
Hackney, 2023

Acknowledgements

Stephanie Maltman and Martin Sugarman obtained access to the wartime London Fire Brigade Registration and Record cards at their records centre in Southwark, and from the approximately 100,000 individual record cards extracted hundreds of Jewish names. We realize that using surnames – and in some cases first names – together with addresses in the East End, and occupations such as furriers and tailors, is not the ultimate proof of Jewish ethnicity, but believe that our experience and common sense ensure it has been a fairly accurate and reliable method of determining Jewish participation. These particular records also enabled the author to cross reference names given to us verbally from families and extracted from the *JC* and *ELA* as well as the LMA registers and AJEX Jewish Chaplain cards. We would like to sincerely thank the archivists of the LFB for their charm and cooperation, especially David Morris and Jenny Dugdale, and also point out that these cards were only for London and only go up to 1941. Were it possible to find records for the rest of the UK and after 1941, the numbers could be potentially hugely increased.

I would also like to thank, for their assistance, Harold Pollins of Oxford (formerly senior tutor at Ruskin College, Oxford), particularly for his work extracting the Jewish civilian deaths from the CWGC website, which can be found online[1]; the staff of the amazing Tower Hamlets Local History Library (THLHL); the editor of the *Jewish Telegraph* newspaper; the many editors of synagogue and Jewish refugee newsletters who inserted our appeal for information around Britain; the editor of the British Jewish Immigrants Association of Israel (Olei Brittania); the editor of the *Essex Jewish News*; *The AJEX Journal*; Charles Tucker of the United Synagogue Archives; the Cemetery Archivists of the Federation of Synagogues, Reform, Liberal and Sephardi Synagogue movements; Joseph John Samuels of Sheffield; Derek Fisher of Jewish Care, and especially the many correspondents from the Jewish community who wrote, telephoned and emailed the details of their relatives who served, often prompted by the indefatigable Dr Saul Issroff of the Jewish Genealogical Society of Great Britain. Thanks to them all and their huge enthusiasm.

Aside from those sources mentioned in the footnotes, I would like to thank the following individuals and organizations for their help with this book:

Staff at the Association of Ex-Servicemen and Women of the UK (AJEX) Jewish Military Museum
The AJEX Journal Editors
Arnold Greenwood of Bristol
Bob Bonner of Greater Manchester Fire Service Museum
Steve Dryden and staff at the British Library
Andrew Caplan, Royal Holloway College, London
Howard Davies at The National Archives, Kew
Carl Goldberg and Lorna Kay of Manchester
Hackney Archives Department
Melvyn Hartog and Leonard Shear of the United Synagogue
Michael Hoffman and Michael Gordon of the Jewish Genealogical Society of Great Britain
Jonathan Levine of the Hull Jewish Community
Rod Bailey and Jane Rosen of the The Imperial War Museum Archives and Photographic Archive
Isle of Wight historians Helen Thomas and Richard Smout
The Jewish Chronicle
Elizabeth Selby and staff at the Jewish Museum
Noson Kahler of the Federation of Synagogues
Harvey Kaplan of the Scottish Jewish Archives, Glasgow
Alan and Sheila Tobias of the Leeds Jewish Community
Phillipa Lester of Leeds (who scoured the West Yorkshire Archives for me)
Johnny Cohen, Arnold Lewis and Jeff Shulkind of the Liverpool Jewish Community
Staff of the London Fire Brigade Museum
Staff of the London Fire Brigade HQ, especially Jenny Dugdale and David Morris
Stephanie Maltman (*Firemen Remembered*)
Staff at the London Metropolitan Archive
Curators at The Museum of London
Staff at the Parliamentary Archives, Houses of Parliament
Harold Pollins of Oxford
Simon Ryan, Liverpool

Paul Settle and colleagues of the Firefighters Memorial Charitable Trust
Dr Freddy Shaw
Firemen at Soho Fire Station, London
Tower Hamlets Archives
Wartime News Magazine
Karen Watson of the Mass Observation Archive at the University of Sussex
Westminster Borough Archives
Kat Hubschmann and Marek Jaros at the Wiener Library
The World War Two Experience Centre, Wetherby, Yorkshire

– and also, of course, all the families who so readily and generously shared information with me about their relatives. Without them, this book could not have been written.

NOTE

1. There are several lists including Jewish civilian casualties in Stepney; and in areas outside Stepney. See website http://www.jewishgen.org/jcr-uk/static/stepney_civilians.

List of Abbreviations

AA	Anti-aircraft
AFS	Auxiliary Fire Service
AJEX	Association of Ex-Servicemen and Women of the UK
ARP	Air Raid Precautions
ARW	Air Raid Warden
ATS	Auxiliary Territorial Service (Women's Army)
BAOR	British Army on the Rhine
BEF	British Expeditionary Force
BEM	British Empire Medal
ELA	*East London Advertiser*
GC	George Cross
HAC	Honourable Artillery Company
IWM	Imperial War Museum
JC	*Jewish Chronicle*
JLB	Jewish Lads Brigade
JMM	Jewish Military Museum
KIA	Killed in Action
LFB	London Fire Brigade
LFCDA	London Fire and Civil Defence Authority
LG	*London Gazette*
LMA	London Metropolitan Archives
LOTS	London Officers Training School
NFS	National Fire Service

OTC	Officer Training Corps
RA	Royal Artillery
RF	Royal Fusiliers
RFC	Royal Flying Corps
RMLI	Royal Marine Light Infantry
RNVR	Royal Navy Volunteer Reserve
SOE	Special Operations Executive
TC	Training Centre
WIA	Wounded in Action

Introduction
Stephanie Maltman and Martin Sugarman

Before 1941, there were many types of Fire Brigades around the country, run by local councils, varying in size, equipment, methods and efficiency. Because the danger of fires from aerial bombardment was realized in the First World War, in the 1930s the government decided to take action to reorganize the Fire Services of the nation, and so in 1938, the Auxiliary Fire Service (AFS) was established to assist the regular Fire Service. The National Fire Service (NFS) was not set up until August 1941, but, by then, the AFS was already ten times their size.

By the time of the Blitz, 5,000 women had been recruited in the UK for the AFS – a first for the NFS – together with 25,000 men. The London Fire Brigade (LFB) alone had 2,500 men. A 1941 article in *The Jewish Chronicle* (JC) announced that the Womens' AFS required 1,300 more women, aged 20 to 50 years, to act as telephonists, watchroom staff, etc., at '£2 and 7 shillings (35p) per week with free uniform and certain free meals', and applications should be made to the London Fire Brigade HQ on Albert Embankment or the WAFS Training offices in Compton Terrace, Highbury.[1]

This study is an attempt to record and remember those Jewish men and women who served in the Fire Service in the Second World War, including those in related units such as Firewatchers, Fireguards and Street Fire Patrols. Not only were many of those who served in these latter organizations also killed and wounded in action, but they did crucial as well as dangerous work, exposed and vulnerable especially atop of buildings during raids while bombs were falling. Even though they were not full members of the AFS or NFS, many were, however, trained by them. During bombing, they would help spot fires and report them, but also begin the extinguishing process with sand, stirrup pumps and water buckets, in very hazardous conditions, often succeeding alone, or coping as best they could during air raids until the Fire Service arrived to take over. As the war progressed, and particularly after the devastating raid on the City of London on the night of 29 December 1940, when the consequences of their absence were only too apparent, these subsidiary units were equipped with increasingly sophisticated machinery. The importance of their positions was demonstrated by cases, often publicised in the press, where members of such units were given severe fines in court if they did not report for duty on time, a sure official indication of the crucial nature of their work.

To complicate matters, other personnel were often drafted in from unlikely places to act as Firewatchers, including regular troops.[2] Also included are those who said they did other jobs at the same time, such as Air Raid Precautions (ARP), with Firewatching duties aswell.[3]

We know that many more Jews served in Aldgate and Whitechapel (it is estimated that 85 per cent of the Civil Defence (CD) in the East End was Jewish), and in London as a whole as many as a third of CD may have been Jewish; also that at AFS substations such as Wellclose Square and Fairclough Street, as many as 90 per cent of the personnel would have been Jewish.[4] An article in the *JC* noted that there was 'a big number of Jewish ARP, AFS and other Civil Defence workers' in the Clydeside area.[5] Another described how the Revd M. Spira of Willesden Synagogue organized a service for Jewish Willesden Civil Defence workers, which included over 80 in ARP and AFS uniform as well as the Commander of the local AFS, Capt. Whiteside, who kindly attended the service but was not Jewish![6] Many of these Jewish volunteers were veterans of the First World War; others were simply too old or unfit for the military. Fire stations in north-west London too had huge Jewish contingents, such as West Hampstead and Golders Green. When using the London Fire Brigade Registration cards to identify Jewish names, a combination of first name, location, home address and occupation (tailor, furrier, shopkeeper and taxi driver, for example) made it clear that even a name such as Harris – a very popular anglicized name taken by Jewish immigrant families – would indicate the man or woman was Jewish.

Completing this task has been a question of researching in archives and obtaining evidence from surviving Firemen and women and their relatives, and accounts left by those since passed away. Fire Service records are notoriously inaccessible, have often been moved around, and those that do survive are also widespread in different archives around the country. Many have sadly been lost or destroyed and so our record will never be totally correct. Where we obtained lists, we used surnames and sometimes first names e.g. Hyman, to indicate those with a Jewish background. We know this can be unreliable as, for example, when Jewish families called Turner and Wilson contacted us to say they served, names which we as authors would never have extracted from a list as being Jewish! Nevertheless, we firmly believe the method is both justified and worthwhile, not least to show our detractors, as well as sceptics, just how many Jews served in the Fire Brigade. It may be in the end that the reality in terms of numbers of Jews who served in the Fire Service nationwide is as much as a quarter again of those we have recorded because their names have been impossible to recognize.

The author and Stephanie Maltman also became aware early on that family names would frequently crop up two or three times in the same Fire Station, a sure indication of members of the same family from the same area joining up to serve together, reminiscent of the famous 'Army Pals' battalions of the First World War. This surely reflected both the close knit nature of the local Jewish communities, and the community nature of the AFS, as well as a patriotic determination 'to do their bit'. But it could also have tragic consequences, as when the Aaron and Jacob Heiser siblings were both killed in the same incident in May 1941 (see below).

Jim Barnard, born in Lowestoft, was a senior London fireman and later Deputy Chief of Essex, who trained auxiliaries and he has testified in his memoirs that of the 400 men he trained in Whitechapel for the AFS, most were Jewish, and he remembers them with respect and affection. Many were Petticoat Lane stallholders and taxi drivers.[7] In common with other schools, the Jewish Free School (JFS) in Bell Lane in the East End was used as a fire station after the children were evacuated from London from 1940.

Very few Jews are known to have served in the Fire Service in Britain until the formation of the AFS. However, surviving records from the early days of recruitment in 1938, when war was still distant but some believed inevitable, show that many Jewish men and women were among the first to enrol.[8] It is well known that even before the outbreak of war and up to the beginning of the Blitz, there was often resentment and hostility between regular firemen and members of the AFS. What is not so clearly recognized is that Jewish AFS personnel, in addition to the normal dangers of the job, had to contend with the usual endemic anti-Semitism of the time as manifested within the Fire Service, and personal research and interviews by Stephanie Maltman also shows clearly that anti-Semitism was a constant background to life in many Fire Brigade stations and sub-stations, laced with the extra portion of British Fascist anti-Jewish propaganda that pervaded society at all levels in those days. In the same way that British Union of Fascists (BUF) members joined the military, many also joined the Fire Service;

the notorious Nazi sympathizer and convicted spy, Anna Wolkoff, who joined the AFS, is one perhaps extreme example.[9]

In his book *London's Burning*,[10] a contemporary account based on his time in the Fire Service in 1940, Maurice Richardson, the journalist and novelist, describes the anti-Semitism latent in his station and points out that it was a constant subject of discussion and often the cause of heated arguments. Many regular men and officers were recognized as Blackshirts and seemed happy, if not in some cases proud, to be so, while members of the AFS were usually allied with the opposite end of the political spectrum. In *The Bells Go Down: The Diary of a London AFS Man* published in 1942, the author,[11] who deliberately dedicates the book to 'the men of the London Fire Service and particularly to those who served east of the fire alarm at Aldgate Pump' – which clearly implies the predominantly Jewish area round Whitechapel – refers to 'N___, the Company Officer who is a Fascist. He spent a long time telling me about Mosley this morning, while I was washing down one of the taxis.'[12] Later on he adds, 'it was nice to get away from N___, strutting about in his leather boots and his specklessly clean respirator case. (I believe that the cleanliness of a respirator case could be taken as a measure of Fascist tendencies ... The cleaner the respirator case the more Fascist the wearer.'

Jim Barnard remembered being appalled when one of his fellow officers at Whitechapel bragged that he was a fully paid up member of the Blackshirts.[13] Such single-minded dedication to the humiliation of Jews could, in those with power, make life uncomfortable in practice, as in the case of Renee Donn: she remembers one of the officers on her station making her return again and again to clean the same toilets she had already cleaned because, he said, 'they had not been cleaned properly'.

Added to this was the general insecurity of working-class non-Jews who met, often for the first time, generally intelligent, capable and educated working-class Jews. Stephanie Maltman also concludes that dozens of those internationalist Left Wing Jews and non-Jews who fought in the Spanish Civil War against Franco, joined the AFS on principle as they refused at first – till Germany invaded Russia – to serve in the army of a capitalist country. Expressing such views would also have brought hostile accusations of disloyal Bolshevism against such thinking and principled Jewish volunteers. In any case there seems to have been an all too ready willingness to blame 'the Jews' for many of the pre-war social and economic difficulties that particularly affected working- and lower-middle-class families. These Jews made easy targets for Right wing agitators and George Wheeler (see Appendix 2), who was born and brought up in the East End and served as a Fire Service messenger in Bow, suggested that once men had a bit of drink inside them it was not difficult to stir them up into believing that all their ills were the fault of 'the Jews'. With such prejudice came the usual accusations, that all Jews were 'Windy Yids', that when the bombing started they would run away, and so on. Although it would seem that direct politically motivated anti-Semitism was at its most virulent in the areas where Jewish communities prevailed, Alf Breck, a non Jew who served in Penge, a small independent brigade on the borders of Kent, spoke of incidents in which Jews at his sub-station were regularly served with bacon and eggs by their non Jewish colleagues, which he defined as 'horseplay'. It would seem however, that further out of London less anti-Semitism was apparent, as indicated by Martin Hichberger who served on the outskirts of Croydon and Sylvia Kay who served in Nottingham. Neither experienced any form of anti-Semitism at all and found most people 'very kind'. In the case of Martin Hichberger, a refugee who came from Germany just before the outbreak of war, he found that it was his German origin that drew more comment than his being Jewish.

Equally interesting is the fact that from the nineteenth century through to the late 1930s it was traditional to recruit London Firemen from the ranks of ex-naval and sea-faring men, not least because several Chief Officers had been in the navy, and 'as they are taught to obey orders, and night and day watches and the uncertainty of the occupation are more similar to their former habits than those of other men of the same rank in life'.[14] If we remember that 'anti-Semitic views were then common in the officer class of the Navy',[15] then the link is not difficult to make. Conversely, Michael Wassey points out that racial stereotypes were broken down when he described how Firemen encountered the kindness of East End Jewish families who often brought them tea and sandwiches during incidents, even though they themselves were clearly poor with very little to spare.[16]

There can be no doubt from contemporary accounts and later testimonies that anti-Semitism was an issue within the Fire Service, in London at least, and that this was a reflection of the wider culture of which it was a part. Based on interviews with many who served in the armed forces it would seem that the unfamiliar circumstances, which men and women were called on to deal with and adjust to, absorbed a great many of the tensions that led to resentment and conflict at home. It may be argued therefore, that on one level the Fire Service was far from an easy option for Jews. The majority conducted themselves with dignity and forbearance and, ultimately, won the respect and affection of the men and women alongside whom they fought. Maurice Richardson wrote that, 'much of the anti-Semitism failed to survive the first month of the Blitz. The few imbeciles who said things like "I wouldn't save a _____ Yid's house from burning" learnt sense at the fires in Whitechapel.'[17] Stephen Spender who came into the Fire Service after the Blitz, summed it up well in reflecting that 'those men who had been through the worst of the Blitz seemed to have been purged in some way, and reborn into the camaraderie of the sub station'.[18]

Several contemporary accounts of the Fire Service illustrate that a common anti-Semitic jibe of the time was that Jews joined as a soft option to the Armed Forces. This unfounded accusation could be levelled at anybody, however, as many men with young families preferred to work on the Home Front if they could. In any case this absurd allegation could never be substantiated, as the higher than average enlistment into the Armed Forces of Jews per head of population shows. In any case there was a very high level of volunteering for the Fire Service from Jews in 1938, long before war was declared, supporting the well known fact that Jews a have a strong sense of public service and civic duty.

Indeed it may be argued that anti-Semitism in the Armed Forces was quite rare after basic training (many Jewish veterans have testified that once posted to and integrated into Regiments and Corps, or Squadrons and Ships, few Jews faced anti-Semitism because the overarching feeling of everyone 'being in the same boat' prevailed, especially overseas or under fire; and usually a stand up bout of fisticuffs would settle a dispute and result in respect and friendship[19]). Indeed, being in Civil Defence was doubly difficult for Jews who faced a lot of home grown anti-Semitism from active Black Shirts who were in the Fire Service, as well as the usual dangers of fighting fires under the bombs.

In addition to this, during the notorious 'Aliens' scare of 1940, there were at first purges of any foreign-born Jews who had already volunteered for the ARP, Home Guard, Fire Service and general Civil Defence units.[20] In June 1940 there were two successive removals of 'alien' Jews from the Fire Service in London and this is borne out by at least one Jewish AFS card that gives as reason for termination of duty, 'Services terminated. Alien 1.7.40', even though this individual had been twice promoted to AFS Sub Officer before the outbreak of war in 1939! These measures were later rescinded, as an item in the *JC* of 1941 stated, 'that police authorities may be prepared to relax the strict curfew restrictions (midnight to 6 a.m.) on friendly aliens so that they may volunteer for fire fighting patrols in their own districts'[21] – but stipulated that they would have to be 'in company with British men or women'. A later item noted that the Association of Jewish Refugees (AJR), in a leaflet, called upon even more Jewish refugees to sign up as

Firewatchers, 'as many had already done so'.[22] By January 1942,[23] local authorities such as Marylebone in London began to ease restrictions that required that Firewatchers and other Civil Defence workers had to be nationals of the UK, especially in the light of manpower shortages in the prosecution of the war, and so in May 1942[24] Marylebone announced that 169 Aliens had been enrolled as Fire Guards.[25]

Richard Gilbert, the grandson of Fireman Morris Lustig, wrote that his grandfather related to him how he was one of the group of LFB Firemen sent to serve in the Isle of Wight, which had become a particular Luftwaffe target as it guarded the approach to Portsmouth.[26] Morris became one of the few survivors of the notorious Shanklin bombing that killed several of his colleagues, including two fellow Jewish officers (see below). Nevertheless on his return to London, where he was asked to do a desk job, he faced unpleasant, anti-Jewish remarks from some of his colleagues, who 'complained' as to how a Jew managed to be one of the survivors of the tragic incident, despite the fact that two of those killed were Jewish.[27]

Conversely, *The Jewish Chronicle* had earlier noted that a *Kol Nidre* Service (for Yom Kippur, the most holy day in the Jewish calendar) was held by Revd S. Levy of the New Synagogue, London, at an un-named Fire Station.[28] This was, of course, with the full support of the Superintendent, there being over thirty Jewish Firemen under his command; he allowed the service to take place in the Station so the men could be on call in an emergency. In a later issue the *JC* noted that The Great Synagogue in Cheetham, Manchester, had held a service in which over 300 CD workers had attended, including AFS of course, conducted by Revd Perlmann and Rabbi Altmann, after which the congregation marched to Albert Square for the March Past the Mayor, together with other CD staff.[29]

The *East London Advertiser* also noted that Stepney's ARP Controller, Mr A.R. Beaumont, issued an order concerning the Jewish High Holydays of September 1941, saying 'a Jewish Fireguard may find a substitute should his regular turn of duty fall on any of the above stated nights [Rosh Hashanah and Yom Kippur]. If unable to find a substitute, she/he must carry out their duties as previously arranged.'[30]

Touching too was the view of Superintendent McDuell of 'C' District (which included Jewish Whitechapel and Stepney) who made the effort to discover the dates of all the Jewish Holydays in order both to plan to accommodate the needs of his mostly Jewish personnel, as well as ease his problems of constantly being asked for leave.[31]

In 1942, the Ministry of Information commissioned a film on the Fire Service, *Fires Were Started*, written by Humphrey Jennings, to especially celebrate the war work of the AFS, telling a fictitious story centred on a day and night in the life of a docklands fire crew during the Blitz, but actually filmed at Wellclose Square Station. One character was played by real-life Jewish Fireman Albert Levy (see below) and although no reference is made to the fact that he is Jewish, he very clearly is, with one remark about him 'getting the samovar going for making tea', as well as a confirmation from Jennings's assistant who was interviewed by Stephanie Maltman on the issue. It is felt that Jennings was in a subtle way telling his audience of the sacrifice Jewish Firemen were also making, and to counter some negative views about Jews from other Firemen, picked up during the making of the film and from other observers.

Sadly, the losses of Firemen and women are regarded as 'civilian' casualties by the CWGC (Commonwealth War Graves Commission) and so the graves are the responsibility of the families (though Stephanie Maltman does know of several killed in the Second World War who have CWGC headstones at Mitcham and Tooting cemeteries, before the policy changed) and so are not cared for by the Commission. However, civilian casualties of 'enemy action' are all recorded by the Commission on their website and in their Registers. Unfortunately, this means that some graves have simply disappeared, i.e. either the location is lost, or the plot is known but the headstone is totally destroyed or disintegrated (for example, see Lennick below). Also most graves that do exist rarely say they are fire service deaths; Joseph Greenberg's at East Ham is an exception. Most say simply 'killed by enemy action'.

Acts of bravery were of course recognized with awards but as in the military, they were not always fair. A current serving police officer, Bob Parker, related to us how his father Henry, a Second World War Middlesex Brigade Fireman, witnessed the courage of Fireman Greenbaum at the tragic Bounds Green Underground Station bombing on 14 October 1940. Many were trapped below ground and a local doctor managed to crawl through the rubble and reach survivors; he was later awarded a medal. However, Bob's father always told him that Greenbaum was the real hero, because, being powerfully built, he supported a large piece of wreckage on his back whilst the doctor and others crawled through his legs. His bravery and strength were never recognized.[32] Renowned reporter Ritchie Calder wrote in *The Lesson of London* of witnessing the heroism of a Jewish AFS squad 'dashing into a fire as fierce as a blast furnace, with foam sprays' during one raid.[33]

Firewoman Charlotte ('Lottie') Eva Sternheim, now Stenham, née Kohn, tells another touching tale. She was born in Hamburg on 18 December 1922 and her step-father had been a First World War hero, earning the Iron Cross before being killed on the Western Front (her mother re-married after the war). Her parents got her out to the UK but they stayed behind and sadly perished in the Holocaust.[34] After leaving Bunce Court School in Kent, she lived in great poverty in London.[35] She got a job with the Jewish Refugee Council and also volunteered as a Firewatcher on their office roof at Bloomsbury House. She later joined the NFS (in 1943) and was attached to Soho Central HQ, and was on duty in Peter Street (near Piccadilly) on a night when land mines were landing in the area. One job she had was standing on the roof tops with a senior officer in Rupert Street, to monitor the number of V1 and V2s and where in London they were landing and exploding.

Having come as a Jewish refugee to Britain, she knew from letters and Red Cross notes from her parents (which she received up until 1941–42) that her Christian former primary school teacher in Germany had tried to help her parents before they were deported to their deaths in Minsk. After the war, Charlotte asked a friend who was stationed in the British Army in Hamburg to trace the teacher, who had been imprisoned by the Nazis for associating with Jews, and was ill and in dire poverty by 1945. The friend found the teacher and despite her situation, the woman had hidden and kept family photos for Charlotte, which she passed to the friend to bring to England. Charlotte, knowing of conditions in Germany at the time, immediately cut the buttons off her Firewoman great coat and sent it to the former teacher. She also later sent her food parcels. The teacher was eternally grateful and they met soon after and remained friends till the teacher died some years ago. Thus a British Jewish Firewoman's coat helped a German Righteous Gentile.

It should also be noted that dozens of Jewish women served in the Palestine Mandate Auxiliary Fire Service in the Second World War and there are photos in archives in the USA and Israel illustrating this.[36]

NOTES

1. *JC*, 25 April 1941, p.6.
2. Helen Fry points out in *The King's Most Loyal Enemy Aliens* (Stroud: Sutton Publishing, 2007) that the whole of 87 Pioneer Company, over 200 men, were drafted in as Firewatchers in March 1941 in Liverpool. These included the German Jewish refugees Colin Anson aka Ascher and Karl Billman aka Bartlett, who later served in the famous No.3 ('Jewish') troop, No.10 Commando. Virtually all of 87 Company were Jewish.
3. So far as the author is aware, no official lists of Firewatchers has survived and so information has come only from newspapers and family contacts; nevertheless it still gives us a picture of the large number of Jewish volunteers in this service.
4. From research and a talk by Stephanie Maltman.
5. *JC*, 18 April 1941, p.12.

6. *JC*, 10 January 1941, p.11.
7. Using Jewish taxi drivers, especially in London, to drive their taxis as towing vehicles and as fire engine drivers, was common, as they of course had 'the knowledge' of the speediest routes to take to fires, particularly in the blackout and when thoroughfares were blocked by debris and alternative ways had to be found.
8. London Metropolitan Archives LFB Registers LFB/WAR/4 series references and the London Fire Brigade Registration and Record cards kept at the LFB HQ in Union Street Southwark.
9. A photo of Anna Wolkoff in AFS uniform can be seen on her Wikipedia page. Another character was Adelbert H. Krugolski a London Fireman detained by MI5 in October 1939 as a suspected Nazi sympathiser. He was British by birth but with a German mother he lived most of his life in Germany, and had been leader of the Hitler Youth branch in England. He was later released as 'harmless' and there is a file on him in The National Archives, Kew (TNA) (see A.W. Brian Simpson, *In the Highest Degree Odious: Detention Without Trial in Wartime Britain* [Oxford: Clarendon Press, 1992], p.74). Yet another prominent Fascist serving in the Fire Brigade was Brigadier R.D. Blakeney (ibid., pp.116–17).
10. Maurice Richardson, *London's Burning* (London: Robert Hale, 1941). The film *Fires Were Started* is based on this work. See Appendix 2.
11. Tom Black, *The Bells Go Down: The Diary of a London AFS Man* (London: Methuen, 1942), p.35.
12. Ibid., p.9.
13. Interview with S. Maltman, 1 March 2006 – see Appendix 2.
14. Sally Holloway, *Courage High; a History of Firefighting in London* (London: HMSO, 1992), p.46.
15. Simpson, *In the Highest Degree Odious*, pp.219–20.
16. Michael Wassey, *Ordeal by Fire* (London: Secker and Warburg, 1941).
17. Richardson, *London's Burning*.
18. Stephen Spender, *World Within World* (London: Hamish Hamilton, 1951), pp.270–1. Though not connected to any anti-Semitism in the Fire Service, another of Stephen Spender's experiences illustrates the racism prevalent in the UK at the time when Spender was serving. Anti-Semitism pervaded all classes and institutions in 1900–50s Britain, and Spender (who had fought against Franco in the Spanish Civil War) describes one vivid and ugly example. He was invited to dine in 1940 in the Dorchester Hotel suite of Emerald, Lady Cunard, socialite and plutocrat, who admired his work. A fellow guest was Sir Joseph Addison, former British Minister in Prague, who boasted that he had succeeded that day in preventing his Club (The Travellers) in electing as a member 'a dirty little Czech Jew', by threatening to resign. Spender, a Socialist Byron, was trying to formulate a witticism to express his disgust, but decided simply to get up and leave; he said he had to return on the Underground to duty at his Fire Station. Addison quipped, 'Well, I hoped you're not crushed to death by a crowd of Yids'. Next morning Cunard telephoned Spender to say that she thought he was right to leave; she did not, however, invite him to dine ever again. Quoted in Matthew Sweet, *The West End Front; the Wartime Secrets of London's Grand Hotels* (London: Faber and Faber, 2011), pp.96–7, and taken from Stephen Spender ,'Waiting for the Bombers', *The Guardian*, 11 February 1989.
19. Many Jewish men had been boxers in their youth clubs and could give good account of themselves in any 'discussion'.
20. See *JC*, 24 May 1940, p.17, and Appendix 3.
21. *JC*, 24 January 1941, p.5.
22. *JC*, 3 October 1941, p.4.
23. *JC*, 9 January 1942, p.9.
24. *JC*, 1 May 1942, p.5.
25. There was an intense debate by letter on the subject of employing 'Aliens' between the Home Office and Foreign Office during this period and with the various Refugee

Associations and Overseas Allied and Neutral Legations, particularly with regard to Firewatching and Fireguard duties; those interested can see TNA files HO207/103 and HO 186/834, for example.
26. Email to author 12 August 2007.
27. Morris had left the mess hall to get some kierchels (Jewish style biscuits sent by his sister Ginnie from London) to share with his fellow Firemen. By pure chance, it was while he was out of the room that the bomb fell, killing his friends.
28. *JC*, 25 October 1940, p.14.
29. *JC*, 20 November 1942, p.10.
30. *East London Advertiser*, 27 September 1941, p.1.
31. Stephanie Maltman interview with McDuell's son.
32. Bob Parker wrote to the author, 'When I was a little boy in the 1950s I lived in Myddleton Road, Wood Green where my father was a Fire Station Officer. One Sunday afternoon we were playing football in the street and along came a man called Aubrey Greenbaum, in his thirties, who had learning difficulties. He lived alone with his mum Naomi in the same road and he liked to play football with us. On the corner was an old street Fire Alarm, and we dared Aubrey to call the Fire Brigade and then hid round the corner. To my horror it was my father who turned up with the Fire crew, but we were surprised when my father spoke very kindly to Aubrey and then sent him on his way. I got a huge telling off and when I later asked my father why he had been so kind to Aubrey, he told me about Aubrey's late dad's exploits during the war as a brave fireman at the Bounds Green underground station incident.'
33. Ritchie Calder, *The Lesson of London* (London: Secker and Warburg, 1941).
34. For Charlotte's full and moving story of her life in the UK, see IWM taped interview 17232 and her testimony at the Wiener Library.
35. At one point she was so desperate, she asked the Home Office to be interned so she would at least have regular food and shelter. They refused because she was low risk as a possible spy.
36. *JC*, 17 October 1941, p.22 and 31 October 1941, p.18. One was Marynra Znamirowska aka Chatteron, *Guardian* obituary 23 March 2010.

Roll of Honour

Introduction

The sources for compiling this introduction and Roll of Honour include back issues of *The Jewish Chronicle* and the *East London Advertiser*, personal correspondence from relatives in the files of the Jewish Military Museum, the CWGC website (Civilian Losses), and some secondary sources such as Cyril Demarne *The London Blitz: A Fireman's Tale*;[1] Cyril Demarne, *Our Girls*;[2] John Astor, *When Sirens Sounded: An Account of Air Raid Precautions in Printing House Square 1937 to 1945* (London: Office of the Times, 1949); Barry Hollis, *37 Fire Forces: Fire and Rescue, S.E. London, 1941–46*;[3] AFS records at the London Fire Brigade Museum/Records Office; the London Metropolitan Archives (LMA); and Fire Brigade records/registers at the London Fire Brigade HQ in Southwark. The Sheffield firemen are named on their synagogue memorial, possibly the only synagogue memorial in the UK to do this. AJEX Jewish Military Museum archives contain a 1940 Fireman's helmet and axe, NFS and AFS badges, original documents and also many photographs of Jewish personnel and many personal testimonies.

The detail on many of those killed can also be found on the Commonwealth War Graves Commission (CWGC) website, www.cwgc.org.uk, civilian section. Extra information came from searching their Fire Brigade Record Cards and a file at the London Metropolitan Archives (LMA) FB WAR/1/177. The graves of some casualties can be found on the United Synagogue graves website. Please note that East Ham cemetery is known as Marlow Road Cemetery. All listed are Firemen/women unless stated otherwise as Firewatchers or Fireguards.

The place of burial where known is given, but despite extensive enquiries and searches by the author, the graves of some of these men and women have not been located.

The casualties include one set of brothers, Heiser, (who were Firewatchers) and two other sets, one of whom died in the Merchant Navy (Millet) and the brother of Hyman Feldman (Louis) who died as a POW of the Japanese.

Note too that many Firemen and women were in the AFS from 1938, but left by 1940–41 as they were 'called to the colours' or suffered ill health owing to wartime bombings. Many were in their late 30s and early 40s.

It is important to note that of the approximately 400 Firemen/women killed in London in WW2, thirty-two were Jewish (8 per cent); yet of the 8.6 million population of London in 1939, only 150,000 were Jewish (1.7 per cent). This astonishing sacrifice – sad but glorious – shows that Jewish fire-fighters were in the forefront of the war and their sacrifice was over four times what would be statistically predicted in proportion to the population of London.

Awards in the Record of Honour are given in bold type;[4] *JC* is *The Jewish Chronicle*; *ELA* is the *East London Advertiser*; b. is buried; WiA is 'wounded in action'; ARP is Air Raid Precautions; St. means Station as in Fire Station; ranks and numbers, where known, are included. If no other description accompanies a name, then the person was in the AFS or NFS. Women have been listed under their single names if they were not married at the time of service.

The Roll of Honour – those Killed in Action or on Active Service, with date of death

George Isaac Abrahams, Firewatcher, husband of Mary, 38 York Street, Northam; Southampton 25/2/43.

Isaac Amiel – Firewatcher (tobacconist) Mile End aged 59, husband of Mary, 154 Mile End Road, killed at 206 Mile End Road on 10/5/41 – b. Edmonton Jewish cemetery, grave V-75-20.

Joseph Applebaum, Firewatcher killed 20/2/42 aged 42, husband of Sophie, buried Rainham Jewish cemetery grave A1-26-29

David/Davis Appleby, born 10/5/07, metal dealer, KIA aged 33 years 14/11/40 at AFS Station Invicta Road School, Blackheath, when a

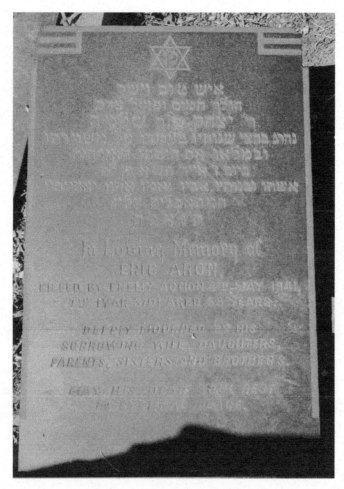

1. Grave of Firewatcher Eric Aron, buried in Liverpool.

landmine landed nearby; husband of N. Appleby, 432 Bancroft Road, Mile End; b. 19/11/40 East Ham cemetery, grave O-20-643.

Eric Aronowsky/Aron, Firewatcher, aged 38, husband of Estelle, 64 Childwall Valley Road, died of injuries at David Lewis Northern Hospital, Taggart Avenue, Liverpool, 4/5/41; b. Long Lane cemetery, grave N8.

Solomon Belinsky, WIA 15/3/41, wounds inflicted at Leeds Museum, Leeds but died at Leeds Infirmary 1/4/41, aged 43. Husband of Rachel of 19 St Alban's Mount, Harehills, Leeds. Left wife and children. Buried New Farnley Jewish cemetery, grave 1-1-4.

2. Grave of Fireman Solomon Belinsky, buried in Leeds.

Simon Berkon, aged 31, of 95 Manchester Road, Chorlton-cum-Hardy, son of Barnet and Dora of 45 Manchester Road, husband of Sadie, injured at Oxford Rd/High St Crossing, AFS Despatch Rider, died at Manchester Royal Infirmary, Manchester, 2/11/40; b. Blakeley Jewish cemetery, grave 5797-E293.

Louis Black, Firewatcher, aged 49, of 13 Parkfield Drive, Hull, husband of Hettie, father of Norman and Stella, killed at 78, Regent Street, 8/5/41; b. Delhi Street cemetery, grave 44N.

George William Blumson, Firewatcher, KIA 10/5/41, son of Mr and Mrs George John Blumson of 147 Vallance Road, died corner of Whitechapel Rd/Vallance Road, aged 15 years, possibly the youngest Jewish casualty (if Coster was not Jewish – see below); of Jewish origin.

Louis Brilleslyper, Firewatcher, son of Rebecca, KIA 10/5/41, of 45 Chadwick Road, Leytonstone; killed at 336 Mile End Road, aged 46; b. Marlow Road cemetery, grave I-6-377.

Abraham Carason, Firewatcher, aged 55, husband of Eva, 54 Rice Lane, Liverpool, 8/5/41 died at 1 Caernarvon Road (TBC if Jewish?).

David Cohen, aged 35, of 7 Grove Road Edgware, son of Mr and Mrs M. Cohen of Strangs Farm, Finstock, Oxon., died 3/1/43 at NFS Station, Landguard Road (Gloucester Hotel) Shanklin, Isle of Wight, alongside Glantzspigel. US and Federation cannot find his grave. His name is on the war memorial at Shanklin, Isle of Wight. HO 192/1568 file map at TNA says it was a low level attack with a 25lb bomb, dropped at 1628 hrs (one of four dropped on Shanklin) at the NFS HQ on the corner of Landguard and Collingwood Road.

George Leslie Cohen, born 24/10/13, of 74 South Lodge, Circus Rd, St John's Wood, London; stalwart of Maccabi sports, builders merchant, only son of Mr and Mrs Lionel Cohen, served West Hampstead Station (death aged 29 in service 19/3/43, buried 21/3/43, announced in *JC* 2/4/43, but not on CWGC site or Fire Service memorial); b. Willesden cemetery, grave P-1-12. (Death Certificate may show death through illness but still on active service. Fire Brigade

3. Fire Brigade Registration Card of George Leslie Cohen, proving his service; he was killed 19 March 1943 and buried at Willesden Jewish Cemetery.

MR. GEORGE LESLIE COHEN

Mr. George Leslie Cohen, who has died at the age of 29, was a member of the N.F.S. since the outbreak of war, and was held in high esteem in that service. He was the organiser of sports for the N.W London Region. Mr. Cohen held office at the Maccabi and won many trophies in boxing and swimming tournaments.

In a tribute, Rabbi Harris Swift, of the St. John's Wood Synagogue, writes that " in the passing of Mr. Cohen young Jewry has suffered a grievous loss." He was the only son of Mr. Lionel L. Cohen (Warden of that Synagogue and Vice-President of the Shechita Board) and Mrs. Cohen.

4. *Jewish Chronicle* article describing the death of George Leslie Cohen.

archivists are aware of this case. Grave gives no further detail; he has a London Fire Brigade card.)

Isaac Cohen, Firewatcher and retired draper, aged 65, of 59 Earle Rd, Wavertree, Liverpool, husband of the late Edith Cohen, injured 3/5/41 at Earle Road, died Rainhill Hospital 3/6/41; b. in the Jewish section of West Derby cemetery, Lowerhouse Lane, Liverpool, plot 2, grave 101.

Monty Cohen, Firewatcher, Stepney (no further information).

Simon Cohen, born 9/5/13, warehouseman, of 57 Cleveleys Rd, husband of Elizabeth, died of illness 11/8/40 aged 27 whilst serving in NFS; b. Marlow Road cemetery, grave N-20-630. Possibly first Jewish Fireman killed as he died on active service.

Jacob Woolf(e) Corby, born 21/12/11, music teacher, son of David and Polly, 12 Well Street, Hackney, of Kingsland Station (38), died 25/9/40 aged 28 at Lamb Lane; b. Marlow Road cemetery, grave O-12-368. His sister Hilda was also in the Fire Service.

[Form image: Fire Brigade Registration Card, A.F.S. 12, No. 2696]

NAME: CORBY Jacob Woolf
ADDRESS Home— 12 Well St, Hackney E.9
Business— Same
Date of birth: 21.12.11
OCCUPATION: Teacher of Music
Initial Training Date commenced: 3.10.38
Date completed: 21 JUN 1939
Stations Appointed to: 38 Kingsland
Killed by enemy action off duty, No. 243, 25...9...40

5. Fire Brigade Registration Card of Jacob Woolf Corby, showing he was killed 25 September 1940; he was buried at Marlow Road Jewish Cemetery.

Albert Victor Coster, Firewatcher and unofficial Volunteer Fireman, aged 14 years (poss. youngest Jewish casualty), son of Harry and Alice of 70 Sheridan Street, E1, nephew of J. Marks and Joseph Harris, KIA at 71, Sutton Street, 9/4/43; b. Manor Park cemetery with officiating vicar – TBC if Jewish or of Jewish origin. Not on CWGC site as death was attributable to an ordinary domestic fire and not enemy action, even though he was firefighting in the Blitz period as a 12 year old. Search for grave unsuccessful.

Harry Coster, age 53, son of Benjamin and Esther, husband of Lily, of 42 Dalkeith Road, killed at Dalkeith Road, Camberwell 3/12/42 (grave says 1943?); b. Willesden cemetery, grave GX-3-133.

Israel Deutsch/Deutch (incorrectly spelt as Isreal, on the memorial but will be corrected in due course), cabinet maker/shoe dealer, husband of Frances, who lived in Richmond Rd, Hackney and 26 Clark Street, Whitechapel, Station 34, Shadwell, killed corner of Cable Street/Backchurch St/Lane, Stepney 8/3/41 aged 33, at 9pm (Federation of Synagogues burial registers); b. Edmonton cemetery, grave V-70-24. Israel was killed on his first call-out by an exploding bomb, having volunteered to take the place of an injured comrade. Killed in the same incident as Alexander Smith (see below). Brother of Alec/Alex, who was also a Fireman.

6. Israel Deutch, AFS (left) killed in action at Cable Street.

7. Grave of Israel Deutch at Edmonton Jewish Cemetery.

Mrs Miriam 'Dolly' Emden, Firewatcher, wife of Maurice, 1A Hughes Mansions, Stepney, died 10/5/41 aged 35, killed at 1A Hughes Mansions; b. Marlow Road cemetery, grave I-6-380.

Hyman Feldman, husband of Rebecca, 85 Amhurst Park, Stamford Hill, killed 19/3/41 at 9pm (Federation of Synagogues burial register) in Stepney (Dod St) aged 32 – his team were hit by an exploding bomb whilst firefighting; b. Edmonton cemetery, grave V-71-2 – sadly his gravestone has disintegrated. His bother Louis was killed as POW of the Japanese. Family belonged to the Jubiliee Street and Philpot Street Great Synagogues in E1.

Philip Freeman/Friedman, Firewatcher, husband of Lillian Freeman, 131 Magdalen Road, Exeter, son of Hyman of Chapeltown Leeds, died 6/5/42 aged 67 at Exeter City Hospital bombing. Believed buried Higher Cemetery,

8. Fireman Hyman Feldman, killed in action 9 October 1940.

Exeter cemetery, grave ZD-250, originally as 'unidentified body' then later identified; new headstone is now on his grave.

Daniel Friedman, Firewatcher, of Kings Head, Bear Street, died aged 68, at Kings Head, Westminster, 16/4/41; probably buried 24/4/41 at Marlow Road cemetery, grave I-5-302 – headstone disintegrated.

9. The once unidentified grave of Firewatcher Philip Freeman/Friedman, originally from Leeds but killed in Exeter. His remains were later identified as being in this grave (plot ZD 250, Higher Cemetery, Exeter) but he now has a new headstone on his grave, organised by Martin Sugarman and Jerry Klinger in December 2022. See P398 (with thanks to James Sprague of Exeter Cemeteries Department).

Who knew this hero?

THE AJEX Jewish Military Museum is searching for the family of a Jewish war hero from Leeds who died seven decades ago.

Philip Freeman was a fire watcher in the Second World War.

He was killed on May 6, 1972, at Exeter City Hospital and buried in Higher Cemetery, Exeter.

It was originally in an unmarked grave. But he was later identified as the son of Hyman Freeman, of Chapeltown.

AJEX archivist Martin Sugarman is seeking family with a view to erecting a headstone.

"Philip's grave was never marked with a Star of David or his name," he explained.

"The city council at the time placed memorials and Philip could not have been identified until later so it is just inscribed 'To a citizen'.

"Philip is buried in the block ZD, which has many victims of the blitz and most have had a memorial placed on their grave."

■ Details from Martin on 07758 621561.

10. Advert in *The Jewish Telegraph* (May 2013), seeking information about the family of Philip Freeman of Leeds, killed later in Exeter.

Benjamin Gaidelman, Fireguard, husband of Rachel Blanche, 64 Bethune Rd, Stoke Newington, injured 18/7/44 at home, died aged 46 at Chase Farm hospital 16/8/44. Gaidelman is buried at Adath Yisroel cemetery, Carterhatch Lane, Enfield as GADELMAN – grave C5 31.

Sydney Gevelb, Firewatcher, son of Morris and Ada, 31 Jubilee Street, died 16/4/41 Stepney, aged 17 years; **his cousin Morris** aged 18, son of Mr and Mrs F. Gevelb, 73 Jubilee Street, was in St Johns' Ambulance and killed in same incident at 297 Commercial Road; they are buried in a double grave at Edmonton cemetery, grave V-74-19/18.

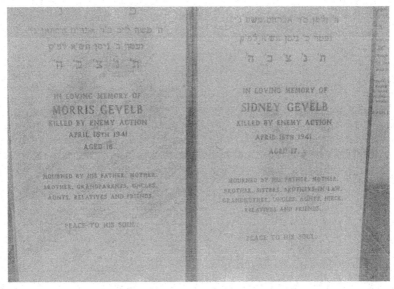

11. The Gevelb cousins (Firewatcher and St Johns Ambulance respectively) killed aged 17 and 18 years old, at the same incident and buried together at Edmonton Jewish Cemetery.

Hyman Gilbert, (named by the CWGC mistakenly as Gilbert Hyman), Firewatcher Liverpool, widower 7 Laburnum Grove, Litherland, killed at Canada Dock, Liverpool, 3/5/41 aged 65. Probabaly buried in a mass grave at Anfield cemetery – see his story in the text below. He was killed in the same incident where Fireman Noel Landau won his BEM.

Harry F A Glantzpe(i)gel aka Lewis, aged 32, son of Mrs Sarah Glantzspegel, 70 Chanctonbury Way, Finchley N12, killed 3/1/43 at Shanklin alongside David Cohen within 48 hours of arrival, by a sneak German bomber raid; b. 8/1/43 at Marlow Road cemetery, grave P-1-32-33.

12. The war memorial at the corner of High Street and Cline Avenue, Shanklin, Isle of Wight, showing the names of the three Jewish firemen killed in one raid – David Cohen, Glantzspigel and Jacobs.

13. *Jewish Chronicle* article of 12 March 1943 reporting the death on the Isle of Wight of David Cohen and Harry Glantzspigel.

14. The grave of Fireman Lewis Glantzspigel, at Marlow Road cemetery with the tribute from his firemen colleagues.

Herbert Benjamin Henry Golden, born 21/7/13 (TBC), theatre doorman, of 10 Sutherland Place, Bayswater, son of Sydney and Annie of Camberwell, worked at Blue Hall cinema, Edgware Road, based at Edgware Road Fire Station; King's Commendation for Brave Conduct (LG 28/3/41); injured 11/5/41 aged 27 at Clifton Road, Maida Vale,

Paddington, when a bomb fell on his team whilst fire-fighting; died at St Mary's Hospital.

B. Goldsmith (TBC – on Fire Service memorial but not on CWGC site).

Neil Goldsmith (TBC – on Fire Service memorial but not on CWGC site).

George Eric Goldsmith aka Goldschmitt, son of Carl and Madeleine née Barrat, of 15 Beechwood Avenue, Finchley, killed Cheyne Court, Chelsea, 16/4/41 aged 27, by a falling bomb whilst fire-fighting; b. 22/4/41 at Islington and St Pancras cemetery, High Road, Finchley, grave 30-RC-5. No religious symbol on grave. A contact at the AJR said the family was definitely Jewish and he was a frequent visitor to their home as a boy. Also information from nephew Erol Goldschmidt of Australia.

15. The original grave register entry for G.E. Goldsmith, registered by his father Carl under the true family name of Goldschmitt (with thanks to the cemetery staff).

Morris Goldstein, Firewatcher/ARP, son of S. and Jane Goldstein, 47 Bigland Street, died 16/4/41 aged 24, corner of Commercial Road/Watney Street, Stepney.

Edwin Goodman (TBC – on Fire Service memorial but not on CWGC site).

Joshua Goodman, Firewatcher Leeds, aged 58 years, died 16/12/43 leaving a son and daughter; b. New Briggate cemetery, grave 26D.

Jack Gordon/Cohen, Firewatcher, son of Lewis and Hetty, 1 Cedra Court, Cazenove Road, Stoke Newington, KIA 17/4/41 aged 30, at 25 Cannon Street, died Barts Hospital; b. Edmonton Federation cemetery, grave V-74-16.

Barnett 'Barney' Greenberg, born 3/2/10, hairdresser, 62a Lyndhurst Grove, Peckham, son of Ada and Morris (Russian Jewish immigrants), killed aged 31, West India Docks Fire Station, Poplar (Station 35K) 11/5/41 at 1 a.m. when it received a direct hit; body recovered at 6 a.m.; b. Rainham cemetery, grave A-22-30. Registration card says he was living at 57, Globe Road, E1 and parents at 32 Napier Road, Luton. Information also from nephew Maurice Davis, with photograph.

16. Fireman Barnet Greenberg.

17. Copy of Barnet Greenberg's Fire Brigade enrolment form.

18. One of Barnet Greenberg's referee letters signed by a Mr V. Cohen.

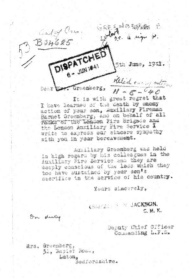 

19. Letter of condolence sent by the Deputy Chief Fire Officer to Barnet Greenberg's mother in June 1941; courtesy of the LFB and Emergency Planning Authority Records Office 2005, Lambeth.

20. Grave of Fireman Joseph Greenberg at Marlow Road Cemetery.

Harry Greenberg, Firewatcher, Stepney, son of Benjamin Greenberg, lived 41 Cable Street, injured 8/3/41, died 19/3/41, London Hospital, aged 35.

Joseph Greenberg, born 25/11/01, greengrocer, husband of Rachel, 14 Greatorex House, Greatorex Street, based at Whitechapel Fire Station, killed aged 39 on 1/1/41, by falling masonry in Fieldgate Street, Stepney, when the engine he was in, driven by Lou Sherman (see below), en route to a fire, was hit by a collapsing wall; b. Marlow Road cemetery, grave O-26-846. Article on front page of *ELA* of 18/1/41.

Nat Greenberg, Firewatcher/Ambulance Driver, husband of A. Greenberg, 204 Smithdown Road, Liverpool, died aged 33, Smithdown Road Hospital, *JC* 07/5/41; b. Rice Lane cemetery, grave B-36-29.

Emmanuel Gush, husband of May, 7 Wonford Road, son of Samuel of Seaton Hose, Exminster, injured Paris Street, died 25/4/42 aged 47, Heavitree Road, Exeter; probably in unidentified grave at Higher Cemetery, Exeter, block ZD, maybe plot 250? – waiting confirmation from Exeter (TBC if Jewish).

Henry Harris, Firewatcher, son of F. Harris, 10, Ruth House, Flower and Dean Street, died 10/3/41 aged 16 years on duty at White Horse

Lane, second youngest Jewish casualty (if Coster was not Jewish – see above); burial place not found

Myre/Moier Harrison, son of Solomon and Sarah, 6 Carment Drive, Shawlands, Glasgow, died Craigiehall Street, 13/3/41 aged 32; b. Cathcart cemetery, grave 136/L36 (?); eight Jewish AFS men acted as pall-bearers at his funeral in Glasgow, and over 3,000 attended his funeral.[5] First Fireman killed on Clydeside in Second World War. (Related to Arthur Lawson, AJEX.)

Aaron (Harry) Heiser, Firewatcher, husband of Sarah, 5 Brookside Road, Golders Green, KIA 11/5/41 aged 57, 95 Old Street (JC 16/5/41); b. Willesden cemetery, grave FX-19-857.

Jacob Heiser, Firewatcher, brother of above, 44 Stanhope Gardens, Haringey, killed same day, same incident at 95 Old Street, aged 55; b. Willesden cemetery, grave FX-19-856.

Leslie Walter Joseph Isaacs, market porter ('pitcher') by trade, husband of L. Isaacs, 37A, Tranmere Road, London, son of Mrs M.J. Isaacs, 31 Freshford Street, enlisted 11/38, killed 16/11/40 aged 39, West Hill Fire Station, Wandsworth when it suffered a direct hit by

21. Grave of Firewatcher Nat Greenberg, killed and buried in Liverpool.

22. Firewatcher Jacob Heiser killed in the same incident with his brother Firewatcher Aaron (Harry) Heiser on 11 May 1941 and buried together at Willesden Jewish Cemetery.

an oil bomb. The incident is described in *London Firefighter* magazine, Summer 2000 – courtesy of Stephanie Maltman, and in a bound mimeograph at the library of the LFB HQ in Southwark, which also describes the unveiling of a memorial in June 1984 in memory of the six men killed that night. It states clearly in the book *Wandsworth and Battersea at War* that Isaacs was given a Jewish funeral, but location of grave so far not found.

Leslie Alfred Jacobs, from Shoreside, The Esplanade, Shanklin, son of Major C.J. Jacobs, killed 3/1/43 aged 39 at the Fire Station, Landguard Road. Name only on war memorial at Shanklin cemetery, Isle of Wight with D. Cohen (above). (TBC if Jewish.)

Hyman Marks Lennick, born 26/2/07, a shop manager of 147 Osborne Road Forest Gate (his AFS card gives 95 Kyverdale Road), worked at 147 Whitechapel Road, husband of E Lennick, West Ham. He was stationed at Stoke Newington and died in Plaistow, 18/6/43; b. Marlow Road cemetery, grave P-14-440, but headstone no longer exists.

Ascher/Arthur (David) Davis Lettner/Latner, born 4/11/05, a musician and a tailor, 38 Coram Street, Russell Square, WC1, stationed at Clerkenwell and mortally injured 17/4/41 in Cannon Street, City, aged 36, died at Barts Hospital. The family say correct spelling is Latner. Brother-in-law of Jack Silver (see below), Ascher served at Cannon Street with Jack. He was killed by a collapsing wall, blown out by a bomb, on the other side of which Jack was standing and his death was not notified for a week as his body was missing. Taken to Barts Hospital. Ascher's wife Erna Helen of 38 Coram Street, Holborn, was not Jewish and she had him cremated in London but she swam out to sea herself and scattered his ashes at sea off the coast of Looe in Cornwall. There is a plaque on his parents' grave in Willesden Jewish cemetery. He was the son of Marks and Shoshana (Jessie) Latner and had returned from the safety of the USA where he had been a musician, 'to do his bit' as his nephew remembers him saying, and then gave his life in the Fire Service.

23. Fireman David Lattner killed in action 17 April 1941 at Canon Street.

24. Memorial for Fireman David Lattner, who has no known grave, on the grave of his parents, Willesden Cemetery.

Albert Levenson, cabinet maker, Hackney, husband of Rebecca of 88 Hindle House, Arcola Street, injured 20/10/42 at Globe road, Mile End, when his fire engine over turned in a skid and he was fatally injured, died 5/11/42 aged 37, at Mile End Hospital; b. 8/11/42 East Ham cemetery, grave PX-12-371.

Abraham Levy, husband of Sarah, 467 Hessle Road, Hull, killed 20/5/42 Scarborough Street aged 54/57; b. Delhi Street cemetery, grave D12. German Refugee? (On CWGC site as a civilian – not on Fire Brigade Memorial. Was he a Firewatcher?)

Samuel Levy, Firewatcher, Bristol, husband of Florence, 12 Hampton Road, Redland, injured 12/4/41 at Park Row, died 13/4/41 aged 38, at BRI. Bristol historian Gerry Nichols says Samuel had Jewish immigrant parents from Russia (1911 census) and married and had three children. His wife Florence died in 1960. Bristol Jewish graves

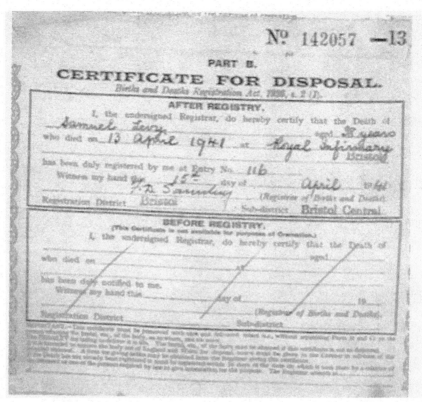

25. Certificate of Disposal (of a body) of Jewish Firewatcher Samuel Levy of Bristol.

expert Alan Tobias confirms that Samuel was buried by the Bristol Chevra Kadisha (Jewish burial society) as the Disposal Certificate from the BRI survives in their records. His grave must be in either the Ridgway or St Philips Jewish cemeteries but it either never had a headstone or it has disintegrated. The grave registers have not survived.

Ms Hetty Lewin, Firewatcher, 105 Clissold Crescent, Stoke Newington, killed at West Central Synagogue Jewish Youth Club, Alfred Place, Holborn, 17/4/41 aged 28; b. Streatham cemetery, grave E-26-35 (see S. Osterer, below).

Abraham Lewis aka Bookatz, husband of Rita Lewis, 84 Fieldgate Mansions, Myrtle Street, son of Mrs B. Bookatz of 49a Golding Street, injured 11/5/41 Trinity Square near The Minories, whilst attempting to extinguish an incendiary when another incendiary fell on him; died 12/5/41 aged 35 at London Hospital; b. Rainham cemetery, grave A-24-24; also noted in the LMA records FB/WAR 4/12 number 1663.

26. Grave of Firewatcher Hetty Lewin, killed in action 1941 and buried at Streatham Jewish Cemetery.

27. The 2003 unveiling of the plaque in memory of Fireman Abraham Lewis who was killed in action. Grandson Andrew Fox and great grand-daughter Talia were present. The event was instigated by Stephanie Maltman.

28. Abraham Lewis served at Whitechapel Station.

32 Jewish Participation in the Fire Service in the Second World War

29. Abraham Lewis, second from left, and colleague Hyman Benstock, second from right.

Samuel Libbert, husband of Lena Tobe (formerly Libbert), son of Anna and Mr I. Libbert, 7 Mayfield Road, Kersal, Manchester, killed 19/9/42 aged 29 by a collapsing wall at a factory fire at Woodville Street, Glasgow, together with another fireman. He is buried at Rainshough cemetery, Manchester, grave 71-A. A Guard of Honour attended his funeral from Prestwich station and Glasgow, where he had served in the Ibrox area. There is a memorial to him at the Higher Crumpsall and Broughton Synagogue in Salford.

Jesse Thomas Massow, Fireman, born 6/4/15, a tailor, 61/54 Leatherdale Street, E1, joined the Fire Service in 1937 and was at Whitechapel station, killed off-duty 19–20/10/40 at 61 Leatherdale Street, Stepney according to his LFB Registration card, with next of kin as L. Massow.

30. Talia Fox (Jewish Lads and Girls Brigade) with the Star of David poppy wreath she laid in memory of her great grandfather Abraham Lewis/Bookatz, killed in action in 1941, at the Fire Brigade memorial in September 2008.

31. Memorial to Samuel Libbert in Higher Crumpsall Synagogue, Manchester.

> **LIBBERT.**—On September 19, 1942, while on duty, Samuel Libbert, N.F.S., of Prestwich, a perfect friend and gentleman. "We cannot say, we will not say, that he is dead; he is just away. With a cheery smile and a wave of the hand he has wandered into another land." His memory will never fade in the hearts of his friends in Woodhill Drive and Woodhill Grove, Prestwich.
>
> *Jewish Chronicle, 2nd October 1942*

JEWISH FIREMAN KILLED

A fortnight after he had been transferred to Glasgow, Mr. Samuel Libbert, a Manchester member of the National Fire Service, died while fighting a blaze at a Glasgow factory. He and a comrade were killed instantly when a wall collapsed.

A guard of honour of N.F.S. men from his local post in Prestwich, where he had served as a volunteer for some time before being posted to Glasgow, attended the funeral at Rainsough Cemetery. The Glasgow N.F.S. was represented by two officers. Rabbi K. Rosen and the Revs S. Hershman, J. Vilensky, and L. Glickman officiated.

Samuel Libbert, who was 29 years old, took an active interest in communal affairs. He was a member of the Higher Crumpsall Synagogue and a founder member of the Literary Society connected with the Synagogue. Before volunteering for the N.F.S., he belonged to a First Aid Party.

He leaves a wife and daughter. His brother, Mr. M. H. Libbert, is Treasurer of the Holy Law Hebrew Congregation.

Jewish Chronicle, 2nd October 1942

> **LIBBERT.**—Precious memories of Samuel Libbert, N.F.S., taken from us September, 19, 1942. So sadly missed by his wife, Lena, and daughter, Joan.—Woodhill Drive, Prestwich, Lancs.
>
> **LIBBERT.**—Fragrant memories of our beloved son and brother, Samuel Libbert N.F.S., who was killed on duty, Tishri 8, 5703—9, New Hall Avenue, Salford, 7.
>
> *Jewish Chronicle, 14th September 1945*

32. JC article about the death of Samuel Libbert, from Manchester but killed in action in Glasgow.

33. Memorial to Samuel Libbert in Higher Crumpsall Synagogue, Manchester.

He is remembered by the CWGC as a Fireman. He appears not be in a United Synagogue cemetery and is TBC if Jewish, although Massow is a Jewish surname. He is not on the Fireman's memorial at St Pauls.

Victor Michaelson, born 27/12/88, an advertising agent from Wandsworth, husband of Justina, 6 St Nicholas Mansions, Trinity Crescent, SW17, died 6/11/40 aged 51 at Cavendish Road School station 86W, Balham, when it suffered a direct hit by a bomb; b. Willesden cemetery, grave FX-13-566 – headstone totally blank/worn. He is commemorated at St John's Wood Synagogue.

Percy Millet, born 12/10/11, a street trader, son of Annie Millet of 45 Fuller Street, and Mr A. Millet, members Bethnal Green Synagogue, stationed at Whitechapel, attached to St Katherine Dock station, killed 8/9/1940 aged 28 at Buckle Street, on Commercial Road, Stepney. Percy was probably the first Jewish Fireman killed (see Simon Cohen above who died of illness), when the walls of a tenement block opposite Buckle Street School collapsed; b. Rainham cemetery, grave A-19-29. (His brother Morris was also killed serving in the Merchant Navy 22/10/42.) JC 20/9/1940 noted that his mother received a letter from the Fire Brigade stating, "If it were not for the gallantry of men like Mr Millet we may well have had another 'Great Fire of London'" – submitted by Yoel Sherensky/Sheridan, of Israel, who knew Percy.

Harry Morris, AFS, son of Solomon. 26 Wetherall Road, Hackney, killed 11/5/41 Rockmead Road, aged 36; b. Marlow Road cemetery, grave I-6-388.

Issac Nyman, Firewatcher, husband of V. Nyman, 162 Redbridge Lane, Ilford, killed 10/5/41 at 206 Mile End Road – not listed as Firewatcher on CWGC site, and not named in *JC*; b. Rainham cemetery, grave A-24-23 with illegible headstone.

Mrs Sarah Osterer, Fireguard, husband of Israel, 21 Howland Street, Holborn, killed 17/4/41 aged 47 at the West Central Synagogue Jewish Youth Club, Albert Place, Holborn, with Hetty Lewin; b. Liberal Jewish Cemetery, Pound Lane, London, grave 3-K-19.

Alexander Paul, Manchester, killed at Parker Street, aged 38 years, during the major Blitz attack of 22–24/12/40. He was injured by High Explosive bombs in the Piccadilly area, on 22/12 and died on 24/12/40. From 36 or 26, Thirlmere Street, Hightown, it appears he had no known family and was buried at the Southern Cemetery, Manchester on 31/12/40 by the local South Manchester Synagogue burial society. Julius Goldberg recalls being a pall bearer at the ceremony. At the time it was not realised he was Jewish and he was re-buried in the Jewish section of the cemetery on 17/2/48, grave D22 or D122.

34. Grave of Alexander Paul at Southern Cemetery, Manchester.

35. Grave of Fireman Pizer Pearl at Marlow Road Cemetery.

36. Grave of Fireman Manuel Rabinowitz, fatally injured in London, but died at home in Edinburgh where he is buried.

Pizer Pearl, born 21/09/08, of 14 Morgan Street, Bow, son of Leah and Abraham, 131 Epsom Road, Cheam, Surrey, post at Northwold Road fire station, killed 26/9/41 aged 32, at 261 Tottenham Court Road; b. Marlow Road cemetery, grave O-13-404.

Manuel (Mendel) Rabinowitz aka Rabinowisky, from Edinburgh, posted to London, when a bus hit him on his bike on the way to his fire station, and died aged 37 of serious head injuries in Edinburgh at 30 Moston Terrace on 17/10/41, whilst convalescing at home. In *JC*, 24/10/41, husband of Esther nee Marcus, father of Jackie/Jacob, son of Rabbi Jacob Rabinowitz. His two brothers were Rabbi Louis and Rabbi Eliezer Rabinowitz, both Jewish Chaplains in the Armed Forces in the Second World War. Buried at Piershill cemetery, Edinburgh, grave C2/48. Not on CWGC or Fire Brigade Memorials, and his grave has no mention of fire service – LFB Archivists are aware of this anomaly.

Max Randal, Firewatcher, husband of Rose, 68 Hurstwood Road, Golders Green, died 18/3/41 aged 48; b. Marlow Road cemetery, grave I-3-141, no headstone, just a disintegrating marker, barely visible.

Jack Raphael, Firewatcher, husband of Violet, 105 West End Lane, Hampstead, died 20/6/44, aged 60. No more is known about this man.

Maurice Sydney Rose, Column Officer, husband of Nora Winifred, 20/204 Woodlands Road, Toller Lane,

Roll of Honour

37. The forlorn marker in place of the disintegrated headstone of Firewatcher Max Randal at Marlow Road Cemetery.

Bradford, son of Mr and Mrs Sydney Rose of 23 Chapel Road, Redhill, Surrey, killed/died of injuries 11/12/43 aged 38, Bradford.

Hyman Roseman, previously in ARP, husband of Elizabeth, 20 Nova Road., Croydon, son of Jesse and Barrett, killed by collapse of heavy pipework, Elephant and Castle, died 12/7/44 aged 35 at Guys Hospital; b. Streatham cemetery, grave F-28-28. Unfit for military service, he was a gentle and cultured man, according to his niece; his wife re-married after the war.

Frederick Charles Salkeld, Section Officer, son of Bessie and William, 166 Amesbury Avenue, killed at Mitcham Lane, Wandsworth, 17/10/40 aged 30, when a bomb made a direct hit on his fire station. (TBC if Jewish.)

Ernest Adam Schneider, born 9/11/07, from Stepney, tailor, was at Whitefriars station, husband of V. Schneider, 3 Chapman House, Bigland Street, Stepney, killed 14/10/40 aged 32, Bunhill Street, Finsbury, when a roof he was firefighting from collapsed when an incendiary exploded

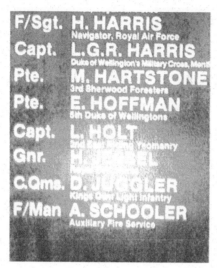

38. Memorial to Fireman Alexander Schooler at Pryme Road synagogue, City of Hull, where he was killed.

39. Fireman Alexander Schooler, killed in action in Hull.

(LMA file 177, which also gives an address at 24 Brockham Street, SE1); his remains were not found until one year after at Bunhill Street, in September 1941, with two other missing firemen killed in the same incident. No grave has been located so far.

Alexander Schooler, No.891, German refugee, husband of Hilda, 2 Norfolk Street, killed 8/5/41 aged 42 at Albert Dock, Hull, first Jewish Hull Fireman casualty; b. Hull Delhi Street Jewish cemetery, grave 44N/S.

Israel Schwartzberg, husband of Sarah, 19 Dunloe Street, Hackney Road, son of Morris and Celia, 26 Blythe Street, Bethnal Green, injured 28/8/43 at Roman Road School station, died 29/8/43 aged 31 at Chase Farm Hospital.

Morris/Maurice (Mossy) Share, cinema owner, served Euston and Soho, 57X substation, son of F. Share, 22 Camilla Road, injured 8/9/40 aged 35, at 256 Southwark Park Road, Bermondsey, died at St Olave's Hospital, same day as Millet; b. Rainham cemetery, grave A-20-14. (Possibly first Jewish Fireman killed.)

Benjamin Joseph/John Sheldon, retired carpenter, husband of Ada, 59 Reidhaven Road, SE18, injured Kings Warren School, Old Mill Road,

Woolwich 11/9/40, died aged 77, St Nicholas Hospital, Plumstead. TBC if Jewish – not in *JC*.

Harry Simon or Simion from Scotland, believed killed 13/3/41 and buried in Manchester South (Reform) cemetery. TBC if this is the correct name/place. (Call from Carl Goldberg of Manchester whose late father gave this information.)

Alec Slipman, Firewatcher, 19 Kingly Street, Holborn/49 Old Hill Street, Stamford Hill, killed 109 Kingsway, 17/4/41 aged 38; b. Edmonton cemetery, grave V-75-23 – gravestone disintegrated. Unmarried, one of his brothers was a stretcher bearer and another a firewatcher.

Alexander Smith, tobacconist, served Shadwell station, husband of Rose, Urswick Road, 6 Kings Market Parade, Hackney, son of Mrs M. Smith of Holloway; seriously injured by an exploding bomb when firefighting, and died of his injuries in hospital 9/3/41; b. East Ham Jewish cemetery 11/3/41, grave I-2-118. Killed in same incident as Deutsch (above).

Miss Helen Sussman, 12 Clydesdale Rd, Kensington, daughter of Morris and Eva, killed 19/6/44 aged 25; b. Edmonton cemetery, grave W-26-19. Her parents were also killed the same night.

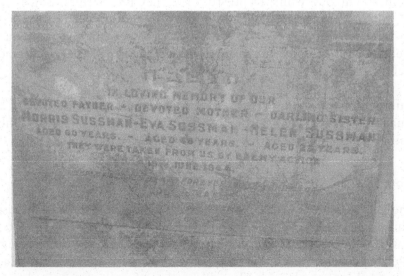

40. Grave of Helen Sussman (Edmonton cemetery), as far as is known the only Jewish Firewoman killed.

Harold Alan Tasho, born in Manchester, died in Hertford County Hospital 21/2/41 aged 27, and living at 9 Central Parade, Hatfield at the time (according to US Burial Register), but served in Southampton (in *JC* 7/3/41, p.17, but not on Fire Service memorial or CWGC site as he died of illness – but is likely he was in the Fire Service at time of illness/death). Buried Marlow Road cemetery 23/2/41, grave O-33-1086 but headstone no longer exists – Fire Brigade (FB) Archivists are aware . AJEX archive box has his death certificate but no mention of Fire Brigade. Fire Brigade card required.

David Viener, of 17 Church Crescent, Hackney, died 23/12/45 in Hackney Hospital, aged 44; b. Rainham cemetery, grave A-39-19. Not on Fire Brigade Memorial but is a Fireman on CWGC – FB Archivists are aware. No mention on his headstone of NFS and not mentioned in *JC*. His LFB Card does not mention his death. It says he lived at 2 Palatine Road, Stoke Newington and was a street trader, born 31/12/01, serving at C36 Bishopsgate Fire Station.

Myer Wand, wife at 14 St Johns Place, Clark Street, Stepney, E1, parents at 71 Imperial Avenue, Stoke Newington, killed 18/9/40 aged 31, at Jackson's Garage, Rathbone Place, Oxford Street, on the same night and same building (direct hit by bomb) where Jewish Fireman Harry Errington won his George Cross; b. Marlow Road cemetery, grave O-10-313.

Herbert Thomas Wolff, Deptford, of Verney Rd, Bermondsey, killed 28/9/40 at Lyndhurst Road School Fire Station, Camberwell. Possibly Jewish but does not appear on the CWGC website with this or alternate spellings as a casualty, but is listed as such in the LMA Fire Brigade archive files. TBC.

Phillip Zage(a)rman, Firewatcher/ARP, husband of Rachel, 26 Quantock House, Stamford Hill, killed 13/1/41 aged 40, at Tenby Buildings, Old Street. Buried Rainham Cemetery, grave A-23-16.

From London Metropolitan Archives – LMA-file – FB/War/1/177)

The following are Jewish Firemen listed as having died of natural causes whilst in service. Given the higher average age of Firemen, it is likely that stress, exhaustion, exertion and danger added to the death rate by so-called 'natural causes' in the Second World War. These men are honoured here as their deaths will not be officially recognized as by 'enemy action' even though their families may know otherwise.

M. Levy 7/10/40, of Station C32.
W. Levy – 12/10/40, of Station B76.

E.C. Louis – 4/4/40 of Station D42 (earliest Jewish Fire Brigade casualty if we accept his death was caused by active service)

This casualty from family contact: **Joel Harris**, born 27/10/1898, street trader, 98 Colvestone Crescent, Hackney, watchroom attendant at Kingsland Station (38) serving from 29/9/38, died 22/11/43 of heart attack whilst on duty aged 45 years at St Olave's Hospital. His death certificate does not confirm he died at his Fire Station. Buried East Ham Jewish cemetery, grave P-24/765. Not commemorated by the CWGC.

From the West Yorkshire Archives: **Robert Stanley Simons**, Fireman, husband of Frances M. Simons, 78 Church Street, Woddlesford, died 14/3/43, whilst on duty at Purston in an accident, aged 33. May have been Jewish.

New casualty **Fireman Simon Woolfe Pinsker** aged 29, kia Colston Ave, Bristol 12/4/41. Of 66 North Road Bishopston, son of Elijah Lewis and R. Pinsker. Brother also a Firewatcher. Buried Ridgway cemetery grave A11 08.

NOTES

1. Cyril Demarne, *The London Blitz: A Fireman's Tale* (Essex: After the Battle 1991).
2. Cyril Demarne, *Our Girls* (Edinburgh: Pentland Press, 1995).
3. Barry Hollis, *37 Fire Forces: Fire and Rescue, S.E. London, 1941–46* (Newport Pagnell: Enthusiast Publications, 1988).
4. For an excellent account of awards to the Fire Service see kfrs_history_medals-awards-decorations_1890-2009.pdf.
5. JC, 28 March 1941, p.4.

THE TESTIMONIES

Chapter One

Bergit Braach (later Forchhammer)

41. Bergitt Braach in later years.

42. Bergitt Braach in the USA Army 1945.

Bergit was a Jewish refugee from Germany who arrived in the UK in August 1939 via Holland, just three weeks before war broke out. She was born in Duisberg in April 1921, the only child of writers Johannes and Emilie née Hirschfeld. She attended the Viktoriaschule (now Bettinaschule) High School in Frankfurt, which had a high percentage of Jewish pupils whose lives were made miserable by a Nazi headteacher.

On arrival in the UK Bergit stayed with family friends in Sydenham Hill and avoided internment as the family vouched for her. After several temporary jobs, she joined the Fire Service in January 1943 and was stationed first at Kentish Town and later at Southwark (as a driver) in the building which now houses the LFB Museum. She was active with the firemen/women artists and a co-custodian of their exhibitions at the Royal Academy. After demob in 1945 she worked as a censor with the US Army in London. She left the UK after the war and lived in Denmark.

One incident she recalls was connected with a huge salvage operation of food at Chambers Wharf grain warehouse in Rotherhithe which was hit by a V1 on 10 August 1944 during the 'Second' Blitz of London, and burnt for days after. Six salvage tenders were needed to gather the loose linseed and peanuts which were blocking the drains as they were washed away by the water used on the fire. It required 210 salvage sheets and twelve special Homelite pumps for fourteen days to pump water away from the food stocks. Bergit was driving the canteen van and attended every five hours day and night to bring food to the firemen. At night during the blackout, with V1's falling, she drove with her colleague from Bermondsey along the Old Kent Road to Surrey Docks, where swarms of flies feeding on the oily grain and the overwhelming pungent smell of burning linseed were a sure sign they were near their destination. The ground was covered with thick, oily grease and parking and walking were extremely difficult; falls were frequent. But the upside was that everyone was able to supplement their diet with nutritious roasted peanuts, which had not been seen in Britain since before the war.

One fireman gave her a gift of a small sack of nuts to take home. Bergit placed them by the fireplace, and she fell asleep dreaming of fresh peanuts for breakfast. But during the night she was woken by something biting her nose and she switched on the light to see the sack crawling with all kinds of worms and insects of every description. It took all her courage to pick up the sack and throw it out the backdoor.[1]

Bergit died in 2011.[2]

NOTES

1. This story appeared in the Winter 2007 edition of *The Roundthreads*, the newsletter of the retired LFB Members Association. Bergit had sent it from her home in Lyngby, Denmark. It is also kept in the archives of the WW2 Experience Centre in Yorkshire.
2. Bergit wrote two books about her life: *Ferne Nahe; Briefe und Erinnerungen* [Far and Near; Letters and Recollections] (Frankfurt: Fischer Taschenbuch, 1997), and *Hjemad; men ikke hjem* [Homewards; But not Home] (Denmark: Siesta Books, 2011).

Chapter Two

Sam Chauveau

Sam was born to an Orthodox Jewish family in the East End in 1912 and became a high ranking Jewish Fireman throughout The Second World War. He joined the AFS in 1938, having already been active fighting the Fascists in the East End in the 1930s, and first served at Bishopsgate Fire Station during the 'phoney war'. He had volunteered for RAF aircrew but the Fire Service refused to release him. When the

43. Station Commander Sam Chauveau in the Second World War.

44. Sam Chauveau in 1996 (centre) unveiling the Fireman Memorial at the Stock Exchange Building in the City of London.

45. Entrance to the Sam Chauveau Room at the London Fire Brigade Museum in Southwark, courtesy of the LFB Museum.

Blitz began he was made Junior Officer in charge at station 36Y at the Stock Exchange.[1] The messroom window faced east so the men could see the huge barrage balloons over that part of the City, and when a raid was impending, they could watch the balloons rapid ascent into the sky on their cables. Soon, twelve months of doing nothing was to turn into enough fire fighting to last a lifetime.

Sam was a trainer and ran five-day courses on incendiaries, high explosive bombs, elementary fire fighting and chemical warfare with raw recruits. He despaired at the way some men responded to these sessions, but this doubt was totally dispelled because when it came to action, his crews turned out to be magnificent.

In September 1939, Sam's fire station took possession of a clapped out London taxi, GU 6804, which was to be driven by Fireman Smith, a former cabbie, to tow one of the fire pumps. Over the coming weeks, Smith expertly overhauled the old cab.[2]

On Saturday 7 September 1940, the men were relaxing after completing their chores about 1 p.m. when at 4 p.m. the sirens went off; soon the first German raiders would appear over the City in the first daylight raid on London. The cabs were started up and the two heavy units (fire engines) and two other pumps were prepared. Sam and his men dressed in their full gear – helmets, boots and leggings, fire tunic, belt and axe, spanner and respirator – and went up to the arched entrance at Shorters Court, near Drapers Hall, where their appliances were parked. But nothing happened except they could hear some distant anti-aircraft fire – and so the men went back up to the messroom on the fourth floor, for tea.

At 5.30pm the phone in the basement watchroom rang from the roof spotter (with whom they had a direct link – these spotters were

Stock Exchange staff who manned the post 24/7 in a rotation of volunteers) and a firewoman answered. The spotter said bombs were falling near Tower Bridge, hoards of German bombers were above and gunfire was heavy. Then the phone connected to Bishopsgate Control rang, and after a short conversation, the firewoman 'pulled the bells down' (set off the alarm). Sam's 5 crew with cab, left for their 'Shout'[3] at the corner of Globe Road and Mile End Road, where they found a two-storey clothes factory ablaze. Other appliances sere sent elsewhere.

The driver reversed to a street hydrant, a fireman removed the cover plate and connected the hose, two more laid out the hose and the leading fireman smashed the door open with his axe. Sam meanwhile went to the street alarm phone and called for more assistance as his men broke into the building, with the hose doing its work. Then a ladder was pitched against a wall and Sam entered the building via a window. He quickly became his station's first casualty as a small burning beam fell across his neck causing a nasty burn. But by 8.30 p.m. the blaze was out, the all clear sounded and the men, wet, tired but elated, began to stack their hoses.

By 9.30 p.m. they were back at Y station but at 10.30 p.m. were called out again to a burning food warehouse in Wapping Lane, believed to be Clarnico's sweet factory. The sirens again sounded as the second wave attack came in, searchlights swept the sky, AA guns opened up and bombs fell. When they arrived, the fire was out of hand and a thick, molten food mass was creeping down the walls into the street as huge clouds of acrid smoke billowed out of the windows. With walls about to collapse the men were told to draw water from the nearby dock. As the water spouted out the men huddled together to grip and control the powerful jet of water. Soaked and choking from the smoke, the men inched slowly forward, screwing their eyes against the intense heat.

By 6 a.m. the fire was under control but the senior officer ordered the crew to reinforce firemen at the East London Rubber Company in Shoreditch, from where a despatch rider had just come. Tired, stinking of smoke, covered in glass slivers, aching, cold and hungry they had been looking forward to a hot meal and a change of clothes. On arrival at Shoreditch they were ordered to prepare their hoses and as the all clear went, they trained the water on the building till the fire went out at about 11.30 a.m. Just about ready to 'knock-off and make-up', they were ordered to go to the rear of the building as a new fire had re-ignited and they were to extinguish it at once. Totally exhausted now, they continued their job. This blaze was huge but the warmth it generated on their chilled bodies enabled them to rally and finally put out the blaze. Sam walked wearily to the pump and there found the driver fast asleep; he did not have the heart to wake him.

Sam plucked up courage to ask the Superintendent if they could now be relieved. 'No you bloody-well can't. You will do the same as I am doing and wait for relief to arrive.' They were finally released at 3 p.m. to go back and drove by the ruined buildings of the East End watching the Rescue teams trying to extricate the dead and injured. At the Stock Exchange they found the surrounding area had been damaged and glass and debris were everywhere. The iron gate at Shorters Court was hanging off its hinges blocking the entrance, so they parked in Bartholomew Lane.

By 7 p.m. everyone had cleaned themselves up and eaten and were fast asleep. But at 9 p.m. the alarms sounded again. It was Sam's first night of the Blitz. Many more fires followed during the following eight months, at timber yards, flour mills, granaries, docks, offices and houses.

On one occasion an incendiary landed on top of an office lift six floors up; instead of running up the stairs, they called the lift down and put the fire out comfortably at ground level. One of the more onerous jobs was cleaning unrefined oil off hoses after refinery fires. In one blaze at Poplar, as a building collapsed, hundreds of rubber balls bounced down on their helmets. One night they were called to a fire in Carlton House Terrace, when a member of The Atheneum Club popped over and said, 'would you be so good as to attend to a fire on our roof?'. They did.

In October 1940, they returned from fires in Poplar at 4.30 a.m. to find that the area round the Stock Exchange was ablaze after a parachute mine had gone through the dome of the Dutch Church in Austin Friars. They of course joined in with the other appliances to put out the blaze. There was then a lull in London and this allowed the crews to replenish and repair equipment. On 27 December they helped at a fire at Woolwich Arsenal, and then came a shock.

Sam led his crew of five on one of the worst nights of the Blitz, 29 December 1940. His grey pumps were parked in Shorters Court on that freezing night. As Sam descended to the Watchroom beneath the Exchange, the sirens went off, the emergency phone rang to issue 'Air Raid warning Red', and AA guns opened up. The bombs began. Sam was soon atop the Stock Exchange clearing flares and incendiaries off the flat roof and described the whole City as wreathed in a ring of fire as German aircraft first dropped flares followed by the bombers who dropped the explosives onto the City's 'Square Mile'. It was, he said then, the Luftwaffe vs. the Fire Brigade! Only St Paul's dome stood above the flames.

Soon Sam and his crew were sent to a blaze at Austin Friars then on to one in Bevis Marks. Back at their station at 9 p.m., a policeman rushed in to report a fire at Tokenhouse Yard behind the Bank of

England. A firestorm was developing as oxygen was sucked out of the air by the flames; the Guildhall and St Lawrence Jewry Church were alight. Amazingly the 'All Clear' sounded at midnight (it is thought that thick fog over the Channel prevented the Germans returning for the second wave) and Sam's crew set to work pulling down dangerous walls. 1,500 fires were burning and Sam and his men were showered with red hot embers and suffocated by smoke.

Unfortunately the tide was out on the river and until 4 a.m. there was virtually no water to fight the flames as the mains had all been burst by the bombing. In addition, there was an unexploded parachute mine in the mud near Tower Bridge, preventing the deployment of fire-boats which relayed water from the river to the fire pumps ashore. Sam said he despaired and called urgently to Control for more pumps and a turntable; an hour later they arrived – one pump from West Ham, one from Bexley and one from Crayford – but still there was no water. As the Thames slowly filled, Firemen struggled across 50 yards of mud and placed hoses in the water, which was pumped by relays into artificial reservoirs in the streets and eventually to the pumps for use by hoses. Soon the fire-boats were operating too. At dawn his men were withdrawn as the 'stop' order was made and they all reported to Barts Hospital that afternoon with 'burnt eye' and had to be treated. Next night they were back again as the raids continued and fires burnt. It turned out to be one of the worst nights of the whole Blitz.

Two nights later, when dealing with a fire at Tower Hill, two Scots Guards from the Tower approached Sam with an offer of a 'wee dram' to celebrate the New Year. He happily accepted; the water on his tunic had turned to ice.

On Saturday 11 January 1941, a bomb crashed into the road at Mansion House and exploded in the Bank Station booking hall; an ARP Warden summoned Sam's crew. It was a charnel house as bits of bodies littered the area. They helped as many of the injured as they could and ferried bodies to Popes Head Alley. They were then summoned to a fire at Drapers Gardens and at 6 a.m. were sent to Liverpool Street to remove dead from the rubble where another bomb had landed outside at a bus stop.

After a short lull, Sam and his men were sent to Norton Folgate on the first Saturday of March to a fire in an umbrella factory, followed on Wednesday 16 April by a heavy raid on London and Sam's crew were sent to Billiter Street; here an office block was alight and it took ten pumps to bring it under control. At 8 a.m. a wall near Sam collapsed and just missed him and another fireman with whom he was chatting. Shaken, the two sat in the rubble and a caretaker from the next building came out with a welcome tot of whisky. On the 19th there was another raid at 10 p.m. and Sam by now realized it was better to stay out than keep going back to his station after each raid; he arranged this with his Control and so they went from fire to fire.

An ARW rushed into the station and, tripping over a wire, fell down the stairs into the watchroom. Before passing out he told them to go to London Wall post office. On arrival they extinguished a magnesium incendiary on the top floor with sand and an extinguisher; then on to Brune Street to a seed warehouse where they forced entry to put out a smoking fire of sacking, which they threw into the street and stamped out; then to Old Castle Street where an incendiary had fallen through the roof of the synagogue and landed on the Holy Ark containing the scrolls. Two Jewish members of the Street Fire Party helped put out the fire and carried the scrolls to safety.

Finally to a printing factory in Commercial Street; when they arrived a pump crew was wasting water by directing the hose from across the street, which was achieving nothing. Sam ordered them to stop and follow him inside the building with a large axe to break down the door. By the appearance of their clean uniforms, they had come from outside London and had not much experience of bashing doors in to get at the root of a blaze!

At the start of March Sam had been made 'Water Officer' and his job was to earmark all emergency water supplies in their Bishopsgate area. This was to become very useful for what followed.

On the night of Saturday 10 May 1941, Sam's crew headed for a fire in Upper Thames Street at a shipping office. After about an hour on the hose, without warning, a bomb screamed down and made a direct hit on the cab; it was totally blown apart and Smith was dead.[4]

Having returned from leave that Saturday, Sam and his men were resting after completing all the cleaning and maintenance chores at the station. He had attended a service at the Dutch church to commemorate the invasion of Holland and had shown his new Station Commander the location of all the emergency water supplies as required. But back at the station the red alert was sounding, and at 11 p.m. they were sent to Parnell Road in Bow where Woolworths in Roman Road was ablaze. They broke in and Ginger Rabinowitz, a former tailor, one of his most trusted firemen, said there was a dead girl behind the counter and he could see her legs. Sam went over to find a wax dummy lying on the floor!

By 1 a.m. they were back at base and awaiting further orders; they were sent to Pudding Lane by the Monument, where there was a blaze at the corner of Cornhill. Sam found one hydrant working but also an artesian well in the basement of a building in Gracechurch Street. With the help of two crews from Walton-on-Thames, they coped with the night's fires. At 8 a.m. a firewatcher asked for help with a small fire in an office at St Michael's Alley. An incendiary was lodged in a large horse-hair chair and was burning furiously; Sam and the fire watcher opened a window and threw it out onto the pavement where it burnt itself out.

As the day wore on they were all over the City – Houndsditch, Throgmorton Street, Fenchurch Street; at the latter there was a big blaze and Sam was ordered to organize a water relay from London Bridge, starting at Billingsgate at New Fresh Wharf, from where hoses came from a fireboat in the river. Then it continued along Fish Street Hill to Gracechurch Street to Fenchurch, into a canvas dam to supply the hoses. That night they were at London Wall fires, being helped by five crews from Bristol, but their pumps could not work as their hose fittings were different from the London types and hours were spent finding the right pieces in order to get them into action. By 3.30 a.m. Sam was leaning against a wall watching Carpenters Hall burn and he fell asleep standing up, hitting the pavement with a bump which woke him up. By 5 a.m. he just had to join his crews and get some sleep; it had been 30 hours non-stop.

In April 1942 Sam was promoted Company Officer and then transferred to C Division to be Staff Officer to the Divisional Officer. But in Summer 1943 he elected to return to active duty. This was to have a fateful consequence.

By June 1944 Sam was co-commander of Burdett Road station in Stepney. Then the VI attacks began but the firemen were working mostly with blast damage issues, not fires, and bringing bodies and injured out of the debris. During this period Sam saw some very harrowing incidents which he did not describe in his memoires. Then in July 1944, he was on alert in West India Dock when a VI hit an army convoy killing many soldiers and hitting his station. Sam was injured in his head, back and legs and had to end his active service. After convalescence Sam was sent to Area Stores in Highgate to work on administration; as stations began to close, as bombing began to peter out, Sam was sorting hundreds of hoses, first aid boxes, ladders, equipment of all kinds, and so on. Finally in April 1946 he was discharged. For many years after when his alarm clock went off he would automatically jump out of bed, and reach for his fire-boots!

In the LFCDA book *Under Fire*, Sam wrote,

> In the docks, strange things were going on. There were pepper fires loading the surrounding air heavy with stinging particles so that when the firemen took a deep breath it felt like breathing fire itself. There were rum fires with torrents of blazing liquid pouring from the warehouse doors and barrels exploding. There were

paint fires, cascading white hot flame, coating the pumps with varnish that took weeks to clean off, rubber fires that belched black smoke so asphyxiating that it could only be fought from a distance, and was always threatening to choke the firemen; sugar that burnt well in liquid form, floating on the water in docklands basins, and tea that burns sweet and sickly and very intense.

Grain fires bring out unexpected offspring – banks of black flies and scores of rats scampering round the feet of the firemen. [p.19]

Shorters Court no longer exists; the only reminder is the huge plate glass door that leads from Throgmorton Street, and above it is written 'Shorters Court'.

In 1967, Sam volunteered to fight for Israel in the Six Day War even though well into his 50s. He appeared in several documentaries in the late 1990s, such as *Blitz* with Professor Richard Holmes in 1997 (BBC/History Channel) and the History Channel film, *I, Witness*.

In July 1996, Sam returned to the Stock Exchange where he was responsible for the unveiling of a plaque to the forty-five brave firemen and women who served in the Stock Exchange fire station in the Second World War. He died in 1998, survived by his children Barry and Helena and their families, whose children knew him as 'Fireman Sam'. A room in the Fire Brigade Museum in London is named after him.

NOTES

1. It held forty-five staff in the deep requisitioned basement of the Stock Exchange, where the Watchroom was located, and equipment included two fire engines, two large pumps and two old London cabs to pull the pumps. The engines were usually parked beneath the arched entrance to the former Shorters Court, a 100 feet long cul-de-sac, and the pumps and taxis at the end of Throgmorton Avenue, outside Drapers Hall.
2. The accuracy of this information needs to be confirmed.
3. Firemen slang for an incident.
4. The accuracy of this information needs to be confirmed.

Chapter Three

Leonard Clements[1]

46. Leonard Clements, Army Fire Service, in later years; and on far left with his two brothers.

Leonard was born in Liverpool but moved to Rectory Road, Hackney in 1931. During the war he was part of the Army Fire Service and landed one week after D Day in France. His first job was putting out the large fires in the huge Allied petrol storage area at Arromanche; it was the size of Hyde Park.

Following the troops into Belgium, Leonard's team befriended a Jewish family who had been in hiding throughout the war, like Anne Frank; he fed them for a month until he was posted to Arnhem and Nijmegen. In Holland he fought many fires caused by the incessant German shelling, day and night. During one fire at a rubber warehouse in late 1944 a German shell landed right in the blaze and Leonard was injured and sent to hospital; two *Daily Mirror* photographers with him were killed.

After recovering he was sent to Kaggervin in Belgium in 1945. There he met some former Belgium Resistance workers who told him about a crashed Canadian plane that had been buried by the Germans with its crew during the war; Leonard reported this and saw that it was exhumed and the men given a proper War Grave burial. He was then sent to Oldenberg in Germany where he befriended the concierge in the billet he was given. The concierge asked Leonard if he could help him find his son who had been in the SS and was missing in Russia. Leonard told him what the SS had done during the war and the man tore up his son's uniform, made a wallet from his son's old jackboots and gave it to Leonard as a memento. Leonard later acted as an interpreter at Belsen concentration camp between the Allies and the prisoners there, as he spoke French and German.

He returned to live in Clapton after the war.

NOTE

1. Taken from an article in the *Hackney Gazette*, 7 September 1995, p.12.

Chapter Four

Harry Errington/ Ehrengott, GC[1]

Harry was born in a tiny, two-roomed flat at 47 Poland Street, Westminster on 20 August 1910. He was one of four children of Yiddish-speaking, poor, observant Jewish Polish immigrants Solomon and Bella Ehrengott, who were tailors from Lubartov, near Lublin. In 1908, fleeing the pogroms, they came to England and soon changed their name to Errington.[2] Educated at St James and St Peters Infants School in Great Windmill Street, after a short time he transferred to

47. Harry Errington/ Ehrengott GC, as a young fireman 1942.

48. Harry Errington on the AJEX Parade in the 1990s with his GC.

49. Harry Errington at the Soho Fire Station on his 90th birthday in 2000. This photo hangs in a place of honour in the first floor corridor.

50. Grave of Harry Errington at Cheshunt Jewish Cemetery.

51. The entire squad of the Rathbone Place sub-station, standing on the roof of Jackson's garage, where Harry Errington later won his George Cross. Harry is sitting centre without hat. The two men he rescued are John Hollingshead (standing just behind but to right of Harry with round glasses and crossed respirator belt and peaked hat), and John Terry (back row, eighth from right). Photo by kind permission from Martin Lloyd-Elliot, *City Ablaze: Life with the World's Busiest Fire-fighters* (London: Bloomsbury Books, 1992).

the Westminster Jewish Free School. His Bar Mitzvah was at the old Manetti Street synagogue in Soho. Harry had vague memories of the First World War – especially sleeping at Oxford Circus underground station to avoid the German bombers, and going on free joy rides along the line to pass the time. Back at Oxford Circus after the raids he would then run about the streets with his gang of friends collecting hot pieces of shrapnel. He recalled policemen on bikes with whistles and rattles sounding the all clear, Zeppelins bathed in searchlights as they bombed London, and 'war tourists' coming from all over the south to see the results of the bombing on London. Of rationing, he said, there was very little.

The West End Jewish community was a vibrant but poor one and faced much anti-Semitism when it came to employment; hence many were self employed in small businesses.

Harry initially trained as an engraver, but the nitric acid fumes used in engraving affected his chest, so instead he went to trade school and

52. The site of Jackson and Allum garage at 7–9 Rathbone Street, W1, as it looks in 2015.

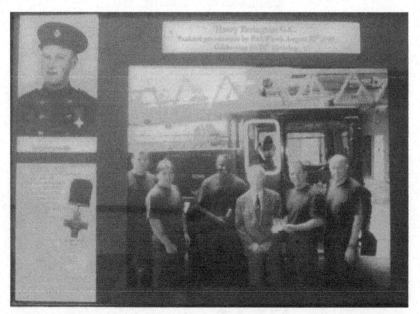

53. Harry Errington at his 90th birthday party at Soho Fire Station in 2000. Today this photo is in a place of honour on the first floor.

became a tailor (at Errington and Whyte), working for his uncle in Savile Row. His job was to take finished articles to Savile Row shops and bring back further work for his uncle's shop ('outdoor tailoring'). Harry later spent the rest of his professional life in that street. After

Numb. 35239   4545

SUPPLEMENT

TO

The London Gazette

Of TUESDAY, the 5th of AUGUST, 1941

Published by Authority

Registered as a newspaper

FRIDAY, 8 AUGUST, 1941

CENTRAL CHANCERY OF THE ORDERS OF KNIGHTHOOD.

St. James's Palace, S.W.1.
8th August, 1941.

The KING has been graciously pleased to award the GEORGE CROSS to:—

Harry Errington, Auxiliary Fireman, London Auxiliary Fire Service.

High explosive and incendiary bombs demolished a building. Errington and two other Auxiliary Firemen were the only occupants of the basement of the building at the time of the explosion. The blast blew Errington across the basement, but although dazed and injured he made his way to the other two Auxiliaries, whom he found to be pinned down, flat on their backs, by debris. A fierce fire broke out and the trapped men were in imminent danger of being burnt to death. The heat of the fire was so intense that Errington had to protect himself with a blanket. After working with his bare hands for some minutes he managed to release the injured men and dragged them from under the wreckage and away from the fire.

While he was so engaged, burning debris was falling into the basement and there was considerable danger of a further collapse of the building. He carried one of the men up a narrow stone staircase partially choked with debris, into the courtyard, made his way through an adjoining building and thence into the street.

Despite the appalling conditions and although burned and injured, Errington returned and brought out the second man.

Both Errington's comrades were severely burned but survived. He showed great bravery and endurance in effecting the rescues, at the risk of his own life.

CENTRAL CHANCERY OF THE ORDERS OF KNIGHTHOOD.

St. James's Palace, S.W.1.
8th August, 1941.

The KING has been graciously pleased to give orders for the undermentioned appointment to the Most Excellent Order of the British Empire, for the following awards of the George Medal and of the British Empire Medal and for the publication in the London Gazette of the names of the persons specially shown below as having received an expression of Commendation for their brave conduct in Civil Defence:—

To be an Additional Officer of the Civil Division of the Most Excellent Order of the British Empire:—

James Foulds Knape, Deputy A.R.P. Controller, Plymouth.

Mr. Knape has given outstanding service to the Plymouth A.R.P. organisation.

54. Harry Errington's George Cross citation in the *London Gazette*, 5 August 1941.

learning to be a cutter he got his first job in 1930 with a famous Dutch tailor called Sholti, who as soon as he discovered that Harry was Jewish, sacked him. Harry described him as 'a real bastard to work for anyway'. When he applied for two further jobs, on hearing his Jewish name, the owners immediately replied, 'we do not want anyone on the J book' i.e. Jews. After, he used the name Errington and found work. His next job in 1936 was with the famous tailors Simpsons of Piccadilly, with whom he stayed for many years. At this time Harry was also manager of the West Central Jewish Youth Club.

Three weeks before war was declared, Harry joined the AFS fulltime, with three friends, at Shaftesbury Avenue area HQ.[3] Harry was highly motivated as he had over twenty relatives in Poland, all of whom he later learnt were murdered in the Holocaust.

There was no waiting on ceremony: he was interviewed, looked up and down, given a quick fitness test and signed on.[4] When he joined up, Harry said, 'we were given our uniform on the spot, but I had such a big head they could not find a helmet to fit me for months. As soon as we were enrolled and kitted out ... we were sent to one of the sub-stations ... and we slept crunched up in the taxis whilst 200 yards away my family slept in the comfort of their lovely beds'. Later they moved to quarters in a school in nearby Hanway Place, about 400 yards away.

He was first based at a sub-station of Shaftesbury Avenue Station, near the present-day Cambridge Circus, at the corner of Rathbone Place and Oxford Street (station 72Z) with his crew of four, the usual requisitioned taxi, a pump trailer and telephone and alarm link to HQ. For several months (the 'phoney war') little happened; they slept in the taxi when on duty and enjoyed their training. Morale was high and as they had good chefs among their crew from the West End restaurants, the mess food was excellent. There were also theatre people in the crew and concert parties were first-rate. One farcical item was a striptease by John Terry (Harry later won his GC saving him), and Harry's role was to push his arm through the curtain to act as a hook on which Terry hung his clothes; 'it brought the house down', said Harry.

In early 1940 he was transferred to Jackson and Allum's garage further along from 72Z, at 7–9 Rathbone Street, not far from where he lived in Poland Street, so he could walk to work. This station now had five crews and larger wagons for towing the pumps. Jackson's had three floors and a basement with a large elevator so that cars could park on upper floors if need be. All the fire vehicles and equipment were parked on the ground floor, so when they got ' a shout' at night, they had to dash from Hanway Place to Jackson's – which was alright for the younger men a but a bit hard on the older ones.

Once the Blitz began, on 7 September 1940, among the incidents Harry took part in were fire bombings at Woolwich Arsenal, Peckham, Camberwell, East Surrey Docks, Great Eastern Street and even chasing a burning barge near St Katherine's Dock. On other nights they were on standby at many other stations in case help was needed, including Long Acre, Clerkenwell, Shoreditch and Farringdon.

The George Cross Event

On the night of 17 September, Harry and his comrades were exhausted and were resting in the basement at Jackson's garage. There were about twenty firemen and thirty civilians in the air raid cellar of the garage. The firemen were in their shirt sleeves and using their tunics as pillows and just a blanket as a mattress on the concrete floor. They slept restlessly as bombs fell in the area. Around midnight the building received a direct hit and the floors above collapsed as the vehicles and the garage petrol store, above, crashed into the basement, creating a fireball. Harry was blown across the cellar floor, and woke and found himself standing up stunned but unhurt; but twenty-six were killed including six (some say seven) firemen, among them another Jewish Fireman, Myer Wand (see Roll of Honour).

When he came to, the cellar was burning and full of smoke and rubble; he tried to get to the stairs, but they were blocked and then he remembered another exit so he made for that. Suddenly he heard screaming and saw his friend John Hollingshead who was lying face down in terrific pain as his legs were trapped by heavy masonry from the waist and his exposed naked back was badly burnt. Placing a blanket over his head to try and protect himself, Harry retraced his steps, and pulled John free by scraping away the rubble with his bare hands even though they were by then burnt and cut and the skin was peeling off in strips; he was in great pain. He then half carried, half dragged John up another rubble-filled stairwell. Meanwhile the fire worsened and the building above heaved and groaned ready to collapse completely.

On the way out he saw another friend trapped; this was John Terry (later Sir John Terry, a solicitor). A radiator lay across his body, and he was semi-conscious with a huge bloodied lump on his head the size of an orange. Having hauled Hollingshead out to the street, and despite the danger of the basement collapsing totally, and the raging fire, Harry then returned to the cellar and freed Terry, dragging him bodily, despite his injured and burnt hands which he knew could end his livelihood. This time he got out by yet another exit – a window that had been blasted away – as the stairs were now blocked with debris and flames. Leaving Terry propped up by a nearby wall, to be cared for by first aid men, he took Hollingshead staggering south towards the women's hospital he knew was in Soho Square; the skin on his back was burnt away. On the way Harry heard a terrific whoosh as a bomb fell very nearby and they both dived to the ground; Harry said he could have dug into the concrete pavement if he had had the strength.

At the hospital, they treated Hollingshead and also washed and bound Harry's right forearm which was both cut and burnt; he was also concussed. Terry meanwhile was taken to the Middlesex Hospital and both he and Harry met up later at Cheshunt Hospital where they had to stay for about two weeks. Harry remembers they were given beer each lunch time because among their fellow patients were Canadian soldiers who did not like English beer and gave it away! Harry also recalled being visited by a Jewish chaplain but could not remember his name.

After four months recovering, Harry was discharged and returned to his family's new flat in Ridgmount Gardens, Greek Street. His cousin was staying there with him as his parents had moved to Birmingham. They decided it would be safer to sleep in the basement as raids were expected and in fact the flats received a direct hit on his first night home. Leaving the basement, Harry worked calmly to rescue people from the building and then he and his cousin made for Goodge Street Station to rest, waking up in the middle of the morning rush hour.

Harry was thereafter advised by doctors to take a long rest.[5] He was actually treated very shabbily by the Fire Service management. The Civil Injuries Act meant that men injured in service could only be kept on full pay for thirteen weeks and as his burns failed to heal in this period, he was compulsorily discharged from the London Brigade.[6] So he went next day to join his family who were staying with an aunt and Uncle Lou who lived in Birmingham Road, Bromsgrove, Birmingham and the AFS invalided Harry out of the service.

Afterwards

For a while he had nightmares about that night of the Soho bombing. He spent his time in Bromsgrove working at Austin Aero helping make Lancaster Bombers and teaching sports at a youth club in the evenings. He then rejoined the local NFS part-time until the end of the war as the Army refused him as unfit due to his injuries during the Blitz.

For his gallantry, Harry was awarded the highest decoration for bravery, equivalent to the VC. Whilst in Bromsgrove he received, much to his amazement, the letter which announced the honour; he had no idea exactly who recommended it, but years later discovered that Terry and Hollingshead had reported events to a senior officer. A Major

Jackson described Harry's act as 'carried out under appalling conditions (he had third degree burns) at very considerable risk and obviously without any thought for self preservation. By his act he displayed exceptional bravery and endurance.'[7] The award was Gazetted on 8 August 1941.[8] Even years after he felt a little embarrassed by the award. Only later did he realize what a celebrity it had made him.

He went to Buckingham Palace in October 1942 to receive the GC from the King. There was a VC given at the same ceremony and the various other awards were given in different rooms in the Palace. Harry's parents and sister Freda came with him but only his parents were allowed in. He was given a hook to place on his left breast in order for the King to pin the medal easily onto his tunic. He was warned not to stand too far from the King in order that the King should not have to stretch too much, and also not to grip his hand too firmly when he shook it.

Harry was one of three Jewish GCs of the Second World War, one of only three given to firemen, and one of only 139 awarded; he was the only London fireman to receive it during that war.

Childhood friend Jack Feldman,[9] who left school to work as a furrier in the 1920s and 1930s, lived as a young boy at the time in the same house as Harry's family at 55 Broadwick Street, Golden Square, W1 and knew the family very well. Harry was the Club Manager at West Central when Jack attended as a teenager. Jack described Harry as a most self-effacing and quiet man and was not surprised when, after the award, he saw Mrs Errington walking round the area with Harry, asking every one of the neighbours she saw if they would like to see Harry's super medal! Needless to say Harry was pleased his mother took such pride in him, but was greatly embarrassed by her showing off his GC to all and sundry.

Harry was a lifelong lover of gymnastics and a sports coach, especially in basketball at the Regents Street Polytechnic; he became Vice Chair and also Life President of the UK Amateur Basketball Association, often travelling round the world with the British team, including at several Olympics. All who knew him described him as a modest, dignified and loving man.

For years after the war he remained in contact with John Terry and every year was invited to stay with him and his family in Exeter for Christmas. Terry's wife used to tell Harry that it was because of him, she was able to have her two children and a happy family life. Harry said this was the greatest compliment he could ever receive; they all remained good friends until they died.

Harry returned to work for Simpsons but eventually set up his own business, Errington and Whyte in Sackville Street. He was an active member (Treasurer) of the VC and GC Association and of Westminster AJEX, often attending the Annual AJEX Jewish Parade in Whitehall. He belonged to the West End Great Synagogue. He never married, retired in 1992 and from 2002 was a resident of the Nightingale Jewish Old Age Home in South London.[10] Harry died on 15 December 2004 and at his funeral at Cheshunt Western Jewish cemetery, three fire engines and a large firemen Guard of Honour with Standards were present at the service and grave side. His photograph hangs still in the watch room of the Soho Fire Station in Shaftesbury Avenue, where the firemen gave him a splendid 90th birthday party in 2000. The Fire Services College at Moreton-in-the-Marsh named a road after him on the site. In 1990 he was one of three GC holders invited to sign a limited edition of 1,000 first day covers (postage stamps on commemorative envelopes) on the 50th anniversary of the institution of the George Cross.

His other medals included the Defence Medal, the Elizabeth II Coronation Medal, the Elizabeth II Silver Jubilee Medal and the Golden Jubilee Medal. On his death they were presented to the Jewish Museum with his miniatures and are on display at the Jewish Military Museum section of the Jewish Museum, gifted by his large extended family. There is also a display about Harry at the LFB Museum in Southwark.

Appendix

The St Marylebone Civil Defence Records at the Westminster Council Archives (file 80) contain about forty original messages on official message-pad paper, charting the events immediately following the bombing of Jackson's Garage. At precisely 14 minutes past midnight (00:14) on 17/18 September 1940, the first of many messages came through from Tottenham Court Road Police Station, scrawled in pencil, reading, 'Incident Rathbone Street ... send ambulances as quickly as possible ... most urgent'.

This was followed minutes later in quick succession by, 'Jackson's Garage ... fire ... gas mains not ignited ... approx. 20 casualties, 10 buried'; then 'Auxiliary Fire Station (hit) – 1 light rescue party'. At 00:56 the message read, 'Fire under control ... Stretcher Parties operating, Repair Party and Ambulance'. At 01:04 a message read, 'All trapped now freed – death van required'. At 04:47 a further message read, 'cries of help from basement can be heard' and at 06:22, 'Hampstead Rescue Party called to help'. Bodies were being found up until 29 September.[11]

NOTES

1. Some detail is taken from Harry's taped interview at the IWM, which he recorded in the year 2000, and the Jewish Museum tape interview No.32, recorded in 1991. Additional information came from a 1985 letter Harry wrote to Jack Lennard in his files, kept at the Jewish Military Museum.
2. Ehrengott means 'honour God'.
3. His sister meanwhile got an important secretarial job with the World Jewish Congress in London.
4. Martin Lloyd-Elliott, *City Ablaze: Life with the World's Busiest Fire-fighters* (London: Bloomsbury Books, 1992), p.57 and passim.
5. *Jewish Chronicle*, 22 August 1941.
6. Neil Wallington, *Firemen at War: The Work of London's Firefighters in the Second World War* (London: David and Charles, 1981), p.101.
7. Arthur Lockyear, *Warriors in Fire Boots: A Tribute to the Valour of Firefighters* (Yorkshire: Jeremy Mills Publishing, 2011), pp.125–7.
8. Not surprisingly the *London Gazette* citation bears only some resemblance to what actually took place. The statements made by Hollingshead and Terry essentially repeat the descriptions of what happened as explained above.
9. Interviewed aged 92 at his home in February 2014. Jack served in the Argyll and Sutherland Highlanders with his twin brother Louis and saw much fighting in Italy 1943–45 and was later in the BAOR in Germany till 1947.
10. When a memorial service was held for the Jewish RN Victoria Cross holder Tommy Gould at St Martin in the Fields, in 2001, the author had the pleasure of meeting and chatting to Harry. Wearing his George Cross alongside many other VC and GC holders, he was a charming and delightful man who left a great impression.
11. Thanks go to Howard Davies of TNA for pointing out this file for me; despite searches by the author at TNA there is no mention of the bombing in the Bomb Census accounts in HO 198. The 17/18 September 1940 appears to be almost the exact date of the start of records that survive, and the Rathbone Street bombing does therefore not get mentioned or described. Despite searches of many local and national photo archives and newspapers, no images of Jackson's garage before and after the bombing, seem to exist.

    In November 2020, a black and gold granite plaque commemorating Harry's George Cross award was fixed on a wall on the site of the incident in Rathbone Place, Soho by the author, funded by Jerry Klinger of the Jewish American Society for historic preservation, and supported by AJEX. See page 398 for photo.

Chapter Five

Sidney Gabriel[1]

Sidney lived at 13 Jewel Street, Stepney, but after it was bombed Sidney and his family were homeless, sleeping on the floor of a nearby school hall until they were ultimately re-housed at 23 Coram Street, Holborn. From there he volunteered as a firefighter, aged 17 years old. He was issued with dungarees, boots, steel helmet, gas respirator and an identity card naming him as a fireman.

He duly reported to his sub-station at the council cleaning depot that night where some men playing cards told him to find a bed in the next room, and he went to sleep. Next day he was told to report on Sunday afternoon for training with ten others; he was shown an old open-topped lorry which was the fire engine! It had a short ladder tied to its side, only long enough to reach to one floor above the ground. A petrol driven pump stood next to it together with some hoses and red fire buckets full of sand. But there was no driver and so nobody knew how they would ever get to an incident.

Later, they placed a hose onto a hydrant and it took three men to control the recoil as it squirted into an imaginary fire in the yard. They also practised placing a bucket of sand on an imaginary incendiary, whilst lying on the ground – to avoid the explosive device which was in the tail of the incendiary blowing up in the face of the fireman. They also learnt how to crawl through a hut full of smoke at face level, to illustrate how there can be sufficient air at floor level to enable you to breath in a smoke-filled room; they entered through a kennel-type door at one end and exited at the other. One volunteer was a bit stout and afraid he could not get in or out of the kennel entrance, so he crept round the shed unnoticed and pretended he had gone through. When nobody appeared at the exit there was a moment of panic as the other volunteers thought he was stuck inside; they later discovered what he had done!

Soon after, during a raid, a call came and the men rushed to a warehouse nearby where the roof had been set alight by an incendiary.

But they could not gain entrance as the door had steel panels and the windows were all alarmed. They had no axes and had to wait till the regular firemen arrived. Next came an office building in the City and the caretaker let them in to fight the fire; but the nearby street water tank was dry and their hoses could not work as the nearest hydrant was too far away for their hoses to reach! Again they had to wait for the regular firemen to arrive.

Later Sidney was able to assist in fighting two real fires but an abiding memory was attending a gutted office block building in the City. They were sent to relieve the night team who had extinguished the fire, but Sidney was amazed to see long, sharp icicles hanging from the ruins. The night had been so cold that despite the raging fires, hose water on the facade of the Victorian building had turned to ice and these were falling and could cause serious injury to passers by. His team helped by rolling hoses and sweeping glass from the roads.

NOTE

1. From Sidney's privately published book, *Recollections*.

Chapter Six

Hyman Gilbert[1]

Hyman Gilbert was born in Liverpool on 4 September 1877/1879, one of eight children. His father, Jacob, who was born in Warsaw, Poland was a shoemaker, and had come to England in the 1850s. The family first lived in Manchester but later settled in Liverpool.

Hyman ran a butcher's outfitters from a little shop at 30a Brunswick Road, Liverpool with his brothers Abraham, Isaac, Morris, Henry and Solly. His sister Rachel also helped out there. Unfortunately the business went bankrupt in 1903.

Hyman was a keen cyclist and was elected as Chairman of the Liverpool Time Trials Cycling Association in March 1924. The Hyman Gilbert Silver Cup was presented to the association by Hyman and it is still raced for today.

Hyman married late in life at the age of 51 to Nellie Silverstone on 21 August 1928 at Princes Road Synagogue in Liverpool. Nellie was 19 years his junior and ran the La Caritas Dancing Academy in Liverpool. Unfortunately, Nellie died five years later of heart disease.

Hyman was a firewatcher in the Second World War and was killed during Liverpool's May blitz on 3 May 1941 when the ammunition ship, SS *Malakand*, blew up after catching fire. The ship was in Huskisson Dock and was being loaded with 1,000 tonnes of munitions when it caught fire from flames from nearby burning warehouses and exploded, devastating the surrounding area. His body was not found until 6 May 1941.

The family story is that the mortuary that he was resting in was also bombed and therefore he was buried in a mass burial at Anfield cemetery on 13 May 1941, section 7, grave 736. However his family have not been able to discover any proof that this story is true. Hyman is mistakenly named on the CWGC site as Gilbert Hyman (i.e. the names are inverted) – see Roll of Honour in the introduction.

NOTE

1. Submitted by his great niece, Sue McFarlane.

Chapter Seven

Joe Gilbert[1]

Joe was born in 1915 into the small Jewish West End community known as the Soho Ghetto, and became a barber like his father before him. His father and uncles all served in the First World War. After marrying Betty Swartzer in 1939 at Philpot Street synagogue, they moved to Stamford Hill and Joe joined the AFS on the outbreak of war.

Joe soon became a qualified driver and was stationed at Kings Cross but was given a special pass so that if there was an emergency he could report to any fire station for duty. Joe remembered one early siren went off on 11 November 1939 and he and his crew were sent to stand by two huge gasometers near Kings Cross. It was a false alarm. There followed some domestic fires, and then when the Blitz began he recalled his first fire at a school in Hampstead. A huge oil bomb had landed and they were not sure how to handle it; through trial and error they discovered that it was easiest to extinguish using sand. Later he fought fires in Tottenham Court Road.

One evening he and his wife were on their way home after visiting friends when the air raid sirens sounded. Having accompanied his wife to a local air raid shelter, he made his way to Brooke Road Fire Station in Stoke Newington. The City and Docks were an inferno and Joe was ordered to drive a petrol lorry to the Docks to re-fuel the fire engines and pumps; given the bombing and fires, this was a very dangerous job. He was directed to take the Blackwall Tunnel route but there he was confronted by a bus that had taken a direct hit and had been blown over the entrance to the tunnel. He managed to steer around it and reached the docks where a senior fire officer congratulated him for getting through so quickly with the badly needed fuel. Seeing Joe's pass, the officer asked if Joe would stay and assist with the pumps to get water from the Thames, as the mains had been breached. Later he was sent aloft on a turn table ladder, directing the hose at the seat of the fire. At intervals he was deliberately hosed with water to keep him from burning.

The warehouses full of molasses and other inflammables burnt, and Joe and his comrades had to slowly retreat as walls collapsed. Joe was there for three nights on shifts, with the Salvation Army supplying food and tea. Much equipment was destroyed and many firemen were casualties.

In 1941 Joe was called up and served as a Sergeant in the Royal Artillery for the rest of the war.

NOTE

1. Jewish Museum, tape 327.

Chapter Eight

Manny Gold

Living in Chelsea and working as a tailor in the West End, Manny joined the Fire service in January 1939, aged 30, and was posted to Soho Station. Every Tuesday and Thursday he had to report for drill and learnt knot-tying, hose and ladder drill and did general PE. He had been told to leave his kit (peaked cap, boots and overalls), which he was given at the depot in Theobolds Road, on a hook at the station with his name on it, and it would be there next session. When he returned, it was gone and when he complained the officer said, 'Well take someone else's then!'

55. Fireman Manny Gold

56. Fireman Manny Gold standing left on the taxi.

57. Fireman Manny Gold at the Royal Academy fire with hose.

Aside from a few drill displays for the public, all was relatively quiet, but on 1 September he was ordered to an empty car showroom at 110 Jermyn Street and arrived with his suitcase to find hundreds of others milling about. Nothing happened but on 3 September he was again posted to the London Pavilion in Piccadilly Circus. Here he became a team with three other men and they were given a London taxi, with twenty lengths of 50-feet hose, ladders strapped to the top of the cab, and a trailer pump to pull along behind the taxi. With four other crews they stayed put for several weeks and then were sent to the Canada Life Building in Charles II Street off Piccadilly, designated Station X. It was a full size station, one of six in Soho, with 10 pumps and catering and sleeping facilities for 100 men and women. Evening entertainment included being solicited by prostitutes hanging about after dark with torches saying, 'Hello darling – like to come home with me tonight?'.

Requisitioned taxis were use to pull the Dennis pumps and also held ladders and hoses. Manny passed tests in driving Bedford trucks and Dennis Fire Engines if needed

When the Blitz began the main centres attacked were in the docks, but in July 1940 came their first call out to Buerk's chemical factory in East Ham. They drove via the City with bombs falling all around them, and when civilians heard their bell, they tried to stop them to attend their house fires. On arrival at Buerk's, they accidentally drove over an unexploded bomb. They got near the river and started to pump out water but the tide was going out and as they were strafed by a German plane, they were forced to run for cover into a nearby shelter. Night after night they were called out with no time for meaningful rest, and it was always devastating to see the smashed streets as the sun rose each day after they had fought the blazes at night. On one occasion in West Ham, he wrote in a letter to daughter Marilyn, he fought a fire in a sulphuric acid and chloride plant. The bombing was so intense they had to shelter in a cellar and let the fire burn itself out, and were only able to return to base from a 12-hour shift next morning at 7 a.m., having not eaten or drunk since lunch time the day before. No leave was permitted in this terrible period, he wrote, and he advised his family to always take to the Anderson shelter in raids.

Soon, Manny was appointed Deputy Station Officer, and so had to direct operations, returning each morning filthy, wet and tired from the air raids. On cold nights hoses could freeze and buildings had to be left to burn. Often they had to travel to old schools or office blocks at one of their six sub stations to help cover for men already out on calls. On occasion a Chief Fire Officer would swoop at 2 a.m. for a drill and Manny had to get dressed, alert the crews, run down to start the engine, alight the crew, and then drive round a square – to prove they were always prepared.

Manny recalled the evening of Sunday 7 September 1940; waves of bombers attacked huge dock warehouses containing essential war supplies, much of which was combustible, and at Whisky Wharf he witnessed an especially huge explosion. Dock work was very dangerous for this reason as it was not always known what the buildings contained. On one occasion the Turkish baths next to Fortnum and Mason was hit. Manny's crews were called out and two colleagues climbed onto the glass-domed roof to dampen the fire. Suddenly another bomb went off, hit a gas main and the resultant explosion blew Manny and his mate hard against a wall and smashed the glass dome just as the two other firemen had moved off it; a lucky escape for them all that night.

To help solve the water supply problem two steel tanks were built as a reserve in Haymarket and Regent Street and contained 5,000 gallons of water each, filled from water hydrants. One night Shaftesbury Avenue station was hit and the commander killed; Manny was part of the Guard of Honour at his funeral.

On a lighter note, although warned never to loot, when Burlington Arcade was hit, two men from his station emerged from the debris with so many shirts on under their tunics, they looked like Michelin men; a blind eye was turned.

In 1944 the second V1 and V2 Blitz began and Manny was stationed at Westminster, mostly working on helping people recover possessions from bombed homes. After the war Manny returned to tailoring and died in 2004 aged 94.

Chapter Nine

Samuel Guttenberg/Godfrey

AFS/NFS 112 Samuel Guttenberg was born on 7 March or February (!) 1909 in Albert Square, E1, the son of Morris Isaac (a master tailor, born in Commercial Road) and Sophie née Goldberg (born in Plotsk, Poland, but brought to England when she was 2 weeks old). Sam went to Malmesbury Road School in Mile End when the family went to live in Cleveland Street near Cambridge Heath Road, now Tower Hamlets. They then moved to 83 Bow Road. Sam had two older brothers (Zola and Jack) and they all left school aged 14 years.

58. Fireman Sam Guttenberg aka Godfrey, taken just pre-war.

When Sam was 5 years old, whilst the family were on holiday at Thorpe Bay, the First World War broke out. Refused by the Army for medical reasons, his father Morris and his brother obtained work for the Government to repair soldiers' uniforms; the family moved to Brighton and Morris commuted each day to London by train. Before this, Sam remembers the Zeppelins bombing London. One bomb landed near their Bow Road house, and Sam saw the very first Zeppelin shot down in flames – it broke in half as it plummeted to earth crashing ultimately in Enfield. The British fighter pilot, Robinson, got the VC.[1] He also recalled digging bomb and shell shrapnel out of the tarmac outside his school with his mates.

Sam attended Mornington Road Talmud Torah but he often 'bunked off' lessons. He was Bar Mitzvah with four other boys on the same day in 1922 at Stepney Green synagogue; five boys together was a record and the story was in the *Jewish Chronicle*.

Sam went to work at a chemist shop in Old Bailey when he left school, then moved to Houndsditch to a shop that sold Swiss embroideries; after that he worked at John Blundell's furniture store in City Road, lying about his age to obtain the job (which paid more) as he was still too young to officially work. Sacked for forbidden use of the company manager's car, he then moved to a firm near the London Hospital and later still found work with Master's Trading Company where he stayed till 1939. He was then offered the managership of their branch in Portsmouth and so he moved there.

Portsmouth

After some anti-Jewish remarks from a member of staff who came down from London head office to inspect the business, Sam walked out and volunteered for the RAF as a Wireless Operator/Gunner. But there was such a long wait for training and so he decided to join the Fire Service around April 1940. His AFS group were mostly Welsh policemen.[2] Sam was both a driver and pump operator, mainly obtaining water supplies from the sea during raids. He shared a rented house with other firemen in Southsea.

The first German raid on Portsmouth[3] hit a major bridge and also cut off the water mains; street water tanks only lasted a few minutes. So they had to pump sea water via three engines to the fire locations in the docks. Sam also witnessed the struggle to get people to leave their homes when fires spread; they often refused. On one occasion a senior fire officer suggested they knock down houses in order to stop fires spreading, but nobody had the explosive skills and the buildings just burnt.

On another raid, he was dragging boxes of live ammunition out of the Victoria barracks as they burnt,[4] when one of the men who had refused to do this very dangerous work told him, 'I never thought a Jew would do that Sam'. Sam's reply is unprintable. For weeks Sam refused to talk to him, but the man felt ashamed and apologized and said he did not realize what he was saying. Sam should have been given an award and he knows an enquiry was made to the Home Office about this. But Sam had made a complaint that the police had taken shelter during the incident with the ammunition, leaving Sam and other firemen to do the dangerous work of moving the explosives. Sam overheard one officer call him a 'black bastard' because he had dark hair – another anti-Semitic remark – and is sure any prospect of a bravery award was quashed because he spoke out. Sam made himself even more unpopular with the officers when he complained that at the height of the Blitz, his crew were always on duty night after night from 6 p.m. in full fire-fighting gear, seated in the engine ready to go, like pilots waiting to scramble, whilst other firemen were directing traffic outside the town in safety. He said that the teams should swap and his crew be given a break. Nothing came of it.

Later, his station in Queens Road was bombed and his crew moved to share the dockyard station where bombing was of course especially heavy. Sam was involved in many fire-fighting incidents there. On one occasion he was 100 feet up on the turntable ladder where he had an all round view of the many fires burning all over the docks; strangely, he said, he felt safe at that height; he recalls that there were 2,000 casualties that night. He used to find bits of bodies on roofs of houses where people had been blown to pieces.

Sam said three other Jewish men were with him in the Portsmouth Fire Service – all received awards except him. One was a Dave Gold,[5] another a Dutch Jewish man whose name he does not remember. Another Jewish fire colleague was Morris Lesser. He attended services in the synagogue on a few occasions when there was time.

The station officer in the docks was also an anti-Semite ('Yiddified bastard' as Sam said, using an old fashioned cockney Jewish expression for an anti-Semite) and whenever possible gave Sam any difficult or uncomfortable jobs that came along. One day he ordered Sam to clean the toilets; Sam threw water down and brushed the floor thoroughly but the officer insisted he scrub it on his knees. Sam protested it was clean and just at that moment a higher ranking officer approached and asked what the problem was. When Sam explained, the senior officer inspected the toilet and said it was indeed clean and ordered Sam back to his post, and reprimanded the other officer. As a result, the man disliked Sam even more after that, but Sam was a tough East End lad and was not bothered by it in any way.

Later a request came from the HQ at the Town Hall for a man to be sent down for a job; usually this meant the messy task of scrubbing hoses from the previous night's bombing. When he arrived he was taken to a private room and was told he was about to be given confidential information, and if he thought he was unable to keep it secret, he should leave the room now. He was told the King and Queen were arriving for a visit to the town next day and he and others were to form a Fireman Guard of Honour. When he arrived back at his station, the anti-Semite asked him what kind of rough job he did, but Sam said it was confidential and he could not tell him what happened. The officer became angry and Sam told him to phone HQ if he wished. When the officer found out what was happening he tried to get Sam replaced, to no avail. On the parade, the Queen (later Queen Mother) stopped at the man next to Sam and asked 'if he was happy in his work'.

One of Sam's crew, called Tom, was their cook. One day as a raid began, he failed to report for duty and so Sam went to his house and found it had been damaged. He called out but there was no reply so Sam ran upstairs and found Tom fast asleep on the bed covered in debris. He had not even woken up. He and Sam were good friends. When rabbit was on the menu, Sam would not eat it as it is not kosher. So Tom would especially buy him a piece of steak instead, something which Sam remembered with emotion.

Sam decided one day to enter the fireman's snooker competition and got to the final and beat the champion, a friend of his with whom he often drank on evenings off. After that he refused to drink with Sam. Sam also saw that a lot of firemen took part in looting empty houses in the wealthier parts of the city, where people had left the area to live in other, safer locations.

Later Sam was moved to the finance section at HQ and after a few days was transferred to the National Fire Service. Whilst working on the Records section he came across a sheet in his file where he had been charged with not taking due care of his boots when they were stolen from him, and using the motorcycle for changing the crews' ration books (an unauthorised use of Fire Service fuel). So he tore the sheet up and carried on work!

Sam also recalled seeing the V1's passing over the city, on their way to other targets; the distinctive engine noise, profile and blue flame from the engine was very recognizable. On one occasion a huge crater appeared in Portsmouth and the authorities passed it off as a crashed aircraft, but Sam and friends believed it was a V1 that had fallen short or been shot down; presumably it was hushed up to prevent damaging morale in the city. On another occasion, Sam's crew were called to a house where an incendiary had dropped through a roof and landed in a bath! When one of the fireman turned a water tap on it, it exploded; he said they ran down the stairs pretty quickly.

For a while Sam was a despatch rider whose job was to ride a motorcycle ahead of an engine when it went to a domestic fire. Just before D Day he worked guiding massive military convoys from all over the south to their departure points on the coast; he said the roads were totally blocked with military traffic of all kinds, and his job was to act as point duty rider to assist their journey by clearing the road ahead. Later he went back onto station work.

After leaving the NFS, Sam joined the Merchant Navy. A friend got him forged references and he sailed from Southampton the day after enlisting on the RMMV *Athlone Castle* as a steward/waiter. After three trips, he resigned and entered civvy street as a tallyman. In 1953 he married Irene née Silver.

Just before Sam died in 1996, he said he had never bothered to claim his medal. So, the author wrote to the Home Office and claimed Sam's Defence Medal for him; it is now proudly owned by his family.

NOTES

1. Captain William Leefe Robinson, 39 Sqdn RFC, was the first pilot to shoot down a Zeppelin (SL11) on the night of 2–3 September 1916 in his BE2c night fighter. Sadly he died of flu in 1918 and is buried at Harrow Weald.
2. Sam said that a certain number of police officers, nationwide, had to make themselves available for Fire Service if the need arose.
3. If it was indeed the first raid, this was the evening of Thursday 11 July 1940. Sixty six more raids would follow over the next four years.
4. These naval barracks were hit several times during the war.
5. The author could find no record of a Dave Gold (Jewish or not) receiving an award, but this does not mean it did not happen. There was a David Gold, Fireman, KIA in April 1944 on Tayside at Broughty Ferry. The Dutch Jewish name was probably Andrew Nabarro.

Chapter Ten

Sidney Hart/Hartz

Sidney was born in East London on 11 September 1914 and rose to become the highest ranking Jewish officer in the Fire Service. One of four children of Amelia Mendes-Coutinho, the family belonged to Bevis Marks Synagogue. After leaving JFS he became a printer and was also a member of the Gravel Lane JLB; he was an athlete and often confronted Mosley's Fascists in the East End.

A part-time fireman, he was called up full time when war began in 1939, to Bishopsgate Station, and served throughout the Blitz. In one fire at Rum Quay in the docks, he testified as to how the men all became light-headed from the fumes of the burning alcohol. His father Samuel was also a fireman and his mother often turned up to fires, braving the bombs, with large pots of tea for the men. Both his wife and sister also served in the wartime Fire Brigade.

59. Station Officer Sidney Hart/Hartz, sitting third from left.

60. Station Officer Sidney Hart Hartz with hose.

Sidney was seriously injured at Liverpool Street Station during a Blitz fire on 11 January 1941, where he was picked out from the debris between two dead people. He was later transferred to Cardiff, and then served in Bangor, Rhyl and Connah's Quay. His wife Edith joined him at Colwyn Bay where their daughter Rona was born.

Post war he was active in the Fire Brigade Union, was secretary of the Colwyn Bay Synagogue and also captain of the Flint fire brigade cricket team. In 1958 he moved to Tilbury as Station Officer, whilst living in Westcliff. He retired in 1969, but then joined the Civil Service, still involved in Trade Union work as well as Jewish Youth Club work in Southend. On his 90th birthday, in 2004, firemen from Hadleigh station (his last command) arrived with flashing lights and sirens to help him celebrate. He died in 2005. His daughter lives in Israel.

Chapter Eleven

Martin Hichberger[1]

Martin was born on 8 August 1922 in Karlsruhe, Baden, an only child. At aged 14 he had to leave school as the Nazis closed all Jewish schools after having forced all Jewish pupils to leave the state schools. After working for a while in a department store he was dismissed under the anti-Semitic employment laws, and again after working in a Jewish upholstery factory. After Kristallnacht in 1938, he came to the UK on the Kindertransport (his parents were able to escape to the USA in 1940 because they knew the leading Nazi in the town and paradoxically he protected them).

61. Fireman Heinz Martin Hichberger, London.

Housed at Butlin's Camp at Dovercourt with hundreds of other Jewish children, a Quaker family eventually got him a job in Croydon as a builder and decorator, but this was interrupted by a spell at Huyton Camp (Liverpool) and Douglas, Isle of Man, when he was interned during the 1940 panic arrests of all refugees. On release he volunteered for the Fire Service in 1942. On finding out he was German, the other firemen used to joke when the bombers came over that Martin's countrymen were coming. But they were all very friendly towards him and he never met any anti-Semitism at all.

He was stationed in a sub-station at a school near the Mayday Hospital in Croydon, near Thornton Heath. He only attended one actual fire when a building was set alight after someone left a burning cigarette in a factory; most of his time was spent dealing with the rescue aftermath of the terrible destruction by the V1s. He was advised to buy gloves as he would be dealing with a lot of bodies. The Croydon area was very badly hit during this phase of the so-called 'Second Blitz' – over 140 rockets landed there.

Martin recalled that they slept on makeshift mattresses on the floor, always in full kit ready to go out on call. He usually worked from 7 p.m. to 7 a.m. three nights per week, and thus was part time. At nearby Whitgift School there were two large water tanks which were used for the men to practice with their pumps; water was pumped out of one tank into the empty tank.

With a watch-out on the station roof, if a 'Doodlebug' was seen, a very loud klaxon was sounded (if it was bombers, the siren was used). This gave some warning at least, so the public could get under tables in their homes or dive into shelters. The firemen, on their appliances, on the other hand, would chase the rockets to get to the scene where the V1 might crash and explode, as quickly as possible. In one incident Martin recalls the horror of taking a little girl in his arms to an ambulance after arriving at the scene, and being told the mother was dead and they were trying to get the body out; he openly wept as he carried the child to the waiting doctors. On another occasion he was at home, which was near the station, and the house behind him suffered a direct hit by a bomb. Martin climbed the fence and saw an arm sticking out of the earth; he dug and pulled out a woman alive. Some weeks later he was in the pub and a woman came over to thank him for saving her life; he was quite embarrassed. She had recognized his strong German accent.

Martin had a girlfriend who lived with her parents and a brother in a nearby street; one night a German bomb hit the house and they were all killed; he found out at work the next day. Another incident he witnessed was when a V1 passed over the roof of the fire station whilst one of the firemen was aloft hanging up hoses to dry from the towers; it had glided right over his head and exploded just a short distance away; when he came down from the roof, the fireman was shaking like a leaf as was a passing American soldier, who was suffering from shock following the blast. Once when walking home one night, he felt a terrific blow on his tin helmet; a chunk of shrapnel had fallen out of the sky and hit him. On another occasion he developed pneumonia and had to spend time at the Mayday Hospital; when the bombers came over the nurse would cheerfully re-assure him and say that as he was on the ground floor, there was a good chance he would survive if the hospital was hit. He was not amused.

After the war Martin joined his parents in America and was married, but returned to live in the UK in 1953 and raised a family.

NOTE

1. Recorded October 2007 by Stephanie Maltman.

Chapter Twelve

Renee Hurst née Gordon

Renee joined the AFS in late 1940 and was posted to Burdett Road station in Stepney, previously a school. On arrival she was met with cat calls and shouts of 'Rookie' by the men. Her then boyfriend, Sid, was already a fireman in Aldgate. She was taken to a dormitory which she would share with five other women. Renee was assigned to Blue Watch.

One of the women, called Winnie, was openly hostile to Renee and said it was because she was 'a bloody Jew', and it was because of the Jews they were in the war. She attacked Renee who defended herself with her fists as they fell to the floor fighting, furniture being flung everywhere. The other four women pulled them apart as an officer barged in and demanded to know what was going on.

Winnie and Renee were confined to their quarters by the Station Commander for conduct unbecoming, for two weeks and all leave cancelled, with extra fatigues to carry out around the station. Forced to spend a lot of time in each other's company, the two women got to know each other better and became a little friendly.

A week later the sirens went at the Burdett Road station and the women were on duty receiving and passing telephone messages during a raid. It was organized, noisy chaos. It was Renee's first emergency. Suddenly there was a terrific explosion nearby and Renee and others were thrown to the floor; Renee hit her head and blood trickled down her face. She hid under the large desk and refused to come out despite threats from her officer. Eventually she emerged and went back to her switchboard. As she sat down the phone rang and she answered with trembling hands and voice; she took the message and passed it to her officer who barked out an order, gently encouraging her with a comment of praise. Thus she continued through the watch until the all clear came.

News came next day of the death of some of her colleagues in other stations and she felt ashamed at how she had behaved earlier on. Both her officer and Winnie consoled her and said many were frightened first time round. Winnie and Renee became friends and kept in touch after the war. Winnie married a Canadian soldier and went to live abroad, sadly being killed in a car crash years later. But until then Winnie and Renee never forgot each other each birthday and Christmas.

Chapter Thirteen

Margaret 'Peggy' Sara Jacobs née Joseph, BEM[1]

Margaret was born in Cricklewood in 1915 and, while she was a manager at the Stepney Settlement Jewish Club, she joined up with the AFS in West Hampstead at the time of the Munich crisis of September 1938. She was sure there would be war and she wanted to be trained and in uniform. In the summer of 1939, her group were told to be prepared to report to the fire station if they saw the news headline, 'Fleet is mobilised'. That is exactly what happened. Margaret drove straight to her fire station from Bognor, where she was on holiday. Most women were watchroom staff, telephonists and drivers so as to relieve men of these jobs to allow them to do the actual fire fighting. In the phoney war period she was the station officer's driver, and the time was used in between to do gas mask drill, first aid classes, PE, squad drill, and men in addition did fire fighting training, with time for concert parties and tennis in between.

62. Firewoman Margaret 'Peggy' Jacobs, BEM, later head of Women's Fire Brigade Section in London.

Peggy recalled the shock and awe when entering her first station when a firewoman accidentally pulled the brass alarm handle and the whole crew careered down the emergency poles to find it was a false alarm. The station commander went into a rage.

In September 1940 Margaret was transferred to the Fire Prevention Department, driving for Fire Officer superintendents. She was on duty on the night of the docks fires on 7 September and ordered to drive to

Surrey Commercial Docks so her superintendent could supervise the fighting of the blaze; she described it as like a scene from a huge Hollywood movie fire set. She watched by the car as more and more fire engines arrived. Around midnight she discovered that there was only one way to drive out of the docks and if the bridge leading out was destroyed, they would be trapped. Her car was parked by a tiny warden shelter big enough for one man only, and he suddenly popped out and said, 'come and shelter in here; it is safer'. But she refused and stood by the car. She remembers being oblivious of the danger of the bombing.

On the night of 7 October 1940, Peggy was driving a brigade staff car down Charing Cross Road in the midst of a heavy raid, but would not stop due to the urgency of her mission; in fact the street was filled with such thick smoke and dust she did not even realise the station at Soho, where she was aiming for, had suffered a direct hit.[2]

Margaret recalls that if women were sleeping in the station – and she remembers one event one night at Southwark station – then if the sirens went, everyone had to go to the shelter and not stay in the building. On another occasion at Euston fire station, where accommodation was poor, the four women drivers in her team and their officers would go to the Hearts of Oak insurance offices which had huge vaults underground and were very safe, but reached only by ladders and in the dark; but when this bolt hole was discovered, the LCC (forerunner of the Greater London Council) ordered them out as the company owners were demanding rent! It seems money overrode safety for the Fire Service personnel.

On the night of 29 December 1940, Margaret had taken her superintendent to observe from the roof of the HAC[3] building in City Road. Around 2 a.m. her superintendent appeared back at the vehicle with a cinder lodged in his eye and ordered her to take him to Moorfields Eye Hospital. She drove to the location and dropped him off. After three minutes he came out and angrily said they would not deal with him; it was a maternity hospital. Margaret had missed the Moorfields door which was a few metres ahead of her. Such was the chaos and smoke in the streets during the raids.

In letters in the JMM files from 1985 and 1986, Peggy wrote, that she was 'taken short' during one midnight raid when driving her Station Commander in Redcross Street. He left to inspect the fire and she had the predicament of where to 'go', as the fires lit the streets like daylight. There were firemen everywhere, bombs falling and the gushing water did not help! She finally found a shaded area behind a wall which she hoped would not collapse on her and got back to her vehicle just as her Commander returned.

In January 1941 Margaret married and fell pregnant; but she was also ill and in University College Hospital near Euston Fire Station. On the night of the 10/11 May 1941 raids, and despite the bombs falling all round the area, Margaret refused to go to the air raid shelter when asked to by the nurses. She told the nurses she felt safe as her old fire station was just round the corner; she slept on and off throughout and to her dying day she does not know how she survived that night, so careless of the carnage around her in Tottenham Court Road, Malet Street and buildings adjacent to the hospital which took direct hits. She recalls that as a firewoman she and her firemen visitors always received special attention and refreshments from the staff.

Sadly her husband, 2nd Lt Bernard Jacobs, RA, was killed in action at El Alamein on 3 November 1942. Margaret went on to serve post-war and was awarded a BEM for services to the Fire Brigade in 1964 as Senior Woman AFS Officer, London AFS.

NOTES

1. IWM, tape 5342.
2. Martin Lloyd-Elliott, *City Ablaze: Life with the World's Busiest Fire-fighters* (London: Bloomsbury Books, 1992), p.69.
3. Honourable Artillery Company regimental barracks.

Chapter Fourteen

Eric Alexander Kaufmann[1]

Eric was born on 24 March 1913 at 263 Goldhurst Terrace, Hampstead, son of Leo and Gerta who had come to live in the UK from Germany in 1907. They were interned on the Isle of Man in 1915 as Enemy Aliens and after the war there was so much anti-German feeling, they left for Dusseldorf in Germany. As Eric had dual nationality, he was able to leave Germany in June 1933 to escape the Nazis, followed by his parents in 1934. Eric ran his father's old business as a grain merchant. After joining the AFS in mid 1938, he was trained and stationed in Hendon and Golders Green at St Dunstan's Church Hall Fire Station, where many of the crews were Jewish. When war started, he was working 48 hours on, and 24 hours off. The large fire engines were kept at the main fire station, but at St Dunstan's they had grey coloured pumps, pulled by vans, each with a crew of four or five men.

63. Eric Kaufman standing with Golders Green station crew, fifth from right.

He was on duty for fifty-seven straight days during the Blitz but he was first sent to a fire in May 1940 in the City at Queen Victoria Street. The hand bell on the fire engine was clanging all the way into town as the crew rushed to the scene. However, when they arrived, there was not enough water as the river was at low tide and could not be pumped, and the street reservoirs were emptied very quickly. The firemen could do nothing but watch the surrounding inferno along the whole street. He even asked his officer if he could check on the family business offices in nearby Marks Lane and when he arrived, he could only watch it burning to the ground. Eventually the tide rose and the men were able to put out the fires all the next day – but the damage had been done.

64. Eric Kaufman.

After this he attended various local domestic fires and sometimes incendiaries fell in the area which they had to deal with. On one occasion whilst on watch duty he raised the alarm when a large barrage balloon came loose. There were always many training exercises, during which, being very short, he played the stretcher victim or the victim being carried down a ladder.

Eric felt that the famous 'Blitz Spirit' was indeed not a myth and in his experience really did exist. He also was unaffected by the Alien scare – and not dismissed from the Fire Brigade – as he had been born in Britain, even though he spent many years in Germany before the war.

Finding there was not much to do, Eric requested a transfer to local HQ in Pinner in the NFS where he took charge of administering food, supplies etc. for all the local sub-stations. In 1944 a V1 landed in Pinner but Eric was not involved and little damage was done.

In Pinner he overheard a lot of anti-Jewish remarks about the common false allegations concerning Jews and the Black Market; this was, however, a very widespread accusation at the time.

NOTE

1. This testimony was recorded by the author in November 2007.

Chapter Fifteen

Sylvia Kay(e)[1]

Sylvia was born on 19 November 1920 in Bow, the youngest of five children. She trained as a hairdresser after school, and well remembers her experiences in shelters during the Blitz in east London. She joined the Fire Service in 1941 in Northampton (her family had moved there to join an older brother after their flat had been bombed in Bow). Her training involved ladder climbing on an extending turntable ladder on a fire engine, which she remembers was quite scary. After full fire-fighting training, including fire hose ('branches') training, she was allocated as a telephonist in the watch-room, receiving messages about fires and directing vehicles to the scene. She lived most of the time in the fire station, getting home only on days off.

She was steadily promoted and became the Chief Fire Officer's personal assistant at the main station, accompanying him on visits and inspections in his car. She spent spare time with other personnel making parties and wooden and knitted toys for local children. She also recalled a 'lovely legs' competition to raise money for children: she won twice. The most serious incident occurred when a bomb hit an outbuilding of her station and killed a young fireman.

Sylvia was of course excused Church Parade, as were all Jewish personnel. Often they held march-pasts in the city with other Civil Defence groups such as the ARP and Home Guard, to keep up morale and 'show the flag'. Sylvia was released in 1944 and the family returned to London.

After the war she moved to Israel with her husband and family, and her son and daughter served in the army there.

NOTE

1. This testimony was recorded in November 2007 by Stephanie Maltman.

Chapter Sixteen

Jack Krisman[1]

Jack Noah Krisman was born on 1 July 1899 in Mile End, the son of Barnett and Fanny (née Lowenthal); he attended Trafalgar Square (Tredegar Square?) school. He was a First World War veteran (RFC/RAF Bomber Air Crew) and married Betsie Goldwater in 1926. Jack joined the AFS in Willesden in 1939 aged 40 and trained alongside the Jewish poet and writer, Stephen Spender.

At this time Jack lived at 5 Anson Road and was stationed at Cricklewood Broadway station in Moon's garage (situated on Cricklewood Broadway, now part of the A5, the old Watling Street) between Walm Lane and Keyes Road. It closed as a petrol supplier soon after war was declared as petrol was rationed.

65. Jack Noah Krisman served Cricklewood Broadway station, taken in 1970's

The Broadway is still there, but is now a very different place. In 1939 Cricklewood was a very Jewish area, and virtually every other house in Anson Road, from the Broadway down to Gladstone Park would have Jewish residents.

Because his base was so near his house, Jack was able to call in most days, even if only for a short while. The service operated on a '48 hours on and 24 hours off' basis, and Jack, like many of the other men, had little part time jobs on their days off (Jack was always in the retail clothing business). His daughter Audrey was welcome at the station. Though aged 9, Audrey was fully aware of the dangers and going to the station was a sort of 'war work' for her. The living quarters were pretty sparse but she never saw the sleeping accommodation – only the Mess.

Jack was always known as Kris or Krissy and was highly respected by the men. Because he was so familiar with the East End and the Docks he became a sort of navigator on the engines. Though small in stature and probably the oldest man in the station, he was invaluable finding ways through the bomb-damaged streets, burst water mains and blocked entrances, when on the way to fires. He was also the station Quartermaster. He saw some terrible sights, but somehow he managed to keep up his morale and make light of the situation.

Audrey recalls that one morning he came round to the house, still in his uniform and waders. The firemen had spent the night in a burning margarine warehouse. The margarine liquefied and they were walking about in the running fat. It flowed over the top of Jack's waders, getting inside his trousers, into his jacket pockets and inside his sleeves. As soon as they came out into the February daylight the fat solidified – and there it was in great swirls on the inside and outside of his uniform. Audrey's mother said if it had been butter she would have scraped it off and used it. But margarine held no charms for her. The incident became known as 'The Great Margarine Melt'.

But there were other occasions when Audrey's mother was relieved to see Jack return from the city, particularly after the fire-bombing of St Paul's Cathedral. He was there and came home in a state of shock – his pal and hose mate had been killed when a burning wall fell on him in St Paul's Churchyard.

Sometime between 1940 and 1942 a string of six or seven land mines aimed at the northern mainline railway, which ran parallel with Cricklewood Broadway, was dropped; it was not the most accurate form of bombing, but could be very disruptive and these particular bombs went astray. Landmines were attached to parachutes and one of these mines was caught in the branches of a tree outside The Windmill Pub, just a few yards from the fire station. Jack was walking back to the station when he saw it hanging there. It was important that an unexploded bomb be protected from vibration, passing buses being a regular hazard. Jack rushed back to the station to alert the crew, stopping whatever traffic was on the road. In the midst of the confusion he found a moment to phone his wife to alert all the people in the house – they would soon be ordered to evacuate and should begin to prepare to leave – and fill the suitcase in the hall with any important documents, passports, etc. His wife filled the suitcase with food and phoned relatives in Golders Green to ask if they could pick them up in Cricklewood Lane, half-a-mile distant.

Jack was the hero of the hour. As it happened this particular land mine did not explode – nor did several of the others dropped that night. Audrey and the neighbours were told that the mines were made in Czechoslovakia by slave labour who worked out an undetectable way of wiring the fuses which would stop the mine from exploding on impact. Post war, this was found to be true.

Bombing raids eventually subsided, but the fire service stayed on the alert because one never knew when the demoralizing campaign would resume. And, of course, it did. Shortly after the D Day Landings on 6 June 1944 the V1 and later V2 arrived. This development had a severe effect on civilians and on the fire service – absolutely no warning and the most terrible destruction and loss of life, as they were quite as likely to fall on a school or a housing estate as they were to fall on a factory. 'This development really shook my father', wrote Audrey. 'He had attended a bombing on a Bakerloo Line train at West Hampstead station – I don't think he recovered from what he saw that day – but to a large extent it meant he was determined to get his family out of London. The bombing only stopped when the Allies reached the launch sites in France. Almost normal life resumed.'

Audrey also recalled that whenever her Dad managed to come round after dark to check them all in, he had a pile of small cards on which he would write a number in black ink, and pin or stick it to the front door. This was to inform the rescue services how many bodies they should look for if the house was bombed. Too gruesome a story for children.

Jack attended a fire at the back of a neighbour's house (Dr Britten) – quite a big one in a yard used for collecting salvage. He was caught in the eye by a hose at full strength and was rushed into Dr Britten's house, treated immediately, and his sight was saved by the good doctor.

NOTE

1. Submitted by his daughter Audrey Jones.

Chapter Seventeen

Noel Landau, BEM[1]

Noel was born on 14 March 1907 in Shanghai as Noach Haimovitch, son of Izik and Itke Haimovitch, who were Romanian and Russian-born respectively and had left Roumania to escape anti-Semitism. Izik and Itke both died in Shanghai in a flu epidemic and Oscar and Debora Landau, who were near neighbours of the Haimovitch family, had previously agreed to bring up the three children Harry, Marie and Noach, and to give them a thoroughly good European education, should anything happen to the parents. The Landau's were British citizens living in Shanghai, and had no children of their own. In exchange Itke had assigned all her property to the Landaus in trust for the children. The deed of adoption appears to have been signed by all parties on 18 September 1922.

66. Fire Station Commandant Noel Landau with crew at Book Street HQ, Bootle, near Liverpool in 1940, standing at centre with civilian on his left.

Noel had come to live, be educated and work in England, alone aged 15, in 1923, but it wasn't until 11 February 1936 that Noach Haimovitch formally changed his name to Noel Landau by deed poll. He initially went to study engineering in Manchester and then later moved to Liverpool. He was a self employed builder, living at 8 Wadham Road, Liverpool, and later at 51 Thornfield Road, Thornton.

At the outbreak of war, Noel was Commandant of Bootle AFS but was then transferred to be a Section Officer with Liverpool AFS. This apparent demotion

67. Fire Station Commandant Noel Landau BEM.

RESCUED WOUNDED IN HEAVY RAID

Liverpool Man Awarded B.E.M.

[From our Correspondent—LIVERPOOL]

Mr. Noel Landau, Section Officer in the Liverpool Auxiliary Fire Service, has been awarded the British Empire Medal for outstanding courage and devotion to duty in particularly heavy air raids on Liverpool some months ago.

He, together with men of his section, at the height of one of the heaviest raids, fought a serious fire at a dock in an attempt to reach a blazing ship which finally blew up, causing many deaths. The ship and large sheds alongside were burning furiously and bombs continued to fall all round. Of Mr. Landau, the official citation says, that he obeyed all commands in the most nerve-testing circumstances; although he knew there would be a second explosion, Landau stayed and attended to the removal of the dead and injured, and personally rescued many of the wounded, showing utter disregard for personal danger.

Mr. Landau, who is the first Merseyside Jew to win the B.E.M., was Commandant of the Bootle A.F.S. from the outbreak of war until June, 1940, and is at present an officer of the Liverpool N.F.S.

He is a Vice-President of the Liverpool Zionist Central Council and Hon. Secretary of the Liverpool Jewish National Fund Commission, and was Chairman of the J.N.F. bazaar held in Liverpool in 1938, when a record amount was raised. For seven years he was the Hon. Secretary and Treasurer of the Bootle Liberal Association, and contested—the Stanley Ward, Bootle, in municipal elections in the Liberal interest. He was also Captain, and later Chairman, of the Bootle Liberal Lawn Tennis Club. Mr. Landau is the son of the late Mr. Oscar Landau, who was a prominent member of the Shanghai Jewish Community, and Mrs. Landau, who has been a generous supporter of Zionist funds and Shanghai Jewish communal causes.

68. JC article about Noel Landau and photo.

may have been at Noel's request, in order to be where the action could be expected, or perhaps was associated with the Aliens scare – we may never know.[2]

On the night of 3 May 1941, during the Blitz on Liverpool docks and city centre, the 4,000-tonne steamer SS *Malakand*, moored at Huskisson Dock, carrying 1,000 tons of explosives and ammunition bound for the Middle East, was set alight by German incendiary bombs which had hit an adjacent warehouse at about 23.30 hours. In addition, part of the deck of the ship had been set alight, possibly by a crashing barrage balloon. In a gallant attempt to try to save the ship, Section Officer Landau took the ship's Master (Captain Kinley) to Acting Deputy Divisional Officer John Lappin (later given the GM) who was the Fire Officer in charge, who then drove off to report the serious situation of the ship to the City Chief Fire Officer, Owen, leaving Noel in effective charge.[3] The fires raged for hours and eventually huge explosions from the ship killed a number of dock workers and firemen at around 0730. The *Malakand* continued exploding till 7 May. In describing the incident later, John Lappin said especial mention should be made of Noel Landau and Officer McColl, who 'by their example and disregard for personal danger were an inspiration to men and officers alike'.

Much later, on 9 January 1942, Lappin recorded his memories of that fateful night for BBC Radio Manchester. He told how the firemen had gone on duty on a glorious evening at about 7 p.m. and Landau had brought his fiddle and had started to play for the men. Suddenly the bombs started to fall. The men tackled the blazing *Malakand* all night. Landau was second in command and shouted for the men to follow him at the double: 'he once dived into a blazing shed because he heard there was someone trapped inside ... he jumped over the red hot debris and looked like a devil as he ferreted around, with the flames shooting about him'. The ship's ammunition was exploding and the adjacent sheds were aflame; each time the flames forced the firemen to retreat, they then later returned to fight back. Eventually the Master decided his ship could not be saved and the fire was abandoned. After it finally exploded, the firemen returned yet again to fight the dangerous fires on the dockside, despite being completely exhausted. Landau 'showed bravery and unyielding devotion to duty, courageously obeying all commands, and although he knew there could be secondary explosions, he attended to the removal of the dead and injured, personally rescuing many of the casualties himself and organising their removal to hospital in improvised ambulances'.

When it was over, Landau found his fiddle – a family heirloom – safe in its case beneath a heavy table in the debris of the firemen's quarters in the docks, which had also been bombed. 'You should have seen his grin as he put it under his chin and it played as good as ever. Somebody shouted, "Not so bad Nero!" That was the spirit of those hours', said Lappin.

Noel Landau was awarded the BEM for bravery and devotion to duty, as were other firemen involved in that night's events. His investiture was at Buckingham Palace on 28 April 1942. His comrades presented him with a leather bound 'Book of Congratulations' which fifty of them signed. It says, 'You have displayed great courage and have always shown ability to take control under most difficult circumstances. Having confidence in yourself, you inspired confidence in others and the whole Division is proud of the honour which has come to you.'

Noel was well known in local public affairs, having been Commandant at Bootle AFS Station, and in local Jewish and especially Zionist voluntary organizations. He was a member of the Greenbank Drive synagogue. He died suddenly on 22 March 1955 aged only 48, leaving a wife (Pamela) and two sons, Robert and Malcolm; he is buried at Long Lane Jewish cemetery. His BEM and the book are still with the family but there are plans for them to be donated on loan to the AJEX Jewish Military Museum.

NOTES

1. Relevant excerpts have been taken from Gavin Bassie's *Liverpool's Finest: The History of the City's Fire Brigade* (Liverpool: Trinity-Mirror-Media, 2008), with thanks to the author, who formerly served with the Merseyside Fire Service; from Arthur Lockyear, *Warriors in Fire Boots: A Tribute to the Valour of Firefighters* (Yorkshire: Jeremy Mills Publishing, 2011); and John Hughes, *Port in a Storm: Air Attacks on Liverpool and Its Shipping in the Second World War* (Merseyside: Merseyside Port Folios, 1993). Further detail comes from Noel's son Robert in St Alban's.
2. Hughes, *Port in a Storm*, p.85.
3. Ibid.

Author's note: It is an amazing coincidence that one of the senior engineers on 'Malakand' on the night of the bombing was Jewish Merchant Navy Officer Stuart Samuel, who served in the MN 1938-1947. Also, Jewish Firewatcher Hyman Gilbert was killed that night in the Malakand incident (see above). His body was never found.

Chapter Eighteen

Leslie Leveson[1]

Leading Fireman Leslie Leveson was born in 1908. He was refused service in the army in 1939 due to a hearing defect. After a chance meeting with a man who he had helped when his car broke down, Leslie was introduced to the Fire Service and volunteered to do his bit. He was called up on 1 September 1939.

He was stationed at Brentford and Chiswick fire stations. Nicknamed 'Levee' he was the only Jewish fireman at Chiswick and had many friends among the men.

Leslie recalled sleeping under a piano at his station, located in a school, as a precaution. He joked about the story of being refused entry to a house in Gunnersbury, to use the telephone to report a fire nearby, because the owner said he had muddy boots! On duty, based in a block

69. Leading Fireman Leslie Leveson's Fireman and Civil Defence card issued in 1939.

70. Leading Fireman Leslie Leveson, second from right, Chiswick and Brentford station.

of flats at Hartington Court, which still stands on the riverside at Kew, he recalled sunbathing on deckchairs waiting for the 'bells to go down'; he was given permission by his commander to fish. One morning at dawn he rose to see many small boats sailing silently down river; he discovered later these were the 'Dunkirk Little Ships' making their way to France to rescue the BEF in May 1940.

Later he was transferred to Kew Bridge Court flats and Hartington Court was bombed shortly after.

He recalled many incidents. A convent in Plaistow was bombed (probably The Sacred Heart of Jesus, Bethell Lane) and he helped carry out the books, statues and other religious items to save them from destruction by the resulting fire. He attended other serious fires in Tooley Street and at London Bridge Station. Called to one blaze in the docks south of West Ham, Leslie took his fire engine on a circuitous route he knew would get them there quicker, along the Embankment; on arrival they had to remove oxygen cylinders from the burning building and dump them into the Thames before they exploded. He died in 2003.

NOTE

1. Submitted by his daughter Sue Selwyn.

Chapter Ninteen

Ben Levinson

Ben, the son of Reverend A. Levinson, was a song writer and pianist from Nottingham. He joined the Fire Service aged 36 when war broke out in 1939, and undertook intensive training. He noted how the fulltime regular firemen looked down on the fulltime volunteers, who in turn looked down on the part-timers, though this gradually dissipated as the men grew to know each other and fought fires together. He worked 'days' one week, and 'nights' the following week, and so on. This later became two days on and 24 hours off. The training was physically very demanding but it paid off when they went into action as stamina mattered greatly when they were struggling to fight fires. The men formed five-man crews, sleeping on two-tiered bunks at the station.

When war was declared, a period of relative quiet followed, but there was always drill, cleaning the appliances, exercises and also alerts on 'stand by' when false alarms were made, or the odd bomb fell somewhere around Nottingham. Then came the Blitz on Nottingham on 8 May 1941. This was Ben's baptism of fire and at 11 p.m. his crew rushed into the city centre to fight the flames amid the bombs. He described morale as very high and there was a complete absence of fear, just a grim determination to save lives and property. The place they were called to was a large burning warehouse which stored ARP equipment. Although already destroyed, they had to dowse the flames as they acted as a beacon for German bombers. To help hold the hose – which was very difficult to handle when under pressure – in the smoke and fumes, they found what looked like a piece of masonry to rest the hose on, and used it as such for some hours. At dawn they were relieved and went to have some tea and sandwiches in the mobile café. They then noticed some army personnel roping off a large object which was an unexploded bomb; it turned out that it was the piece of so called 'masonry' they had been leaning the hose on for hours before! Ben was also sent with his crew to deal with fires in Birmingham and Liverpool.

So inspired was Ben that he later wrote a song called *Keep Smiling* which became quite famous. From 1943–45 he worked at the War Office.

Chapter Twenty

Albert 'Bert' Levy[1]

Albert joined the Fire Brigade because he didn't want to join the forces as he was against killing – but not a pacifist; he wanted to fight the Nazis somehow. As he had been recently sacked from his job, he decided to join the Fire Brigade in 1938, spending the year on intense training and going to domestic fires. When war was declared he was about to start his new regular job one night, when he received the order to take a pillow and three blankets and go to his nearest fire station, which was a sub station in a garage at Aldgate, and like many such stations was centred at a fire alarm post. (Albert pointed out in his testimony that the pump trailers, hoses and equipment for a five-man team were so heavy that the clutches of the commandeered taxis often burnt out as soon as they reached a small incline. Eventually Bedford trucks replaced many of the taxis.)

Soon after being allocated to his sub-station, a number of such small posts were amalgamated and located at Camperdown House sub-station, Aldgate, which was also the HQ of the Jewish Lads Brigade, and where Albert was sent. From here he was sent to Buxton Street station (known as the punishment station because of its poor facilities), near Vallance Road, and later to Wellclose Square (off Cable Street) where he spent most of the war.[2]

At the time of the phoney war, he remarked that it was quite common for passers by to hurl insults and rotten fruit at the firemen when on domestic calls, as they were seen as dodging the forces, but once the bombing began they received applause and high praise. Albert himself was twice wounded with blows on the head during his service. At a burning factory in Wormwood Street near Liverpool Street, Albert was holding a branch (hose) alone when a bomb nearby hit the mains and the water pressure suddenly dropped. Albert was naturally leaning forward against the pressure and so ended up being jerked violently forward without warning and ended up face down in the fire; he was dragged to safety by a comrade.

Evening roll call in the stations was held at 10 p.m. each day and if there was no 'shout', the men were allowed to go and have a beer or play cards. There were also sudden mock alarms called during the night to see how fast the men could muster for the real thing; one and half minutes was the usual target to be at action stations. But Albert said 'you never slept in the fire brigade anyway; you just rested'.

Sometimes other spare hours were used doing PT and ladder drill with hook ladders or the large turntable ladder. On one refresher course, a senior instructor was demonstrating the hook ladder to his station, at some height, and failed to hook it properly over the window sill; he fell and broke his leg and later was medically discharged from the service.

Albert explained that many of the station officers had only been ordinary regular firemen who had been rapidly promoted when war began, to command stations and teach the auxiliaries. Many were not suitable and at the start of the Blitz, it was often noticed by the AFS men that the regulars would be sleeping during call outs whilst the AFS men were sent off to fight fires during the bombings as soon as they came on duty. This soon stopped. It was often common to be at a fire for twelve hours as 'damping down' followed the extinguishing of the blaze. The rule was that no tea was to be provided by brigade canteen vans till four hours had passed. But the Salvation Army or Quakers always came along with their own refreshment vans and provided hot soup or tea for whoever needed it whenever it was wanted.

Among the incidents he recalled was fighting the huge fires at Shellhaven, and at Rum Quay Dock where they were surrounded by fires and unable to leave the area. The burning alcohol even set the river alight and Albert thought that he and all his comrades would be killed that day.

One evening at Wellclose Square, he and his men were playing poker when bombs started to fall nearby and the men had to rush to take shelter as doors and windows were blown out; one man who was an incessant gambler refused to budge as he had four jacks! Later Albert took the chickens he was rearing in the station (for the eggs) back to his house in Nelson Street, in order for them to recover from the blast.

On one occasion his team were sent on duty to Kingsland fire station in Stoke Newington when suddenly a massive oil bomb hit a house nearby. The building was a blazing inferno and they could not get near it; sadly the whole family, including a baby who Albert carried out, were asphyxiated by the smoke, having sheltered in the basement. Albert said this was only one of dozens of similar incidents he witnessed.

In another incident Albert remembers sitting on the eaves of a tall building in a railway depot, chopping at the eaves with his axe to get at an incendiary that was dangling and burning. Suddenly it blew up in his face and burnt his uniform quite badly. Nevertheless, he finished the job and the building was saved. After rescuing a publican and his wife from their bombed pub off Cable Street, Albert and his mates got free drinks for weeks afterwards!

It was common during the '24 hours off' period for men to take part-time jobs to supplement their income of £3 per week; Albert and a friend used to deliver coal and earn 12 shillings (60p) per day; but they then had to go to the Turkish baths (steam baths) and spend that much on getting the grime out of their skins! They soon gave that job up.

Albert's station were frequently sent to St Katherine's Dock after the big bombing, to pump out the basements which were full of massive amounts of water; there was often the opportunity to leave with a few bottles of alcoholic refreshment which were found floating around, as this dock had many alcohol bonded warehouses. Once, when using suction hoses to drain the basements, using a wire cage to catch solid objects, dock police came to check their progress. They had to explain the presence of several full bottles, but a blind eye was turned.

Another incident Albert recalls was in 1944 when a V1 hit one of the London (West?) Docks where petrol was being loaded by dockers for D Day. The dockers were wearing felt slippers over their boots to prevent sparks accidentally igniting the fuel, whilst the firemen were sitting in a nearby shelter on call, in case. As the engine cut out and the V1 began to fall, the dockers scattered and the missile glided between the two masts of the ship that the dockers had been loading and exploded in the water, throwing up the most appalling filth, stench and mud from the river bed. Fortunately, nobody was hurt, save, said Albert, the pride of the dockers, for the firemen had of course, as ever, stayed bravely out in the open as they made for their equipment.

He explained that when making the film, *When the Bells Go Down*, many of the locations were deliberately mis-named for security reasons and that actual pubs and warehouse locations were altered and re-labelled. He said the film company told them that between and after takes they could go to The Artichoke pub (now renamed) and have as many free drinks and cigarettes as they wanted. As they were not being paid, this is a perk they fully used. As the film was made after the worst of the Blitz, it was actually, said Albert, a good use of their spare time.

Albert left the NFS just after VE Day.

NOTES

1. IWM, tape 11345/2. Albert was a star of the wartime film, *When the Bells Go Down* (with actor Tommy Trinder), about the wartime Fire Brigade, as well as being a real fireman of course.
2. Author's note: the tape interview includes detailed descriptions of Albert explaining the exact layout of the Wellclose Square station as he looks at photographs of the station and surrounding area with the interviewer, as well as identifying photos of locals who appeared in the film.

Chapter Twenty One

Renee Malin née Titton

Renee spent four years in the AFS, mainly based at the London Fire Brigade HQ on the Albert Embankment, Lambeth. Her father Jack was a First World War veteran in the London Regiment who served in France. She lived in quarters behind the main building, which pre-war had been condemned as unfit for human habitation. Her job was administration by day and radio operator for officers' incident control cars by night. This meant that as soon as a

71. Firewoman Renee Titton, wife of Myer Malin, third from left at Lambeth station.

72. Renee Titton standing on the left with a fire engine.

73. Renee Titton portrait with forage cap.

raid began, they would be woken by telephone and she would get up and put on her helmet and uniform over her pyjamas, and run hell for leather down four flights of stairs to accompany senior officers in their cars and head to the scene of a raid as directed by the main HQ. The women would radio the incident report back to HQ, then be directed to the next scene of a raid – and so on through the night.

Of course she witnessed many traumatic sights and would return at dawn exhausted, when, after a cup of hot cocoa and a few hours sleep, she would return to the administration desk to work. The strain was quite intense given it was the usual fire service pattern of 48 hours on and 24 hours off; this later changed to a slightly less gruelling 24 hours on and then 24 hours off, she recalls. Renee remembered that the East End population were absolutely resolute and tough, despite the death and destruction that surrounded them; often bombed out and homeless, they would nevertheless ask the fire personnel if they could get them 'a nice cup of tea'. Despite their relative poverty, they tore up sheets to use as bandages and used their own blankets to help the wounded and shocked during raids – and always with an irrepressible sense of humour.

In 1944 Renee recalls the first V1s and how at first the fire brigade HQ staff thought the cut out engine meant it was an enemy plane being shot down, and cheered accordingly; they soon realized this was a missile falling to earth to wreak mayhem. Renee said the camaraderie was incredible and kept them all going despite utter exhaustion and constant tension for years. She said she was honoured to have served with the fire brigade heroes.

Post-war Renee worked for two years in Brussels for ECITO (European Central Inland Transport Organisation), returning all modes of transport (trains, buses, cars, etc.) stolen by the Nazis, to their rightful owners. Her unique NFS dog tag (ID tag) and her badge are in the family archive.

Chapter Twenty Two

Leonard (Jonas) Marks[1]

When he first joined, Dad had to learn how to go up ladders safely to rescue people from windows and was taught first of all many different kinds of knots, including a Fireman's Chair/Lift, a sheep-shank etc. This was to tie ropes safely when lowering rescued people.

On his first practice ladder climb, when he reached the top, two of the more experienced firemen holding the base of the ladder, moved it away from the building with him still hanging on the top and gave him a terrible fright because he had no control over it. They moved it across with him on the top to another window. Apparently this was part of the initiation procedure!

74. Leonard Jonas Marks.

In their spare time while they waited for an emergency call out, they often played cards – a gambling game called Slippery Sam, at which our dad was very inexperienced and the others were ready to take him for a ride. But by a spot of luck, he won and they brought the prize to him which was a chicken. He thought our mum would be delighted as chickens were hard to get in those days. He was shocked however to find that it was a live one in a bag and was told that it laid eggs. He took it home but couldn't kill it, so he put it in the bathroom while he built a chicken pen in the garden. He returned to find that it had completely wrecked the bathroom – broken the mirror and left lots of unpleasant mess everywhere. Mum was horrified but pleased with the eggs that it eventually laid. He then proceeded to win several more chickens with his Slippery Sam prowess until finally he won a prize chicken which they said laid double-yolk eggs – which it did. However, they failed to let him know that it also ate its own eggs immediately! So he built a device inside the hen house, so that as the chicken laid its egg, it would roll down a slope and into a trapped area where the hen could not get to it. A few days later, the other firemen asked him how he got on with the new chicken and to their surprise he took one of the double yolk eggs to show them and said that the eggs were really wonderful and he was happy. He mentioned nothing about the hen eating them because he knew they were previously aware of it! When Mum, my younger sister Elaine and I were evacuated, dad would send us parcels of the chickens' eggs by post, wrapped so carefully that they were never broken.

Dad said solid blocks of coconut oil were used to grease the Rolls Royce engines being built in the Kemps factory during the war, because it was extremely pure – and it also made very good cooking fat at home!

In his spare time, Dad was also chairman of the local Civil Defence organization which met in our flat in Honeypot Lane, Stanmore two or three times a week, to discuss emergency procedures and to have first aid lessons. I was the dummy and had lots of people put splints on me and breathe air into my throat whether I wanted it or not.

He attended a lot of fires within the Kemps factory and the surrounding factories.

NOTE

1. These memories of Leonard (Jonas) Marks, AFS, Burnt Oak, were submitted by his son Derek and daughter Gina.

Chapter Twenty Three

Hyman 'Hymie' Mesnick[1]

Hyman was born in May 1912 and lived at 26 Cable Street, the son of Abraham and Rebecca.[2] In 1938, Hymie was newly married to Esther Kanerick and 'on the knowledge' to be a taxi driver, whilst working in a bank to support the family. He and his wife lived at 20 Alcaster Crescent, Clapton, E5. Believing war was inevitable, and wanting to do his bit, he joined the AFS as a driver, as he had 'the knowledge' of London. Training involved evening lectures, and films of the bombing in Spain to illustrate what to expect should war come to Britain. Hymie recalled the thrills of going out with the regular fire brigade on their fire engines to watch them at work on domestic fires. But on 1 September 1939 he was suddenly called up to the AFS and given overalls, tin helmet, boots, belt and axe. Not till after the Blitz did they receive a proper waterproof tunic, so all through the Blitz they returned from fires soaked and then had to go out again wearing wet clothes.

On 3 September, when war was declared, Hymie was stationed at Whitechapel and put in charge of a group of men in a requisitioned private lorry with driver, to go and collect thousands of sandbag sacks from a warehouse south of the Blackwall Tunnel and deliver the sacks to another warehouse, just near the north tunnel exit in Bow. Suddenly at 11 a.m. the sirens went off. Hundreds of people in the area panicked and seeing some men in uniform, rushed to Hymie and asked him what to do; he advised them all to go to the nearby Blackwall Tunnel and take shelter. The lorry driver ran off and was never seen again. Suddenly the 'all clear' was sounded, and Hymie finished the job himself, proud they had come through their first 'incident'.

During the phoney war, their real enemy was the IRA who were bombing targets in central London, and they were on duty all night to fight this threat. At his East End station was a regular fire engine, a 'green goddess' and a taxi pulling a pump, all located in a school. Each appliance had a team of four led by a Leading Fireman, and each man had a specific task, but it would rotate between the four on each call out, as directed by the Leading Fireman. Each man knew all four jobs. It was, said Hymie, very efficient.

Every day there was 8 a.m. roll call and checking that all appliances were working properly. Before the Blitz, there were the regular domestic fires to deal with. Generally, Hymie said the NFS regulars got on quite well with the AFS volunteers but the public's attitude to men in the Fire Service was not always so sympathetic, the reasoning being that all men should be in the army. This view soon changed once the Blitz began. At one stage, feeling a little guilty about this situation with no real work to do, Hymie went with four friends to enlist in the RAF at Upminster. They were refused as they were doing important work in the Fire Service and the recruiting officer warned, 'Your time will come son, go home!'

Hymie's first big incident when the Blitz started was at the bombing of the big oil refinery at Thameshaven, near Chatham. Hundreds of firemen had been sent from all over London to try and contain the ferocious blaze; Hymie said that they did not really understand then that water hoses were useless against burning oil, and foam was what was required. The fires just had to be left to burn out. He was there all day. From there he was sent almost at once to massive warehouse fires at St Katherine's Docks by the Tower, where they stayed all night till early morning trying to extinguish the fires. Hymie said they could not really see that they were achieving anything because as they put one fire out, the bombs were falling and starting new fires.

On being relieved and arriving back at their station, they just fell fully clothed onto their mattresses and fell asleep. This continued for several days until they were given 24 hours leave. Then back to the fires – for almost fifty continuous days of bombing. Eventually Hymie said mobile canteens providing tea were brought in at fires where it would be possible at least for the Civil Defence workers to get some refreshment during incidents.

At this time Hymie's wife was pregnant, but their house had been bombed and they lost everything. She was living in a shelter and was asked by the family to accept evacuation to Hitchin for her safety, whilst Hymie stayed on duty.

Three of Hymie's friends were killed during this period. One was a very strong Welsh lad with him at a fire on Tower Hill; while bending down to attach a hose to a hydrant, a falling German incendiary hit him directly on his body and broke his back. He was rushed to the London Hospital, and when Hymie went to visit him later, his friend asked him for a drink. Hymie checked with a doctor who said he can have what he wants as he was dying.[3] He passed away later that day.

Where possible the men tried to relax between call outs and Hymie was keen on organizing physical training; he himself had done some boxing and PE training and he tried to involve the men in this with considerable success.

Hymie recalled an incident at Ludgate Circus when they were called to a fire at Bravingtons jewellers in Ludgate Hill; he said there were more police there than firemen owing to the danger of looting. One of his colleagues boasted later that he had liberated a diamond ring by hiding it down his boot, but Hymie was never sure whether this was just bravado. Hymie himself admitted to 'accidentally on purpose' taking a small leather writing case from the ruins of Strakers stationers during a call out, remarking that for poor, low-paid firemen, risking their lives daily, this was a great temptation.

Hymie recalls that at a fire in Kensitas cigarettes store in City Road, cigarettes were stolen by firemen of the previous watch, and brought back to his fire station. On arrival at base, the culprit was sharing them out among his three mates in a dark corner of the station, when he spied another pair of legs in the group. He swore and said that the man should move along as he wasn't in this deal; when he looked up, it was the Station Commander, who was also a Fire Brigade champion boxer. He told the men he would give them five minutes to clear this up whilst he turned his back. They ran off and all Hymie knows is that these four men were coughing for the next four months as they consumed their loot.

At Stoke Newington, Hymie attended a terrible incident where a shelter had been blown up and the mains alongside burst and drowned the people inside. He did not say in the interview but this was almost certainly the Coronation Flats/Imperial Avenue disaster of 13 October 1940, when 170 people died in the shelter. There is a mass grave of many of them in Abney Cemetery in Hackney; a large number were Jewish families. Hymie recalls assisting in bringing out the many drowned bodies, which showed no sign of blast damage at all. He also remembered the destruction of a public toilet in Bishopsgate where people had taken shelter and the basement received a direct hit; again he had the job of recovering, this time, blown up bodies.

Asked how he coped with these sights, he really had no idea; it was expected that they would see and endure such things and they dealt with it as part of their job and way of life. In essence there was no escaping it and there was a job to be done. He felt that Churchill's leadership and feelings of patriotism kept many people going. He never recalled any firemen being discharged for shell shock or what we now call Post Traumatic Stress Syndrome (PTSD), though many would argue this may have manifested itself in later life. The fact is that dealing with the bombing had become much more serious and devastating than anyone had ever contemplated it would be; great conflagrations which burnt for days, unrelieved fighting of fires, terrible loss of life.

On occasions during calls, people would wave down a fire engine on its way to a blaze and get them to put out a local bombing fire; once on the way to a blaze in the King George V Docks a man stood in the road and stopped their engine and asked Hymie's men to put out the blaze in his pub in return for free beer; they duly, but briefly, obliged. It was quite common for locals to emerge from their homes with tea and biscuits for the firemen whilst they were working – Hymie said the solidarity was always amazing.

Hymie clearly recalled being present on the notorious 29 December 1940 bombing of the City as it went up in flames when the Thames was at its lowest ebb; the pumps could thus not get at the water (the mains had been destroyed)[4] and the City burned. Whilst in the middle of this conflagration, he received a message that his wife was seriously ill and about to give birth. His sympathetic Company officer, Mr John, could only give him 12 hours unofficial compassionate leave, saying he would cover for him. When he got to Hitchin on the 1st of January, his daughter had been born and all was well. When he got back to his station, he discovered that his machine had been blown up by a bomb and two of his friends killed, one his best friend. Had he not gone to Hitchin he would have been killed with them. He named his daughter Joan after Joe, the man who was killed. His other colleague who survived the hit and had replaced him was Lou Sherman (see his testimony), another Jewish fireman.

In another incident, again at St Katherine's Dock, it was Hymie's turn to go up to the top of a mechanical extension ladder about 100 feet above the street, playing his hose on a burning building. The procedure was for a searchlight below to pin the fireman in its beam so he could be seen, whilst he gave instructions to the controller below by telephone on where to manoeuvre the ladder and platform in relation to the blaze. It was a terrifying experience to do this as enemy planes could see the searchlight beam and it engendered a feeling of being totally exposed to enemy bombs and guns, as well as the burning fire. Indeed it was the turning of night into day by the burning fires and German flares which gave the worst feelings of total vulnerability to German aircraft. Toppling buildings were the other great danger and of course took so many lives. Hymie said, however, that it was all taken in their stride and as the Blitz went on men became fatalistic and just got on with their dangerous but essential work.

Hymie's worst experience was when on call waiting by a railway bridge near the docks. They did not know that there were anti-aircraft guns in the area; when they opened fire the noise was astonishing, the ground shook, walls vibrated. He said that the shock from the guns was worse than the fire fighting. He heard later that some were heavy naval guns and they were moved along the railways on flat cars to fire from varying positions during air raids.

Hymie recalled the journey home each dawn, on their appliances, bumping along through devasted London streets covered in debris and glass. People still went to work amid the smoke and ruins, as best they could; uppermost in the minds of the firemen was to simply get back, wash and sleep.

Food was delivered to the stations each week and was both plentiful and nourishing; they also improvised and kept chickens and rabbits to supplement their rations.

After January 1941, there was a quiet period and then a resurgence of bombing in April. Hymie was called out to a mass of fires at King George V and Victoria Docks and the firemen noticed parachutes coming down. Thinking these were shot down German airmen, they made for them, with murderous intent, incensed and angry as they were at what these bomber crews were doing to London. One was caught on the huge chimney stack of a building, and they suddenly realized these were not men descending from the sky, but huge containers they had been warned about – landmines. Within seconds they reversed and ran for their lives.

Later the Germans added explosive devices to the incendiaries so that attacking them became very dangerous; all the firemen and firewatchers – as well as the general public – were told to wait till the incendiary had gone off before approaching with a sand bucket or water. The potential of these devices to damage was thus much increased.

At another incident, at a burning school in the East End, Hymie's good friend Bert Watkins – their Leading Fireman and a very heroic man – made his way to the roof with a hose to get to the seat of the fire, and went to cross a beam; the beam could not hold him and he fell and broke his back. He was taken to hospital but was paralysed for the rest of his life. Some years after the war, when Hymie had returned to being a cab driver and was at Euston station, he saw coming towards him a man in a wheel chair pushed by a woman. It was Bert, and they fell into each other's arms. The lady was his wife and had been his nurse during his long stay in hospital, and they were living in the south west in retirement. Hymie always regretted that he never got his address.

After the Blitz Hymie was invited to apply for a position in administration and as he had some training in a bank, he was offered the post of a Section Leader (Finance). His salary doubled over night from £3 to £6 per week, working in a small team on the payroll of firemen. He was then transferred to Ilford HQ, based in a large school, and asked to take a special post training mostly young offenders – with a team of two assistants – to be firemen messengers before they joined the armed forces. They were 'tearaways', as Hymie described them, but he liked them and they got on well; he took them on an army assault course and they thoroughly enjoyed the challenge and discipline involved. He also trained them to take part in a local boxing tournament. Their job would ultimately involve being sent to various fires with messages whenever communications broke down. One night in June 1944 they had a red alert and Hymie took these youngsters in an engine to the East End where they saw a falling aircraft caught in a cone of searchlights, fire coming from its engines. They gave chase at speed, bell clanging, to a location in Grove Road, Stepney, where the aircraft crashed into the railway bridge there; they began immediately looking for the pilot but it became known next morning that this was not a crashing plane but the first V1 rocket to fall on London.

Hymie remembered that one day a contingent of WAAFS moved into the station in Ilford where he was working with these young men; they were involved with installing and test firing secret new rockets for use against the V1 and V2 threat. Hymie discovered later that it had been the earlier test firing of these totally inadequate rockets that had caused the panic at Bethnal Green Underground Station when 172 people were killed in the disaster there in March 1943.

On duty in the East End near some typical terraced houses and sweat shop tenements, Hymie heard the sirens sound to warn of a V1 approaching. Often these rockets passed over an area and fell somewhere else. At this time in 1944 interruptions by sirens were so frequent, that people in factories and houses often did not heed them and stayed at work or in their homes, especially as the sound of the rockets overhead often meant that the missile was flying away from them. On this occasion, the cloud was low and the rocket motor was clearly heard, but this time it cut out and as Hymie looked up he could see it coming straight through the low cloud, where he was standing in the street. He dived for cover as it hit the tenements and he and his men were pulling out the dead and injured for hours afterwards. After some time a boy approached them shouting and crying that his parents were still in the rubble; they had sent him on an errand and he had just returned. Hymie and his men dug frantically in the area where the boy indicated and they eventually found the parents in each others arms, under a piano where they had sheltered, but they were, sadly, dead.

Hymie said that the comradeship among his men would be the thing he would never forget; by his own admission he was a disciplinarian but it was necessary if the firefighters were to work efficiently as a team in very dangerous circumstances – and it paid off. He deeply regretted that the government never really recognized the work the Fire Service did with a specific service medal to wear on Remembrance Day, though most did receive the Defence Medal if they claimed it. But he took great satisfaction from a job well done and was grateful he had survived and all his family were together and safe in the peace that followed, no matter how great the austerity. He said, it all now appears as if it was one long dream.

Hymie took the view that after the Blitz began, he personally sensed that many people in London had soon had enough. In contrast to the accepted view looking back, there was a strong feeling that surrender would be better than this and that the 'Blitz spirit' was to many a bit of a myth. But he agrees that this is a controversial area and he can only speak about what he heard.

Hymie and Esther had twins in 1944 and after discharge from the service in 1945 he returned to cab driving; he died in July 2002.

NOTES

1. From a DVD recorded by the IWM probably in 1995, donated by his daughter Joan Manning.
2. Hymie was the cousin of Sidney Solly Goldman, of Colditz fame; see the chapter on Jews at Colditz in Martin Sugarman, *Fighting Back: British Jewry's Military Contribution in the Second World War* (London and Portland, OR: Vallentine Mitchell, 2010).
3. Fireman Abraham Lewis (Bookatz) was killed in the same way at a fire in Tower Hill – see his testimony.
4. Later Hymie described how the authorities placed 5,000-gallon canvas water containers on bomb sites to prevent water shortages when the Thames was at low tide; also special fire lorries were introduced specifically to carry hundreds of feet of hose to ensure there was enough to move water from the Thames itself, to fires distant from the river bank, by relay pumping water long distances by hose.

Chapter Twenty Four

Marie/Miriam Morris née Garcia[1]

Marie was born on 23 October 1921 near Victoria Park, Hackney. After moving to Hammersmith where she went to school, she did short-hand training at college and when war began she was in Portsmouth where her parents owned confectionery shops called 'The Chocolate King'.

Marie was called up in 1940 and chose the Fire Service (AFS), and reported to Petersfield in Hampshire, about 20 miles away, located near to a large Canadian Army base. Here she was billeted with a family and worked

75. Firewoman Maria Garcia later Morris.

two days on and one day off (when she went home to her parents in Portsmouth). Marie was a telephonist at the local fire station area A4, and sometimes went to work at stations in the surrounding villages. If there was an emergency, she would give the order to 'Put the Bells Down', i.e. sound the alarm, and then firemen would slide down the pole to man their engines. After some 18 months she was sent to be a telephonist at the fire officers training centre. She recalls seeing convoy after convoy of American vehicles along the roads, in the run-up to D Day. Also she remembers evenings in local pubs playing darts. After being forced to leave the service in late 1944, when her parents became ill, she worked till war's end in a food distribution shop to complete her National Service.

NOTE

1. This testimony was recorded by the author in November 2007.

Chapter Twenty Five

Ruth Myers née Carne[1]

76. Firewoman Ruth Carne on telephonist training on right, from a local news cutting 1942.

77. Firewoman Ruth Carne as the then married Mrs Myers, as a Leading Firewoman, B Division HQ 35 FFHQ, Ealing.

Following training, Leading Firewoman Ruth Myers née Carne, NFS (B Division HQ), moved from an HQ at a private house in Hampstead, to a block of flats in Ealing. She was in the catering section from 1942–45 responsible for providing food for the fire crews numbering hundreds of personnel in the North West London area.

NOTE
1. This testimony was recorded by the author in November 2007.

Chapter Twenty Six

Andrew Nunes Nabarro, GM

Andrew was born in Wadebridge, Cornwall in 1910, the son of Simon N. Nabarro (of Amsterdam) and Sarah (née Jass) of Southsea, and the family are long associated with the Bevis Marks Spanish and Portuguese Synagogue. Andrew was a Leading Fireman in Portsmouth when he won his GM.

The GM citation reads,

> Houses were demolished by a bomb in Reginald Road and fires broke out. Two people were trapped beneath the debris, in which a gas main was burning furiously. Nabarro took charge of the operations, and despite great danger from collapsing buildings,

78. Leading Fireman Andrew Nunes Nabarro, George Medal, Portsmouth; painting by Bernard Hailstone, courtesy Imperial War Museum.

79. Nabarro's photo and mention in *The War Illustrated*, 10 October 1941.

the people were rescued and the fires brought under control. He then went to other fires at the Curtis Furniture Depository and the Electricity Supply Depot, and showed initiative in finding and organising water supplies. This resulted in the saving of much valuable property.

In fact the citation is understated as it was Nabarro who entered the building and personally pulled out the two trapped victims.

Photos of him appeared in *The War Illustrated* magazine, the *JC* and *Portsmouth Evening News*.[1] A painting of Nabarro in full fireman's gear, by Bernard Hailstone, is at the Imperial War Museum.

NOTE

1. *The War Illustrated*, 10 October 1941, p.188; *JC*, 18 July 1941, p.5; *Portsmouth Evening News*, 28 April 1941.

Chapter Twenty Seven

Abraham 'Alf' Nathan

Alf was based at several stations during the Blitz including Red Lion Yard. He was once on duty on the outside balcony of the dome of St Paul's with bombs raining down all around, and related how frightening that was. On another occasion, whilst directing his hose at a fierce fire, he was ordered to report at once to the First Aid post; when he looked down he saw he was bleeding heavily from a huge piece of glass that had embedded itself in his thigh boot and into his leg. He passed out. Firemen often had to rest between fires and their clothes were invariably soaking wet; this caused all kinds of illnesses. After catching pneumonia whilst on duty, he was for a time in St Leonard's Hospital in Hackney.

80. Abraham 'Alf' Nathan.

Alf also worked hard in between shifts for the Firemen Benevolent Society and saw that all widows and sick men received their payments. He died in 1993 aged 87 years.

Chapter Twenty Eight

Morris Nathan

B/5417 Leading Auxiliary Fireman Morris Nathan, aged 27 years, a builder, lived at 520 Mile End Road, E3, and was posted at station 28, Whitechapel, 27 Commercial Road. Here are excerpts from the recommendation for an award.[1]

> Near to this officer's station (28 X sub-station, Crutched Friars, EC3, a portion of the City at great fire risk through bombing), at 2114 hours on 8th Sept 1940, a heavy HE bomb caused severe damage to Carlisle Avenue buildings and gas mains. There were explosions, falling walls and much debris. Ten pumps were present and it was brought under control. On the 11th September there were further fires in the same area (Lloyds Avenue and Northumberland Alley) and 5 pumps attended whilst bombs continued to fall. Several firemen were injured. Again fires were rapidly brought under control. On the night of 17th September there was a further incident in Clare St EC and with one pump and during heavy bombing fires were again brought under control.
> During these incidents, LAF Nathan rendered energetic and valuable support to senior officers so that men and appliances were used to the best effect. By his example and his conduct, regardless of his personal safety, Nathan imbued the other Auxiliaries with a spirit of confidence and so restricted the fires. [Signed by the Deputy Chief Fire Officer, LFB, 13/5/41]

On 16 April 1941 the Chief Superintendent of District C, surname Norman (partly illegible in the document) suggested the recommendation was 'mild' and that it should not proceed. On 18 April 1941 the Divisional Officer, Northern (F.W. Freeth? – illegible) replied and rejected Norman's claim and pointed out that the Home Office and the previous Chief Superintendent, named May, had supported the conclusion of the exceptional work of Nathan, and suggested more evidence be gathered from the men present in order to substantiate the claim for an award. On 6 May Norman replied he had carried out this order and attached the new evidence for Freeth to consider.

This included a signed statement by Superintendent H. Hydes, confirming what Nathan had done, writing that he saw 'the untiring and courageous efforts of Nathan to support the fireman in charge (Henry E. Shaw) and much of the work accomplished was in a large measure due to the energy and help given by Nathan and the example he set to others'. He had no hesitation in supporting an award. Hydes continued that Nathan had exhibited coolness, initiative and great leadership whilst under enemy bombing. Nathan and Shaw had shown more than 100 per cent initiative and gallantry, he said, and had effected entries on either side of burning buildings and had placed branches (hoses) on surrounding roofs to cover the fires, with promptitude, efficiency and leadership, so the fires could not travel in any direction. Hydes concluded that these men had prevented what would have been a City conflagration.

Shaw himself, in his own statement, the senior of the two men and a regular fireman, had said Nathan had been particularly courageous; Nathan in turn praised Shaw in his own statement.

Despite the witness accounts, it appears that neither man received any recognition for what they had done.

NOTE

1. Taken from LMA FB/WAR/1/203.

Chapter Twenty Nine

Rudolf Peierls[1]

Professor Rudolf Peierls was a German Jewish physicist, born in Berlin in 1907, who came to the UK in 1933. By 1939 he was Professor of Physics at Birmingham University and wanted to do something for the war effort. He joined the AFS and received his uniform, helmet and axe and was posted to a sub-station near his home. He recalled in his book that in the early days old cars were purchased to pull the pump trailers and often would not start or broke down during training runs. Sometimes a rag had to be forced into the air intake to start the motor. Later proper fire engines were introduced.

81. Professor Rudolf Peierls, German Jewish refugee and atomic physicist, AFS Fireman in Birmingham, taken in New York in 1943.

During the 'phoney war' many idle hours were spent drinking beer, but Rudolf told his mates he preferred wine. To tease him they one day offered him a dark liquid as wine, but it was actually a mixture of every kind of liquor they could lay their hands on; they expected him to be laid unconscious after drinking it. But as he sipped and smelt it like a true expert, he described it a good and mature wine and drank it straight down. They never teased him about wine again after that.

Rudolf attended many large fires in Birmingham, his first role being that of laying out the hoses to canals and other water sources to see to the supply. At one factory fire he was directing a branch with a comrade at the ground floor source, when the roof caved in and bricks came flying in their direction. One hit his helmet and severely dented it;

another badly bruised his friend's arms. Often his team was sent to other parts of the city to reinforce over-stretched stations. One night, with bombs falling, shrapnel flying, AA guns firing and bombers overhead, they were lying on the ground resting and waiting to be called to assist, when a Cadbury's factory van drew up, staffed by two women wearing tin helmets, and served everyone hot chocolate drinks – much to everyone's delight. Often when driving through the streets at night to fires, he felt the whole city was alight and being destroyed; the absence of traffic was both depressing and eerie and he never forgot the constant sound of smashed glass being ground underfoot everywhere.

In 1943 he was seconded to the Atomic Bomb project in the USA and later returned to the UK to teach at both Birmingham and Oxford universities.

NOTE

1. Taken from his autobiography, Wiener Library collection.

Chapter Thirty

Charles Poulsen/Paulsen[1]

Charles Poulsen/Paulsen aka Kopel Polsky was born on 15 October 1911 in Stepney Green, the son of poor Russian immigrants and one of four children. His father (born in Grodna) was a photographer and mother (born in Riga) was a milliner; relatives helped his father re-establish his photography business in a shop and for a while they did well enough to move to Croydon, where Charles went to a local boys school till he was 11. When the business collapsed they returned to live in the East End in great poverty in two rooms on the third floor in Old Montague Street. Charles then attended Old Montague Street Elementary School till he was 14 years old. His parents had a love of education and his father was a Hebrew scholar. He recalled in an interview with the Museum of London the influence of his head teacher, Captain Harry Kahn, a Jewish First World War veteran.

82. Charles Poulsen in later life.

On leaving school he had various 'boys' jobs and then became a furnailer and eventually by 1935, a taxi driver; he was by then married to his first wife and living in Stoke Newington. But he had a lust for learning and immersed himself in books at Stepney Library, and went to the theatre and concerts; joining the Scouts had also given him a love of countryside walks.

Charles became a Communist in 1929, but did not totally reject his Judaism and maintained a great respect for its values all his life. He was an active Trade Unionist among the cab drivers and fought the Fascists at Cable Street in 1936.

Just before the war, a Home Office official came to the taxi drivers Trade Union offices and asked cab drivers to be prepared to volunteer for the Fire Service in the event of war because their knowledge of

London streets as drivers of fire appliances would be essential in the defence of London during the anticipated bombing. Clearly, the ability to get from fire to fire and know how to by-pass streets blocked with bomb debris, which cab drivers and their intimate knowledge of the back-doubles could guarantee, was going to be of huge importance to the Fire Service.

Charles shortened his holiday in Wales to return to Dalston in London to volunteer, the day war was declared, because he wanted 'to do his bit', despite the official Communist Party (CP) line of not fighting an 'Imperialist War'. For Charles the evil of Hitler superseded this and he also noted the inactivity of the military during the 'phoney war'. The fire brigade were recruiting and he was immediately accepted; they seemed to be doing something positive for the war effort. In addition the CP were very much in favour of Civil Defence as they knew only too well what Franco had done to the cities of Spain in the Civil War, to the ordinary citizens with whom the CP politically identified. So Charles served as a fire engine driver from 1939 till 1944; in any case his cab had been requisitioned for the Fire Service for the duration.[2]

Their station commander was an overweight, cynical regular fireman who was almost illiterate and over-promoted only because of his long service; he gave pompous lectures and was a brute of a man, though a good fireman said Charles. In one inane talk about 'salvage' the commander explained to the men that 'items in danger of water damage during a fire were to be saved, and if not you will be charged with negligence; if you are unsure it will be damaged then you must break in and check, but will be charged with damaging the door or window; therefore always take a bucket of water and if the salvage was not in danger, throw the water over it a bit and then salvage it, thereby avoiding criticism'.! Such was the logic of salvage![3]

For the first several months they did nothing but train. He served mostly in Haggerston School sub-station in Queensbridge Road (station 38W). There was a 5,000-gallon dam (reservoir) of water for drill purposes, and the appliances were kept under the roofs of the old school playground sheds, with sandbag walls built to protect them from bomb blasts. They had four pumps and four taxis to haul them, with five men per pump; each cab was laden with the crew and ladders, axes, saws, hoses, ropes, etc. There was also a salvage van for rescuing valuable equipment and materials from buildings before they were destroyed. They were paid £3 per week and all the men were local working class. There were three Jewish lads but the remainder of the men were uncompromising Mosleyites who openly expressed anti-Semitic views but in an impersonal and political vein. Charles said they disagreed but it was never personal and during the actual raids, everyone respected everyone else and worked together; men were judged by their deeds and as the bombing went on, some of the Mosleyites lost faith in their 'German friends', for obvious reasons.

When the first raid occurred, on Saturday 7 September 1940, Charles was off duty and was immediately called to his station. There was a feeling not only of fear but also of helplessness as the Germans bombed with impunity while feeble AA fire responded. Before the Blitz began, standing orders were for firemen to rush to their shelters and wait out the bombing. However, as explained below, this was soon changed.

After two hours of sitting in the shelter, the men told their officer they wanted to go out and fight the fires; it was 4 p.m. according to Charles. The commander said no, but they went anyway as they were not prepared to stand by and do nothing. On leaving the building they saw the sky glowing, enough, as he discovered later, to read a newspaper in the dark, and they rushed to St Katherine's Dock. On arrival at the docks, they found dozens of pumps at work and reported for duty. Charles took his allotted place on the pump, where his personal equipment was also kept. (This went on right through to December, virtually non-stop.)

On another occasion, bombs were falling heavily on the docks and Charles's pump was sent out; orders would be shouted from the watch room to each pump to attend at a certain location, under the orders of the Fire Officer in charge who directed operations. But on this day the tide was out so the river was not available and hydrants not functioning due to the mains having been blown up – so the men had to watch warehouses and houses burn. Fire barges in mid river had to draw water for the hoses to relay to the pumps; existing dams of water were also used. But it was not sufficient. Burst burning gas mains were the worst as they could not be extinguished except by sand or until the gas had been turned off.

In one fire at Kings Cross Charles was atop one of the six-storey gasometers; the burning gas shot out from holes blown in the gasometer like giant flamethrowers, and was totally unpredictable and thus very dangerous as it would flare in whichever direction the changeable wind blew it. The only way to tackle it was from the roof of the gasometer and play the water onto the joists and wheels to cool them so they did not jam and then prevent the lowering roof of the gasometer from expelling the gas (until it burnt itself out). If the parts jammed, oxygen would get in and the gasometer would explode – and of course take the firemen with it. The danger was if the pump failed or the roof was hit by a bomb, for then all was lost. Meanwhile AA guns were firing, bombs dropping, bombers flying over, splinters of shrapnel raining down and orders being shouted. The only protection from jagged steel dropping as shrapnel was the tin helmet. And the only remarkable thing was the dramatic view from the top of the City burning. Nevertheless, Charles said that when he was in an air raid shelter off duty, he was even more scared than fire-fighting, because he was at least outside and happy to be with his mates doing what he knew how to do, and fighting back.

Charles recalled the dockland fires in spirit/liquor warehouses which he attended, where the river and road surfaces, flooded with this inflammable material, were literally on fire and an immediate danger to the firemen as it could explode at any time. High buildings, seemingly safe, in fact were often just the front edifice with the back areas completely destroyed by fire or bombs – the slightest vibration would bring the whole edifice down and firemen again would be in mortal danger at such sudden collapses. The answer was to stand well back – though some firemen were able, said Charles, to judge where a large window may collapse and stand in such a spot that the building would miss them and they would be left standing unharmed where the window aperture fell.

Fighting fires later in the city and residential areas was thus more straightforward as it was possible to predict how the burning material would react as it was consumed. But he recalled the massive incendiary raid on the City of 29 December 1940, and how the thousands of German incendiaries were not merely burning but contained an explosive charge that could kill. This forced firemen and firewatchers to be wary when approaching them with sand and bucket attached to a long pole. Leaving the incendiaries thus to burn just increased the level of fire damage and reignited fires that had just been put out.

In addition Charles pointed out that the regulations that stated that firemen would only be required for health reasons to be at any one fire for two hours and then be relieved to rest, dry out, eat and sleep for two hours, before rotating back, had to be totally abandoned once the full force of the Blitz hit the country; often a fireman could expect to be at a fire for two or three days and nights and be rested and fed 'on site', as Charles frequently experienced. In addition the number of fire brigade refreshment vans turned out to be totally inadequate to meet the needs of the crews, and drink and food often never arrived for many hours at a time. In cold weather and soaked through, this was extremely demoralizing for the men and it was the brave women of the Salvation Army who came to their rescue in great danger, to serve the men tea and sandwiches in specially designed vans. Later, the brigade resolved this problem.

Charles recalled that as his family were out of London, and his home was damaged, he simply left with a rucksack and wandered the air raid shelters at night to sleep, as did many other firemen. Inevitably the fire station soon became their obvious 'home' and many men lived there permanently until things normalized as the first Blitz ended by 1942.

Friction between auxiliaries and professional firemen was sometimes acute, because the professionals had often been over promoted to train and command Auxiliaries and they were frequently not up to the job, according to Charles. They became 'little Napoleons' and when the often more able auxiliaries reacted, the officers became dictatorial and discipline could break down. Resentment grew between the two groups and rank was often abused. Later, however, this situation resolved itself as everyone became more highly trained and experienced and shared the common dangers of the air raids. Forming the National Fire Service (NFS) helped with this transformation as LFB/AFS/NFS boundaries slowly disappeared and the whole brigade became more integrated. Charles was particularly aware of and sensitive to these issues as he was Secretary of his local FBU (Fire Brigade Union) branch.

A major issue was uniform: according to Charles, the LFB had all the modern personal equipment required, especially the two thick, felt uniforms, but the AFS were only given one uniform, as more simply did not exist. Once wet, the uniform was useless for further wear until it dried, but there was never time once the Blitz began and men were constantly on call in wet uniforms. This had a huge negative effect on the men's health and morale, especially as winter approached, and added to the already dreadful burden of loss of sleep. So the AFS were given firemen gas capes and hoods, trousers and masks (meant to be used in case of the gas attacks that ultimately never came) and this sufficed very well until new uniforms were made. In fact Charles said they could not have gone on without these capes. One further stop gap was the order given on the second day of the Blitz by the Home Office to divert twenty thousand pairs of navy blue post office trousers ordered by the GPO, to the AFS firemen. And so they at least had a second pair, albeit slightly inferior in quality! This was followed shortly after by the issue of long rubber leggings which helped enormously. Most of the AFS boots were just Wellingtons and proper boots came much later. In all this, the FBU were hugely influential in representing the AFS men, especially in these and other matters such as over-bearing officers, social and educational matters, work conditions and so on.

Charles also took a prominent role in establishing the Fire Brigade discussion groups – modelled on the idea used in the Armed Services –

where time was found to encourage the men and women to meet and argue about the kind of Britain they wanted to see at war's end.

Charles recalled a dockland fire where he was one of several relief crews:[4]

> It was past 10 p.m. and no alert had been sounded. Relieved, the Fire Station settled down to a peaceful night; to the cosy click of the billiard balls ... happy at just not being at work, soaked and frozen, or hot and choking. For they had had their fill in the last 48 hours. Few of the men had had much sleep, and many fires were still burning at the docks.
>
> Though hoping that none would be called that night, the station messenger suddenly appeared ... 'No. 1 trailer pump. Hammett's Wharf at 1 a.m. For cooling down' ... 'Damn!' said Charles, who was driving. (The other crews laughed) ... but Charles' crew were not amused and climbed into their bunks for two and a half precious hours.
>
> At 12.30 the night patrol woke them ... they gaped and stretched, and pulled on their top boots and fire gear. The night air struck coldly ... not so bad in the drivers seat ... but the three men behind were shivering ... one dim headlight shot its anaemic beam and they went through the back doubles of Haggerston ... between the little houses empty spaces gaped ... in each gap people had died ... lost homes and loved ones ... most known to the crew as neighbours. There was plenty of debris ... the heavy trailer pump dragging like an unwilling captive ... on both sides were great buildings, now ruins. Many were 'old jobs' of theirs and they talked about them as they passed. As East Enders they knew every corner and in this area they had fought mad night-long battles with the flames and the bombs ... the destruction was a personal loss.
>
> Their engine turned into a narrow cobbled way with the dock wall on the left, blasted into tumbled piles of bricks every so often. Suddenly a policeman and a Home Guard appeared in the headlights to wave them on. Whilst the area outside the docks was silent and deserted, inside there was bustle and activity; scarlet, burning storehouses, shooting tongues of fire which burnt the eyes. There was a bedlam of rushing firemen, roaring pumps, hissing water and collapsing walls and roofs. The air was hot, heavy and full of a thousand smells, whilst the Thames rolled silently by, burnished like copper as it reflected the fires. Bumping over the hoses, hard as iron when full of water, they reach the towering brown brick building of Hammett's Wharf, with its empty windows belching smoke. Here is the pump they have come

to relieve, with its operator black and grimy from head to foot leaning against its roaring engine.

'Are you 24Z', says the leading fireman. The other, exhausted fireman nods wearily, his face totally blackened, smiling. 'We are 38W come to relieve you', says Charles' boss. 'About time', says the fireman. 'Have you been here long?' says the boss. Gently but sarcastically comes the reply, 'Depends – what day is it?'.But there is no hard feeling; Charles' crew knew what it is like; men working full out for 12 hours, and relief not sent when other men are lolling in their stations!

'Come on, I'll show you the job', says the fireman. They sniff the air and it stinks of hides. 'It's hides, wool, soya and veneers', he says. They enter the building and the fire is under control but not dead yet; it flares here and there and must be fought relentlessly until drowned with water and 'cooled down'. Suddenly a bank of thick, yellow, acrid smoke from burning leather hits them and they start to cough and stumble and their eyes and noses stream; they bend down so they can breathe some air as the smoke rises aloft. All interior walls had collapsed so the building was one large 'hall', piles of goods smouldering and smoking, despite inches deep water on the floors. In the middle Charles remembers the men standing wearily with hoses flowing, stooped low to breathe, sending two glittering arcs of water thudding into the fire; the men they were about to relieve.

The roar of the pump stuttered and then stopped ... silence, and the jets of water lost their strength and died ... the men they were relieving straightened their backs and rolled cigarettes ... and joked and laughed ... Charles continued, they tell us the danger spots, weak walls and roofs... 'and remember – anything (a bomb) drops within half a mile and this lot's coming down for sure', says one man. We change over gear and relieve them.

24Z leave us with a cheery cry; we start our pump and leave one man to operate it and return to the nozzles ... but flames are breaking out in many places. We stand, two of us, at the end of each hose, tucking them firmly under our arms, getting a good stance on our feet. The pump operator emits a huge whistle with his fingers and yells, 'W-a- t-e-r!' and the nozzles begin to sing as the air drives out in a fierce hissing gust. We stiffen to take the strain and the water follows in a great roaring jet. Under such pressure the hoses become alive and wild, struggling with great strength to be free. We press them to our sides and throw all our weight forwards, wrestling with the backward thrust. They then lash sideways but we grip the nozzles. If they break loose like shrieking serpents, the heavy brass attachments can snap a man's thigh. Every few minutes, the spare man has to relieve one of the two hose holders, so great is the strain. The relieved man then uses the spike of his axe to break open bales and timber to disperse the flames. When saturated, the hose passes to a fresh 'bull's-eye' of flame. We sweat as we move forward with the hose, against its back-thrust. The heavy air is like a wet blanket and spray soaks our tunics. The acrid smoke forces us to take breathers in turn, in the rear.

Suddenly above all the noise of jets and pumps, the air raid sirens ('flutes') are heard. Enemy bombers are overhead – again. One man pales, as he is still suffering from a blast shock that hit him a few nights before in Leman Street when he was blown 50 yards down the road. Their team leader deliberately turns to him and calmly asks him to grab his hose and help; a wise and humane move as it eases the man's nerves a little. The noise of the aircraft fills the air and soon follow the crashing AA guns and this is followed by the equally pounding 'quick-fire' guns, chattering like monkeys. They wait for the first bomb to drop.

There is a sudden rush like an express train, which becomes a whine and then a shriek. A roar bursts through my eardrums and punches my skull. The ground leaps a foot into the air; a heavy girder falls to within 6 feet of us, on our left, and we are momentarily showered in dust. When it clears we are all standing covered in white, like millers, but grimly holding our hoses ('branches'). 'Five-hundred pounder; eighty yards away', says one man. 'Near enough', says another.

Bombs continue to fall but we stand to our hoses and slowly the fires die away. After checking, the order comes to stop the pump. Suddenly a huge burning beam falls through the roof onto bales of wool and the fire flares again. They start once more. Suddenly the aircraft are gone and the guns die away. The 'All Clear' sounds and the men cheer. Dawn breaks and their Relief arrives.

Charles drives the pump back to base through newly shattered streets, one tyre is flat and the windscreen smashed. The others doze as they pass through the Jewish ghetto near Charles' old school, its roof blown away.

Charles was present at the terrible bombing of Bank Station. He had just returned from a full 24 hours of fire-fighting to his base, soaked and hungry and exhausted, when they were called to Bank Station. His engine with seven men was first on the scene and they had to crawl on their stomachs into the huge crater and over many dead bodies and bring out the huge number of injured survivors, as well as tackling the gas main fires, with their hoses stretched long distances from the pumps into the disaster area.

In 1940 Charles wanted to join the RAF to really have a crack at the Nazis, and was accepted to train as an RAF Ferry Command pilot. But the AFS refused to release him on grounds that his work in the Fire Service, as with others, was of national importance. He was also quite clear in his testimony that anti-Semitism was rife in the London Fire Brigade at this time and many firemen were Mosley supporters; this is substantiated by many other testimonies, both Jewish and non-Jewish.

Charles also recalled a proposal from Exeter Brigade to send a crew to Haggerston on an exchange to get some war time experience as Exeter had never been bombed. At the same time the London crew could have some respite. This duly took place but it turned out that the Exeter crew came at a very quiet time in London and did nothing, whilst the London crew endured the notorious Baedekker raid on Exeter. Such is fate.

After the Blitz, Charles was transferred to Watford where things were quieter and he could go home and sleep at night, loss of sleep being the most stressful problem firemen faced. He was busy helping demolish dangerous ruins in London, and then applied for transfer to East Anglia to assist at Bomber Command aerodromes to help with crash landings. He thought that this was where the war now was and wanted to be involved as the allied bombing campaign began against Germany. At the same time, his superiors were happy to be rid of him due to his Trade Union activism and his criticism of the Fire Brigade management in a journal.

This work involved much more mobile equipment as 'Flying Columns' and their unit of six men travelled when required up and down the east coast, often living in tents. He attended the crashes of hundreds of bombers returning from raids.[5] The first job at a burning aircraft was to ascertain if any crew were in the aircraft and if they were alive. They knew how many crew should be in each aircraft type and where in the plane they should be located. Any air crew not accounted for had to be searched for, and brought out, when the aircraft might explode at any moment. It was very dangerous work. Many was the time he had to remove the charred remains of brave airmen.

On one occasion his crew went to the site of an American Flying Fortress crash near Hemel Hempstead. All eight airmen were burned to death and they placed the remains on stretchers and covered them with ground sheets, as standing orders were not to 'spread shock' to any civilians. An American crash crew also soon arrived, and all the remains were put on one stretcher and loaded onto an ambulance to take to the aerodrome mortuary. But there was one survivor and he was in shock and insisted on finding his pal. Charles told him there were no more survivors but he insisted on pulling back the sheet; on seeing the horrible sight of body parts, the airman collapsed on the ground.

Charles said that such experiences eventually have little effect on you when you see them day after day. The first time, during the Blitz, seeing burnt bodies was sickening, but ultimately you get used to it, otherwise you could never do the job. Charles's view was that you could not dwell on the horrific experiences of moving burnt corpses from buildings and aircraft, or you would never be able to live a normal life afterwards. Charles said out of the forty-eight firemen he served with at Haggerston/Queensbridge Road, nine were killed and this he would never forget.

Eventually, Charles was made Quartermaster of the east coast columns and for several months enjoyed the luxury of his own billet, own office and restful nights based at Beccles in Suffolk.

From Autumn 1944, Charles volunteered for the elite Allied Services Overseas Fire Column (International Fire Column) in Europe,[6] following the Allied Advance from D Day. He was anxious to discover what the war was really like and take part in the 'Second Front' the CP had so long called for. They did full military training bar weapons training, and were seen off with a rousing speech by Minister Herbert Morrison. Charles moved from Belgium to north France, then back to Belgium and then on through southern Holland and into Germany. They were actually attached to Patton's US 3rd Army, who called them 'The Limey Fire Department'. The 700 or so men were equipped with special army fire trucks and were all Blitz veterans and highly experienced with a strong sense of camaraderie, self discipline and excellent relations between officers and men. Life was basic and they often lived in waterlogged trenches. Charles was once hospitalised in Belgium with the effects of exposure from this.

Much of the work involved extinguishing fires on the front line started by the retreating Germans, to try to stop the Allied armoured columns continuing their advance. They also dealt with fires from crashed aircraft and with protecting of, and checking for fires near, Allied ammunition and oil dumps. They were of course unarmed and civilians, but subject to military law. They followed transports of ammunition convoys, and wherever ammunition or oil dumps occurred, they would provide fire protection for a week or so whilst the dumps emptied; when the Germans were shelling, this was extremely dangerous work. There were many fires and they always carried 5,000 gallons of water in a huge tank mounted on a lorry, and refilled it as it was used up, by relay hoses from local water supplies; they also carried one tanker of foam for chemical and petrol fires. Crashed aircraft were the most difficult to deal with because they usually crashed in dense woods or the middle of huge ploughed fields and were extremely tricky to reach. One great fear was napalm – adhesive liquid fire which stuck to targets and burnt with a fury.

At one of the Rhine crossings, Charles found himself in a long queue with several appliances and about twenty men, waiting with many army vehicles to cross the river. Meanwhile they were being shelled by German long-range guns, and strafed and bombed by the Luftwaffe.

Charles said he felt a particular need to be in Europe to help defeat the Nazis who had done such cruel things to the Jews. His crew always tried to persuade him to hold back when near the front lines in case he was captured by the Germans; they were touchingly aware of what this could possibly mean. But he would have none of it and wanted to face the Germans head on.

Whilst Charles and his crew knew of political concentration camps, they did not expect to see what they found of the full horror of the Holocaust against the Jews. He was present at the Liberation of some of these camps, but did not name them on his tape.

At Namur in Belgium, Charles witnessed the Americans try to blow the bridge to cut off the German retreat by dropping bombs from high level bombers, but succeeded only in utterly destroying the town and countryside. In contrast, when the Germans tried to blow the bridge to stop the American advance they sent one plane at very low level and blew it up.

On one occasion in the Ardennes hills, near the front line, Charles's men came across several large dumps of American petrol aligned along a wooded road, that were being sniped at from the forest by German soldiers and Belgian 5th columnists fighting with them, who had been cut off from enemy lines. Every so often these enemy troops would rush into the two nearby villages in the valley and shoot up shops to steal food. The Americans of course fired back. The danger was that if the dumps had been hit by the exchanges of fire, or the raiding German aircraft that often came over, the burning petrol would flow down the valley and into two nearby villages and destroy them. Charles, as senior fireman, sought out the American Commanding Officer of the 110th Georgia Engineers, and explained that the dumps had been dangerously located. Asking what he should do, Charles replied that pits needed to be built around each dump so any ignited fuel would flow into them and burn itself out. He offered to use his firemen to dig these pits, one each day, and asked if he could have a few American soldiers to help. The Officer said he could do better than that and handed over 100 German prisoners! The job was done by these sullen and unhappy POWs.

At war's end Charles finished up in Frankfurt. After their return to East Anglia in May 1945, via Bruges and Boulogne, his crew were sent back to Regents Park in London to be demobbed. Then an order came from the FBU to call a meeting to bid formal farewell to the roughly 700 men of the International Column in a large hall. Charles was on the platform with other union officials and the senior NFS Officers were to arrive to speak after the Union meeting. However, there was a misunderstanding and the LFB top brass suddenly came into the hall in the midst of the speeches. To save the day, Charles did an extraordinary thing – probably never done before or since – by giving a military order to his union men –'Brothers, Attenshun!' – and the whole hall rose and the proceedings went well.

Charles was also a novelist and through the Socialist Unity Theatre met his second wife to be, Edith, an Austrian Jewish refugee, whom he married in 1949. After the war he worked for five years as a sub-editor of books for various publishers, and then returned to the cab trade after publishers black-listed him for being a Socialist activist in the past and also because, Charles said, of the fact he 'looked Jewish'. In the 1960s he became a very popular history teacher at Further Education College Evening Classes in Walthamstow and Essex, specializing in walking tours of London. He died in 2001.

NOTES

1. Taken from tapes at the Museum of London (92.153), the Imperial War Museum (12508), British Library (C518/08/01) and other written sources.
2. Charles' Fire Brigade Registration card describes him as Charles Albert Alexander Poulsen b. 5 March 1910 and living at 16 Torbay Road, Willesden and based at Kingsland Fire Station in Hackney. Charles pointed out that in fact about three quarters of London cabs were 'called up' for service.
3. Charles names the officer but it would be inappropriate to reveal this here.
4. Taken from H.S. Ingham (ed.), *Fire and Water; An NFS Anthology* (London: Lindsay Drummond, 1942), pp.157–65, paraphrased from Charles Poulsen's testimony,
5. On the tape Charles made in 1977 for the British Library, he said it was known that the Germans used captured damaged Allied planes and sent them up with English-speaking German crews to slip into bomber streams and then shoot down Allied aircraft on their way to and from Germany. This was not widely known until the 1990s, as far as this author understands, but Charles knew it then and in the 1970s.
6. For more detail on this see the pamphlet 'Overseas against Fire' at LMA 23.2 HIC.

Chapter Thirty One

Sir Lou Sherman[1]

Lou was born in the East End on 23 May 1914 and became a cab driver in 1936. On 3 September 1939, a Fire Service officer came and told all the cabbies in his garage that all taxis were requisitioned for the Fire Service – no arguments. He never saw the cab again.

Lou said all prospective firemen had to pass the hook ladder test – that is, taking a 12-feet ladder and hooking it on to the first floor window ledge of a building, climbing up it, pulling it up to the next floor by hooking it to the second level and climbing up

83. Fireman (Sir) Lou Sherman, in later life.

that. His two brothers failed; he passed. He was posted to a sub-station in Fairclough Street School opposite the main Commercial Road fire station, and became a driver of the heavy unit pump. As a result he took part in some of the worst fires. But to begin with in the phoney war there was nothing to do and many wanted to leave and – like Lou – join the army; but it was not permitted as the Government knew what was coming. At one point Lou started a farm at the station and they had 150 chickens and many rabbits – to provide extra food – and the skins of rabbits they pinned and sold to local fur shops. At Millwall they kept pigs; all in all it kept the men busy. At St Botolph's Church by Aldgate Pump, there was a bomb site and Lou got permission from the vicar to have an allotment there; the vicar even gave him £5 to buy tools for his team of horticulturalist firemen. They also had a firemen discussion group, started by Bob Darke, a leading member of the Communist Party. Then came the Blitz.

On the first night they were fighting a fire in Whitechapel Road when a runner came to get them to go to a fire in Plumbers Row off Commercial Road; the men did not bother to climb inside the engine but hung on to the engine sides for speed. When they arrived, a demolition squad had got to work pulling down a dangerous wall and it fell right in front of Lou's engine causing two men to fall off the engine side; they were both killed, hit by falling masonry and Lou was concussed and had an injured finger. He was taken to the London Hospital and then allowed home.[2]

Lou particularly remembered the Thameshaven oil fires on 29 December 1940; they toiled in vain for three days and nights, hosing the unexploded oil containers in the hope they would not explode like the others. For two days they thought they were forgotten and had no food; then finally on the third day they were relieved and sent on leave.

On one 'Shout', soon after Thameshaven, Lou was playing cards in the canteen and winning, when the 'bells went down'. He grabbed his money, wrapped the coins in a handkerchief and shoved it in his pocket. All the men dashed for their pumps and took off to the East India Docks at high speed, as many as thirty vehicles from several stations, in convoy at high speed in the pitch black using only slit headlights. Lou was in the lead and suddenly he saw a huge hole in the Commercial Road where an unexploded bomb had made a large crater. The convoy halted and everyone had to wait until the last vehicle turned around and one by one the vehicles in the convoy could all turn and find an alternative route. Whilst waiting, Lou needed to wipe his nose and, forgetting, whipped out his handkerchief, whereupon his 15 shillings – a small fortune then – flew out into this huge crater right onto the bomb! He hesitated; should he or shouldn't he? He remembered, 'Like an idiot I crawled down and retrieved the sixpences!'

Later his station was on a call to the City but was stopped at Adler Street in Whitechapel where a huge fire was blocking the road; their ten pumps dealt with it and they then proceeded to Bank where the whole City seemed on fire from incendiaries, followed by high explosive bombs which cut the mains and destroyed the emergency water tanks in the streets. Then just as they were working on the fires, the Thames water level began to drop and the hoses ran dry. Pumps then had to be taken onto the mud to obtain the water and get it pumped all the way to Moorgate by relay; they actually drove pumps into the Tower of London and dropped hoses where the guns are today and broke the railings down in order to do it. Ultimately they just had to stop as the Thames receded and the City burnt. Suddenly Lou was hit by a small bomb splinter in his hand and had to be relieved to have it dressed in hospital.

Lou said that the men were very inexperienced at first, but they came to learn certain tricks of the trade. For example, when fighting a fire on a burning upper floor, and it was impossible to see through the smoke and flames where the building ended, you would throw a stone ahead of you. If it disappeared you knew then you had reached the edge and you stopped and went no further with the hose.

In a fire at John Lewis in Oxford Street, the young man next to him fell through a burning floor and broke his spine. After the main Blitz, they were sent again to John Lewis; the fire was out on this occasion but Lou was asked to go up to the roof to determine if it was a dangerous structure; whilst he was on the roof it collapsed and he was taken to Middlesex Hospital with a splintered spine. After being discharged from hospital a week later, he continued in the service as a driver only, but after two years it became so painful he had to spend six months in traction and at the end of 1943 he was pensioned off. By war's end he was driving a cab again.

Lou considered all the men he served with were heroes. The cab drivers especially had a great sense of humour and high morale, always laughing in the face of adversity; they set up cab shelter style canteens in their fire stations to bring some home cooking and comfort to the men on duty, and this attracted men from nearby stations to eat with them. Lou also used to edit a little newssheet which was read by several fire stations in the area and contained articles on how jobs at work could be done more efficiently, making the most of spare time when on duty, and so on.

Post-war Lou became active in public life; he was a Labour Mayor of Hackney, and sat on the GLC and various public bodies such as the Housing Corporation. He was made OBE in 1972 and Knighted in 1975, alongside Charlie Chaplin. The Queen asked him what he did and he said he was a cab driver. She said, 'Are you really? I see so many of them but you are the first one I have ever spoken to.' After he was Knighted, a customer accidentally called him 'sir', and Lou said, 'How did you know?' Lou died in 2001.

NOTES

1. Taken from the online Fire Brigade Forum, 1995, courtesy of John Farrell.
2. The incident is described on the front page of the *East London Advertiser*, 18 January 1941; the men killed were Jewish Fireman Joseph Greenberg and his friend Alfred Strange; Jewish fireman Max Abrahams was injured.

Chapter Thirty Two

Reuben Wilner[1]

Reuben Wilner was born to an orthodox Jewish family in Manchester, son of Solomon and Mrs Wilner, on 14 August 1916 and attended The Jew's School, Derby Street, Cheetham. He left school at 14 and worked in the tailoring trade and then later became a cinema projectionist. In 1939, Reuben tried three times to join various Army Corps in Manchester (Artillery, RAMC and Signals) and was told each time they were 'full'. When he tried the Navy, they said they did not want anyone with glasses. He was told to wait till he was called up and when he finally was, the Army doctor turned him down as unfit. Finally he was accepted by the AFS at London Road HQ, after a quick medical with a Dr Coldheart, and proving he could climb a 30-feet ladder.

84. Reuben Wilner in his later years, Manchester fire brigade.

Reporting to brigade headquarters, Reuben carried out drills in a big yard under the watchful eye of a Sgt Brown: 'He used to be watching carefully. If anybody would shout "OK" like for "Water on", he'd be charging round the yard … "Water on!" Oh yes, he was a right bully. He was an ex-army man I think. But he was a proper fireman. So, that's how I became a member of the AFS.' Reuben continued,

> We did training in some of the large ponds outside the factories … you got pump experience there, because we thought, you just hold the end – holding the nozzle, and it's a cakewalk. My word, it's not a cakewalk. Especially when there's a pump behind it. It takes you, the hose and the whole hog … but it was good. I

enjoyed what we did. But when I told my mother – 'What, you a fireman?' she said.

I got a nice uniform, with a hatchet, and a key. For the first time in my life, I realised what those plates are on the wall. They are the hydrant diameter and distance from the hydrant; I liked the job very, very much. And the only reason I left was because the cinema projection job was interfering. I wasn't full time AFS then, but I realised that if I want a full-time job, I won't be able to carry on in the AFS. And I liked it, you see. But I could only work evenings with the AFS and on Sundays (either a morning or afternoon, whichever was required). But I liked being in the AFS you know. Perhaps it was something with wearing the uniform.

First we were at headquarters, but not for very long. From there, we moved to the Blair's Corset Factory in Knowsley Street and then Julia Street; they had a little garage which they leased to the AFS, and from there we went to Ash Street in Harpurhey. What I do remember is that we drilled. Especially on a Sunday. We used to go to the bottom end of Collyhurst, to these factories, and go inside. We certainly got to know how to hold a nozzle.

The only real fire I went to was one that we were called out to at the bottom of Robert Street. That area I think still has got a lot of factories, near Salford bus station.

In every one of the offices that I worked in we had a book. And everything which happened during our tour of duty was put down. The time, the place, and the details. And they called it the 'Occurrence Book'.

Engineers used to come every month, to service the equipment – that was part of the agreement – but I used to do a lot of the maintenance myself. It was frowned upon by the management – 'The engineers get paid for doing that'. But I liked doing repairs – I liked to be on the ball.

I lived not far from Julia Street and lot of Jewish men worked at Julia Street station.

When asked if being Jewish made him think especially about beating the Nazis in the war, Reuben said,

I will tell you that I was so steeped in, so engrossed in my work, that although I used to take notice of what's going on outside, in the papers, and on the radio – I didn't give it the thought that perhaps I should have done. When I left the AFS – mainly because the job interfered with it – I missed my nice uniform, the fellows that I worked with – they were very nice people, very nice people.

We were purely voluntary. I don't remember getting any pay – and if you were near home, most of the time, and I lived with my mother – so she made sure that my sandwich bag was ready.

I think there was one place where we slept. Because of Fire-watching; we had to do a little bit of that too, in the actual duties. But not on a regular basis. You had to make sure if any incendiary bombs dropped, you'd be there to put them out.

NOTE

1. From an interview with Rob Bonner of the Greater Manchester Fire Service Museum.

Short Stories

Leonard Eliezer Abrahams (later Graham)
Leonard was born in June 1912 and served at Station 39Y, Albion Road, Stoke Newington. He had been a cab driver pre-war. Married to Amelia née Silver, they lived at Imperial and Coronation Avenue. One night before going on duty Leonard told Amelia to shelter in the cellar in the block of flats during the raids, but she refused and went elsewhere. The flats received a direct hit in the notorious disaster and Leonard believed Amelia had been killed. Amelia survived but he never quite forgave himself for giving her the bad advice and as a result never spoke about his wartime experiences.[1]

David Adam aka Adaminsky
David was a Leading Fireman in Leeds. Whilst helping fight a very dangerous blaze at Barn Bow armaments factory, news went out that a fireman had been killed during the incident. David's wife walked repeatedly through the night to his fire station – a two mile round trip – to see if there was news of her husband. Just as dawn broke, her mother persuaded her to go one last time, so Mrs Adams set off through the ginnels (narrow streets) and on her way saw a fireman coming towards her, with a completely black face. She approached him and asked if he had any news about David Adams. He stared at her and said, 'Don't you know me Mary?' It was David, safe and sound, but completely unrecognisable.[2]

Harry (Harold) 'Barney' Barnett
Harry often spoke of his many slides down the fire pole at his station in Kingsland, Hackney and stories including crawling along burning beams when out at fires during the Blitz. He always kept his trousers

right by his bed at night in case of emergency call outs and this habit stayed with him till the day he died.[3]

Ron Berger

Ron was born on 13 November 1923, son of Jack and Bessie of 4 Baker Street, E1, and he attended Rutland Street and Dempsey Street schools; he sang at Philpot Street in the synagogue choir, and was a member of Victoria Boys Club in Fordham Street.

In 1939 he immediately joined the AFS as he was still under age for the army. His uncle, Israel Deutch (his mother's brother) also joined up and was later killed in the Blitz. Ron was a messenger boy in the AFS attached to Whitechapel station at a sub-station called 28X made up of all Jewish taxi drivers who had their cabs requisitioned to haul fire pumps. This station was located at the German owned, Jacobs lager factory at Tower Hill, opposite the Tower of London. The men secretly found a way in and got drunk on a few occasions, so Customs and Excise had to come and seize all the stock and close the building up.

Ron cycled messages to Whitechapel station and also Fire Brigade HQ in Lambeth, but his mother insisted he leave as he was still underage and Ron had to find a job. But he eventually volunteered for the RAF as soon as he was 18 years old in 1941. After training in Blackpool, he was embarked via Greenock to Gibraltar and the Middle East.

Leon Blumenkehl

Leon was a very portly man who joined the Fire Service in Acton. He was often teased for not being able to slide down the fireman's pole during training. As a firewatcher before this, his daughter aged 5 or 6 used to accompany him on his duties at night for short periods, and she recalls the searchlights and the noise of guns and bombs being like Guy Fawkes night. She was allowed on occasion to wear his tin helmet. On one occasion an incendiary bomb landed on their house and the neighbours all gathered round to extinguish it whilst she was whisked away to a nearby house for safety.[4]

Sidney Joseph Braham

Sidney is remembered by his family returning home in the early mornings soaked through and exhausted in his uniform, having what he described as bad food and often having to sleep on straw. He taught his family how to put out incendiaries and there was always a bucket of sand and of water, a shovel and an extinguisher in their house, ready for action if he was on duty.[5]

Walter Brunner

Walter was born in Austria on 1 March 1922 and came to the UK aged 16, as one of the famous 'Schonfeld' kinder. He arrived with only a suitcase and a large sausage, given him by his parents 'in case'. From a very orthodox family, he had been at a Yeshiva (Rabbinical seminary) at Nitra in Czechoslovakia, and was taken to Gateshead Yeshiva near Newcastle. To earn his keep he worked as a machinist in a raincoat factory but was then interned on the Isle of Man in 1940 as an enemy alien (at the famous Hutchinson Square Camp in Douglas). He was released and went to work again in a clothing factory – this time in Manchester – where he was a regular firewatcher in Bury Road. On many occasions he witnessed heavy bombings and incendiary incidents; he often fell asleep and had to be woken by comrades, so exhausted was he after working all day.[6]

Rebecca Caplin

Rebecca was a firewatcher in the Golders Green area during the Blitz. As she was only 5 feet tall, the family said she looked like a mushroom in her large tin helmet. One night whilst on duty with an older male firewatcher, with bombs falling all about, he leant over and whispered to her that they must talk quietly as they might disturb his sleeping wife![7]

Henry (Isidore) Cohen

Henry, later called Henry Coe, was born on 12 April 1913. He was son of Simon and Rachel and brought up in Southwold Road, Clapton. Based at Bishopsgate, he was fire-fighting one night during the Blitz and as dawn came, Winston Churchill appeared and talked to the men. Henry featured in the film *1940* talking to Churchill.[8] Henry later moved to the River Service and escorted merchant ships from US convoys into the Port of London as fire protection boats. He was a veneer merchant by trade.[9]

Lewis Cohen

Lewis was an upholsterer by trade, and related how at one fire in a sugar warehouse, he and his colleagues had to walk in slow motion through the treacly, inches-deep melted sugar which held down their boots.[10]

Mendel and David Cohen

Mendel and David were brothers and firemen in Belfast; Mendel lived at 44 Indiana Avenue and Morris at 16 Marmont Gardens. They were two of eight children of Joseph Tevye and Tobe Mina Cohen, shop keepers in fancy goods. They joined the Fire Service on the outbreak of war and served through the terrible bombings of that city and its docks and shipyards.

On 4/5 May 1941, a high explosive bomb hit the house of their sister Jenny's family at 30 Eglinton Street. When the sirens had gone off, Jenny and her husband Morris Jacobson were sheltering in the under stairs cupboard and their two daughters Fay and Clare under the heavy dining room table. Previous raids had been with incendiaries, so Morris left the cupboard shelter to check the rooms upstairs and at that moment the bomb hit and the house collapsed.

As rescuers arrived, Firemen Mendel and David Cohen were among them and helped pull Jenny, their sister, and her daughters out of the rubble, comparatively unharmed; but it was hours before they reached Morris and he was taken to Mater Hospital nearby, where he sadly died next day.[11]

Gisela Eisner née Spanglet

Gisela was born in Berlin in 1925 and was sent to Britain in 1938 on the Kindertransport.[12] After a month at Dovercourt refugee children's camp she was fostered by two Jewish families in London. Later she moved to foster parents (named Gwinnett) in Chesterfield. In 1943, after completing college, she was moved to Nottingham to work by order of the Ministry of Labour, and here she joined the Fire Guard Service.

Posted to a ramshackle building in the city centre, Fire Guards were locally based auxiliaries to the Fire Service and went to assist wherever required during bombing raids, often arriving first to deal with fires using small pumps, whilst the few fire engines available made their way to the incident. Her office had a small canteen providing mostly buttered spam sandwiches and hot, syrupy tea. Otherwise most of the time was spent on extensive exercises as the main Blitz on Nottingham had occurred in 1941.

Post war Gisela got a degree and became a teacher; her brother Stephen was captured but survived the war. They both married and had families but their parents perished in The Holocaust.[13]

Louis Ellis[14]

Louis recalled that those on the night shift in Leeds had a special treat when they came off duty ... bacon and eggs for breakfast. This was a particular delicacy because bacon was rationed. His crew always liked it when he was on, because, being Jewish, he didn't eat the bacon and eggs and was happy for his non Jewish colleagues to have his share.

Louis Ellis was in the fire service because the family business was making flying jackets for the Royal Air Force, which was considered a 'Reserve Occupation'.

Solomon Engelsman

Solomon was a Superintendent Firewatcher in Petticoat Lane, and responsible for the issue of stirrup pumps and sand buckets to his team, and directing them to locations during raids. He was often accompanied by his teenage son Henry on these occasions, who recalls how at 2 a.m. it was often possible to read a newspaper by the light cast by the enormous fires in the City nearby. Solomon's brother-in-law Hyman Pollack was on the same watch, and one day they received an Electric Trailer Pump and had to be instructed in its use. Henry remembers the fireman trying to explain the Venturi principle on how the pump worked (the end of the hose was dipped into a water tank and the pump pushed the water into the hose) and Boyle's Law of physics. Hymie could hardly speak English and sold cucumbers in the Lane and Henry, then at grammar school remembers laughing till his sides ached as poor old uncle Hymie tried to grapple with the complicated theory of water pressure.[15]

Rivie Erskine

Rivie was a firewatcher in Stamford Hill and at Warren Street/Euston Road. She told how she saw the V1 that hit Shoreditch market fly right over her office windows in Euston.[16]

Nicholas Farago

Nicholas was born in Budapest in 1896 and served in the Austro-Hungarian Army in the First World War. He came to England in August 1939 and was interned on the Isle of Man but later released into the AFS, where he served in Amersham. He fell victim to the issue of whether aliens could serve (see Introduction), but it was resolved and he stayed in the force till war's end.[17]

Hans Nathan Feld

Hans was a Jewish refugee from Europe and a firewatcher where he lived in Highfield Road, Golders Green. Although technically an enemy alien, he was elected Captain of his street team. Great was the amusement at the amount of paperwork that had to be completed so that he could be exempted from the Curfew for Aliens, in order for him to perform his fire-watching duties.[18]

Hyman Feldman

Hyman lived in Stamford Hill and was a 32-year-old cabinet maker. He married his wife Rebecca at Jubilee Street synagogue in 1937 and joined the AFS on the outbreak of war, and was originally at Burdett Road station in Stepney. He was later based at Poplar Fire Station.

On 19 March 1941, his crew of five went to the three-storey ship's chandler's warehouse at 5–9 Dod Street near Limehouse Cut, and were fighting a fire on the roof. When the roof collapsed during the blaze Hyman was killed alongside two other firemen, and two others were seriously injured. It took two weeks to find Hyman's body in the canal and he was buried in Edmonton.

In June 2004 Hyman's widow unveiled a plaque in memory of her husband and his two colleagues George Cook and John Munday, in Poplar; Rebecca was 98 and living in the Woolfson OAP home in north London. Her daughter Gloria Stern and all the family of grandchildren and great grandchildren attended. The other two families could not be found. Sadly his brother Louis was killed whilst a POW of the Japanese in the Second World War.

Solomon Fine

Solomon was born in 1905 and served in the Blackburn AFS from 1939 as an engine driver. He often was moved to fight fires in Liverpool and Sheffield and told how on one occasion he and his crew were able to save the *Sifrei Torah* (Scrolls of the Law) from the Sheffield synagogue when it had been hit and was on fire.

Jack 'John' Franklin[19]

Jack 'John' Franklin was born at 45 Hackney Road in 1908, the son of Polish/Rumanian Jewish immigrants, who sold timber and wood products in Hackney. Jack was one of twelve children and attended Scawfel Street School, Hackney Road. His Bar Mitzvah was at Bethnal

Green synagogue, and he joined the Jewish Lad's Brigade and the Hutchinson House Youth Club in Whitechapel. He at first became a wood turner with his father, and then left and did a variety of sales jobs. He was in the Merchant Navy for a short while, until he eventually he became a taxi driver in 1928 aged 20. He was a prominent member of the East London cab drivers union based at Toynbee Hall. He married Gillian at Hackney Synagogue in 1937, and they lived at 12 Navarino Rd.

When war came he joined the AFS before call up to the forces in order to 'do something useful' and was based in a school in Shoreditch High Street. At first he was refused membership of the FBU, but he insisted and eventually all AFS men were accepted after Jack organized a local campaign for all firemen to be able to join. He was a driver in the AFS and recalled that there were many Jewish cabbies in the Force. Meanwhile Jack put his own cab into storage for the duration.

One of his fire posts was right opposite the family business in Hackney Road and so he often got permission to work at the business and sometimes sleep at home, so long as he gave a telephone number for recall.

Michael Friedberg

Michael was born in 1913 and lived at 211 Victoria Park Road and 49 Penshurst Road in Hackney, husband of Yetta (Nita) Marmelstein. He joined the Fire Brigade in 1939 and served in Lauriston Road and Burdett Road stations. When Michael married, he wore his uniform and his Fire Brigade comrades formed a Guard of Honour outside the synagogue. One story tells how he and his brother Joseph (also a fireman) skipped work one day, and the fire engine on which they would have been was blown up by a bomb. The two were posted missing and the wives thought them dead. When they returned home, unaware of the incident, the wives were dumbfounded. It is not known if disciplinary action was taken but certainly bunking off work saved their lives.

In 1943 Michael was called up and served in the Army in Egypt and India. He died in 2011.[20]

Ernst Frischler/Frinton

Ernst was a Jewish refugee from Czechoslovakia, born in 1917. Whilst studying medicine at Glasgow University he worked as firewatcher four nights per week on the roof top of a textile factory in Bridgeton, Glasgow, to help pay his fees. His partner was a portly elderly Jewish man with whom he shared a primitive shack on the roof, containing two old beds and coarse blankets, and a table with two chairs. He witnessed several firebomb attacks on the city.[21]

Louisa 'Libby' Frumkin (later Sacks)

Louisa was a former pupil of Skinners Girls School in Stamford Hill. She was a fire guard in Stoke Newington when she clearly recalled the V1s flying over London. She was later mother of the former Chief Rabbi, Lord Jonathan Sacks.

Rosalie Gassman-Sherr, BEM[22]

Rosalie was the first person to win the BEM in April 1941. She was 29 and living with her parents (Mr and Mrs N. Gassman) in Fairfield Road, Hornsey. A bomb fell on her substation (a garage) in Hornsey, and it collapsed. She volunteered to stay at her telephone to keep contact with the Control centre and several casualties were brought in to her office. She calmly stayed at her post all night, both receiving and sending messages and caring where she could for the injured, using her first aid skills. During all of this the lights were cut off and she used a torch to do most of her work, whilst burst water mains soaked the floor. When she arrived home exhausted that morning, she assisted her parents clearing debris at her house which had also been bombed.

Rosalie was a secretary by profession, Chair of the Zionist Women (WIZO) Youth Centre of Great Britain, a member of the Bayswater Synagogue choir and a swimmer and musician. Her sister and brother in law were also in the AFS.

Alfred Bernard Gold

Alfred served at Euston Fire Station. At one fire in the docks, he was as a Leading Fireman, first up the ladder to place a hose though the window/roof of a burning building. Suddenly there was huge explosion; he was blown off the ladder and somehow landed unhurt, but his tunic was blown to shreds.[23]

1521 Julius 'Judd' Goldberg

Julius was from Manchester and lived at 45 Esmond Road. He joined the AFS in 1937, serving in Manchester, Liverpool, Birmingham and Glasgow. On 5 March 1940 he was heavily involved in a huge fire at Messrs. Simoles factory in central Manchester. When Salford Fire

Brigade arrived, Julius was already in the burning building with his hose. He received a Letter of Commendation from Chief Superintendant Stranaghan of Salford Fire Brigade. Julius was also a fire engine driver and first aider. He helped at serious fires in warehouses at what is now Piccadilly Plaza.

By 1941 he was fighting fires in Liverpool Docks. When a bomb hit one of the fire engines near which he was sheltering, he was badly wounded, suffering a fracture to his right leg, and was taken to Broadgreen Hospital. When Julius married in 1944 he was still in the Service.

Herbert Golden

B/15620 Aux Herbert Benjamin Henry Golden lived at 16 Kay Court, Shrewsbury Road, W2, and was based at station 11Y St Paul's Hall, Harrow Road, W2 (Edgware Road). He was Commended on 28 October 1940 for assisting in the rescue of a woman on 28 September 1940 at 73 East Side, Kensington Gardens Square, W2, by means of a line from a position on the third floor of a house partially demolished by a bomb that night. The woman was pinned to a bed by debris and the house was cut in half by the bomb, exposing the bed; the floor was about to collapse. Fireman Barker crawled out to her and tied her in a chair knot as Firemen Golden and Cousins swung her in to safety, dangling in space, and hauled her in. As they all gained the ground, moments later the house collapsed. An article described the incident in the *Daily Mirror* of 1 October 1940.

Herbert received the King's Commendation for Brave Conduct, but was sadly killed in action in May 1941 (see Roll of Honour).

Morris Goldstone

Morris was born in 1912 in Great Ancoats Street, Ancoats, Manchester. He served in the NFS during the Blitz from 30 June 1939 till 25 October 1942, in Manchester, Liverpool and Sheffield, broken by a short army service between July and October 1940. In October 1942 he rejoined the army where he served in Belgium, Holland, France and Germany, till demob in December 1945. B. O'Connor, Morris's Divisional Officer, wrote in a letter of 25 October 1942, that Morris had taken part in many serious alerts and operations and gave exemplary service.

Morris married Clara, the sister of fellow Jewish Firefighter Asher 'Arthur' Geller. Another friend was his Ancoats Street neighbour, Sgt Goodman 'Tony' Copitch (1913–72), Army Fire Service.

Strangely, Copitch's daughter married Morris's son just before Morris died in January 1972.

Samuel 'Benny' Goodman

Sam won a prize of a weekend away, organized by the *News Chronicle* newspaper and went to stay in a large house in Godalming; after a fine lunch served by the owner's maid, he went to the cinema in his fireman's uniform and they let him in for free. But he was in for a shock as the newsreel showed the bombing of Soho. He described seeing the burning buildings as 'a very funny feeling' watching it on the silver screen (we might these days describe it as surreal).

A firewoman, Violet Parsons, was posted from Shaftesbury Avenue to the watchroom at Station X; here she met Sam, and they fell in love and eloped (as she was not Jewish) and were married for over fifty years. Sam remembered many good friends from Soho: 'Bryan Gibbens, later a judge; Eden the pianist; Richard Selby a Cambridge lawyer; Mr McIntevy, Irish, ex-Navy, old LFB man, strong as an ox, hard as nails, heart of gold. There was also a very fine portrait painter by the name of Briggs. He actually painted my portrait, but my dear mother used it to help draw the fire at home (i.e. using a piece of card to encourage air flow to light a coal fire at home), so that went up in smoke.'[24]

Isidore Green[25]

Isidore Green was born in 1906, the son of poor Polish Jewish immigrants, who eventually owned garment-making factories in Bishopsgate and other locations. He attended Grocers School, Hackney and University College School where he was in the OTC. He left when he was 16 and joined the family business. The factories were bombed during the war. Isidore was turned down as unfit for the Forces and so joined the AFS. He served right through the Blitz, and was greatly distressed to witness the East End clothing industry being almost totally destroyed by the Blitz. After being injured in the AFS, he joined the Home Guard till war's end.

Dr Georg Heim

Georg (1878–1947) was a Jewish refugee from Vienna, who lived in Cleve Road, London NW6. After internment on the Isle of Man, and being too old for the army (Pioneer Corps), he became a firewatcher and was involved in removing many incendiaries from roofs during numerous night-time Blitz raids. When not on duty, he was a night watchman or played in orchestras entertaining troops; he was a violinist with Norbert Brainin, who went on to set up the world famous Amadeus Quartet after the war.[26]

Mick Hyams[27]

'Sub-Officer Mick Hyams (station 82U) was at a fire at the 'Grange Works' in Grange Road, Bermondsey. This was a wooden floored tannery, and well alight. He was directing a jet into a loophole (where goods were lifted up and into a building) two floors up in the wall, but decided to change his position. He sent his number two to get the water knocked off and was standing on his own when the wall of the building fell out like a piece of board. Luckily it did not snap and Mick was bracketed by the loophole which fell around him. He escaped with just bruising to his legs from the bouncing bricks.'

Chaim Keiner

Chaim was a German/Polish refugee born in 1901, who escaped to England in 1939. He became a firewatcher in Stepney and served throughout the terrible Blitz period. Whilst standing on top of a block of flats on the corner of Commercial Road and Cavell Street, he saw a landmine parachuting down and watched as it destroyed the top half of Watney Street across from where he was standing. For weeks after he suffered from the effects of the blast which injured his neck.[28]

Joe and Evelyn Kerbel

Joe and Evelyn were a couple who joined the AFS in 1938 and served in the same station in a paint factory in Well Street, Hackney. Having been a taxi driver, Joe was made a fire engine driver. Joe was later transferred to Pound Lane in Willesden and Evelyn worked as a telephone operator, directing fire engines to incidents, until becoming pregnant in 1943. Joe related how the lack of radios meant that after dealing with a fire they had to find a phone box and get directions to the next one; if the phones were not working they dealt with any fire they saw along the way until they found a way of communicating with HQ. After the war Joe was asked by the Home Office to stay on and develop the use of two-way radios but he declined.[29]

Eva Hedwig Klopstock, later Evans

Eva was born on 9 March 1924 in Berlin, daughter of Dr Felix Klopstock. After living in London and Devon, Felix got a job in Barrow-in-Furness where Eva joined the Fire Brigade and was sent to Preston. Being an 'alien' she was, however, not allowed to visit her parents, as Barrow was a sealed military area (Vickers Armstrong ship builders were located there); this was later rescinded in her case. One of her jobs was to calculate the weekly rate of fuel use on the fire engines; she said she always felt apart from the local firemen, even though they were friendly enough.

One of the most bizarre events occurred at war's end when German scientists and their families were brought to work at Vickers and many became friends of her family as Felix was a well known GP and hugely admired by local people; whether these scientists had ever been true Nazis, Eva could not say. However they caused a huge local controversy when they were allowed to send food parcels to relatives in Germany, as there were still drastic shortages in Britain.

Alf Levy (by Harold Walker)[30]

> Among persons I became quite friendly with [at a Hendon College course] was Fireman Levy [note – probably Alf] of the River Section, a member of the Communist Party and part time librarian of the now defunct newspaper the *Daily Worker* [now the *Morning Star*]. He failed to persuade me to his join his 'Party', but had a great sense of humour and was helpful in providing information on the USSR [now Russia], that being one of my lecture subjects. His humour was typified when he remarked 'he would get me circumcised before he was finished'.

Harold relates how, against orders to attend incidents only at night whilst on their lecture course, he and Alf Levy were in the vicinity of a V1 rocket attack and went to help (it is not clear where).[30] They were conveying injured people to Charing Cross Hospital and laying them on the only space available, the casualty section floor, and watched surgeons with the almost impossible job of knowing where or how to begin treatment on some of the worst wounded; all they could do was pacify the conscious victims.

Abraham Lewis aka Bookatz

Abraham was born in Leeds in 1907, the son of East European immigrants; he was a baker by trade like his father. He joined the AFS in 1938 and was already married and by then living in Myrdle Street, Stepney. He was based at Whitechapel Fire Station when three appliances were ordered to Tower Hill to fight a blaze there on the night of 10/11 May 1941, the last night of the bombing raids on London (the Blitz). A stick of 10–15 incendiaries dropped directly in front of the vehicles in Mansell Street en route, but they continued and drove straight through the flames. At Tower Hill when they arrived, they were surprised to see a fourth crew with one fireman kneeling by a hydrant on the corner of Trinity Square and Coopers Row, trying to attach a standpipe to the outlet. The fireman, 1163 Abraham Lewis, warned that the mains were dry from being damaged the night before. Suddenly another cluster of incendiaries hit Abraham's back and he was fatally injured. Other firemen rushed to his aid and he was taken to a concrete first aid shelter directly opposite the fire, and medical help was called. Sadly, Abraham died next day at the London Hospital. He was 33 years old and left a wife and two children. Helena Fox (daughter of Abraham) told me that on his last leave, which would have been in the April or early May of 1941, Abraham Lewis appeared in the local paper of the town where she and her mother and younger brother had been evacuated, Eton Wick near Windsor. Although very young at the time, she remembers what happened. She and her younger brother were sharing the same bed. A bombing raid started and what must have been an incendiary bomb came through the roof of the house and into their bedroom causing their bed to catch fire. She remembers hearing her mother scream, "Abraham, the children ..." and Abraham, like a good fireman, managed to save them both. The incident was considered heroic enough to have been written about in the local newspaper, a copy of which should be in the archives of the Slough Local History Library.

In July 2003, Trinity House Trust agreed a plaque should be placed in the building, just above the Merchant Seamen Memorial Book, in memory of Abraham, who died trying to save it.

Samuel Libbert

Samuel was born on 22 June 1913 in Cheetham, one of six children, the son of Israel and Annie Libbert. Samuel was a garment manufacturer and lived at 29 Woodhill Drive, Prestwich in Manchester, husband of Lena/Lenor (née Silverman) and father of Joan. Within just one month of joining the NFS, he was transferred to Glasgow. On 19 September 1942 he was killed fighting a three-storey factory fire, when a wall collapsed on him and a comrade, William Jackson of Glasgow, who was also killed.[31]

Samuel was buried at Rainsough cemetery where both Glasgow and Manchester firemen attended his funeral, officiated by Rabbi Kopel Rosen and Revs Hershman, Vilensky and Glickman.[32] Samuel had been an active member of the Higher Crumpsall Synagogue and taken courses in First Aid. Both the Manchester Jewish Community and the Glasgow NFS erected memorials to him in Higher Crumpsall Synagogue in Manchester

Rae Lubart (later Fieldman) and Larry Fieldman

Rae and Larry served in the London Fire Brigade. Rae was born on 16 June 1920 in Kingsland Road, Hackney, moving to Ilford in 1924 where she attended Gearies School. She was a telephonist in the Fire Brigade, at Senrab Street School fire station (off Commercial Road), despatching firemen to incidents, and reporting when they returned, throughout the Blitz. Larry was born at 75 Copley Street, Stepney on 10 March 1914.

Larry first met Rae at an inter-station dance on 10 May 1941. Back at work later that night Larry (who was based at Dempsey Street, no longer there, but also off Commercial Road) and his crew were preparing to leave to fight a fire when a bomb made a direct hit on his station just as he was pulling on his boots. All his crew around him were killed and he was knocked down but otherwise uninjured. News of the blast reached Rae at her station and she was greatly saddened that the nice young man she had met the night before was killed. Meanwhile an unexploded bomb had also been found at Larry's station and he was transferred by chance to Rae's station at Chadwell Heath (near Ilford) – so a bomb reunited them and they married in 1942.

One incident Rae recalls occurred when two appliances from Canterbury were sent to her station to help during the heavy raids. On one particularly bad night, Rae noticed the men from her station returned tired and soaked through, and were being immediately sent out again, whilst the Canterbury crews were lying around and playing cards. After a while Rae became so incensed, that when her men returned from the next raid, she deliberately did not report them back in, but let them rest for a while; as a result when the next call out came, the Canterbury crews were despatched so giving respite to her own home crews. Technically she could have been in trouble if this had been noticed by senior officers, but there were no repercussions.

Rae also clearly recalled watching the dog-fights between the RAF and the enemy by day and cheering when a German bomber or fighter was shot down; and by night watching the searchlights 'coning' bombers and the distinctive hum of the German bombers and the horrific flashes of bombs landing and exploding on London.

After the war Rae and Larry moved to the USA where at time of writing (2013) they both live, with Larry aged almost 100 years old.[33]

Morris Samuel Lustig

Morris was born in May 1908, son of Jacob and Esther. He enlisted in the AFS and was trained at University College Hospital station; he was at the bombing of the Mount Pleasant Post Office sorting office in 1940; he said they were there for five days trying to dowse the fire. He and several other firemen were sent for some respite to Shanklin station on the Isle of Wight and it was there that he narrowly missed being killed (see the Roll of Honour for details of this incident). He and some colleagues had gone on an evening tour of the island to check the window black-outs, and on arriving back went to have a wash in another part of the station. Morris went to his locker to collect some biscuits to share with his friends, and it was then the bomb dropped and many officers were killed. Morris only ever kept his fireman's badge, of which he was enormously proud; he was greatly traumatized by the Shanklin incident and never went to the Isle of Wight again.[34]

Victor Michaelson

Victor was born on 27 December 1888 and was married to Justina of 6 St Nicholas Mansions, Trinity Cresent. He was an advertising agent by profession and joined up in September 1939. He was in the AFS class 3, meaning he was not fit for fire fighting but could do administrative work.

Victor died aged 51, on 6 November 1940. He was at his Fire Station 86W (at Cavendish Road Primary School, now Henry Cavendish) when a stray German plane dropped its last few bombs on Balham on its way back to France. The last bomb fell onto the mess room in the school just as the crews were eating their evening meal, at about 8 p.m. Fire Brigade historian Stephanie Maltman spoke to a 93-year-old eye witness who was in a nearby fire station in Tranmere Road and was one of the first rescuers on the scene. He said that thirteen fire crew were killed, including one woman; others were injured. The blast, he said, did strange things; he dug out two men sitting opposite each other at a table; one had not a scratch but was dead; the other was grazed but alive and well. Several were still standing as in a queue but were all dead leaning against a wall.

Victor is buried at Willesden Cemetery in grave FX 13 566, but sadly the headstone is totally blank/worn.

On the 60th anniversary of the incident in 2000, a plaque was unveiled at the school to remember those killed. One survivor attended and at the end after a question and answer session, the children stood and sang some war time songs to the many older people in the audience. Every year the names of the dead will be read out at assembly on the anniversary of the bombing.

Muriel Nyman

Mutiny at Lambeth! Muriel Nyman confronts Group Officer Gold:[35]

> The pool of women drivers at Lambeth Fire HQ was in revolt! They had been given notice that they were to be transferred to Westminster School to make way for a party of firewomen from the provincial cities, but they bitterly complained because their cars would still have to be kept at Newport Street garage. This meant that in the event of emergencies, at any hour of the day or night, they would have to run almost a mile to get to their vehicles.
>
> At this time London was under constant V1 and V2 attacks and this scheme was deemed to be unacceptably dangerous, as well as causing a huge delay when a car may be needed in an emergency. But pleas fell on deaf ears. So Firewoman Muriel Nyman with her twenty plus colleagues, marched to the Group Officers room, formed a circle and each one smashed a plate outside the door. Gold appeared and coolly asked, 'Is anything wrong? I thought I heard some noise' and then retreated to her office. This deflated the protesters mood and feeling down, they had to make the move. However, a short while later Muriel testified that the order was rescinded and they were returned to their old quarters; victory to the mutineers.

Jack Oliver

Jack was stationed at Cricklewood and was fire fighting mostly in the London Docks. When he was badly injured on his hand, he was sent to St Mary's Hospital, Paddington. When the surgeon, Mr Dickson-Wright, discovered Jack was a tailor, he took especial care and saved the hand.[36]

Arnold Perlmutter aka Philips

Arnold was a refugee from Poland who served in the 1930s in the Haganah and Palmach in Israel and then came to live and study in Manchester. During the war, before joining the tank regiment, he was a firewatcher. He recalled being on top of exposed buildings during the bombings, where his job was to spot fires and using a radio/telephone, coordinate the fire fighters below by directing them to the fires. He said that being a *Shomer* (guard) in Israel had prepared him well for the long, lonely nights on roof tops, whilst others slept soundly in their shelters.

One vivid memory he had was a bird's eye view one dawn of the streets of central Manchester completely covered in smashed glass after a raid, as though the roads were covered in glittering water. Being used to sleeping through noise, he also remembered waking up one morning in his attic room completely smothered in smashed glass from the windows; he hadn't heard or felt a thing.

Alexander 'Sunny' Pinner

Alexander was recruited with many other taxi drivers in 1939 and was a pump operator. Sent to the East End he served all through the Blitz. After one incident he suffered severe shock and was on leave, then returned to work. Soon after he broke a bone in his back when he fell from an air raid shelter he was standing on whilst fighting a fire. He was in the London Hospital for several weeks, and was invalided out of the Fire Service. He then worked for Vickers making Wellington Bombers till war's end.

Manfred Plaut

Manfred was born in 1912 near Frankfurt and came to the UK in 1929. In 1938 he joined the Fire Service and was stationed at Belsize until 1945. On many occasions he was sent to fight fires in the East End and one morning when he arrived home after a particularly gruelling night, his wife asked him if he had been around the cooking of bacon, as his uniform smelt of cooking. He replied that he had been removing burnt bodies from bombed buildings.[37]

Peter Prager

Peter was born in Berlin in 1923 and came to Britain on the Kindertransport. Aged 18, while studying at university, he stayed in a hostel in Primrose Hill and took his turn as firewatcher, often staying up all night to report fires from the roof of the building as trained. He recalled one night when a bomb landed on houses 100 yards away in nearby Adelaide Road and the whole of the hostel building shook; he immediately sounded the alarm and he watched horrified as the Fire Brigade arrived in minutes and the flames engulfed the houses.[38]

Barney Prever aka Brifor

AFS/NFS Fireman Barney Prever (1910–84) was originally stationed at Bow, but sent to Weymouth in Dorset. Here he attended a large fire at a peanut factory hit by a bomb and he and a comrade went up to the roof to fight the fire, but the roof collapsed beneath them. Barney fell outside of the building but his friend sadly fell inwards and was killed. Barney was missing for six weeks, out of contact with his family, and they thought he had been killed, but he was finally able to contact them in Edgware where they were living. After a long period of recovery in hospital, Barney courageously returned to duty to Mill Hill station (he recalled his station officer there was a Mr Boyle) for the rest of the war until 1946.[39]

Doris Rath (later Moritz)

Doris was born in Germany and came to Britain on the Kindertransport in April 1939, and was sent straight to Cambridge. On leaving the Perse School in 1941, she completed a clerical course and joined the NFS at 12D Division HQ at Trumpington Hall, Madingley Road, Cambridge in February 1943 as a clerical assistant, because she wanted desperately to do war work for the cause. Her only 'war wound' was a crushed finger in a door at the HQ. She left the service in 1946 to do Teacher Training at Aldenham near Watford.

Harry Alfred Ree, DSO, OBE[40]

Harry was born on 15 October 1914 in Manchester. His father was a manufacturing chemist and an active member of the scientific community with relatives in Hamburg, Germany, to which city they had moved from Denmark years before. His mother was American. Harry went to Shrewsbury School and then Cambridge where he became quite left-wing. He then became a French and German Language teacher in Beckenham High School in 1937, which is where he joined the Fire Service. However he says nothing about his Fire Service in his memoires other than that he served.

Being a conscientious objector ('conchie') he volunteered for minesweeping but this never materialized. After the fall of France he dropped his conchie views in response to the persecution of the Jews, and joined the RA in 1940, training at Topsham, Exeter. His brother Eric was a trainer in the SOE and persuaded him to transfer to Field Security and later SOE wireless school. Harry, married with a family, became a heroic member of the SOE, serving in France and awarded the DSO and OBE among several French decorations. His full story is told on tapes at the Imperial War Museum.

Betsy Rubins

Betsy was born in 1918 and married to Solomon Fine (above). She was a switchboard operator also in Blackburn AFS but was posted to Portsmouth where she clearly recalled the massive build up of troops for D Day. However her claim to fame is that when she saw the fire in the station fireplace going out, she thought she would liven it up with some paraffin and almost burnt the fire station down![41]

Claire Elizabeth Salaman

Claire was born on 7 September 1908 in London to Isidore Jacob Rozelaar and Dollie aka Alice Dora Morris of Glasgow. She married Alfred Salaman in 1929 at Hampstead Synagogue and had two daughters, but was divorced in 1938. Claire joined the AFS in 1939 in Lancing, Sussex, and trained at Lancing Manor in the use of stirrup pumps, dealing with incendiaries, how to perform a 'fireman's lift' on injured people, and so on.

Their house was requisitioned as it was in the potential invasion zone and so the family were evacuated to stay with cousins in South Wales where Claire joined the Crickhowell Fire Service. The leader of the Fire Service, Goronwy Jones, gave her a job in his garage as a telephonist but she preferred repairing cars, and then soon was also given the task of touring the local villages and teaching the locals, mainly women, how to use stirrup pumps and deal with incendiaries. This was important work as it was thought that if incendiaries set the moors alight, it would provide a marker for the Luftwaffe to guide them to the important docks in Cardiff, Swansea and Newport. After the war the family moved back to Sussex, and Claire remarried (to Major Harold Warren). She died in 1967.

Morris/Moshe Sheratsky (aka Sherrick)

Morris was born in 1899 and was a First World War veteran who served in the 38th bat. Royal Fusiliers (The Jewish Legion). In the Second World War he served in Fairclough Street School fire station. During one air raid in the docks, he attended a huge house fire where the residents were too frightened to move, so he and a comrade went into the building to bring them out safely; he was given some kind of award for this action but the family has no record of it today. In another incident he was badly injured in the stomach by a bomb and sent on convalescence for many weeks after; the effects of the injury stayed with him all his life.[42]

Ronald Singer

Ronald Singer joined the AFS at the beginning of 1942 in Marlow, Buckinghamshire, where his firm, Odeon Cinemas, had been evacuated. Trained on mobile pumps, he also learnt ladder drill, procedures for carrying men and women from buildings, hose handling and how to take and obey orders at once. He was called up into the army in April 1942.[43]

Isaac Speck

Isaac was from Lynford Gardens, Edgware. Refused for military service he joined the AFS and was at a sub-station in what was Hillwoods jewellers and the neighbouring timber yard which is now The Broadwalk. His daughter remembers that when she was a little girl he would come home night after night covered in grime and dirt, utterly exhausted from fire-fighting in Docklands and the City.

In August 1940, aged 11, she was playing in the garden when she heard a loud aeroplane engine making strange noises and when she looked up saw it trailing black smoke. As the plane zoomed just above their house two men baled out, and she and her family dived for cover under the kitchen table. The plane crashed in Broadfields Avenue nearby, with a huge explosion. She went at once with her family to see what had happened. Flames were leaping from a huge crater and wreckage was scattered everywhere. Two houses were hit and Air Raid Wardens arrived. The airmen were British and had landed in an allotment. Soon the firemen arrived to fight the flames and suddenly there was her dad directing a hose onto the crash site. She felt very proud and called out loudly, 'There's my dad!'[44]

Teddy Steinman

Teddy, from Sheffield, was very short at 5 feet 1 inch. As a driver he was ordered to take a fire engine to Newcastle and had to stand all the way in order to see over the windscreen. He was so exhausted, he went to stay overnight with a relative in Newcastle, who was a rabbi, and parked the engine outside the house. Soon neighbours appeared with buckets of water – they though the house was on fire.[45]

Harry Stern

Harry worked at a large furniture store in Ealing, called 'Lamertons'. He was a German Jewish refugee who had been a lawyer. After arriving in the UK he got a job as a labourer in the store and then was promoted to be an accountant. One night he was on fire watching duty but off shift, resting in the warmth of the boiler room in the basement. Fumes from the boiler overcame the men resting there but Harry managed to stay conscious – although very groggy – and ran across the road to the police station to raise the alarm, thereby saving the lives of the other men. After a short stay in hospital, all returned to their jobs and fire watching. For his calmness and bravery, Harry received a Letter of Commendation from the local Civil Defence organisation.[46]

Joseph Simon Stock

Joseph was born in 1908 and lived at 14 Parfett Street, E1. He was stationed at London Bridge (probably Cannon Street) station from 1940–45. His sons Ray and Stanley remember him telling them that he fought many horrendous fires in the City and particularly recalls a huge bomb at Bank which demolished a police station, and how he had to spend hours bringing out the mangled bodies of dead police officers killed in the explosion. One evening when walking home after a night of fire fighting he was stopped by a rather pompous City policeman who demanded to know where he was going so late at night. Joe lost his temper and asked the policeman where HE was whilst Joe was out fighting fires all night.

On a lighter note, Joe was an accomplished saxophonist and clarinettist and often played in the Fire Brigade bands, sometimes travelling round the country in quieter times. One evening his station comrades were due to play an important darts final against another station; Joe had never played darts in his life but they insisted he try as they would otherwise be disqualified if they did not field a full team. So he obliged and in the last round they needed a double three to win and he got it! He was the hero of the station thereafter.

David Usiskin

David was a fireman and stationed inside St Paul's Cathedral during the height of the Blitz. He slept, when off duty, in the crypt over the grave of a certain 'famous person'. In any spare time he used to make children's toys from scraps of reclaimed wood from the bombings and these have been handed down to this day in the family.[47]

Mendel Wander

Mendel served in Manchester when he was in his early 40s. When asked by his friends why his dad was not in the army, his son would say, 'He is a Leading Fireman!'. He recalls clearly when Mendel would return home on many occasions covered in black dust and smelling of smoke following his attendance at huge fires. His dad would give him playful fireman's lifts, and tell how he would have to slide down a pole to get to his fire engine.[48]

Leslie Wilson

Leslie saw active fire service in the docks. On the night of the big raid in the London Blitz, 29/30 December 1940, he was blown into the River Thames by the force of a huge explosion and was not rescued from the water for some considerable time. A talented jazz violinist, he often gave fire station concerts for local people in the area during lulls in the bombings. His brother Irving Wilson was prominent in the Fire Brigade Union and often represented colleagues in disciplinary hearings, until he was demobbed in 1945.[49]

Derrick David Zimmerman

Derrick was stationed at Cannon Street fire station, was a driver and worked in the area around the Bank of England. His daughter says he met Winston Churchill (either at a Parade or whilst they were clearing debris?) and once entered a tunnel to clear many dead bodies after a fire had occurred during bombing. Awards were given for this incident and Derrick and a colleague tossed a coin for who would receive it and Derrick lost! He also played rugby for the Fire Brigade first 15.[50]

NOTES

1. Submitted by his daughter Frances Newman.
2. Submitted by their daughter Shirley Holton.
3. Submitted by his daughter Hilary Vogler
4. Submitted by his daughter Ella Marks.
5. From an interview with Museum of London staff, reference 2011.2, by son Gerry Braham.
6. This information comes from a Wiener Library testimony audio tape.
7. Submitted by her daughter Ruth Howard.
8. The film, produced by J.B. Priestley, was not shown in cinemas till 1965.
9. Submitted by his son Robert Coe.
10. Submitted by his son-in-law Hymie Lipman.
11. Submitted by Fay Jacobson, née Cohen, who survived the bomb.

12. Her brother Stephen later served courageously in the SOE as Stephen Dale, real name Heinz Spanglet.
13. Wiener Library testimony unpublished memoirs, 4161-67.
14. Submitted by his children, Rose and Richard Ellis.
15. Submitted by Henry Engelsman.
16. Submitted by son Robert Erskine.
17. Submitted by his son John.
18. Submitted by his son Michael Feld.
19. Jewish Museum, tape 453.
20. Submitted by his daughter Frances Hagan.
21. From Ernst Frinton, *Memories: An Autobiography* (Vancouver, BC: Deskside Publishing, 1994).
22. Taken from an undated *JC* article in the JMM Archives.
23. Submitted by daughter Karen Cohen.
24. From Martin Lloyd-Elliott, *City Ablaze: Life with the World's Busiest Fire-fighters* (London: Bloomsbury Books, 1992), pp.65–8 and passim.
25. Jewish Museum, tape 135.
26. Submitted by his grandson John Francken.
27. Barry Hollis, *The Forgotten Front Line* (Newport Pagnell: Enthusiast Publications, 1985), p.270.
28. Submitted by his daughter Judy Keiner.
29. Submitted by their daughter Maureen Maynard.
30. From Harold W. Walker, *More Memories: Waltham Abbey in War and Peace – A Fireman's Recollections* (London: Sewardstone, 1993), p.98.
31. *Dundee Courier*, 21 September 1942.
32. See various entries in the *JC* of September and October 1942.
33. Submitted by Rae and Larry.
34. Submitted by grandson Richard Gilbert.
35. Taken from Cyril Demarne, *Our Girls* (Edinburgh: Pentland Press, 1995), pp.166–7.
36. Submitted by his daughter Maureen Kafetz.
37. Submitted by his wife Vera.
38. Peter Prager, *From Berlin to England and Back* (London and Portland, OR: Vallentine Mitchell, 2002).
39. Submitted by his son Ivan.
40. IWM, tape 10858.
41. Submitted by son David Fine.
42. Submitted by his grand-daughter Ruth.
43. Submitted by his son.
44. Submitted by his daughter Frances Charles.
45. Submitted by his son.
46. Submitted by his daughter Hanna Singer.
47. Submitted by nephew Robert Erskine.
48. Submitted by son Daniel Wander.
49. Submitted by his sister Shirley Kaufman.
50. Submitted by his daughter Delia Halpern.

Epilogue[1]

Charles Poulsen's words are a fitting end to these testimonies, and pay tribute to the Fire Service – and especially its Jewish members – and the victims of the bombings in the Second World War.

October 1940

It was a mid twentieth century townscape, and might well stand for a symbol of this epoch. Not in a backward, desolate part of the world, but in London, one of its greatest and wealthiest cities.

Although it was midnight no lamps or shop windows lit up the streets. Yet they were so bright that one could have read a newspaper with ease. A violent throbbing red fire-light, with great flames leaping above the roof and reflecting a sky gleaming scarlet, illuminated the district with the hues of a thousand sunsets. Many of the buildings along the streets were merely walls, with nothing behind them, like a film set, and the red glow streamed through the empty window spaces. Vast columns of curling black smoke made their way leisurely upwards.

Rosy clouds floated overhead and from above them came the roar of powerful engines, desynchronised into strange rhythms, and sometimes the swift drone of a fighter plane and the rapid iron tapping of machine guns against the sky. Long silver beams of searchlights silently probed clouds and space, gleaming on nothing but round-bellied barrage balloons tugging at their cables.

At intervals began a strange hissing, rising to a shrieking whistle followed by a great crash and the thrust of blast as small streets or large structures leaped into the air and disintegrated, falling to earth with a long rumble like a cross between a roll of thunder and an Alpine rock fall. The greenish-white glare of incendiary bombs showed where soon the flames would rise anew.

The visible inhabitants of this city of terrors seemed weak and puny against the vast forces of high explosives and fire. They were mostly small parties of blue-clad firemen, busy with their ladders, pumps and jets. The infrequent traffic that bumped along over the debris, consisted of ambulances, rescue vans and fire appliances. The citizens were hiding in the tube stations, in brick or iron shelters, in reinforced cellars, or optimistically under the stairs in their passages. Some had already lost everything except the things they had with them. Others feared and expected that when dawn came and all-clear sounded, they would find their homes reduced to piles of debris and everything that they had worked and saved for, destroyed.

The music that accompanied this devils opera was loud and violent, befitting the scenery. Great guns roared in unison, light guns stuttered, drowning the hissing of fire and water. The deep vibrations of the fire pumps at full throttle made a constant ground-bass to the aircraft noises overhead. The sheer volume of sound was felt inside the head, rather than heard with the ears. Shattered shell splinters tinkled everywhere, like iron raindrops, and the shouting of human voices was quite drowned in the mechanical and chemical chaos.

Nights like this passed one another in rapid succession, until to the weary men and women of the Fire Service, both Regular and Auxiliary, they came to seem the natural order of things. Leave, sleep and leisure belonged to a period long ago, to another world. Every day the new light shone on fresh areas of ruin where formerly people had lived and worked, and where the nation's wealth was made and stored.

The dead and wounded were taken away, to make room for the next night's victims. The new homeless were put up somewhere, somehow. And the defiant phrase was made – 'London can take it'.

At this time in the war, October 1940, there seemed little hope of survival. Britain stood alone against Nazi Germany, all her allies defeated and occupied. The sea was no longer her moat. The world awaited her surrender. Then it was that London became the first city in the world to stand up to and defy the horror of prolonged bombardment from the air. This was thought to be the ultimate weapon that led to certain conquest. London proved that theory false, and with its new allies went on to win the war. And in that victory the AFS, with the London Fire Brigade, played its part.

NOTE

1. Written by fireman and writer Charles Poulsen (aka Kopel Polsky), taken from *Under Fire* (London: London Fire & Civil Defence Authority, n.d.), p.9.

Record of Honour

The London Fire Brigade war-time Registration Cards were used for finding Jewish surnames but also forenames, for example, 'Hyman' as in 'Hyman Bull'. Also professions given on the cards and addresses gave further clues, such as furriers living in Whitechapel or Hendon. Some names could also be checked against the AJEX Jewish Chaplain cards as many men and women were 'called to the colours' or volunteered as the war went on. This expression is used on many of the cards but I have only recorded some. Addresses are in London unless specified.

Whilst many of these men and women served in the Fire Brigade from early 1938, many would have left to 'join up' or been invalided out through illness, stress and injury or simply due to family or work pressures by 1941. However, the number of names discovered will be a large under-estimate as we will never know how many anglicized their names to such as Brown, Rogers or Smith, for example, and would thus have been disregarded as Jewish by the author. Many names appear duplicated in the list, but this is because names such as Abraham Cohen were so common. However, each entry is an individual as evidenced by completely different Registration numbers, dates of birth and address on the Registration Cards.

The letters and numbers (where known) refer to the Fire Stations served in, and the key to these can be found on internet sites; when ?? occur, this means the station was not recorded on the card.

Mr A. Aaron, Whitechapel
Morris Aaron, Kingsland
Abraham Aarons, Bow, C32
Doris Aarons, Manchester Square
Isaac Aarons, Kingsland
Sidney Mark Aarons, Euston
Harry Ameen Abdallah, Redcross Street, B68 – TBC

Frederick Abdela, Battersea, probably on the Massey Shaw fireboat; later served RN Reserve at sea
Henry Abel, HQ, TBC
Joseph Abel, Liverpool
B. Abelson, Leeds NFS
Isaac Mendel Abelson, Liverpool
Ellen Abraham, Islington
Richard Abraham, Firewatcher; photo of him appears on the inside page of *Front Line 1940–41: The Official Story of the Civil Defence of Britain* (London: HMSO, 1942).
A.W. Abrahams, B67
Albert Abrahams, Brunswick Road, C24
Alfred Abrahams, Burdett Road
Barnett Abrahams, Shadwell
Benjamin Abrahams, Hammersmith, A9?
Benjamin Abrahams, Stoke Newington, A9?
Bernard Abrahams, AFS
Blanch Eva Abrahams, Enfield
Eleazar Abrahams, Stoke Newington
Enid Abrahams, West Hampstead, Firewoman Artist
Harry Abrahams, Manchester AFS, posted to South England; suffered from depression after the war due to his fire-fighting experiences
Harry Abrahams, E90
Henry Abrahams, New Cross
Henry Abrahams, Streatham
Henry James Abrahams, Euston
Henry Abrahams, Bethnal Green
Isadore Jack Abrahams, Soho
Joan Abrahams, A20
John Joseph Abrahams, Shadwell (B13095??), WIA burns to wrist at Hungerford Road School
Jonas Abrahams, Redcross Street
Leonard Alexander Abrahams, Brighton
Leonard Eliazer Abrahams, later Graham, fire engine driver
Leslie Abrahams, Shoreditch
Lewis Fish Abrahams, Kingsland
Lillian Abrahams, A5
Mark Abrahams, Redcross Street
Max Abrahams, husband of Gertie 'Gerry' Grant, Leeds (see below)
Menassa Abrahams, Whitechapel, WIA 12/1/41
Muriel Abrahams, Plumstead
Percy Abrahams, Westminster, WIA 27/12/40
Phyllis Abrahams, West Hampstead

Ralph Edward Abrahams, C34
Rubin Abrahams, Liverpool
S. Abrahams, Firewatcher, Ilford
Sam Abrahams, Bow, called to the colours 10/9/40
Sam Abrahams, C39
Sam George Abrahams, Shoreditch, called to colours 30/6/40
Sam Gluckstein Abrahams, West Hampstead
Samuel Abrahams, Stoke Newington
Sarah Abrahams
Sidney Abrahams, C35
Sidney Barnet Abrahams, No.1 Headquarters
Arthur Abrahamson, Mile End/Bishopsgate, called to colours (Army) 1/7/40
Kurt Abrahamson aka Karl Aubrey, German Jewish refugee Firewatcher
Abramovich
Abramovitch (above two from Barnard memoirs, a former fireman, as recorded in interview with Stephanie Maltman)
Tobias Abramovitz, Whitechapel, WIA night of 29/12/40
Jack Abramowitz, Whitechapel, B13981 (??), WIA in foot, night of 19/3/41, C28, at Zetland Street
Harold Walter Abrams, Kentish Town, called to colours 22/5/40
Sam Abrams, C34
Harry Abramson, Liverpool
Phoebe Acht, Cannon Street – TBC
Esther Ackerman, Fireguard, Whitechapel
Solomon Ackerman, discharged as unfit after training
Harris (Harry) Adelman, Wembley, C39
Jack Adelman, Stoke Newington, Station Officer, but dismissed as Alien 1/7/40
Jacob Adelman, Burdett Road
Louis Adelman, River Service, Blackfriars
David Adams/Adamsky, Leading Fireman, Leeds
Mr B. Addleman, AFS Leeds
Mr J. Addlestone, Leeds
Alfred 'Fred' Adler, Firewatcher in Oxford Street workshop – former prisoner at Buchenwald, internee as a refugee. Born in Frankfurt in 1897, he was a Medical Officer in the German Army in the First World War.
Frederick Charles Joseph Adler, West Hampstead
George Albert Ernest Adler, Burdett Road
Miss Jean Adler, C28
Maurice Adler, Burdett Road
Richard Frank Adler, Burdett Road
Rose Adler/Howe, West Hampstead

William Frederick Adler, 7/38 till 12/40, St 22
Daisy Adolph, Clapham – TBC
Jack Adolphe, A12
Edward Joseph Agass, Homerton
Joseph Agass, Bow
Charles Henry Ahronson, Dockhead
Emmanuel Aisenberg, Redcross Street
Emmanuel Aizen, Burdett Road
Chaskiel Ajbeszyc, Belsize
Aaron Albert, West Hampstead
Assistant Group Officer Beatrice Albu, West Hampstead
Joel Joseph Allenbick
Zena Allenbick, C23
Jacob Alexander, Liverpool
Jacob Morris Alexander, Manchester Square
Myer Alexander, Stoke Newington
Phineas Alexander, Whitechapel
Hyman Alfman, Station 30
Abraham Allison, Stoke Newington
David Allweiss, C30
Abraham Alman, Kingsland
Rudolf Almenrader, A20 – TBC
Rudolf Almenrader, Leading Auxillary Fireman, West Hampstead
Mr N. Almond, AFS Leeds
Miss L. Alpert, C30
Doris Althoff, F60 – TBC
Myer Altman, Stoke Newington
Mr L. Altshuler, AFS Leeds
Lionel Alvarez, Stoke Newington
Hyman Amd, Holloway/Bishopsgate
Sarah Amstell, West Hampstead
Albert Angel, Shadwell
Alfred Ronald Angel, Kingsland
Edward Angel, Soho
Edward Arthur Angel, New Cross
Esther Applebaum, C32
Harry Joseph Angel, Stoke Newington
Hyman Angel, Whitechapel/Homerton, C28
Leonard Arthur Angel, Kentish Town
Morris Edward Angel, A2
Bernard R. Angell, D54
Leslie Angell, D54
Henry Anish, Whitechapel

Charles Anker, Whitechapel
Samuel Albert Anker, C30
Emanuel Ansell
Solomon Ansell, Soho/Clerkenwell/Redcross Street, B72
Barnett Ansher, Stoke Newington/Brunswick Road
Sybil Antrich, Camden, later Mrs Wayne
Sid Apatoff, Millwall
Maurice Appel, Bethnal Green C30
Maurice Appel, Whitechapel
Benjamin Appel, Shadwell
Philip Appel, C34
Maurice Apple, Euston
Solly Appleby (Appel), Clapton/Kingsland
Louis Appleton, Whitestone Pond Station, Hampstead
Harold Arbeiter, A11
Albert Maurice Arbib, West Hampstead
Richard Arbib, West Hampstead – brothers
Sub Officer Leon David Arditti, Hammersmith, A9
Emanuel Aron, A11
Miss Evelyn Aronson, West Hampstead
Lewis Aronson, later Allison, C39
Frances Charles Arrenberg, 10/38 to Assistant Sub Officer LFB 11/40, F60
William Arren(s)dorf, Clapham, WIA
Mark Asenstein, Whitechapel, C28
Isidore Ash, Homerton, C23
Joseph Ash, Bow
Sydney Ash, C23 – TBC
Cecil Ber(n)ard Asher
John Asher, West Hampstead
Ben Assenheim, Whitechapel
Fireman Isaac Assenheim, Fairclough Stret/Millwall
Nat Avon, Edgware Road
Frederick Rudolf Axelrad, West Hampstead
Alfred Axelrod, Kensington
Eileen Axelrod, C32
Arthur Aziz, Liverpool

Michael Anthony Baatz, Streatham
David Bacal, Whitechapel
Jacob (Jack) Morris Bacal, Blackfriars
M. Bader, Whitechapel
Benjamin Ballon, Whitechapel

Alfred (Abraham) Banes (Bernstein), Brixton
Harry (Hershel) Bar – Manchester
Doris Bard, Brixton, WIA
Gladys Barden
Jack Barden, Firewatcher, Cambridge Heath Road, E2
Barnet Barger/Berger, Bishopsgate
Rafael Isidore Barkoff, Kentish Town
Barnett Barlum/Burlum, Kingsland
Leading Fireman Cecil Gustave Hyam Barnet, Blackfriars/Cherry Gardens/South Wharf (River Service)
A. Barnett, Islington
Philip Barnet, Bethnal Green
Abraham Barnett, Homerton
Alexander W. Barnett, Bethnal Green
Annie Barnett, Bermondsey/Colchester, wife of Stanley below
Benjamin Barnett, Bow
Bernie Barnett, Soho/Clerkenwell
David A. Barnett, Homerton
Diana Barnett, Edgware Road
Emmanuel Barnett, Whitefriars
Eve Barnett, C23 (to ATS)
Gordon Barnard Barnett, West Hampstead
Harold (Harry) Barnett, Kingsland (furrier)
J.T. Barnett, C28, Whitechapel
Jack Barnett, Liverpool
John E. Barnett, Belsize
John R. Barnett, Bishopsgate
Joseph Barnett, C34
Joseph Barnett, C39
Joseph Barnett, Liverpool
Mark Barnett, North Kensington
Mark Barnett, Tooting
Morris Barnett, MBE (this may be a confusion with the RAF Bomb Disposal MBE also called Morris Barnett)
Myer Barnett, C30
Phillip Barnett, Liverpool
Divisional Officer Stanley George Barnett B63, aged 37 years, of 23 Nevin Drive, Chingford, joined the Fire Service in September 1938. He was responsible for training part-time personnel in his area engendering a fine spirit among his staff. He also served in France after D Day as a Fireman and post-war. When he died in the 1980s his body was taken on a fire tender escorted by fellow firemen, to Hoop Lane Jewish cemetery. Recommended for BEM but not clear if it was awarded (LMA/FB/WAR/1/211).

Wolf Bernard Barnett, Brixton, E85
Alfred Barofka, C28 Whitechapel
Benjamin Baron, Millwall
Philip (?) Baron (name from Eric Kaufman), St Dunstan's, Golders Green
Samuel G. Baron, Old Kent Road
M. Barouch, E84, West Norwood
Sylvia Barras, Kensington – TBC
Daniel Barry/Beary, River Service/Norwood
Lothar Baruch (later Prof. Leslie Brent), Firewatcher, Birmingham University; German refugee, later Captain RAMC and Royal Warwicks Reg
Sidney Barzilay, Bow
Alfred Bass, Grimsby/Cleethorpes
Gertrude Bass, C23
Maurice Bass, Whitechapel
Moses Marks Bass, Manchester Square
Betty Basser, Homerton
Phyllis Basser, Bishopsgate
Henry Baum, B72
Jack Baum, Whitechapel
Joseph Baum, Brixton, E85
Morris Baum, Whitechapel
William C. Baum, B73
George Bauman, Liverpool
Jack Baumgarten, Clerkenwell
Section Officer Therese Bayerthal, Belsize – TBC
Cecil Bayzler, Kingsland, to Army 18/6/42
John Robert Bayzler, A2
David Bean, Whitechapel
Isaac Bear/Behr, Cannon Street
Harry/Henry Bebber B66
Gladys Beck/Meyers, Dulwich – TBC
Abraham Becker, HQ
Ernest Leopold Becker, Euston/Edgware Road
Frederick Herman Becker
Israel Becker, North Kensington
Joseph Becker, Euston
Mark Becker, Brixton, WIA 11/12/40
Sidney J. Becker, Fulham
William Becker, Euston
Joel Beckerman, Shoreditch
Sidney Beckerman, Stoke Newington, trans. to ARP 12/9/39
Constance Beckman, Clapham

Michael Beckman, Kingsland
Percy Beckman, Woolwich
Samuel Woolf Beckman, Kingsland
Violet Beckman, Manchester Square
Miss Erna Beer, West Hampstead
John Beer, 1939–40 then 1945–47 after being invalided out of Army, North London, brother of Sylvia;
Samuel Beer, D40
Sidney 'Sonny' Beer, North London, brother of Sylvia
818022 Sylvia Beer, later Dorff, Northampton, Tilbury, etc. and often attended crashed/shot down aircraft and the attendant carnage of bodies
John David Beerbohm, Manchester Square
Jack Behar, Hammersmith, A9, WIA
David Sidney Beherie, Dulwich, WIA 21/9/40
Carl Julius Behrens, Liverpool
Maurice Jack Behrman, Whitechapel, C28
Ernest Beisiegel, Lewisham
Isaac Beitler, Bethnal Green
Max Belchack, Shoreditch and Kentish Town
Jack Belevitch, St 30, Bethnal Green
David Belinfante, Kenton
Jacob Belinfante, Firewatcher, North Kensington
Samuel Belinfante, Stoke Newington
Michael Belinsky aka Burton, C28
Joe Bellnikoff, Stoke Newington
Belofsky – more not known
Reuben Bemofsky, Stoke Newington
Jules Ben-Nathan, West Hampstead, A20
Victor Ben-Nathan, A20
Victor Ben-Nathan, West Hampstead; to LFB 24/6/41
Sidney Maurice Benavente, Clapham, WIA three times
Isaac Bender, Clerkenwell
Louis Bendoff, Whitechapel
Lewis Benezra (B15814??), WIA in foot, Lea Bridge Road, E5
Morris Benezra, Hammersmith, WIA
Morris Benezra, A9
Bernard Benjamin
Betty Rebecca Benjamin, West Ham
David Benjamin, Perry Vale, D55
Edward Adrian Benjamin, Hampstead – to Forces 30/5/40
Elizabeth Benjamin, Clerkenwell
Gerald Benjamin, Whitechapel

H. Benjamin, Euston
Hannah Leah Benjamin, West Hampstead
Harry Benjamin, Stoke Newington
Harry Benjamin, Streatham, E90
Hubert Benjamin, C28
Hyman Benjamin, Wandsworth
Station Officer J. Benjamin, Lauriston Road, Hackney (see B. Rubin wedding)
Joseph Benjamin, Islington, B67
Leon Philip Benjamin, Edgware Road
Nathan Benjamin, Cannon Street
Reuben Benofsky, Shadwell
Henry Benovich, Homerton
Michael Louis Benovich, Clerkenwell
Wolf Benstein aka Bruhstein, aka Bernstein? Shoreditch
Alexander Benstock aka Beenstock, Homerton
Jack Benstock, Brunswick Road, to HM Forces 13/5/40
Woolf Bensusan, Whitechapel
Samuel Bercovitch, Whitechapel, C28
Benny Berenson, Bow
Louis Berenstein, Bethnal Green
Alfred Berg, Whitefriars
Charles Berg, Whitechapel, wounded in fall from ladder; called up to RASC 1943
Jack Berg, Bethnal Green and River Service Blackfriars Bridge
Mark Berg, Whitechapel
Nathan Bernard Berg, Wanstead and Woodford-Gates Corner Station
Sidney Robert Valentine Berg, Red Lion Lane, Woolwich, D42
Carl Berger, Belsize, A13
Louis Berger, Islington/Holloway; also Fireman's dance band leader, B67, WIA
Michael Montagu Berger
Ronald Berger, C28, Whitechapel; bicycle messenger boy aged 15 years, from Jacobs lager factory at Tower Hill, to Lambeth HQ, later to RAF 1943
Mr H. Bergman, AFS Leeds
Louis Bergman, Belsize
Maria Bergman, C39
Henry Bergner, West Hampstead, WIA
Miss N. Bergson, C30
Francis Josef Berhang, Clapham, 80
Samuel Berizensky aka Berry, Millwall, C35
Abraham Max Berk, B76 – TBC

Pearl Berkovitch, Finchley
Sidney Berlin, Whitechapel, C28
Walter Berlin, German refugee, Firewatcher, Manchester Square, London 1941–45
Joseph Berlinsky, Whitechapel
Marks Berlinsky, Whitechapel
Morris Berlinsky, Burdett Road, C22
Debbie Berlofsky, Bow
Morris Berlyn, Shadwell and Greenwich
Anne Berman, Stoke Newington
Cyril Berman, Grimsby/Cleethorpes
David Berman, St 72 Soho
Frederick Berman, Pageants Wharf/Camden Town F50
Lew Berman, Shadwell
Louis Berman, Brunswick Road
Morris Berman, St 72 Stoke Newington
Morris Berman C39
Stanley Berman, Company Officer
Sydney Berman, C28
Sydney Berman, Whitechapel
Mr T. Berman, AFS Leeds
Joseph Bernadout, Hammersmith, former member Cambridge and Bethnal Green Jewish Boys Club
Gerald Bernard, NW3
Isaac Bernard, Middlesborough NFS
Louis Bernard, Forest Gate
Maurice Bernard, NW8
Harold Berners, North Kensington, A12
Sub Officer Philip Stanley Berners, West London
Francis Bernhard, Fulham (is this Fritz Bernhard at Soho?)
Charles Bernhardt, Liverpool, First World War veteran
Barnett Bernheim, Whitechapel
Elizabeth Bernheim, Edgware Road
Margaret Bernheim, Edgware Road
Woolf Bernheim, Whitechapel
Annie Bernor, C28
Abraham Bernstein, aka Alfred Barnes, Buxton Street
Abraham Bernstein, Redcross Street
Abraham Bernstein, Shadwell
Abraham Alfred Bernstein, C28
Abraham Alfred Bernstein, Stoke Newington
Abraham Alfred Bernstein, Whitechapel
Alfred Bernstein, East London

Benjamin Bernstein, Wanstead and Woodford
David Bernstein
Eli Harry Bernstein, Stoke Newington, C39
Harry Bernstein, Catford
Harry Bernstein, Shadwell
Isaac Bernstein, Cannon Street
Jack Mark Bernstein, Stoke Newington, C39
Joseph Bernstein, C34
Joseph Bernstein, Whitechapel
Lily Bernstein, C36
Peter James Bernstein, River Service Blackfriars/Cherry Gardens
Samuel Bernstein, Stoke Newington, C39
Sidney Bernstein, Stoke Newington, C39
Solle Bernstein, Shadwell
Solomon Bernstein, Kingsland/Shadwell
Solomon Bernstein, Whitechapel
Cyril Isidore Bertish, Manchester Square
Louis Berzon, Shadwell
Harry Beskin, Soho/Camden
William Beskin, Whitechapel
Montague Besser, Burdett Road, 22
Joseph Best, Kingsland
Sub Officer Paul Rudolph Bezak, Soho, B72
Louis Bielski, Manchester Square
Barnett Billig, Kentish Town
Freda Bilsky, Bishopsgate
Phillip Binder, Burdett Road
Gerald Binderman, Bethnal Green
Sidney Bindon, C35 – TBC
Asher Binger, Holloway/Camden, WIA Long Acre, 8/9/40
Harry Binick, West Hampstead
Hymie Binstock/Benstock, Whitechapel 28, taxi driver of 15 Basil House, Berners Street – also acted in the film *Fires were Started* (1943).
Miss Vivian Birn, C37
Bella Birnbaum, Bishopsgate
John Birnbaum, later Burnham, Firewatcher St Mark's Hostel, North Kensington – see Overman (below)
Charles Birnhak
Sidney Birnhak
Frank Ephraim Bitterman, Bethnal Green
John/Jacob Bitton, Burdett Road/Homerton
Marcus Black, Kenworthy Road

Maurice Black, Burdett Road, C22
Nathan Black, HQ Hose Laying Station and ARP
Oscar Black, Whitechapel
Sidney Black, Stoke Newington 39
David Blackman, Bethnal Green
Julius Blackman, Belsize/Lambeth HQ
Maurice Ephraim Blackman, Edgware Road
Howard D. Solomon Blaiberg, Manchester Square
Reuben Montagu Blanks, Perry Vale, D55
Ronald Charles Blanks, Brixton, E85
(Prof.) Hermann/Hugh Karl Felix Blaschko/Blashko (1900–93) German Jewish refugee, working at Cambridge University (Pharmacology), at first refused for Fire Watching service as an 'enemy alien' but later accepted and recalls extinguishing incendiaries during the raids on Cambridge University buildings; later became group leader of Fire Watching detachment in his street (IWM tape 4497).
Mr Ellis Blaskey, Sheffield
Simeon Sam Blatt, Redcross Street, Woolwich, River Service at Cherry Gardens and Blackfriars
John Blint, Islington, 67
Abraham Blitz, Bow
Alfred Abraham Blitz, Whitefriars
Walter Eugene Blitz, C37 and Coventry
Eileen Bloch, B66
H. Bloch, West Hampstead/Surbiton, A20
Ernest Block, Brompton, A6
Spencer Alan Block, B73, Euston
Isaac Blodowsky, Bow
Rosemary Blom, West Ham
Albert Ernest Blomberg, Pageant's Wharf, Army 16/5/40; F50
Charles W. Blomfield, D40
Woolf Blondin
Charles Sewell Bloom, Edgware Road/Stoke Newington
Elizabeth Bloom, Woolwich
Harry Bloom, Shadwell/Bow/Whitechapel
Harry Bloom, Stoke Newington
Isaac Bloom, Whitechapel
Jack Bloom, Battersea
Jack Bloom, Bow
Leslie John Bloom, Soho/Euston B72
Maria Bloom, West Ham
Chief Officer P.A. Bloom of Malden and Coombe Fire Brigade, was recommended for the Kings Police Medal for rescuing firemen in

a blaze, but it was disputed and the award apparently not given (LMA FB/WAR/1/181).
Stanley Bloom, Burdett Road – Army 13/7/40
Walter Bloom, Coburn Street/Burdett Road/ East London (*ELA* 7/10/39), C22
Benjamin Bloombaum, Bishopsgate
Frederick Isadore Bloomberg, Whitechapel, C28
Lewis Bloomberg, Shadwell/Kingsland, C38
Myer Bloomberg
Sybil Bloomberg, Sub Officer, E80
Florence Bloomfield/Vogil, C32
Mr I.J. Bloomfield, Leeds
Jack Bloomstein, Wolverley Street
Doris Bluston, Stoke Newington
Sadie Boam, Manchester Square
Miss Rachel Bobbroff, Cricklewood with Hazel Pearl
Heinz Ludwig Bock, Firewatcher, Chelsea
Harry Bluestein, Whitechapel, C28
Julius Bluestein, Shadwell
Frank Emmanuel Blum, Wandsworth
David Blumenfeld, Stoke Newington
Henry Blumenthal, Westminster
William Blumenthal, Bishopsgate
463937 Leon Blumenkehl, Acton
Thomas George Blumson, Kingsland
Reginald Blumson, Belsize
Joseph Boaz, Liverpool – TBC
Leslie Ivan Bober, Streatham, E90
Nochem Bockmuz, Millwall
Joan Renee Boesche, West Hampstead – TBC
Aux. B/17481 Solomon Bogush, aged 34, men's clothier – lived Blackstock Road, Holloway and 42 Ravensdale Road, N16, based at station B76 at YMCA Hostel 110, Hornsey Lane, Commended for Courage (*LG* 3/10/41) when he fought fires for several hours to help stop the flames reaching an unexploded bomb nearby (*JC* 21/10/41). On the night of 16/17 April 1941, large numbers of incendiaries fell on Charing Cross Station and hotel; a one and a quarter ton landmine landed near the Charing Cross signal box. Despite the danger of it exploding, the firemen fought the blaze to prevent it reaching the signal box, Government buildings and Hungerford Bridge timbers, finally extinguishing the fire only 15 feet from the unexploded mine. Station Master F. Bassett described the firemen as fearless and courageous (LMA FB/WAR/1/207). Lt

E.O. Gidden, RNVR Bomb Disposal, said in a letter to the Fire Brigade, that the explosive in the mine was exposed to the flames as its protective plate had broken open. Although only 15 feet away from the bomb, the firemen continued fighting the blaze and had to be ordered away by Lt Gidden, and they left only reluctantly.

Oscar Bohman, A11
August Bohn, Manchester Square
James Bohn, Battersea
Julius Joseph Bolderman, D40
Marcus (Mick) Herbert Bolen, driver and fireman, Chigwell
Joseph Bonn, A11
Joseph Leslie Bonn, Belsize/Edgware Road
Albert Bookman, C37
Joshua Boor, C28
Philip Boorman, Kingsland
Abraham Israel Borenstein, Fire Guard Party Leader at home, 42 Darville Road, Hackney N16
Nathan Borenstein aka Renn, brother of above, Firewatcher bombed out twice, Hackney E8
Barnett Bornheim, C28
Woolf Bornheim, C28
Nat Borr, Mobile, Manchester
Jack Bowman, C22
Josephine Bowman, Burdett Road
Rachel Bowman, C28
Rebecca Bowman, C28
Sidney Bowman, C28
Tanhoom Boyars, Liverpool
Lewis/Louis Boyask, Bethnal Green, C30
Jack Bozman, Liverpool, First World War Veteran – TBC
Bergit Braach, later Forchhammer, German refugee
Nathan Brackner, C24, Brunswick Road
Sidney Joseph Braham, (sub-officer) B73, Euston
Sydney Braham, Liverpool
Bertha Brand, A13
Betsy Brand, West Hampstead
Dorothy Brand/Eated – TBC??
Miss Frances Brand/Seymour – TBC??
Lillian Brand, B76
Nathan Brand, C38
Olive Brand, C22 – TBC
Barnett Brandon, Bishopsgate
Daniel David Brandon, Stoke Newington

David Joseph Brandon, Euston/Holloway/Clerkenwell
Eric Gustave Brandt, 72 (Soho)
Rudolf Alexander Brandt, B1, Whitechapel
Jack Isaac Braunstein, Kingsland – Army 14/2/39
Alfred Braunstone, Kingsland/Shadwell
Gilbert Bravo, London
Firewoman Ms I. Brazil, Leeds
Marks Brendon, Kenworthy Road/East Greenwich
Alec Brenner, Euston, B73
Isidore Brenner, Dulwich
Jack Brenner, Stoke Newington
John Brenner, Whitechapel
Judith Brenner/Goldberg ??
Lilly Brenner, C23
Paul Brenner, Euston
Louis Fabian Bresh, C34
Isidore Breslovsky, Whitefriars
David Bretstein, Burdett Road/Millwall
Arnold Brewer, Sunderland Deputy Chief Fire Officer
Louis Brier
Barnett Brifor, aka Prevor, Burdett Road, WIA Weymouth
Jack Brightbart (Filey), Leading Fireman, discharged injured in 1943
Marks Brilliant, Shoreditch/Kingsland
Jack Brinks, Hammersmith
Firewoman Brockman, Pageant's Wharf
Morris Brockman, Bethnal Green, C30
Hyman David Broder, Stoke Newington C39
Morris Brodsky, Bishopsgate
Eli Brody aka Michael Martin, Manchester
Arnold Bromberg, Bethnal Green, C30
Davis Bromberg, Bethnal Green/Homerton/Whitechapel
Morris Bromberg, Brunswick Road
Abraham Bronstein, Bishopsgate, WIA
Miss Minnie Bronzeit, later Groth, Firewatcher, City Road
Queenie Brookner/Yellin, Bethnal Green
Hyman Brooks, St 23
Hyman Brookstein, C28 (Prof. Boxer)
Morris Brookstein, C28
Hyman Brotsky, East Greenwich
Brown, West Ham Firewatcher
Abbie Brown, B68, Redcross Street
Bernard Asserson Brown, E88
Moss Brown, C28

Solomon Brown, C35, Millwall
Rabbi Dr Solomon Brown, Firewatcher, London Jewish Hospital; later Jewish Chaplain to HM Forces Germany 1947–50.
Leah Brownhood, Whitechapel
Gershon Brozel, Lee Green
Wolf Bruhstein aka Bernstein, C37, Shadwell
Walter Herman Brunner, Austrian refugee, Firewatcher, Manchester
Vera Brusch, Hampstead?? – TBC
Harry Bruskin, Redcross Street
Betty Bryett/Singer, Manchester Square
Barnett Bubchin, Bow, C32
Joseph Buchwald/Buckwald
Solomon Buffman, First World War veteran, Firewatcher, Leeds, brother Dave in Spanish Civil War.
Hyman Bull, C28, WIA
Lionel Bernard Buirski, Clerkenwell/Holloway
George Gustav Bunzl, River Boat Service, Cheltenham and Dewsbury/Bately, Yorks (Austrian Refugee)
Walter Barnett Burchell, 1938–45, later Chief Fire Officer, Euston Station
Joseph Burdes, Redcross Street
Solomon Burdes, Burdett Road
Sub Officer Nora Burger/Meyers, Wandsworth – TBC
Hyman Burkoff, Whitechapel
Lewis Burlem, B62
Barnett Burlum, Kingsland
Burman, Liverpool – TBC
Benjamin Burman, Burdett Road
Joseph Benjamin Burman, Stoke Newington
Lewis Burman, Homerton
William Burstein, Millwall
Jack Bushkes, Brompton, A6
Charles David Butchoff, B66, Clerkenwell
Hyman Lewis Butchoff, Shoreditch
Reuben Butters, Euston/Soho, then to Army
Joseph Bye, Shoreditch, then to Army

Colin Benjamin Cahen, Belsize
Raymond Cahn, Sheffield
Moshe Cailingold, Firewatcher, Stamford Hill/Whitechapel
Alec Calbier aka Gelbier, Stoke Newington
Aron Calmus, Islington
Harry Camelmaker, Stoke Newington, then to Army

Louis Cannon, Southwark
Joseph Canter, Whitechapel
Philip Canter, Brompton and RS Blackfriars
Awyas Cantor, Liverpool
Evelyn Cantor/Moody, B74
Herbert Cantor, Camden
Mr B.G. Capel, AFS Leeds
J. Capelovitch, AFS Leeds
Abraham Caplan, Stoke Newington, Brunswick Road
Abraham Louis Caplan, Liverpool
Alfred Caplan, Bishopsgate
Miss Bella Caplan, Manchester
Ms Frances Anne Caplan, East London
Jack Caplan, St 3, Shoreditch
Raphael Caplan, C28
Abraham Caplin, Whitechapel
Alec Caplin, Shadwell
Fireman H. Caplin
Hyman Caplin, Shadwell
Jack Saunders Caplin, West Hampstead
Miss Rebecca Caplin, Firewatcher, Golders Green
Jack Cappell, B68
Samuel Carkosky (father of Jean Carr below), Firewatcher; First World War veteran and Hon Major during demobs 1945–46
Harold Carlowe, Kingsland Road
Lewis Carlton aka Kolsky, Clerkenwell, then to Army
Firewoman Ruth Carne (later Myers), Ldg Firewoman, Highgate/Stormont Road and Ealing
David Carpus, training
Jean Carr, telephonist, aka Carkosky, Stillness Road School, Honor Oak Park, SE23
Alec Carriger aka Zalic Karger, Bow
Isaac Cartz, C32, Bow
Margaret Carvalho, Brompton
Alexander Casson, Liverpool
Leonard Casson, Liverpool
Miss Jeanne Castelberg ??
Joseph David Cazes, Knightsbridge, to RAF
Sidney Celnik, C39, Stoke Newington
Henry Chachkas, Bishopsgate
Sidney Chalfin, training centre 'B'
E.H. Chalk, after being invalided from RA
Harold Chalk, Bishopsgate (same as above?)

Sidney Chaplin, B16077, B5, Millwall
Henry Samuel Lewis Chapman, Tooting
Sidney John Chapman, Shoreditch
Jack Gerald Charfelt, A20
Arnold Charig, A11
Stanley Bernard Charik, Stoke Newington, Brunswick Road
Jack Charing, Islington
Mark Chasit, Redcross Street, WIA
Jack Chason, Whitefriars, to Army
Mark Chason, C39 (brothers?)
Elvira Chauveau, C28
Company Officer Sam Chauveau, C36 (his archive is at the Fire Service Museum, London)
Sheila Chauveau, aka Jackson, A2
Jacob Woolf Chaveau, St 37
Arthur Cheaveau, Sub Officer, Stoke Newington
Leslie Cheney, Kensington – TBC
Firewoman Olga Cherney/Charnie, Barnet
Sidney Cherney aka Tcherney (?), West Hampstead
Abraham Chess, Clapton
L. Chestenoff, 57U – TBC
Ben Chizron, Manchester Square – TBC
Solomon Chowchett aka Chowcat (?), Shadwell
Harry Churnin, C36, Bishopsgate
Jack Citrin, Stoke Newington
Annie Citron, C30
Ben Citron, A2
Eric Sidney Claff, West Hampstead
Jack Gerald Clarfelt, Hampstead
Isaac Classis, Clapton
E. Clayman, Middlesborough NFS
Hyman Clifford, Stoke Newington
Edward T. Cline, C30
Jack Cline, St 28
Alfred Abraham Clopper, Fulham, A7
Montague Alfred Closs, 86, Tooting
Morris Cobfeld aka Coblinsky, Firewatcher, London
Minnie Coblentz, Stoke Newington
Simon Cobrin, Stoke Newington
Harry Hyman Coffer, C28
Isaac Coffer, C28
Elliott Coffman, Plumstead
W. Cogan, SE9

Sec. Ldr Cohen, St Dunstan's, Golders Green, given by Eric Kauffman
Abraham Cohen, C34, Shadwell
Abraham Cohen, C28
Abraham Cohen, 36 Cannon Street
Abraham Cohen, 38 Kingsland
Abraham Cohen, 39 Stoke Newington, WIA
Abraham Cohen, Kentish Town, 75
Section Officer Agnes Cohen/Cowen, West Hampstead
Albert Cohen aka Dale, D40/D2, New Cross/Stillness Road (brothers Emmanuel and Jack – see below)
Alexander Cohen, 22 Burdett Road
Alfred Cohen, St 23 (i)
Alfred Cohen, 23 (ii)
Anne Cohen, B76
Arthur Cohen, Trafford Park Manchester/Liverpool
Augustus Albert Cohen, 22 Burdett Road
Mr B. Cohen, Leeds
Barnet Cohen, 38
Barnet Cohen aka Bernard Cowan, 35 Millwall
Barnett (Bernard) Cohen, 63 Cannon Street
Beatrice Cohen, Stoke Newington
Beatrice Cohen, C34
Miss Bena Cohen, C28
Benjamin Cohen, 39
Benjamin Cohen, 38, Stoke Newington
Benjamin Cohen, stations 36, 37, 39
(One of above Benjamin Cohen's is aka Coville)
Bernard Cohen, 12 North Kensington
Mr C. Cohen, AFS Leeds
Caroline Cohen, C40
Charles Cohen, A12, North Kensington and West Ham
Charles Cohen, C38/39
Charles Cohen, 39
Charles Isaac Cohen, C28
Coleman Cohen, Worveley Street
Daniel Cohen, 23 Homerton
Daniel Cohen, Sub Officer, D55, Perry Vale, 7/38 to 6/41
David Cohen, 28
David Cohen aka Keen, 35 Millwall
David Cohen, 38
David Cohen, C39 (i)
David Cohen, C39 (ii)
David Cohen, Belfast

David William Cohen aka David Williams, 54, East Greenwich
Davis Cohen, 30/28
Edward Cohen, 38/101/22
Edward Cohen, B68 (i)
Edward Cohen, B68 (ii) – joined colours 15/12/40
Edward Henry Cohen, 88
Edward John Cohen, C37
(In LMA FB/WAR/1/208 and 211, there is a recommendation for an MBE to an B28435 Aux. Fireman Edward Cohen (of 224 Bethnal Green Road), aged 33 years, and based at No.22 X Station, in New Years Honours 1942. It was proposed because 'during intensive air raids displaying commendable operational efficiency in connection with relaying of water, at times having complete charge of the water unit'. It states that he also attended fires at Thameshaven and in Portsmouth. The MBE was not granted but a gallantry award was suggested instead, though it is not clear it was given.)
Emmanuel Cohen aka Dale, 34 see Albert above
Esther Cohen, Shoreditch
Freda Cohen, Kingsland
Gabriel Cohen, 11
Mr H. Cohen, Leeds, Henry Hyman – (info from Robert Dyson, Leeds)
H. Cohen, 86
Harold Harris Edward Cohen, 20
Harry Cohen, Liverpool (Allerton)
Harry Cohen, 1HQ, WIA twice
Harry Cohen, C38 (i)
Harry Cohen, 38 (ii)
Harry Cohen, 38 (iii)
Harry Cohen, C39 (i)
Harry Cohen, 39 (ii)
Harry Cohen, 39 (iii)
Harry Cohen, C28 (i), WIA
Harry Cohen, 28 (ii)
Harry Cohen, 62
Harry Cohen, 72
Section Officer Hazel Cohen, Edgware Road
Henry (formerly Isadore) Cohen, later Coe, Bishopsgate and River Fire Service, appears in the BBC2 film *1940* (1965, J.B. Priestley) talking to Churchill during Blitz.
Herbert Cohen, Firewatcher, Stamford Hill
Herman Cohen, Camden Town
Miss Hilda Cohen, Firewatcher, Luton
Hyman Cohen, 34

Hyman Cohen, 39/24
Hyman Cohen, 35
Ms. Ida Cohen, Liverpool (Firewoman)
Isaac Cohen, 24
Isaac Cohen aka Ivor Collins, 22; joined colours 22/2/40
Isadore Cohen, 39
Isidore Cohen, 12
Israel Cohen, 38
Israel Cohen, HQ Hose laying, previously ARP warden
Israel Cohen, 35
Ivy Cohen, Brixton
Mr J. Cohen, Leeds No.1978
Mr J. Cohen, Leeds No.23593
Mr J. Cohen, Leeds No.121097
Mr J. Cohen, AFS Leeds, 38144
Mr J. Cohen, AFS Leeds, 373150
Jack Cohen, C30, previously ARP Warden
Section Officer Jack Cohen, C34
Jack Cohen, C63/28
Jack Cohen, Swansea
Jack Cohen, Whitechapel
Jack Cohen ??
Jack Cohen aka Dale, D40, LFB, brother of Albert above
Jacob 'Jack' Cohen aka Clifford, Walthamstow, previously stretcher bearer
Jacob Cohen, 34
Jacob Simon Cohen, 30/22
John David Cohen, 28
Jonas Cohen, 22
Joseph Cohen, C37/28
Joseph Cohen aka Cork, C37
Joseph Cohen, C28
Joseph Cohen, A11
Joseph Cohen, Durning Road, Liverpool
Joseph Cohen, 60
Judah Cohen, 35/30
Judah Cohen, 32 Bow and West Norwood
Judah Cohen, 36
Judah Cohen, 28
Mr L. Cohen, Leeds
L. Cohen, S. Wales
Laurie Cohen, 13
Lawrence Cohen, 30

Leslie Cohen, 32, 35, 28, to colours 2/12/40
Leslie Cohen, 72/73
Leslie Lewis Cohen, 28
Lewis Cohen, 28
Lewis Cohen, C39
Lily Cohen, Stoke Newington
Lily Cohen aka Greenberg, C23
Louis Cohen, 22/28
Mr M. Cohen, Leeds
Mark Cohen, C28
Mark Cohen, 39
Mark Cohen, Whitestone Pond Station, Hampstead
Maurice Cohen, 7/2, called to colours 7/9/40
Maurice Cohen 28
Mendel Cohen, 101/22
Mendel Cohen, Belfast
Montague Cohen, 62/66
Morris Cohen, 24
Morris Cohen, 34
Morris Cohen, C35
Morris Cohen, C36 (i)
Morris Cohen, 36 (ii)
Morris Cohen, 39
Morris Cohen aka Morris Collins, 73
Sub Officer Nancy Cohen, A2
Nathan Cohen, Central Liverpool
Miss P. Cohen/Jacobs ??
Miss Patricia Cohen, Despatch Rider, Stepney
Pauline Cohen, Homerton
Miss Pearl Cohen (sister of Pauline, above)
Philip Cohen, 32/34
Philip Cohen, C35
Phillip Cecil Cohen, Firewatcher, Manchester
Miss R.V. Cohen, Firewoman Leeds
Ralph Reuben Cohen, 35, to colours 19/6/40
Reuben Cohen ??
Rivie Cohen aka Erskine, Firewatcher, Stamford Hill/Euston
Firewoman Rosalind/Rosamond Cohen, Hendon
S. Cohen, 5804, AFS Leeds
Sadie Cohen, B62
Sam Cohen, B68/66
Samuel Cohen, C28, to colours 3/10/39
Samuel Cohen, 20

Samuel Cohen, Speke, Liverpool
Samuel Cohen, 22
Samuel Cohen, 23
Samuel Cohen, 32
Samuel Cohen, C35
Samuel Cohen, 38
Samuel David Cohen, 30
Sid Cohen, London, 28
Sidney Cohen, 34
Sidney Cohen, 39
Simon Cohen, C28
Simon Cohen, 34
Simon Cohen, 30 (i)
Simon Cohen, 30 (ii)
Simon Cohen, 22
Simon Cohen, Leeds, also served Liverpool
Simon Sydney Cohen, C22
Solomon Cohen, 22/38/28
Solomon Cohen, 2
Solomon Cohen, 39
Solomon Cohen, 38
Sophie Cohen, Bethnal Green
Stella Cohen, B72
Susan Cohen, WIA
Sydney (Simon) Cohen, London Road, Manchester AFS; formerly
    Jewish Legion Sgt in the First World War, 39th Bat.; later served
    in the Home Guard; father of Phillip Cecil Cohen, above
Sylvia Cohen (later Garelick), Firewatcher, Cardiff
Firewoman Sylvia Cohen, injured in Manchester when she fell through
    a skylight while fire-fighting – see JC 20/2/42 page 12
Tobi Cohen, 34, to colours 6/6/40
Violet Cohen, Ealing
W.D. Cohen
Wolf Cohen, 36
Woolf Cohen, 65, River Service
Woolf Cohen, Salford, Manchester
Woolf Cohen aka Gershgorin, 28
Woolf Cohen, 20/68/73
Yvonne Cohen/Goldberg, Manchester 1939–48
Miss Susan aka Sophie, Cohn, Warwick, refugee from Germany
Eleazar Coleman, Kingsland, Messenger
Phyllis Coleman, Belsize
Rosetta Coleman, Bethnal Green

Samuel Coleman, Clekenwell
Sidney Samuel Coleman, Battersea
Sam Collier (name given by Eric Kaufman, St Dunstans, Golders Green)
Bernard Collins, Whitechapel
Morris Collins aka Cohen, Euston
Reuben Collins, Southwark, called to colours 28/7/40
Samuel Collins, Stoke Newington
Sidney Colman, Shadwell and Bow, later to Luton
Miss D.M. Compertz, Eltham
Charlotte Conn, later Stenham. Soho 1943–45, German refugee
Edna Conn/Townsend, Greenwich – TBC
Mrs Sarah Conn, née Gabrel, Firewatcher, Sloane Square/Holborn
Sidney Conn, C30
Jack Connick, C30
Sidney Connick
Florence Conradi, Deptford
Harry Conras, Bethnal Green – TBC
Samuel Coon, Shadwell
Barnett Cooper, C28
David Cooper, Burdett Road (lived Stepney Green Buildings)
Israel Cooper, Kentish Town and Clerkenwell
Samuel Cooper, Whitechapel
Solomon Cooper aka Copperstein, Millwall
Harris Cooperman, St 39, Stoke Newington
Hyman Cooperman, C23
Sadie/Sarah Cooperstein, Leman St, wife of Woolfe
Woolf(e) Cooperstein later Cooper, Shadwell
Henry Copleman, Kingsland
Beatrice Cops, Bishopsgate – TBC
Joseph Coral, Kingsland
Isaac Corb, C32
William Corbett (1908–79), Queens Park and Govans Dock, Glasgow, invalided out 1943
Aaron Coren, St 37
Samuel Coren, Stoke Newington
Isadore Cornberg, Liverpool
Maurice J. Corper, A20
Marks Coslover, Shadwell
Miss Milein Cosman, Firewatcher, Oxford, German refugee art student
Joseph Costa, Bethnal Green
Sydney Coten, St Katharine's Dock
David Cotliar, Brunswick Road
Harry Courts, Stepney, later RAF and POW of the Japanese

Samuel Cousin, Wellclose Square
Reuben Coverman, Shadwell
Mr I. Covitch, AFS Leeds
Albert H. Cowan, Old Swan, Liverpool
Alfred Joseph Cowan, West Hampstead
George Cowan, RAF, saved three people in Newcastle from a burning building, whilst on leave (JC 13/11/42)
Isaac Cowan, Central Liverpool
Louis Cowan, West Hampstead
M. Cowan, West Hampstead
Harold Cowell/Bernstein, Blackpool and Tottenham
Mrs Craig, Firewtacher, Golders Green (Jewish Museum tape)
Cyril Percy Cramer, A11
Herman Cramer, Wandsworth
Jack Cramer, Burdett Road
Morris Israel Cravitz, Kingsland
Emmanuel Crego, Whitechapel, C28 (hairdresser)
Lewis Cronick, Bishopsgate (presser)
Kopel Crook, Lambeth
Samuel Crystal, Liverpool
Sophie Crystal, Enfield
Joseph Crystall, C28
Harry Cudish, C35, Millwall, tailor of Stepney
Mark Cudner, C54, East Greenwich, from Stepney
Harry Cymbalist, Acton and Portsmouth
Davis Cyviak, Cannon St, C53

Harry Da Costa, Bethnal Green, C30
Hyman aka Harold Da Costa, A5
John Da Costa, Bethnal Green
Michael Da Costa, Bethnal Green
Moses Da Costa, C28
Moss Da Costa, Bethnal Green
Jack Dacosta, C22
Bernard Dagul, C39, Stoke Newington
George Dagul, C39, Stoke Newington (brothers?)
Joe Dagul, C62, Whitefriars
Bert Dale aka Cohen, New Cross (different from Albert Cohen above)
Emmanuel Daniel, Clerkenwell, B66
Myer Daniel aka Ganyeh, C39, Stoke Newington
Ms Cissie Daniels, C30
David Daniels, West Hampstead
Gabriel Danovitch, Whitechapel/Bishopsgate

Mr Dansky, Southport Fire Brigade
David Danziger, C34, Shadwell
Nathan Daren, East Ham; later KIA in RAF 5/7/41, Runnymede Memorial
Barnett Darwinsky of Burdett Road, C23, Homerton
Harry Darwinsky (brother)
Hyman Darwinsky, C23, Homerton (brother) – all above joined 28/10/38 and all tailors
Samuel Dautch, Manchester
Ruth David, B74
Samuel J. David, C39, Stoke Newington – TBC
Harry Davidoff aka Davis, B73
Louis Davidovitch aka David Lewis aka David Leib, Shadwell, C34
David Morris Davidson, C28, Whitechapel, LFB 28/11/40, presser
Nathan Davidson, C35, Millwall
Jack Davies, A12, North Kensington, furrier – TBC
Jessie Davies, Islington (from N5)
Reuben Davies, Liverpool
Saul Samuel Davies, Liverpool
Woolf Reginald Davies, C36, Bishopsgate
Percy Perry Daving, a barber from Manchester, served Harpurhey
Bernard Davis, C28, Whitechapel, tailor
Cyril Harris Davis, BEM (see Harry Harris, BEM, below)
Emmanuel Davis, C28, Whitechapel
Hyman Davis, C30/C22
Hyman Davis, C22 of Burdett Road (different ages and addresses)
Irving Davis, Bishopsgate
Joseph Davis, C38, Kingsland
Leon Davis, Hanbury Street
Louis Benjamin Davis, Liverpool, First World War veteran
Marks Davis, B68, Redcross Street , furrier
Morris Davis, C38, Kingsland
Morris Moses Davis, Training Centre (TC)
Nathan Davis, C54, East Greenwich – TBC
Samuel Davis, Stoke Newington, cabinet maker –TBC
Samuel Joseph Davis, C60, Southwark, of Waterloo Road – TBC
Solomon Davis, C32, Bow, of Burdett Road
Sydney Albert Davis, C24, Brunswick Road, cabinet maker – TBC
Marie De Beer, B68
Katherine De Groot, A13
Enid De Souza, Soho – TBC
Freedman Decoski, Training but unfit
Thomas Defies, Bethnal Green
Louis Dehaan, Bethnal Green

Michael Dehaan, Bethnal Green
Israel Deitch, Whitechapel
Stanley Deitch, Stoke Newington
Harry Dekotsky, Kenworthy Road
David Dela Fuente, Burdett Road
Joseph and Louis Dela Fuente, Burdett Road
Jacob Louis Delaal, Streatham (Alien, reinstated)
George Delmonte, C28, Whitechapel, presser
Harry Demetz, C22, of Burdett Road
John Dennerstein, C23, Homerton, butcher
Nathaniel Dennerstein/Dinerstein, C23
Harry Denton, C38, Shoreditch, Laburnum Street
Hyman Denton, E17
Morris Dester, C39, tailor
Alex/Alec Deutch aka Duke, East End and Plymouth, bother of Israel Deutch, KIA
Mrs Alec Deutch, wife of above, Plymouth
Andre Deutsch, Firewatcher, London (publisher)
Berthold Deutsch, Firewatcher (Austrian Refugee)
Bertram Deyoung, Edgware Road
David Deyoung, Shoreditch
Rosina Deyoung, Burdett Road
Sydney Deyoung, Westminster
Jack Diamant, C39, shoemaker
Betty Diamond, Bethnal Green
Jack Diamond, Shoreditch
Jay Joseph Diamond, A2
Ruth Diamond, Training Centre (TC)
George Dias, C28, Stepney, handbag maker
Jack Dias, C23
Samuel Dias, C30, shoemaker
Leon Diaz, C90
Robert Leon Diaz, C62, to RAF
Harry Dickenholt, Burdett Road, WIA
Mark Dickenholt, Whitechapel
Morris Dickenholt, Millwall
Dorothy Diesch, C23
Jacob Diker, C68, furrier
Abraham Dikofsky, Manchester, stationed Liverpool Docks
Ms E. Dimond, Wood Green
Bernard J. Dines, C30 – TBC
Leslie Dismore, Camden Town
Sylvia Dloogatz/Douglas, later Kaye, Northampton AFS, 1941–45

Miss E. Doberman, Middlesborough NFS
Jack Dobin, C68, tailor
Samuel Dobinsky, D40
Firewatcher Harry Dobkin, Dalston (sadly he was convicted later of murdering his wife Rachel in Navarino Road, *JC* 27/11/42)
Albert Bernard Dobres, C68
Kitty Dobrin, Homerton
Ann Dobrin, Homerton
Hyman Joseph Doctorsky, C34/39
Fanny Doffman, Burdett Road
Sub Officer Samuel Doffman, C22, 11/38 to 9/39
Zoe Dominic, Firewatcher, professional photographer, b. Streatham
Hyman Donn, C38/28
Firewoman Renee Donn aka Glambotsky, motorbike despatch rider at Homerton
Ephraim Dorson, Westgate Street Fire Station, Newcastle
Isaac (Joe) Dorson, as above – brothers
Max Dreen, C28, tailor, called to colours 12/11/40
Sydney Dreezer, C39
John H. Dresler, C68/66, from Ilford
Myer Dubinsky, C28
Ben Dubrowsky, No.1 HQ, Hose Laying
Company Officer Arthur Duchin/Duchinsky, Lambeth HQ and C13
Ellen Duhig, Millwall – TBC
Alf Dulin, Shadwell
Lou Alec Dvorkin, C38

Cynthia Eastman-Nagle, Clapham – TBC
Beatrice Eberst, Stoke Newington
Berthold Maximillian Ebner, AFS
Henrietta Eckenstein, Manchester Square
Maurice Eckstein aka Eichenstan
Leslie Edelman, Bethnal Green
Adolphus John Edelstein, C68
Benjamin Edelstein, C38
Hyman/Himan Edelstein aka Anthony Eldon, C39, called to colours 20/6/40
Israel Edelstein, C39, WIA 30/12/40
Florence Edelstone, C28
Ms Edlina Edlin aka Bone, Edgware Road
Jack Edoloff, C39
Gustav Otto Ehrmann, C20
Morris Eichenstan, C39/23 – TBC

Sidney Eisbruch, C30/32
Reginald Eisler, C40
Peral Eisner, Stoke Newington
Harry Elbaz/ Henry Elboz, C28
Israel Elfman, C37
Assistant Group Officer Rosemary Elias, C28
David Louis Ellis, of 52 Grange Avenue, Leeds, son of Phillip and Rose, wife of Gertie Carnovsky of Glagow; clothing manufacturer of Sheepscar. He was a firefighter and engine driver and often sent to fight fires in Sheffield as well as in Leeds.
Maurice Ellis, Leeds, brother of David Louis above
Harry Ellman, C68, to Ambulance Service 5/9/39
Joseph Ellman, C39
Abraham Elman, Central Liverpool
Simon Elman, C39
Ms. Aleida Elsinga, Shoreditch – TBC
Charles Elstein, C35
H. Emanuel, C13
Elias Joe Emden, Lambeth HQ
Mr H. Emden, Fire Guard, Hughes Mansions, WIA
Joseph Emden, AFS Section Leader and Fireguard, later to RAF in 1942
Miss Julie Emden, Firewatcher/Fireguard, Hughes Mansions, daughter of Miriam KIA
Mrs K. Emden, Fire Guard, Hughes Mansions, WIA
Mr E. Morris Emden, husband of Miriam (KIA), in charge of Fireguards and ARP at Hughes Mansions, Stepney
Philip Emden, Whitechapel
Henry Emmanuel, C22
Jack Emmanuel, A9/28
Sydney George Engel, C38
Joan Engelbach, North Kensington – TBC
Henry F. Engelmann, C2
Solomon Engelsman, Superintendent Firewatcher, Petticoat Lane/ President Sandy's Row Synagogue. Son Henry remembers as a teenager standing alongside him in the raids.
Sidney Enlander, Fireman at Donaghadee, County Down, from Belfast
Alexander Ephron, Stoke Newington
Herman Albert Eppler/Eppeler, A3
Esther Epstein/Denoff, C22
Gladys Epstein, A2
Hyman Epstein, C39/34
Hyman Lewis Epstein, C47, called to colours 24/10/41
Jack Epstein, C76

Leon Epstein, A13
Maurice Epstein, C62
Max Epstein (note – not 'British'?)
Mordecai Epstein, Firewatcher, Nesbit House, Hackney E9 (served Zion Mule Corps and Merchant Navy in First World War)
Sidney Epstein, St 39
Solomon Epstein, C28/35
James Epstine, B72
Emmanuel Ereira, Bow, C2
Henry Ereira, C30
Joseph Ereira, C30
Morris Ereira, C28, WIA 17/5/41
Samuel Ereira, C32
William Albert Ereira, C37, called to Navy 18/1/42
Derek Erlebach, Westminster
Scout Patrol Leader Herbert Ermann, 15th Bedford – Certificate of Gallantry from Chief Scout for dealing with a serious fire during an air raid on 30/7/42 (*JC* 13/11/42) (German Jewish refugee)
Emil Wilfred Ernst, C2
Fireman Harry Errington aka Ehrengott, GC (only one of three GCs to firemen, and the only one awarded in London) – *JC* 22/8/41. WIA. Harry was one of three GC's won in the Second World War by Jews – others being Commander Harold Newgass (RN Bomb Disposal) and Captain Simmon Latutin, Somerset Light Infantry att. Somalia Gendarmerie. When Harry died the LFB provided a large Guard of Honour with a fire tender and standards flying.
Israel Essenberg, C39
Willi Essinger, Firewatcher, Priory Road, Kilburn, b.1884 Ulm
Harry Esterman, C28
Theodore Esterman, C66
Samuel Estrin, C74
Mrs F. Etkins, Sub Officer, E90
Abraham Ettinger, St 28
Harry Evankovsky, C28/37
Doris Evanguloff, Dagenham – TBC
Philip Evans, Formerly Even, Gorbals/Glasgow
Harry Evinson, Leeds
Edmond/Esmond David Ezra, A20
Esmond Davis Ezra, West Hampstead
Margaret Ezra, B68

Ms Steffi Fabian, later Elias, Firewoman, German refugee
Samuel Fairer

Walter Fairman previously R Navy, served FB 1931–42 Southwark and
    Surrey
Sidney Fairmaner, Redcross Street
Alex Falk/Faulk, Warrington/Manchester
'Lazzie' Lazarus Falk, Warrington, three brothers
Maurice Falk, St 38
Max Falk, Warrington, also served aboard ships as Fireman
Rolf Falksohn, Firewatcher Hoxton/Finchley, Kindertransport refugee
Nicholas Farago, AFS Amersham, Bucks 1940–45, served First World
    War in Hungarian Army, refugee interned 1940
Michael Farbman, C13, called to colours 1/8/40
Louis Farman, C32 – TBC
Stanley Farman, HQ
Albert Sydney Fassenfeldt, C28, called to Navy 8/3/40
Maurice Faust, C28
Colman Faver, C30
Lily Featherman, E90
Nancy Featherstone ??
Charles Colman Feinmesser, Wanstead
Harold Feinmesser, C62
Harris Feinsilver, C54
Michael Felberg, Whitechapel
Jack Felby, Whitechapel
Joel Felcher, C39
Mr Hans Nathan Feld, Firewatcher, Highfield Road off Golders Green
    Road
Kalmar Feldelman, C28
Abraham Feldman, C28/35
Abraham Feldman, C20/68
Bessie Feldman, Shadwell
Daniel Feldman, E89
Edna Feldman, West Hampstead
Area Sub Officer Emmanuel Feldman, C28
Frederick Feldman, C30/23
Gabriel Feldman, C39
H. Feldman, C22
Harris Feldman, C39
Isaac Feldman, C28
Mr J. Feldman, Leeds
Jack Feldman, Firewtacher in Soho, later to Argyll and Sutherland
    Highlanders in Italy
L. Feldman, B67
Louis Feldman, C36, WIA

Louis Feldman, Shadwell
Mark Feldman, Shadwell
Morris Feldman, C39, WIA 31/12/40
Sidney (Simon) Feldman, 1939–45, London, Station Officer Tower Hill
Simon Feldman, C35
Simon Feldman, B72
Solomon Feldman, C36
Harris Felgate, C39
Henry Felgate, C22
Issy (Isadore?) Fellaman, Petticoat Lane
Israel Fellman, C54
Margery Felsenstein, A20
Sydney A. Fendt, C7 – TBC
Louis Fenton, Ilford
Joseph Ferber, Liverpool
Yaacov Feuchtwanger, London; he was later interned as a German Jewish refugee then released
Lewis Fialko, Homerton
Ernest L. Fidderman, C37 – TBC
Dora Fiddleman, C39
Cecil Louis Fidler, St 80
Louis (Lazarus) Fidler, Kinning Park School, Glasgow, nr. Govan docks – often cooked Jewish food for fellow Firemen and recalled when on a call, seeing the tender in front of him exploding when hit by a bomb.
Philip Fidler, Manchester
Alf Field, Kensington
Louis Field, Kentish Town, WIA
Mark Field, Firewatcher, Hull
Louis 'Larry' Fieldman, Senrab Street School station
Mark Fieldman, stationed Limehouse, lived 262 Burdett Road E1 (siblings)
Louis Fienberg, B67
Emmanuel Filstein, C39
Samuel Filvar, Liverpool
Sydney Finburgh, Euston
Israel Fine, served Finchley and Docks areas, lived in Hampstead
Jack Fine, Canning Town and Plumstead (brother of Israel)
Solomon Fine, Blackburn, Liverpool, Sheffield; in Sheffield rescued *Sefer Torah* from burning synagogue
Reuben Finebaum, Shadwell
Barnett Fineberg, North Kensington
Harry Fineberg, C38

Joseph Fineberg, Stoke Newington
Nathaniel Fineberg, E85
Samuel Fineberg, Stoke Newington/Millwall
Barnett Finegold, 'C'
Harry Finegold, Homerton
Ralph Finegold, Greenwich
Harry Fineman, C38, later Lieutenant in RA, POW, escaped, North Africa
Bernard Fink, HQ
Ms D. Fink, A11
Hyman Finkel, Homerton (3, Brenthouse Road)
Harry Finklestein, Whitefriars
Lazarus Finklestein, C28
Charles Firestone, Manchester
Mr J.S. Fischoff, AFS Leeds
Samuel Fischoff, C28
Herbert Samuel Fish, Bishopsgate
Morris Fishberg, C38
Victor Fishburn, Ickenham/Uxbridge/East End
Isaac Sidney Fishel, B73
Adolphus Fisher, Bow
Barnett Fisher, C36
Gershon Fisher, C28
Hyman Fisher, C38
Isaac Fisher, Liverpool
Joseph Fisher, Credon Road, Plaistow
Marcus Fisher, B75
Morris Fisher, aka Fischer C35
Samuel Fisher, Liverpool
Abraham Fishgold, Liverpool
Dora Fishman, Shadwell
Morris Fishman, Bethnal Green
Solomon Fishman, Stoke Newington
Sub Officer Syd Fishman, London, C39
Stanley Louis Flack, C36
Sub Officer Louis E. (Ansell?) Flatau, F65R
Morris Flatt, C23
Joseph Flax, Shadwell
Alf Abraham Flenner, Stock Exchange station, WIA
Barnett Flenner, C28
Alfred Louis Flexman, A7
Rose Fligelstone, Manchester Square
Deborah Flitman, AFS Streatham

Samuel Fogel, J1, Bromley
Simon Fogel, E48
Alec Fogelman, C22
Reuben Foreman, C1
Barnett Forman, Shadwell
Lewis Forshman, C38
Miss C. Fortuin, Sub Officer, E84
Abraham Fox, C28
Anne Fox, C28
Bernard Fox, C28
Benjamin Fox, Dempsey Street motor cycle messenger
Gershon Fox, C28
Harry Fox, C30
Coy. Off. Harry Leonard Fox, formerly Coldstream Gds, b. 3/2/01 served 1926–48
Hilda Fox, C34
Hubert Fox, Kingsland
Lazarus Fox, Lee Green
Leon Fox, Shadwell
Leon Frederick Fox, HQ
Maurice Fox, C30
Max Fox, East London
Morris Fox, C28
Muriel Pearl Fox, C37
Reuben Fox, Whitefriars
Sidney Fox, West Wickham, J5
Solomon Fox, Whitefriars
Judah Franco, C35, WIA
Philip Samuel Frank, C28
Till Frankal, Enfield
Mr G.I. Frankel, a printer of Commercial Road, led 50 men and women in a Supplementary Fire Party in Stepney, throughout the Blitz; mentioned in F. Lewey, *Cockney Campaign* (London: Stanley Paul, 1946).
Matilda Frankel, Shadwell
Nathan Frankel, Burdett Road
Simon Morris Frankel, Water Unit 'E'
Clarence Colman Franklin ('Frank'), Clapton, despatch rider
Harry Franklin, C39
Jack Franklin, C32
Jack Franklin, C30
Jack 'John' Franklin, C37
Barry Barnet Franks, Liverpool

Irene Franks, Clerkenwell
Jacoby Franks, Liverpool
Reuben Franks, C28
Ms Telcie Franks, Whitechapel
Zoe Franks, Brompton
Daniel Franks, C39
E.A. Franks, A7
Eleanor Franks, Clerkenwell
Joseph Henry Franks, F45
Lew Franks, Camperdown House sub-station, Whitechapel
Louis Franks, C28 – aka Flansky – WiA twice, fell through a roof
Charles Fredenfall, Whitefriars
Cyril Fredenfall, Whitefriars
David Freedland, Firewatcher, Dalston
Alec Freedman, Shadwell
Alec Nathan Freedman, Brixton
Alfred Freedman, C28
Archibald Freedman, A6
Esther Freedman, Kingsland
Miss H. Freedman, later Harris; only Jewish woman in Bury St Edmunds Fire Brigade; often drove Fire Engines to US Air Bases when they were bombed
Harris Freedman, B67
Harry Freedman, taxi driver and Firewatcher, London
Hyman Freedman, B62
Israel Freedman, Homerton
Jack Freedman, B76
Joseph Freedman, C28
Leon Freedman, E90
Louis Freedman, C39 (i)
Louis Freedman, C39 (ii)
Max Freedman, Burdett Road
May Freedman, Shoreditch
Morris Freedman (22891) C35, Millwall; he played actor Tommy Trinder's body-double in the film *Fires were Started*
Nuell Freedman, West Hampstead
Philip Freedman, C24
Ms Raie Freedman, C22
Sid Free(d)man, City
Sydney Freedman, Sheffield
Woolf Freedman, C38
Woolf Freedman, C28
Arthur Freeman, Liverpool

Barnet Freeman, B63
Dorothy Freeman, Belsize
Edgar Samuel Freeman, East Greenwich
Harry Freeman, Liverpool
J.L. Freeman, Leeds – TBC
Mr J.L. Freeman, AFS Leeds
Nathan Freeman, F61, Dockhead – TBC
Section Leader Nathan Joseph Freeman, C38
Sol Freeman, Soho
Sydney Freeman, C28
Sydney Frank Freeman, C38 – TBC
Woolf Freeman, Cannon Street/St Pauls
Herbert Samuel Freestone, B68
Sydney Henry Freestone, Southwark
David R. Fresco, Sub Officer, C28
Henry Fresco, North Kensington
Harry Aaron Freshwater, C36
Louis Freshwater, Soho
Michael Friedberg, Lauriston Road, Burdett Road
Louis Friedenfall, C39
Esther Friedlander, Edgware Road
John Friedlander, Clerkenwell
E. Friedman, C38
Freddy Friedman, NFS, Jewish Refugee
Mr G.I. Friedman, AFS Leeds
Michael Friedman, C39
Eric Friedrich, Manchester Square
Hyman Friend, Sheffield
Leslie Herbert Friend, A20
Maxwell Louis Friend, A20
Ms M. Frischaver, TC –TBC
Ernst Frischler aka Frinton, Firewatcher/student Glasgow, b. 1917 Czechoslovakia
Harold Fromberg, HQ
Freda Frosh, Stoke Newington
Miss Irmgard Fruchtzweig aka Broniatowski, Firewatcher London and Merseyside
Libby Louisa Frumkin, later Sacks, Senior Fire Guard, Stoke Newington, died 2010 – mother of Chief Rabbi Lord Jonathan Sacks
Phyllis Frusher, Wandsworth – TBC
Leonard Fryde, C34
Fred Robsahn Fugelsang, A8

Morris Fulberg, B73
Max Futrofsky, Euston

Saul (Solomon) Neil Gabe, based Tower Garage, Hendon, driver in East and West End fires
Isaac Gaber, Stoke Newington
Sydney Gabrel, brother of Sarah Conn (above)
Arnold John Gabriel, Edgware Road
Sidney Gabriel, Holborn/Westminster, previously stretcher bearer ARP, WIA Stepney
Abraham Galinski, B66
Maurice Galinski, Stoke Newington
Mr D. Galinsky, AFS Leeds
Frank Galinsky, C34
Lionel Myer Galinsky, C34
Isidore Galizer, Kingsland
Mark Galler, C39
Isaac Galman, East Greenwich
Louis Gameroff/Gameson, Stoke Newington
Aryeh Gans, London
Charles Leslie Gansler, Ilford (formerly ARP warden)
Myer Ganyon aka Daniel, Stoke Newington
Max Garadofsky, Bow
Miss B.F. Garagofsky, C30
Harry Garber, C28
Nathan Garber, Manchester Square
Sam Garber, C28
Ms Marie Garcia (later Morris), 1939–45, Petersfield (Hants) Fire Officer Training Centre, from Portsmouth
Station Officer Philip Honig T. Garcia, V Sub Station, LFB C37 (*ELA* 14/10/39)
Benjamin Garfinkle, C34
Sub Officer S. Garfinkle, B92
Barnet Garnet, C28
Assistant Group Officer/Firewoman Rosalie Gassman-Sherr, BEM (first Jewish woman ever to win BEM) – Hornsey (*JC* 2/5/41; *LG* 24/4/42). Rosalie was an AFS/NFS telephonist in the watchroom; she remained at her post after a bomb led to the collapse of her station around her, continuing to take incoming emergency calls and passing them to the Central Control, so assuring that all fires were being attended; she also meanwhile administered First Aid to all those injured around her.
Miss Gassman's sister (name not known)

Miss Gassman's brother in law (name not known)
Annie Gasson, A8
Lesley Cyril Gasson, Belsize
Rebecca Gasson, Stoke Newington
Samuel Gasson, Tooting
Sidney Gasson, E89, Battersea
Walter Gasson, Tooting
William Gasson, Perivale, WIA twice
Max Gastwirth, C28
Zelda Gatoff later Fisher
Lillian Gatoff, sisters, both at Westgate Street Station, Newcastle-upon-Tyne
David Gaus, Plumstead
Jacob Moses Gaus, East Greenwich
Max Pizer Gauston, Shadwell, WIA
Aubrey Gee, Manchester Square, WIA
Hyman Geffen, Shoreditch
Isaac Gehr, Burdett Road
Gerald Geiger, Major (Ret.), Westminster
John Geiger, Clapham
E. Geist, C28
Reginald Gelding, Cardiff/London, Camden
Harry Geldman/Gildman, Shadwell
Reuben Gelfer, Kentish Town
Asher 'Arthur' Geller, Manchester
Hyman Geller, Stoke Newington, WIA
Victor Geller, C28
Mr S Gelman, AFS Leeds
Jack Gelstern, Bethnal Green
Louis Genis, Redcross Street
Reuben Genis, B68
Isaac Joseph Genyon, Stoke Newington
Ernest Gepstein, C28
Joseph Gerber/Gerbitch, Kentish Town
Ana Gerharz, Hammersmith – TBC
Henry Lewis Gerlack, D42, Woolwich, WIA
Philip Gerlack, Old Kent Road, F82
Albert Gerngross, E86
Frank Gerngross, Tooting
Solomon Gerofsky, C28
Barnett Gersh, 'C'
Woolf Gershgorin aka Cohen, C28
Simon Gershman, Stoke Newington

Sylvia Gershman/Duzzy, Stoke Newington
Alfred Gershon, Firewatcher, Hendon
Eli Gershon, Soho
Jill Gershon, Edgware Road
Mike Myer Gerstenblatt, Stoke Newington
Berwin Gertler/Gurlter, D55
Bertha Gestenberger, TBC
Harris Gevelb, C28
Harry Gewirtz, Islington
Leonard Gewitzke, Old Kent Road
Joseph Gilbert, Kings Cross
Nathan Gilbert, Bishopsgate
Solomon Gilbert, C28
Vera Esther Gilbert, Islington
Mrs Gilbert née Guggenheimer, AFS, German refugee
Abraham Gillman, Liverpool
Woolf Gillon, B63
Alfred Ginsberg, C38
Mr H. Ginsberg, AFS Leeds
Judah Ginsberg, Shadwell, WIA
Mr M. Ginsberg, AFS Leeds
Abraham Ginsburg (later Alfred Gilbert), Whetstone district, London
Ms R. Ginzburg, Hornsey
Morris Gittleson, Shadwell
Albert Giwelb, C34
E.H. Glaisyer, Kensington
Marcus Glaser, C28
Harold Basil Glaskie, Manchester
Barnett 'Benny' Glass, Whitechapel Station, Commercial Road C28, WIA
Frederick Sydney Glass, Islington
Philip Glass, Whitefriars
Alex Glassberg, Brixton
Lewis Glassof, C22
Marcus Glaubenfeld, East Greenwich
George Roman Glauser, Euston
Sub Officer/Section Leader Mark Glazer, Fairclough Street, C28
Ms Cissie Glazerman, C28
Emmanuel Glazerman, Stoke Newington
Sylvia Glazerman, C28
Oscar Gleinser, Southwark
Minnie Gleissoff, Bishopsgate
Solomon Glen, Homerton

E. Glick, S Wales
Benjamin Glicksman, Shadwell
Anne Gliergevert, Kingsland
Leslie John Glikstein, Homerton
Column Officer Norman Jack Gliksten, HQ
George Gluck, Islington
Israel Godasewitz, Bethnal Green
Women's Group Officer Gold, Lambeth
Alfred Bernard Gold, of Southgate, driver in docks and Euston Fire Station; WIA when he was blown off his ladder by a huge explosion in the docks, and his jacket torn to shreds.
Benjamin Gold, C22
Dave Gold, Portsmouth, allegedly given a bravery award (evidence of Sam Guttenberg who served with him)
Elijah Gold
Harry Gold, C23
Harry Gold, Shoreditch
Ivor Gold, Shoreditch
J. Gold, Fire Guard, Hughes Mansions
Jack Gold, Shoreditch
Jack Woolf Gold, Stoke Newington
Louis Gold, Soho
Manny Joseph Gold, Shaftesbury Avenue Station, tailor (see *Wartime News*, November 1997, p.9 – B72)
Maurice Gold, Lambeth
Myer Gold, Bishopsgate
Philip Gold, C39
R. Gold, Bow
S. Gold, Bow
Samuel Gold, Euston
Revd Sidney Gold, London, Firewatcher (*JC* obituary 6/4/12)
Sonny Gold, Soho
Terence Gold, Hammersmith
Abraham Goldfarb, C39
Morris Golding, C28
Mr A.A. Goldberg, AFS Leeds
Abraham Goldberg, Glasgow
Albert Goldberg, C36
Alexander Goldberg, West Hampstead
Benjamin Goldberg, Stoke Newington
Cecil Goldberg, Speke, Liverpool
Colman Goldberg, C38
David Goldberg, C35

David Goldberg, C28
Fanny Goldberg, Firewatcher, Manchester
Harold Joseph Goldberg, A20
Harry Goldberg, Shoreditch
Mr I. Goldberg, AFS Leeds
Irene Goldberg, C34
Isaac Goldberg, C28
Israel Goldberg, East Greenwich
'Issy' Isidore Goldberg, Manchester
Jack Goldberg, Bishopsgate
Jean Goldberg
Joseph Goldberg, Shadwell
Joseph Goldberg, Shoreditch
Joseph Goldberg, Essex Street, Liverpool
Judith Goldberg, née Brenner, Bow
Julius 'Judd' Goldberg, Oxford Road, Manchester, also Liverpool, London, Coventry, Glasgow, WIA, Commended for Bravery; brother of Issy above
L. Goldberg, C28
Lazarus Goldberg, C28
Louis Goldberg, C37
Louis Goldberg, C23, WIA
Marie Goldberg, Burdett Road
Maurice Goldberg, Homerton
Morris Goldberg, Bow
Morris Goldberg, Streatham
Morris Goldberg, Firewatcher, Manchester
Pinkus Goldberg, East Greenwich, WIA
Reuben Goldberg, Clekenwell
Mr S. Goldberg, AFS Leeds
Samuel Goldberg, Shadwell
Simon Harris Goldberg, Durning Street, Liverpool
Samuel Goldberg, Swansea
Sidney Goldberg ??
Sophia Goldberg, C28
Toby Goldenberg, Stoke Newington
Abraham Goldfarb, Stoke Newington
Barney Goldfine, Manchester
Julius Goldflust, Bethnal Green
Alfred Isidore Goldhill, C35
Frederick Golding, Stoke Newington
Hyman Golding, TC
Louis Golding, Perivale

Morris Golding, C28
Alfred Goldman, C38
Bernard Goldman, E86
Ms H. Goldman, Bethnal Green
Harold Goldman, Hammersmith
Harry Goldman, Bow
Louis Goldman, Dockhead
Ms Renee Goldman/Gill ??
Samuel Goldman, Durning Street, Liverpool
Henry Judah Goldner, C22
Jack Goldner, Burdett Road
Harry Goldrich, C24
Alec Goldring, C28
Cecil Goldring, Stoke Newington
Jack Goldring, Knightsbridge
David Goldsack, Lee Green
Norman Goldsack, Kentish Town
Stephen Goldsack, previously RAMC, served FB 1919–38 Woolwich – TBC
Morris Goldshaft, Bishopsgate
Goldsmith, believed Jewish, named on Pollins photo of No 36 FF Area course, 1943
Tom Goldsmid, Caversham fire station near Reading (from Alan G. Sandall, *Are you 17?* [Frome: Private Publication, 1993])
James Charles Goldsmith (junior) – 1930s to 1966, Lee Green and Chief Fire Officer Broad Street 1960s; cited for courage Broad Street Station Fire 21/12/1951; Green Howards Second World War. One of six brothers. The memorabilia of this family were donated to The Forties Experience museum in Bushey, London.
Joseph Goldsmith, C28
Lottie Goldsmith/Sternberg, C36
Sidney Goldsmith, brother of James Charles above, Plaistow
Patrol Officer Joseph Goldson, Liverpool Docks, 'BEM for bravery; displayed outstanding leadership and resource, when on one occasion he made rapid arrangements for relaying water from the docks, and by astute tactical positioning of the appliances and firefighting equipment, prevented fire spreading to adjacent buildings. He was undeterred by unexploded time bombs, and he constantly exposed himself to falling debris whilst ensuring the safety of the men under his command' (Arthur Lockyear, *Warriors in Fireboots* [Huddersfield: Jeremy Mills, 2011], p.214) – TBC if Jewish.
Aaron Goldstein, Belsize

Aaron Ronald Goldstein, Edgware Road
Abraham Goldstein, C38
Alec Goldstein, C38
Alec Louis Goldstein, C30
Alfred Aaron Goldstein, C37
Charles Goldstein, Dockhead
Davis Goldstein, Clerkenwell
David Goldstein, Burdett Road
H. Goldstein, North Kensington
Helen Anne Goldstein, TC
Hyman Goldstein, Westminster/Islington
Jack Goldstein, Stoke Newington
John Schier Goldstein, Brunswick Road
Lillian Goldstein/Nash ??
Mark Goldstein, Old Kent Road
Mark Goldstein, C38
Maurice Goldstein, A6
Morris Goldstein, C38
Morris Goldstein, Shoreditch
Moss Goldstein, Kingsland (B2361??), WIA in arm in Roman Road, E2
Pearl Goldstein, Homerton
Philip Goldstein ??
Samuel Goldstein, A9
Sidney Goldstein, C38
Simon Goldstein, C28
Simon Goldstein, C39
Sydney Goldstein, C22
Sylvia Goldstein, B72
John Goldston, Kingsland
Abraham Goldstone, Manchester and JLB
B. Goldstone, AFS Leeds
Ernest Albert Goldstone, 26Z/D40
George H.W. Goldstone, D40
Maurice Goldstone, Manchester
Sam Goldstone, Manchester, stationed in Glasgow
Samuel Goldstone, Allerton, Liverpool
Daphne Gompertz ??
Lucy Gompertz, Perry Vale
Leading Fireman Goodman, Heckford Street Station, Stepney
Alfred Goodman, C35
Anne Goodman, Brixton
Barry Goodman, Soho

Mr E.A. Goodman, Leeds
Edward Goodman, C23
Edwy Goodman, Sheffield
B16346 Frank Goodman, A12, BEM: 'During an air raid, bombs demolished buildings at the junction of Cannon and Broad Streets, damaging two fire appliances of a stationary fireman convoy killing and injuring members of the crews. Goodman, although injured, and in shock, immediately went to the assistance of his more seriously injured comrades, and worked with others unceasingly to remove casualties and render first aid. Goodman then carried on fighting fires in the neighbourhood until he collapsed and had to be removed to a first aid post for treatment.' (*LG* 28/11/41, p.6822)
George Goodman, C38
Harry Goodman, C28
Henry Goodman, A9
Ivor Norman Goodman, C28
Jacob Goodman, Shoreditch
John Goodman, Homerton
John Goodman, Shadwell
Joseph Goodman, A6
Joseph William Goodman, E85
Kopple Goodman, Belsize
Leon Goodman/Garfield, Firewatcher, John Lewis store (Anglo-French)
Maurice Goodman, Wandsworth
Max Goodman, C34, attended at Bethnal Green tube disaster 1944
Max Goodman, Bishopsgate (B7016??), WIA in eye and leg in a collision
Michael Goodman, Stoke Newington
Michael Goodman, Burdett Road
Morris Goodman, Forest Gate, invalided out 1943
Moss Goodman, A11
Reuben Goodman/Goodwin, Bethnal Green
Rose Goodman, New Cross
Samuel Goodman, Stoke Newington
Samuel Woolf 'Benny' Goodman, Soho, WIA
Sonny Goodman, Manchester
Miss W. Goodman, Firewoman 887594, AFS Leeds
Fireman W. Goodman, 2876, Leeds
Horace Sydney Goodrich, Westminster
Jack Goodstein, C28
Sidney Goodstein, C28
Florence Goold/Dale, C28

Meyer Goolnik, Whitefriars
Woolf Goorvitch, Burdett Road
Samuel Gootnick/Gilbey, Belsize
Albert Gopstein, C30
Alex Gopstein, Bethnal Green
Hyman Gopstein, Bethnal Green
Hyman Jack Gordon, Ilford
Solomon Gordon, C38
Joseph Gordon, Hull
Renee Gordon, C22
Stella Gordon, West Hampstead
Jack Stanley Gorowski, Lambeth
Morris Gorsch, Clapton
Ldg Fireman Gossenberg/Gosen, St Dunstans, Golders Green (given by
    Eric Kauffman)
L. Gotlieb, Burdett Road
Walter Gotlieb, Stoke Newington
Philip Gotlop, Manchester Square
Barnett Gould, Fulham
Eva Gould, Stoke Newington
Harold Gould, E85
Harriet Rosanna Gould, Burdett Road
Henry Gould, Liverpool
Mr J. Gould, AFS Leeds
Jack Gould, Streatham
Maurice Gould, NFS (*Guardian* Obituary 2/9/10)
Maurice Gould, Allerton, Liverpool (duplicate of above?)
Abraham Gouldman, Manchester
George Goulstone, B63
Lazarus Grablof, Islington
Benjamin Gradus, C23
Louis Gradus, C28
Cyril Graefe, A13
Barney Grant, St Katherine's Dock
Gertie 'Gerry' Grant, telephonist, Leeds
Green, first name unknown; given by Rabbi Salasnik of Bushey
Benjamin Green, C28
David Green, Clerkenwell
Doris Green, Burdett Road
Emmanuel Green, Bethnal Green
Hyman Green, Shadwell
Isidore Green, A2
Miss Jessie Green, Manchester

Maxwell Green, A2
Rosina Green, C32
Woolf Green, Hendon (former ARP)
Robert St John Green-de-Woolfson, Parsons Green
Fireman Greenbaum, unsung hero of the Bounds Green tube disaster (see introductory story) – perhaps Charles of 62 Coldharbour Lane, SE5?
Abraham Greenbaum, Burdett Road
Bessie Greenbaum, Millwall
Charles Greenbaum, Brixton (see above)
Ezriel Jacques Greenbaum, Islington
Jack Greenbaum, C28
Joseph Greenbaum, Clapham
Judah Greenbaum, C39
Louis Greenbaum, Clapham
Solly Greenbaum, Whitechapel
Abraham Greenberg, Belsize
Abraham Greenberg, Shadwell
Alfred Greenberg, 'C'
Barnett Greenberg, Clerkenwell
Benjamin Greenberg, C34
Beanna Greenberg, Shadwell
Charles Greenberg, Shadwell
Godfrey Greenberg, Kingsland
Harry Greenberg, Woolwich
Isaac Greenberg, Kingsland
Jacob Greenberg, Bishopsgate
Julius Greenberg, Liverpool
Ms L. Greenberg/Cohen ??
Lily Greenberg, C23 (same person?)
James Greenberg, C39
S. Greenberg, Middlesborough NFS
Samuel Greenberg, C28
Nathan Greenblatt, Stoke Newington
Emmanuel Greenhill, Clapton
Morris Greenspan, Burdett Road
Morris Greenspan, Enfield
Morris Greenstein, Stoke Newington
Maurice Greenwold, Clapham
Cecil Louis Greenwood, Belsize
Clara Gregory, Cannon Street – TBC
Lewis Grill, C28
Barnett Gritz

Milly Gritiz née Demy, Manchester, husband and wife
Israel Gritzman, Stoke Newington
Michael Groffman, C30
Julius Groschler, later Gale, AFS, b. Jever, Germany, refugee
Anthony Gerald Gross, B63
Charles Henry Gross, A9
Lionel Gross, Stoke Newington
William Oscar Gross, E84
Barry Grossman, Shoreditch
Harry Grossman, C38
Chief Officer Joseph Grossman, Elstree Fire Brigade was recommended for a New Years Honour list MBE in November 1941, but the Home Office decided that as 'he had St Vitus Dance, the award would not be appropriate [!!!] despite his excellent work with recreational, social and Benevolent Fund matters with the London Fire Brigade' (LMA FB/WAR/1/181).
Phillip Grossman, Whitefriars and Horninghold (Leicestershire) station, WIA 1942 by an explosion
Sim (Simon?) Grossman, Bournemouth AFS
Guildford Hospital, all Jewish Fire crew of European refugees led by Jimmy Vasha (?) – to be investigated
Lily Grun, West Hampstead
Elizabeth Grunewald, Peckham
Solly Guise, Queens Road, Manchester
Sam Gudelovitch, Greenwich, aka Gedalovitch. His wife Molly was killed in Blitz 11/5/41
Vera Guggenheim, Belsize
Edward Guiterman, Edgware Road
Berwin Gurtler, Southwark
Sam Gurvitz, C28
Dora Gushinoff, Kingsland
Mr Gusterson, Stock Exchange station
Ilse Guttenberg, later Sinclair, NFS Guildford, b. Hamburg 1922
Samuel Guttenberg/Godfrey, served in Plymouth
Fireman Guttman/Goodchild, St Dunstans, Golders Green, given by Eric Kauffman

Montague Haberfield, Burdett Road
Benjamin Hacker, St 52
Henry Joseph Hacker, Bishopsgate
Joseph Hacker, Old Kent Road
Joseph Hackman, C30
Philip Hackman, Bethnal Green
David Albert Hahn, Old Kent Road

Reginald Hahn, Homerton
Coy. Off. Charles Bernard Haisman, 1914–42, Bishopsgate and HQ – TBC
Lawrence Norman Haisman, Lee Green – TBC
Frederick Charles Halon, Manchester (later REME)
Lawrence Isaac Halon (brothers)
Harris Halpern, Shrubberies Fire Station, Prestwich
Julius Halpern, Southwark
David Halpin, formerly Inniskillings, served FB 1922–46, Shoreditch, Belsize, etc. –TBC
Cecil Halter, Birmingham, Spark Hill (Stratford Road) and Moseley Road
Doria Hambourg, Edgware Road
Jack Hamburgh, Burdett Road – TBC
John Hamburgh, Blackfriars – TBC
Alfred Hammarberg, Whitechapel
Sam Hammerstein, Firewatcher, Grimsby
Isaac Hanken, C23
Kathleen Hankin, Stoke Newington – TBC
Rev Leslie Hardman, Firewatcher Leeds, later Jewish Chaplain to Forces in NW Europe, liberating Belsen
Philip Haring, Bethnal Green
Gabriel Haring, Bow
Harry Harowitz, Liverpool
Joseph Harowitz, Liverpool
Samuel Harowitz, Liverpool
Barnett Harris, Blackfriars
David Harris aka Landrofsky
Enid Lillian Harris later Perez, telephonist/control van, Hendon/Barnet during V1/2 attacks, daughter of Harry Harris BEM (below)
Harry Harris, West Hampstead
Harry Harris, Shoreditch
Harry Leslie Harris, B62
Harry Harris aka Hednitsky, Stoke Newington
Harry Harris, Firewatcher, Leeds, Area Coordinator, First World War veteran
Section Leader/Officer Harry Harris BEM, aged 49, of Golders Green. In WW1 he served in Gallipoli, Mesopotamia and India. Harry joined the AFS in 1938 and served till 1945, stationed at St Peter's Hall, Cricklewood. Awards to Harris and Davis (see above) 'for remaining at their posts pumping out water from the site of an unexploded magnetic parachute mine – which the men knew might explode at any moment – whilst it was being defused by RN bomb

disposal men, in November 1940; incident at 24 Hocroft Avenue, Cricklewood'. Harris lived at 13 Powis Gardens, Golders Green; originally from Hull, he served in the AFS from May 1938 till the end of the war (*LG* 24/4/42), investiture 19 May 1942 at Buckingham Palace. He died in May 1948 and is buried at Bushey.

Jack Myer Harris, A2
Joel Harris, Kingsland
Joseph Harris, Kingsland
Leonard Harris, C35
Lionel Harris, C30
Louis Harris, Parnell Road, Bow, WIA (lost eye), badge 'For Loyal Service'
Louis Harris aka Zugzie, Blackfriars
Louis Harris, Shadwell
Louis (Lew) Harris, uncle of Fl. Sgt Jack Nissenthal of Dieppe raid fame
Mark Harris, Bishopsgate
Maurice Harris, Belsize
Meyer Harris, Shoreditch
Michael 'Mickey' Harris, Bow and Greenwich
Michael Harris, West Hampstead
Michael Harris, East Greenwich
Michael Harris, Clerkenwell
Morris Harris, Bow
Myer Harris, Islington
Nathan Harris aka Novgorod, C28
Section Leader Oscar Edward Harris, Brixton 1938–45
Philip Harris, Stoke Newington
Rufus Jacob Harris, West Hampstead
Sadie Harris, Bethnal Green
Samuel Harris, C28
Samuel Henry Harris, Whitechapel
Sidney Harris, Liverpool
Sydney Harris C39
Sydney Harris, Islington
Zena Harris, Whitechapel
Reuben Harry, C34
Mr A. Hart, Fireguard, Stepney
Ada Hart, Southwark
Arthur Hart, C35
David Hart, C34
Emma Hart, B74
Ethel Hart/Lanceman, C32
Isaac 'Mick' Hart, Docks

Harold Hart, C35/36 – TBC
Harry Hart, 'C'
Henry Harry Hart, Brunswick Road
Henry Hyman Hart, Kingsland
Edith Hart née Bernstein, Tel-y-Cafn, Llandudno (wife of Sidney below)
Elizabeth 'Betty' Hart, later Mrs Walvish, Shadwell, sister of Sidney Hart (below)
Isaac Hart, Kingsland
M. Hart, Fire Guard, Hughes Mansions
Michael Hart, C28
Nathan Hart, C30
Norman Hart, West Hampstead
Norman David Hart, St 20
Raphael Hart, Whitechapel
Raphael Hart, 'C'
Samuel Lionel Hart, Bishopsgate fire station, father of Sidney (below)
Sidney Saul Hart, C36
Sidney Hart/Hartz, D40, 1939–69, Bishopsgate fire station/Cardiff, North Wales (Bangor/Rhyl) till 1957, then Westcliffe on Sea till 1969 (WIA at Liverpool Street); later post-war highest ranking Jewish Fire Officer (Station Officer), Fire Brigade Union Official.
Saul Alexander Hartman, St 47
William Hartman(n), Soho –TBC (is he the music hall artist known as 'The Drunken Wizard', who used to entertain the Soho station crews?)
Emma Hartogs, Manchester Square – TBC
Eric Hauser, North Kensington
Joan Hauser, North Kensington
Doris Haussmann, Islington – TBC
Sidney Hayman, Bethnal Green
Miss Stella Hayman (later Gold), Firewatcher, Chiswick
Bernard Hecht, Firewatcher, father of Michael Howard, MP
Nathan Hecht, Firewatcher, Manchester
Sec. Ldr Ernest Hermann Hegele, C36, LFB 1936–48, served 12th Royal Lancers – TBC
Sec. Ldr Victor Frederick Heier, 1949–58 – TBC
Dr Georg Heim, Firewatcher at Cleve Road, NW6, Austrian refugee
Richard Heimer, Edgware Road
Winifred Heine, Kensington – TBC
George Heinzman, New Cross
William Heiser, later Hayes, Cockfosters
Abraham Heitner, Stoke Newington

Samuel Heitner, Islington
Albert Heitzer, Streatham – TBC
Henry Joseph Heitzer, Whitechapel etc., formerly RN, served 1906–41 – TBC
Reuben Helfand, HQ – TBC
Harry Helfgott, Firewatcher Finsbury Park, brother of Paul (below)
Paul Helfgott, Firewatcher Finsbury Park 1940–41, later to Paras, German refugee
Hyman Heller, Homerton
Philip Heller, Kingsland
Simon Heller, Whitechapel
Simon Heller, C28
Abraham Helman, Stoke Newington
Charles Henick, Clerkenwell
Harold Henkewich, Liverpool
Charles Henkleman, Bow
Cyril Henneberg, Wandsworth
Felix Henneberg, Clapham
Zena Henneman/Markson, Lee Green
Felix Herman Hennenberg, E80 – TBC
Ann Henriques/Shewell, Brompton
Sub Officer H.L.Q. Henriques, A6
Louis Henriques, Belsize
Peter Ralph Quiseans Henriques, Belsize
Harold Henry, Stoke Newington
Joel Henry, A9
Charles Henshaw, Liverpool
Frederick Hensher, Bow
Gustav Hentschel formerly RN, served 1928–44 – TBC
Abraham Herman, C28, WIA
Alfred Herman, Bethnal Green
Bert Herman, C23
David Herman, West Hampstead
Harry Herman, Euston
Hyman 'Henry' Herman aka Hermon, C22 stationed Limehouse, of 262 Burdett Road E1, axe donated to Leytonstone Fire Brigade after Second World War
Jack Herman, C39
Mark Herman, Piccadilly Fire Station, Manchester
Maurice Herman, Piccadilly Fire Station, Manchester (brother of Mark); Mark's wife took kosher food each day to the Fire Station for the brothers.
Nina Herman, B76

Philip Herman, C28
Richard Herman, Bromley
Robert Herman, Whitechapel
Sydney Herman, Southwark
Walter Philip Herman, A7
Doris Hernandez, Westminster – TBC
David Herschman, Old Kent Road
Joseph Herschman, HQ
Miss R. Hershkovitch, C28
Samuel Hershman, C35
Sidney Hershon, Liverpool
Yetta Herskovitch, C39
Myer Hertsis, Homerton
Ben Hertzberg, Whitechapel
Ben Hertzberg, C28
Sidney Hertzberg, C22
Karl Herzberg, Firewatcher, Hampstead Garden Suburb, German refugee
Miss Frieda Herzfeld later Wollmerstadt, later to ATS
Miss Martha Herzfeld, sister of Frieda, German refugees
Joseph Hessel, 'C'
Firewoman Judith Heyman née Carlebach, German refugee, location not given (Wiener Library archives)
Heinz Martin Hichberger, 513308, NFS 1943–45, Kindertransport 1938
Benjamin Hildebrand, Whitechapel
Emil Hill, Firewatcher, Soho
Louis Hill, London Docks
Maurice Hillel, Stoke Newington
Cyril Hillelson, Grimsby/Cleethorpes
Mark Himmelman, C34
Harry Himmelspring, Stoke Newington
Jack Himmelspring, Stoke Newington
Percy Himmelspring, Stoke Newington
Margarete Hinrichsen, Firewatcher London, German refugee
Albert Hintz, Soho/Enfield
Elizabeth Hintz, Bethnal Green – TBC
Gustav Benjamin Hirsch, E89
Jack Hirsch, Whitechapel
Otto Hirsch, Millwall
Charles Joseph Hirschle, Westminster, WIA
Ronald Hirschle, Westminster, WIA
Harold Hirsh, Blackfiars

Harry Hirsh, C35
Norman Hirshfield, Hendon
Victor Hirschfield, River Service
Philip Hiseman, Clerkenwell – TBC
Frederick Hiser, Islington
William Hiser, Millwall
Harry Hockberg, Burdett Road
Simon Hoepelman, Bow
Cecil Hofman, Lee Green
Frederick S. Hoffman, F82
Harry Max Hoffman, B62
Hilda Hoffman, Stoke Newington
Israel Hoffman, C23
Ms L.M. Hoffman, Section Leader, Leeds
Maurice Hoffman, Stoke Newington
Oscar Hoffman, C37
William Henry E. Hoffman, C23
Peter Hoffman-Swedlow, Euston
Theodore Henry Hoffmeyer, served 1932–44, formerly RN – TBC
Rosina Seibt/Holman, Clapham, Commended *LG* 1941
Max Holt, Holloway
Max Holt, Shadwell
Sydney Holt, Shadwell
Edward Homberger, F58, Cherry Garden
Mark Honickberg, Edgware Road, former ARP
Joan Honig, Wimbledon
Abraham Horenstein aka Ornstein, Kingsland
Ronald Horley, Edgware Road
Davis Hornstein, Shadwell
Marks Hornstein, Shadwell
Israel Horewitz, Redcross Street
Louis Horvitz, Homerton
Jack Horvoitz, Kingsland
Harold Horwich, West Hampstead
Sub Officer Richard Horwitz, B76
Hyman Hoser, C38
Harry House, Shadwell
Henry House, Holloway
Nathan House, Whitechapel
Station Officer Cyril Huber, Lambeth
Marie Humplemann, Burdett Road – TBC
Lena Hunziker, Westminster – TBC
Mrs Renee Hurst

Sidney Hurst aka Issy Hescovitch, Stoke Newington, C34, later 8th
 Army, husband of Renee
Benjamin Hyam, F41
Reginald Hyam, A5
Albert J. Hyams, F82, to LFB Sub Officer 11/40
Edgar Hyams, Liverpool, First World War veteran
George W. Hyams, Kentish Town
Henry Hyams, Old Kent Road
Hyman Hyams, C30
Hymie Hyams, Firewatcher, Hull
James Hyams, C39
Joseph Hyams, C34
Section Officer Joseph Edward Hyams, Stoke Newington, commended
 for work in Coventry and Birmingham (JC 5/1/45, p.5)
Kate Hyams, Southgate
Michael 'Mick' Hyams, C30, Sub Officer (see Short Stories)
Myer Hyams, Stoke Newington
Mr P. Hyams, Leeds
William Hyams, B67
George Lawrence Hyman, E80
Israel Hyman, Edgware Road
Ivan Hyman, E88
John Hyman, Lauriston Road
Joseph William Hyman, E80
Louis Hyman, New Cross
Mark Hyman, fire engine driver in London Blitz
Morris Hyman, Kingsland
Reginald Hyman, Hammersmith
Mr P. Hymans, AFS Leeds

Isaac Ikin, C34
Alfred Imhof, Euston
Vera Instone, New Cross
Station Officer Miss Isaacs, known to Ruth Carne (above), first name
 unknown
Albert Edward Isaacs, B66
Asher Isaacs, C34
Barnett Isaacs, Millwall
Benjamin Isaacs aka Lakumsky, Stoke Newington
Daniel Isaacs aka H. Gallett, Stoke Newington
Daniel W. Isaacs, C39
Dave Isaacs, Soho
Ms E. Isaacs

Edward Isaacs, HQ
Ernest Isaacs, Soho
Florence Isaacs, Wandsworth
Ms G.D. Isaacs, Wandsworth
George Isaacs, Belsize
Head Fireguard H. Isaacs, Stepney (?)
Harold Charles Isaacs, F60
Harry Isaacs, A2
Harry Isaacs, Southwark
Jacob Isaacs, Redcross Street
John Isaacs, Bishopsgate
John Isaacs, Shoreditch
John Isaacs, Wandsworth
John Isaacs, Islington
John Sydney Isaacs, E88
Joseph Isaacs, Stoke Newington
Joseph Isaacs, C36
Joseph Isaacs, Bishopsgate
Leon Isaacs, Kingsland
Leslie Isaacs, Wandsworth
Mr M. Isaacs, Leeds/Harrogate
Michael Isaacs, Cannon Street, formerly ARP
Michael Angel Isaacs, Belsize
Noah Isaacs, South Tottenham
Phyllis Isaacs, Brixton
Renee Isaacs, Shoreditch
Robert S. Isaacs, Shadwell
S. Isaacs, B62
Sadie Isaacs, Whitechapel
Leading Fireman Samuel Isaacs, Heckford Street Station, Stepney
Barnett Harry Isaacson, Liverpool
Sub Officer Henry.G. Isaacson, D52
Lucy Isaacson
Stella Isaacson, Bow
Lawrence Isaaman, Shadwell
Mark Isaaman, Stoke Newington
Solomon Isbitsky (B24633??), Millwall, WIA twice, in eyes, at Millwall Dock
Sadie Isbitsky aka Joel, Kentish Town
Leonard Isenberg, Stoke Newington
Beatie Israel, Whitechapel
Jacob Israel, Kingsland
Lesley Israel, Finchley, brother of Sydney (below)

Robert Israel, Shadwell
Sydney Israel, pump operator, Finchley, uncle of Jeffrey Rose AFS
Woolf Israel, C28
Albert Itzinger, Dockhead
George Izenman, C24
Harry Izenman, Whitechapel
Louis Izenman, C34

Lou Jackson, Firewatcher, Ilford
Walter Jackson, Glasgow
Eileen Jacob, Streatham
Harry Jacob, Liverpool
Howard Jacob, Belsize
Sydney Norman Jacob, A34
Hilda Jacobovitch, C34
Abraham Alfred Jacobs, Northwold Road
Alex Jacobs, Millwall
Alexis Jacobs, E90
Alfred Jacobs, St 'B'
Alice Jacobs, Brompton
Arnold Jacobs, C22
Arthur Jacobs, Stoke Newington
Barnet Jacobs, C39
Bernard Jacobs, West Hampstead
Bernard Jacobs, Whitechapel
Bernard Jacobs, Red Lion Square
Bertram Jacobs, Soho
Charles Isaac Jacobs, D40
Coleman Jacobs, Kentish Town
David Jacobs, C28
David Jacobs, D44
Edward Jacobs, C38
Edward Ernest Jacobs, B76, WIA
Edwin Charles Jacobs, D54
Ella Jacobs, B73
Elliot Jacobs, Edgware Road
Elwa Jacobs, A8
Eric Jacobs aka Young, B66
Evelyn Jacobs, Soho
Frank Jacobs, Invicta Road
Frederick Jacobs, Mina Road
Frederick W. Jacobs, F60
George Jacobs, Southwark

George Jacobs, A9
Harold Jacobs, Camden Town
Henry Jacobs, Plumstead
Herbert Jacobs, Shooters Hill
Hyman Jacobs, 'C'
Jack Jacobs, Burdett Road
Jack Jacobs, C30
Jacob (John) Jacobs, Blackfriars
James A Jacobs, B62
John Jacobs, 'C'
John Jacobs, C30
John Jacobs, Bow (i)
John Jacobs, Bow (ii)
John Jacobs, Holloway
John Jacobs, Brunswick Road
John W. Jacobs, C24
Joseph Jacobs, 'C'
Judah Jacobs, C28
L. Jacobs, New Cross
Laurie Jacobs, C28
Lily Jacobs, Hendon
Louis Jacobs, Millwall
Louis Jacobs, Bethnal Green
Student Rabbi Louis Jacobs, Firewatcher, Manchester (many of the Manchester Yeshiva students were apparently Firewatchers according to Jacobs and Turetsky – see below).
Mrs Margaret 'Peggy' Sara Jacobs, West Hampstead, BEM for services to Fire Brigade (*LG* 1/1/65), NFS driver 1939–45, Senior Woman AFS Officer in London Fire Brigade, Assistant Group Officer in charge training of women, 1953, Lambeth HQ, 1950–68 (husband Lt Bernard Jacobs KIA Alamein)
Mark Jacobs, C60
Maurice Jacobs, West Hampstead
Michael Jacobs, Enfield
Michael Jacobs, Peckham Road
Michael Jacobs, Southwark
Miriam Jacobs, C36
Morris Jacobs, Homerton
Morris Jacobs, Brunswick Road
Nathan Jacobs, B66
Newman Jacobs, B60
Ms P. Jacobs/Cohen, C28
Philip Jacobs, Bow

Philip Jacobs, St A2, joined in 1938 and 'called up' to Manchester Square station on 1/8/39; he later became 1250062/25058 Fl. Sgt/Sqdn Leader 88 Sqdn Bomber Command RAF and was shot down and became a POW in July 1942. His extensive archive about his POW experience is at the Mass Observation Special Collection at Sussex University.
Mr R.H. Jacobs, Leeds
Ms Ray Jacobs, Ilford
Reginald Jacobs, Islington
Ronald Jacobs, Streatham
Rose Jacobs, Hendon
Ms S.J. Jacobs, Finchley
Samuel Jacobs, Stoke Newington
Seymour Sydney Jacobs, E85, WIA
Sidney Israel Jacobs, Liverpool
Sidney Jacobs, Perry Vale
Sidney Jacobs, Wolverley Street
Simon Jacobs, Burdett Road
Solly Jacobs, C28
Solomon Jacobs, Stoke Newington
Thomas Jacobs, East Greenwich
William Jacobs, St 'E'
Adele Jacobson, B72
Albert Jacobson, Brompton
Alfred Jacobson, West Hampstead
Barnett Jacobson, C28
Cecil Jacobson, Kensington
Daniel Jacobson, St 85
Lily/Lillian Jacobson, Edgware
Louis Jacobson, Westminster
Marcus Jacobson, Woolwich
Morris Jacobson, Firewatcher, Belfast
Myer Jacobson, Lee Green
Myer Jacobson, Shadwell
Nathan Jacobson, Clapton
Sidney Jacobson, C34
Louis Jacoby, C28
David Jacques, Bishopsgate
Thomas Jacques, North Kensington
Leslie Jaeger, Battersea
Morris Myer Jaeger, East Greenwich
Eric Jaffa, Middlesbrough NFS
Ms J. Jaffa, C38

Rabbi Maurice A. Jaffe, Firewatcher, severely burned, January 1941, Manchester (JC, 10/1/41, p.12); later a Jewish Army Chaplain to the Forces in the Second World War
Charles Jaffee, A12
Joseph Jaffee, Homerton
Fireguard L. Jaffee, Stepney
Leonard Jager, Battersea
Nathan Jager, Whitechapel
Walter Jager, Dockhead
J. Jakobs, Camden Town
Harry Jameson, Firewatcher, Wembley
Oscar Janke, Wandsworth
Sidney Janke, HQ
Raymond Japhet, Perry Vale
P. Jappell, Shadwell
Sydney Jaque, River Fire Service, WIA
Leon Jaques, Brompton
Maude Jaques, B62 – TBC
Sidney Jay, Soho
Henry Jesberg, C35, WIA
George Jessel, B25
Barnett Joel, Southwark
Charles Joel, C28
John Joel, Hammersmith
Edward Jofeh, Manchester Square
Harold Jolowicz, Manchester Square
Daniel Jonas, Shadwell
Lewis Abraham Jonas, Bishopsgate
Sydney Jonas, Stoke Newington
Jehudah Jonkler, Whitechapel
Abraham Joseph, Kingsland
Arthur Wolfe Joseph, Birmingham, stationed Coventry Road, Smallheath
Augustus Joseph, C30
Barney Joseph, Newport Road, Cardiff, formerly a Reserve Policeman
Caroline Joseph, Shadwell
Colman (Carl) Joseph(s), Millwall
Daniel Joseph, Burdett Road
Edward Joseph, Penge
Harry Joseph, E85
Hyman Joseph, Shadwell
Isaac Joseph, C28
Jack Joseph, Bethnal Green (i)

Jack Joseph, Bethnal Green (ii)
Joseph Gerald Joseph, C23
Joshua Joseph, Burdett Road
Julius Joseph, Cannon Street
Lesley Edward Joseph, Wembley district
Leslie Joseph, Islington
Levi Joseph, Norwood
Louis Joseph, Whitechapel
Louis Joseph, Millwall
Mark Joseph, Westminster
Mark Morris Joseph, St 2
Maurice Joseph, A11
Morris Joseph, C30
Morris Joseph, C36
Morris Joseph, Bishopsgate
Moss Joseph, Bishopsgate
Nina Joseph, Clerkenwell
Samuel Joseph, River Service
Samuel Joseph, Liverpool
Sidney Joseph, Kingsland
Sydney Joseph, Bishopsgate
Victor Joseph, B72
Percy Josephs, Burdett Road
Polly Julius, Brunswick Road

Barnett Kaczka, Islington, WIA
Stanley Israel Kaddes, Lambeth
Station Officer Basil Kahn, 1931–48, to Norfolk Fire Brigade
Dorothy Kahn, HQ
Joseph Kahn, born Tottenham, WIA as Fireman, served against Franco
    in Spanish Civil War, died 2010
Annie Kaizer, Soho
Mille Leah Kaizer, Whitefriars
Mark Kalikman, New Cross
Louis 'Leslie' Kalisky, C34, 1939–47, Shadwell/Addlestone (Surrey),
    served RAF 1941 but recalled to fire service
Harry Samuel Kallmeier, Westminster
Sidney Kalms, C28
Harry Kamaurice, Whitechapel, later to Army 'Desert Rats'
Leonard Kamm, Euston
Alexander Kammer, Clapton
Joseph Kamovitch, Stoke Newington
Hyman Kanarienvogel, Whitechapel

Reuben Kanter/Kantrowitz, Covent Garden/Odhams Press
Charles Kapinski aka Kaye, Shooters Hill
Jack Kapinski, Shooters Hill
Benjamin Kapinsky/Kapinski aka Kaye, D44, Shooters Hill
Edward Kaplan, A2
Gerald Kaplan, Stoke Newington
Raphael Kaplan, Homerton
Samuel Kaplan, A20
J. Kappel
Jacob Karbel, Clerkenwell, WIA
Morris Karchick, C38
Harry Karet, Stamford Hill
Rose Karet, Stoke Newington
Alec Karger/Zalic Carriger, Bow
Simon Karlatsky, Whitefriars
Augustus Karlo, Bethnal Green
David Karmel, B63
S. Karminsky, SE5
Doris Karn, West Norwood
Harry Karn, Lee Green
Sidney Karn, Lee Green
Ivan Karno, Burdett Road
Goodman Karp, Bethnal Green
Joe Karvitz, Brunswick Road
Max Kashdan, Whitechapel
Herman (Harry) Kasherman (Kaye), Firewatcher, later Fireman, later REME
Henry Kasket, Euston
Joseph Kaslaukas, Shadwell
Sam Kasminsky, Lewisham
Woolf Kassovitch, C28
John Kastenbauer, Isabella Road
Firewoman Betty Katanka, Liverpool
Arnold Kattel, Stoke Newington
Harry Kattner, B75
Bernard Katz, Stoke Newington
Betty Katz, Stoke Newington
Harry Katz, Whitechapel
Joseph Katz, St 86, 7/38 to 8/41
Louis Katz, Shadwell
Nathan Katz, C39, WIA
Reuben Katz, C23
Robert Katz, Camden Town

Sidney Katz, C34
Solomon Katz, C28
Harry Katzovsky, Stoke Newington
Abie Kaufman, Islington
Albert Kaufman, Knightsbridge
D. Kauffman, NW10
Reuben Kauffman, C38
Samuel Phillip Kauffman, E80
Eric Kaufman, 190308, St Dunstans, Golders Green 1938–43; Pinner 1943–45, German Refugee
Godfrey Kaufman, Blackfriars
Harry Kaufman, Fulham, WIA
Nathaniel Kaufman aka Martin, C66, then to Army
Izzy (George) Kaufman, B25171, Station C28, Fairclough Street, twice WIA; see LMA FB WAR/1/181 – chest injury following a collision
Sub Officer William H. Kaufman, B63, WIA
Bernard Kay, North Kensington
Harold Kay, Knightsbridge
Henry Kay, Knightsbridge
Jack Kay, Camden
Julius Kay, Blackfriars
Myer Kay, B66
Harry Kaye, Redcross Street
Hyman Kaye, C28
Leslie Kaye, Souhwark
Louis Kaye, Stoke Newington
Michael Samuel Kaye, C23
Reuben Kaye aka Kodiesh, Beckenham
Simon Kaye, Shoreditch
Solly Kaye, B74
Sydney Kaye, Shoreditch
Frank Kehl, A8
Chaim Keiner, Firewatcher, Stepney, WIA Commercial Road/Cavell Street
Isaac Keizer, Bethnal Green
Sidney Kelner, St 23
Lottie Kempster, Manchester Square – TBC
Henry Keppler, Old Kent Road
Mrs Evelyn (Eve) Kerbel, C23, wife of Joseph
Joseph Kerbel, taxi driver/fire engine driver, Docks, Hackney, Willesden
Hyman Kerbel, Homerton
Louis Kerman, Fulham/Westminster
Louisa Kerman, 58R

Anna Kern, Hammersmith
Ernest Kern, Hammersmith
Nathan Kern, Cannon Street
Mary Kerner, Epsom
Joseph Kershinbaum, Homerton
Alfred Kerstein, A7
Gertrude Kerstein, Stoke Newington
Marks Kerstein, Whitechapel
Henry Kerstin, Edgware Road
Louis Kesner, Whitechapel
David Kessler, Blackfriars
William Kessler, Battersea
Harry Kesten(baum), London
Israel Ketchenoff aka Sidney Kitchen, Blackfriars
Harold Kevin, Whitechapel
Hyman Kevin, Fulham
Sidney Keye, Kingsland
Simon Keye, Whitechapel
Philip Kifenstein/Kivenstein, Edgware Road
Max Kilner, Burdett Road
Sub Officer Theodore Kimche, A20, Alien
Benjamin King, Liverpool
Isaac George Kinsky, C28
Mark Woolf Kintzler, Shooters Hill
Sub Officer Albert Kircher, previously RW Surreys, served FB 1919–
   43 – TBC
Morris Kirkelwitch/vitch, Shadwell
H. Kirsch, Florence Road, Northampton
David Kirschenbaum, Whitechapel
William Kirschner, Brunswick Road
Bernard Kirstein, C22
Sidney Kirstein, C38
Hymie Kisner, Burdett Road
Alex Kistenmacher, Cannon Street
P. Kiverstein, Elgin Avenue, W9
Jules Louis Klass, Liverpool
Maurice Klass, Redcross Street
Philip Klass/Glass, City 1939–46, 35 Area HQ, lived Clapton
Frederick Kleeman, A9
David Klein, C39
David Klein, Stoke Newington
George Klein, Lee Green
Igor Klein, Lee Green

Sidney Klein, Kingsbury, later to Army
Moshe Kleinberg, Whitefriars
Nathan Kleiner, C36
J. Kleinman, Firewatcher, Stoke Newington
Reuben Kleinovitch, Whitechapel
Jack Klensberg, D52
Rachel Kligerman, Shadwell
Albert Kliman, C28
Jack Zeal Kliman, Liverpool
Leslie Kliman, Kingsland
Elie Klinghoffer, F60
Isidore Klinghoffer, Woolwich
Goodman Klingo, Burdett Road
Lewis Klofacz, Clapham
Eva Hedwig Klopstock, now Evans, 896959 Lightfoot Lane, Preston HQ, German refugee living in Barrow-in-Furness
Joseph Klyne, Mobile, Manchester
Doris Kneuss, Fulham – TBC
Ernest Knopp, Bethnal Green
Coy. Officer Alfred Koch, Stepney, C28, later to RAF air crew
Alfred George Koch, FB 1933–48, previously Mercantile Marine
Israel Kochinsky, C38
Jacob Kodesh, HQ
Morris Koenick, A12
Gershon Koenigsberg, Manchester Square
Cecil Koffman, Stoke Newington, WIA
William Kogel, Burdett Road
Lazarus Kohen, C39
Irene Kohn/Parker ??
Mark Kolanier/Kolanizer, C28
Frereick Harold Kolb, Liverpool
Lewis Kolsky/Carlton, Clerkenwell
Benjamin Koltinsky, C34
Lois Konantz, Edgware Road
Ronald Konski, Edgware Road
Isaac Konskier, Shadwell
Sam Konyn, HQ and St 28
Barnet Koplovitch, East Greenwich
Henry Kopp, Peckham
Bernard Korman, Whitechapel
F. Korn, AFS Leeds
Jack Jacob Korn, Southgate
Lazarus Korn, C23

Victor Korner, E88
Maurice Kosberg, C28
Barnett (Bert) Kosky, C37
Harry Kosky, C30
Harry Kosky, Shoreditch
Henry Kosky, Shoreditch
Israel Kosky aka Kingsley, C35 (B16100??), WIA in hand, Marylebone Street, Stratford
Maurice Kosky, Brunswick Road
Nathan Kosky, Stoke Newington
Pizer Kosky, C28
Jacob Kosrovitsky, Fulham
Alec Kossoff, C37
Elizabeth Kossoff/Kennedy, C39
George Koster, Stoke Newington
Deputy Commander Jane Koster, District Officer, A13
Morris Ivan Koubel, C28
Ichiel Kovler, Bishopsgate, aka Julian Kovler
Phillip Kozinsky, Edgware
Harry Kramer, Stoke Newington
Hyman Kramer, B73
Isaac Kramer, Shadwell
Israel Kramsky, South Wales, also a miner and steelworker
P. Kransky, Atherton Road, E7
Frederick Kranz, Holloway
Ernest Kratz, HQ
Harry Kratz, Westminster
Trevor Krauhaus, Woolwich
Kenneth Krauhaus, Woolwich
Hyman Kravitz, C23
Gerald Krejzl, Euston
Miss Johanna Krekmeyer, TBC
Joseph Kremel, Shadwell
Arthur Kremer, West Hampstead
Bernard Kremer, North Kensington
Firewoman Elsie Krengel, Liverpool
Theodore Kressman, Streatham
Alan Krett, C34
Douglas Kreutzer, Liverpool
Samson Krimgoltz, Shadwell
Alexander Krisman, Shadwell
Jack Noah Krisman, Moon's Garage in Cricklewood Broadway
Nathan Kritz, C39

Albert Krogolski, Kingsland
Adelbert Herman Krogulski, C36?
Montague Kroll, Homerton
Alfrd Kromer, Euston
Sam Kronengold, Stoke Newington
Nathan Krongold, C28
Miss Nita Krotosky later Greene, Cardiff AFS
Albert Kruger, Cherry Garden
Millie Krupka, HQ – TBC
Philip 'Philly' Kruyer, served Millwall and Bristol, son of Louis and
    Milly Kruyer of Hackney (cousin of the author)
Abraham Krystal, Kingsland
Otto Kubie, Firewatcher, Glasgow, interned German refugee
**Herman Frederick Kubsch, Ldg Fireman, Croydon AFS, Commended
    for Brave Conduct (*LG* 29/4/41), TBC if Jewish**
Walter Kuch, Shadwell
George Kugele, North Kensington
Frederick Kuhn, North kensington
Nathan Kunick, C22
Maurice Kunz, Dulwich
Thomas Kupferoth, Homerton
Lillian Kupers, Camden Town – TBC
Sub Officer Joseph Kupperblatt, F61, served 1939–64
Hyman Kurasch, Whitechapel
Joseph Kurlaer/George Kurlander, Westminster College Street, WIA
Lazarus Solomon Kurlander, Bethnal Green
Harry Kurtz, E85
Deputy Senior. Fireguard L. Kurtz, Stepney
Felix Kurstow, Southwark
Eric Kury, West Norwood
David Kutner, West Hampstead
Maurice Kutner, B62
Stefan Kuttner, Firewatcher, London, Austrian refugee
Alfred Kyte, Euston
Ernest Kyte, Euston

Barnett Labofsky, C28
Ms B. Labovich, AFS Firewoman, Leeds
Albert Reinhold Lachner, Edgware Road
Jack Lakumsky, later Lacey, Firewatcher, Hackney (brother of
    Benjamin)
Benjamin Lakumsky-Isaacs, later Lakum, C39, Stamford Hill
Bernard Lampert, C28

Saul Lampert, Homerton
Maurice Lan, Burdett Road
Montague Land, Whitechapel
Aaron Landau, C36
Barnett Landau, C28
Bernard Landau, Homerton
Bernard Landau, C28
Ernest A. Landau, A7
Gustave Landau, A9
Jack Landau, C28
Maria Landau, Manchester Square
Noel Landau BEM, Commandant, Bootle AFS and Liverpool NFS, 'for bravery and unyielding devotion to duty, obeying all commands in the most nerve testing circumstances ... although he knew there would be a second explosion, he attended to the removal of the dead and wounded to hospital in improvised ambulances' (when an ammunition ship – SS Malakand – was bombed May 1941, Liverpool Docks) (*LG* 19/12/41). Son of Oscar Landau of the Shanghai Jewish Community.
Ronald Landau, Hammersmith
Sydney Landau, West Hampstead
Theresa Landau, North Kensington
Leon Landaw, Hammersmith
Cecil Landeau, A5
Arthur William Lander, served FB 1920–48, formerly RA
Harry Sidney Lander, C28
Maud Lander, Manchester Square
Sidney Lander, Streatham
John Landers, Invicta Road
Aaron Harry Landesberg, C39
Ernest Landsberg, H1, Ilford
Lister Landsberg, Edgware Road
David (H.?) Landrofsky/Landosky aka Harris, B7471, C24, WIA when burnt on legs at Hungerford Road School
Albert Lane, C28
Harry Lane, C28
Phillip Lane aka Levinson/Levinberg, London/Luton/Coventry
Jack Lang, C28
Reuben Lang
Samuel Lang – three brothers from Hull
Louis Langdon, Bethnal Green
Walter Langdon, C28
Joseph Langleben, C28

Samuel Langleben, 'C'
Danny Langley aka Riginsky(?), Manchester
Julius Langley, Manchester
Miss Hannah Langsman, later Hoffman, West End
Morris 'Mick' Larn
Henry Laskey, B72
Ivy Laskey, Brixton
Mr Laskie, Mobile, Manchester
Harry Lassman, Shadwell
Sheila Latner, Enfield
Sheila Latuske, Dockhead – TBC
Jack Lawrence, Burdett Road
Sid Lawrence, Kingsland, band-leader, information from Hilary Vogler
   via Harry Harold Barnett
Simon Lawrence, C28
Roger Lazar, Belsize
Samuel Lazarovitch, C28
Leading Fireman Lazarus, Stepney
Charles Lazarus, B73
Daisy Lazarus, West Hampstead
Doris Lazarus, Bethnal Green
Miss Doris Lazarus, later Nayman, Firewatcher, East End
Edith Lazarus, Manchester Square
Deputy Fireguard F.G. Lazarus, Stepney (?)
Harry Lazarus, Holloway
Harry Lazarus, Euston
Henry Lazarus (M.M.), C28
Jack Lazarus, St 28
Joseph Lazarus, Shoreditch
Deputy Senior Fireguard Mrs K. Lazarus, Stepney (wife of Jack above)
Michael Lazarus, Edgware Road
Nathan Lazarus, Bethnal Green
Philip Lazarus, 1HQ
Phineas Lazarus, Kingsland
Samuel Lazarus, C28
Simon aka Chanaka Lazarus, Millwall
Joseph Lazinsky, C28
Lily Lazinsky, Shadwell
Harry Leader, St 54
Jacob Leaf, Euston
Nathan Leaf, West Norwood
Winifred Leaf, Southgate
Edna May Leaman, Harrow

Diana Leapman, later Benjamin, became LFB PT Instructor for women
Harry Leaver, Cannon Street
Henry Leaver, C30
Barnett Lebovitch, C28
Nathan Lebozur, Redcross Street
Lebowitz, Stratford
Louis Lebus, Manchester Square
Felix Lederer ??
Ronald Lederman, C28
Sidney Lederman, Shooters Hill
Benny Lee, St 90
Bessie Lee, Bishopsgate
Lewis Lee, Millwall
Jack Leewarden, C28
Isidore Disraeli Leffel, Kingsland
Barnet Lefkovitch, A3
Edie Lefkovitch, Whitechapel
Kolman Lefkovitch, C28
Marx Lefkovitch, C28
Matthew Lefkovitch, Shadwell
Alfred Erasmus, Leftwich F1
Ellen Leftwich, Bethnal Green
George Leftwich, Bethnal Green
Sidney Leftwich, E80
Bertha Lehmann, Edgware Road
Betty Lehmann, HQ
Frank Lehmann, Battersea
Sub Officer Harry Leibu, D55
Edward Leigh aka Morris Levy, West Hampstead
Hyman Leigh, C39, WIA
Maurice Leigh, Euston
Ralph Leiserach, Kensington
Albert Lemberger, St 30
Bernard Lempert, C28
Olive Leno, Hornsey
Reuben Leno, Kentish Town
Alfred L. Leon, E88
Louis Leopold, Bishopsgate
Arthur Lerner, Stoke Newington
David Lerner, Holloway
Jack Lerner, C36
Simeon Lesler, HQ
Leslie ('Aaron') Leslie, Tower Garage, Hendon, West and East End fires

Moss Leslie, West Hampstead
Moses Aaron Leslie, A20
Vivian Leslie, served 1920–48, formerly RA
Lionel Lesser, C39
Morris Lesser, Portsmouth
Mrs Beena Lessing
Nat Lessing, Highway, Wapping, husband of Beena
Leslie Lester, Bishopsgate
Nathan Lester, Kingsland
Murray Leton, A11
Maurice Letsky aka Lester, Millwall
Jessie Leuers, E85 – TBC
Dudley Maurice Leuw, Belsize
Solomon Levack, C28
Ldg Fireman Leslie Leveson, Brentford/Chiswick
Jack Morris Levey, C23
B. Levene, C28
Barnet Levene, Old Kent Road
Barnet Levene, Stoke Newington
Daniel Levene, A20
Harry Isidore Levene, Liverpool
Israel Levene, CTC
Joseph Levene, Lee Green
Joseph L. Levene, Soho
Marl Levene, Whitechapel
Philip Levene, C22
Rufus Levene, Woolwich
Victor Levene, Blackfriars
Zena Levene, E48
Mendel Levensohn, Liverpool
Albert Levenson, C30
Jack Levenstein, C38
Anne Lever, Manchester Square
George Reuben Hollander Lever, West Hampstead
Group Officer Ethel Leverson, HQ
Jane Leveson, A3
Marjorie Leveson, Westminster
Albert G. Levey, D56
Firewoman C.R. Levey, Typist, Leeds
Jack Levey, Homerton
Jack Levey, Liverpool
Mr D. Levi, AFS Leeds
Ernest Levi, A9

Hyman Levi, A6
Karl Levi, Blackfriars
Mr L.M. Levi, AFS Leeds
Miriam Levi
Elsie Levie, Clerkenwell
Ena Levicki/y, Hammersmith – TBC
David George Levin, E89
Joseph Levin, Stoke Newington
Mr A.H. Levine, AFS Leeds
Abraham Levine, Millwall
Daniel Levine, West Hampstead
Henry Levine, Tooting
Hyman Levine, Euston
John Levine, Cannon Street
Joseph Levene, Shadwell
Mr M. Levine, AFS Leeds
Myer Levine, Millwall
Nathan Levine, Homerton
Phoebe Levine, TC
Ms S. Levine, Leeds
Mr S. Levine, 381880, AFS Leeds
Samuel Levine, Burdett Road
Samuel Levine, C22
Samuel Levinger, C38
Ben Levinson, Nottingham
Jack Levinson, Stoke Newington
Morris Levinson, Stoke Newington
Morris Levinson, Homerton
William Levinson, Kingsland
Henry Levison, Walthamstow
Ms J. Levison, C30
Jacob Levison, Cannon Street, WIA
John Levison, West Hampstead
Celia Levitas, C34
Aaron Levy, C38
Abigail Levy, C28
Ms Abigail Levy, Wellclose Square Fire Station, Stepney
Abraham (Jack) Levy, Manchester
Albert Levy, New Cross
Albert Levy, Bethnal Green, played himself – aka 'Jacko' – in film *Fires were Started* 1943 (photo box 380.1 THLHL, *London Fireman*, Winter 1983)
Alf Levy, Penge

Alfred Levy, Walthamstow
Alfred Levy, Homerton
Anne Levy, despatch rider, Stepney
Arthur Levy, West Hampstead
Barnett Levy, Clapham
Barnett Levy, Bow
Basil Levy, Whitechapel
Bella Levy, Edgware Road
Ben Levy, Firewatcher at Itshide Rubber Company, Petersfield, Hants
Bernard Levy, Whitechapel
'Bobby' Levy, Redmans Road (*JC* 21/11/41)
Celia Levy, Euston
Charles Levy, C32
Charles Levy, Burdett Road
David Levy, C38
David Levy, Redcross Street
Ms E. Levy, Bethnal Green
Edward Levy, C24
Edward Levy, Brunswick Road
Elizabeth Levy, Brunswick Road
Emmanuel Levy, Whitechapel
George Arthur Levy, joined FB 1927, Shadwell/Southwark, to RAF 1943 and KIA 27/7/44
George M. Levy, A6
Harry Levy, Edmonton
Harry Levy, Stoke Newington
Harry Levy, Stoke Newington
Henry Levy, F60
Henry Levy, Southwark
Henry Levy, East Greenwich
Hyman Levy, C30
Hyman Levy, Shadwell
Mr I.H. Levy, AFS Leeds
Irene Levy, C28
Isidore Levy, (B16104??), C35, WIA in fingers, Millwall Dock
Israel Levy, C39
Mr J. Levy, Leeds
Jack 'Julius' Levy, badly burnt by an incendiary on duty at Coldharbour Lane, was a Navy and Army veteran of the First World War
John Levy, Stoke Newington
Joseph Levy, BEM, awarded whilst an Air Raid Warden but also a parttime Fireman, rescuing six people from a bombed and burning house in Fortune Green Road, Finchley (*The Times*, 15/2/41, *LG* February 1941). Medals at Jewish Military Museum.

Joshua Levy, C38
Joshua William Levy, B66, Sub Officer
Leon Barnett Levy, C36
Lew Levy, Shadwell
Lewis Levy, Whitechapel
Lewis Levy, Liverpool
Lindo Levy, Kensington
Lionel Levy, Homerton
Lucien Levy, Stoke Newington
Madeleine Levy-Marsden, Kensington
Mark Levy, Bow, died on active service
Mark Levy, Dockhead
Mark James A. Levy, F60
Maurice Levy, A2, to Act Sub St Officer LFB 28/11/40
Maurice Levy, Shadwell
Michael Levy, St 34
Miriam Levy, 'B'
Morris Levy, Shadwell
Sub Officer Morris Levy, Horseferry Road
Morris Elijah Levy, C23
Myer 'Mick' Levy, C22, Docklands, once pulled two men into a doorway during an air raid and one of them was Deputy (later Prime) Minster, Clement Atlee
Myer Levy, Stoke Newington
Myer Levy, PerryVale
Nathan Levy, C34
Nathaniel Levy, Bethnal Green
Pauline Levy, E90
Section Leader Percy Levy aka Gilbert, 1922–48, West Norwood, etc
Philip Levy, Kingsland
Philip Levy, Stoke Newington
Philip Levy, A9, died on active service
Philip Levy, Bishopsgate, WIA
Philip Levy, Liverpool
Ronald Levy, West Norwood
Rose Levy, Homerton
Miss Ruth Levy, later Crosby, Firewatcher, City of London
Samuel Levy, C39, WIA
Samuel Levy, Whitechapel, WIA
Stephen Levy, Blackfriars
Sydney Levy, Stoke Newington
William Levy, Kingsland
William Levy, Redcross Street
William D. Levy, B72

Woolf Levy, Holloway, died on active service
Woolf/Wolf Levy, C28
Woolfe Levy, C39
Woolfe Levy, Stoke Newington
Leonard Levy-Teesdale, Lambeth
Isaac Lewbitz, Millwall
Jack Lewin, Whitechapel
Mona Lewin, Euston – TBC
Alec Lewis, Whitechapel
Alec Lewis, West Hampstead
Barney Lewis, C36
David Lewis, North Kensington
David Lewis aka Pizer, Whitechapel, WIA
Dora Lewis, Shoreditch
Fay Lewis, C37
Harris Lewis, Manchester
Henry 'Harry' Lewis, Homerton
Jack Lewis, Manchester Square
Joseph A. Lewis, E86 – TBC
Launcelot Lewis aka Wartski, Shadwell
Louis Lewis, Whitechapel
Louis Leonard Lewis, 1HQ
Rose Lewis, Stoke Newington
Sydney Lewis, 'B'
Solly Lewis, Burdett Road
Solly Lewis, C22
Stephen Lewis, Stoke Newington
Herbert A. Lewisohn, A8
Samuel David Lewisman, C28
Katherine Lewkowitsch, West Hampstead
Phyllis Lewkowitsch, West Hampstead
Lewis Lewson, Bishopsgate
Gershon Liansky, Stratford/Stoke Newington
Adriana L'Heimer, South Kensington – TBC
Karl Heinz Libenau later Charles Leigh, Firewatcher, Brighton, later to Sussex Reg.
Eli Liberman, Euston
Max Liberman, Brompton
Solomon Libouzer, Bow
Joseph Libowitch, Bishopsgate, WIA
Libowitz, Stratford
Hilda Librach, Shoreditch
Sam Lichtienstien, C28

Sam Lieberman, Bishopsgate
Sam Solomon Lieberman/Liebman, St 28, Tyson Street, Manchester
Ralph Liermann, B68
Joseph Limberg, Stoke Newington
Lionel Limburg, West Hampstead, WIA
Fredman Ellis Lincoln, Blackfriars
John Linden, Edgware Road
Norah Linden/Lyndon ??
Norman Linden, Edgware Road
P.J. Linden/Lyndon, A5
Phyllis Linden, Hammersmith
Reuben Linder, Stoke Newington
Anna Linderman, Belsize
Mr B. or I. Lindley, AFS Leeds
Paul C. Lindo, A6
Emanuel Lion, A2
Alfred Lipman, A20
Barnett Lipman, Knightsbridge
David Lipman, C28, Truman Brewery area
Edward Herbert Lipman, C38
Joseph Lipman, Soho
H.W. Lipman, Stoke Newington
Morris Lipman, Stoke Newington
Firewoman Rita Lipman/Chadwick, (Finchley/Hendon)
William Lipman, Euston
Jack Jacob Lipschitz, C30, WIA
Israel Lipstein, Clapton
Lewis Lipstein, C28
Joel Meir Lipton, Homerton
Kenneth Lipton, Stoke Newington
Daniel Liptz, Brunswick Road
Samuel Liptz, Whitefriars
Edward Maurice Lisboa, Kensington
Kathleen Lisbona, B72
Barnet Lishner, Plumstead
Rosa Liss, Stoke Newington
Nathan Lissack, Brunswick Road
Jack Lissner, Stoke Newington
Joseph Lissner, Stoke Newington
Morris/Maurice Lissner, C39
Alfred Litman, Whitechapel
Hyman Litman ??
Arnold Littman, B67

Charles Littman, Southwark
John Littman, Southwark
Lazarus Litwin, Shadwell
Louis Litwin, Kingsland
Sidney Lobatto, Edgware Road
Edward Lockspeiser, Belsize – TBC
Ivan Lodic, Bishopsgate (Palestine Wine Coy.)
Leonard Loeber, Plumstead – TBC
Helen Loewenfeld/Leslie, Clapham
Jack Isidore Loft, Lee Green – TBC
Howard Loft, Bromley – TBC
Harold Lohr, Knightsbridge – TBC
Gertrude Lombard, A3 – TBC
Patricia Lombard, A3 – TBC
Lew Lonis, Whitechapel
William Lorberg, Wandsworth
Harry Loshak, Cannon Street – TBC
Bella Losner, North Kensington
Samuel Lotheim, Tooting
Lillian Lotinga, West Hampstead
Queenie Lotinga, Edgware Road
J. Loubell, NW10 – TBC
Ernest Louis, A11
George Louis, A7
William Loupa, Bishopsgate
Bernard Lovick, Cannon Street
Betty Lubart, C34
Miss Ray 'Rae' Lubart, C34, later married Fireman Louis Fieldman
Abe Lubin, Bow
Deborah Lucas, Streatham
Freda Lucas, North Kensington
Gertrude Lucas, B66
Leila Lucas, Edgware Road
Joe Ludaman, Northwold Road, Stoke Newington
Joseph Ludaman, Kingsland
Doris Ludeman, Wimbledon
Bernard Ludwig, C38
Jack Ludwin, C38
Alf Luhman, Redcross Street
Lelsie Luhr, Soho, WIA
Morris Samuel Lustig, survived the direct hit in Shanklin which killed
    David Cohen and Harry Glantzpegel, attended fire at Mount
    Pleasant sorting office, Holborn, when fire burnt for five days

Barnett Lutovitch, C22
Abe Lutsky ??
Rebecca Lutsky, Whitechapel
Henry Lutz, Manchester Square
Louis Lux, Burdett Road
Lucien 'Bobby' Luz aka Lewis, Firewatcher/ARP messenger
Charlotte Lyon, TBC ??
Mark Lyon, Shoreditch
Mark Lyon, C37
Roma Lyon, C28
Alison Lyons, Manchester Square
Cicley Lyons/Dennis, West Hampstead
Gladys Lyons, West Hampstead – TBC
Harry Lyons, C28
Henry Lyons, Burdett Road
Henry Lyons, C22
Henry Lyons, Shadwell
Henry Hyman Lyons, Stoke Newington
Hyman Lyons, North Kensington
Hyman Lyons, Stoke Newington
Jack Lyons, C28
Jack Lyons, Whitechapel
Joseph Lyons, Shoreditch
Joseph Lyons, C34
Section Leader Leslie Louis Lyons, C38, served 1926–48
Ms Louie Lyons, 'W'
Michael Lyons, C36
Morris Lyons, B72
Muriel Lyons, C34
Sydney Lyons, A11
Sydney Lyons, Shadwell
Divisional Officer Walter Lyons, Hammersmith

Brigid Maas, Edgware Road
Joyce Macklin, C38
Catherine Fortuin/Madely, Holloway
Nison Mader, Clapton
Fireman Louis Madlin, of Bethnal Green- lost his eye in action in London
J. Maginsky, Liverpool
Ada Magnus, Battersea
John Magnus, Whitechapel
Nellie Garcia Magnus, Manchester Square
Philip Magnus, HQ
Ralph Magnus, Brunswick

Cyril Mahler, C38
Sam Mail, Glasgow
Julius Main, Kentish Town
Theresa Majer, Cannon Street – TBC
Udel Makofsky, Burdett Road
Margaret Makower, Shooters Hill
Nathan Malach, Brunswick Road
Alice Malin, West Ham
Beral David Malin/Malinski, Firewatcher, Shaftesbury Ave., Montpelier, Bristol, ASC veteran First World War
Betty Malina, C35
Laurie Malina, Docks/Bow
Solle Maliney, Shadwell
Bernard Stanley Malkin, B66
Florence Seger/Mallows, C22 – TBC
Brian Eugene Malschinger, A20
Marie Benita Henson/Malschinger, Belsize
Alfred Manches, Southwark
Emmanuel Manches, West Hampstead
Herbert Joshua Manches, Southwark, later founded Everest Double Glazing
Bernard Mandel, Lomond Grove, former Canadian Army
Mark Mandelberg, Chiswick
Emmanuel Manning, C34
Amos Manton, Lewisham
Hyman Marcovitch, C30
Joseph Marcovitch, Stoke Newington
Joseph Marcovitch, Shadwell
Michael Marcovitch, Shadwell
Nathan Marcovitch, Millwall
Nathan Marcovitch, Bethnal Green
Alf Marcus, C28
Alf Marcus, Whitechapel
Alf Marcus, Bow
Emmanuel Marcus, C39
Emmanuel Marcus, Stoke Newington
Freda Marcus, Whitechapel
Henry Marcus, Shoreditch
Madge Esther Marcus, A8
Nat Marcus, Cannon Street, WIA
Pearl Marcus, Stoke Newington
Abraham Margolis, Bishopsgate
Samuel Margolis, Whitefriars
Solly Margolis, C39

Alexander Markl, Shadwell
Alfred Markovitch aka Isaac aka Alf/Ivor Murray, C32, transferred to
 army fire service, who he testified were known as 'the jam labels'
 because of their colourful and distinct arm badges. From Catterick
 he was sent to Nijmegen at the time of Arnhem and then went on
 into Germany.
David Markovitch, C38
Harry Markovitch, CTC
Harry Markovitch, Hammersmith
Louis Markovitch, Bow
Marie Markovitch, Bow
Michael Markovitch, C38
Solomon Markovitch, Shoreditch
Dorothy Markowski, Brixton
Albert Marks, 40U
Albert Marks, A11
Albert Marks, C37/39 etc., served 1926–46, formerly RN
Alexander Marks, Bow
Alfred Marks, B68
Alfred G. Marks, D55
Alfred Marks, Millwall
Alfred J. Marks, Redcross Street
Archie Marks, Soho
Arthur Marks, 1HQ
Betty Marks, F61
Colin Marks, C88 etc., served 1939–48
D. Marks, Stratford
David Marks, Stoke Newington
David Marks, Westminster College
Davis Marks, Southwark
Dorothy Marks, Penge
E.J. Marks, Whitechapel
Edith Marks, Bethnal Green
Edwin Marks, Dulwich
Ernest S. Marks, B5226, C23, WIA right hand at Lathams Timber Yard,
 Clapton
Frank S. Marks, D46
Frederick Hyam Marks, St 84
G.A. Marks, Erith
Geoffrey N. Marks, A11
George Marks, Northwold Road
**H.A. Marks, of Tottenham, station 35, Commended for Bravery on
 23/24 April 1941 in Plymouth (LMA FB/WAR/1/181)**
Harry Marks, C30

Harry P. Marks, Cherry Garden
Harry R. Marks, Shadwell
Harry T. Marks, Deptford
Henry Marks, C28
Herman Marks, C38
Isidore Marks, Bow
J.F. Marks, 8RTP
Jack Marks, C22
Jacob Marks, Kingsland
James Marks, Old Kent Road
Joan Marks, C5
Joe Henry Marks, F60
John Henry Marks, C23
Joseph F. Marks, D40
Judith Marks later Shaw, NFS telephonist, Holdenhurst Road, Bournemouth
Leonard (Jonas) Marks, AFS and later Firewatcher, De Haviland aircraft works, Burnt Oak, London; also served in Scotland
Martin Marks, Blackfriars
Maurice Marks, Homerton
Maurice Marks, Manchester
Morris Marks, Bishopsgate
Nat Marks, Whitechapel
Percy Marks, served 1929–48, formerly RN
Raymond Marks, Bethnal Green to Northampton
Reginald Alfred Marks, aka Reuben Meyerovitch, North Kensington, Commended for Bravery (Vol.2 LCC War Diary London/*LG* 28/11/41)
Ronald Marks, HQ
Samuel Marks, Liverpool, Driver, badly injured by blast of a landmine at Piccadilly in Manchester and spent seven weeks in hospital; he kept the tassle of the landmine parachute that nearly killed him
Sidney Marks, C30
Simon Marks, Stoke Newington
Solomon Marks
Sydney Marks aka Martin, C39
William George Marks, E48
Sadie Markson, Edgware Road
Cyril Marock, Stoke Newington, TBC
Jacob Marock, Kentish Town, TBC
George Marsden-Levy ??
Harry Marshall, Clerkenwell
Louis Marshbaum, Burdett Road
Bernard/Barnett Alexander Martin/Osofsky, Stepney/Shadwell/Enfield

Joseph Martin, Chigwell, First World War Grenadier Guards veteran
Leslie Martin, brother of Bernard, as above
Samuel Martin, Stoke Newington
Enid Marx, Belsize
Edward Marx, Edgware Road
Lily Marx, Brompton
Bessie Maskin – TBC
Beatrice Maslin, Fulham
Sidney Massin, Belsize
Ronald Aaron Masters, Bishopsgate, WIA
Phyllis Matkin, HQ
Mervyn Matz, West Hampstead
Harold Mayer, Manchester Square
John Mayer, Millwall
Robert Mayer, Bethnal Green
Stanley Mayer, Shadwell
Thomas Mayer, Bethnal Green
Alfred Mayers, Millwall
Isaac Measure, Shadwell
Ruby Meddick, A11 – TBC
Harry Mednitsky aka Harris, Stoke Newington
Station Officer Murray/Moss Medway, Commercial Road
Simon Medwed, Homerton
Barnet Meisler, C23
Abraham Melamed, Stock Exchange station
Simon Melamed, Cannon Street
Cyril Melandovitch, Bishopsgate
Abraham Meltzer, Bow
Edward Meltzer, Stoke Newington
Lionel Meltzer, Stoke Newington
John Hyman Mendel, C22
Philip Mendel, C35
Marks Mendelsohn, Shadwell
Alfred Mendeson, Enfield
P. Mendelson, Southall
Leon Mendoza, A7
Michael Mendoza, Burdett Road
Emanuel Mercado, Whitechapel
Nathan Mercer, C22
Abraham Mermenstein, Blackfriars
George/Gasal Meropolsky, Shoreditch
Section Leader Hyman Mesnick/Masnick, Whitechapel/East Ham AFS, 1938–45
Carl Messenbrinck, Soho

Nathan Messer, Shadwell
Samuel Messer, A13
Alfred Messias, Euston
Benjamin Messias, East Greenwich
Samuel Messias, C28
Basil Messing, Fireguard, Barts Hospital, witnessed the burning of The
    Old Bailey, German refugee
Isaac Metchick, Bethnal Green
Ronald Meth, Bethnal Green
Simon Metselaar, C39
Lewis Metz, E2
George Metzler, Hammersmith
D.V. Meyer, SW9 – TBC
Joan Meyer, West Hampstead
Gladys Meyers/Beck ??
Mary Meyer, C32 –TBC
T.W. Meyer, Highbury – TBC
Dorothy Meyers, Wandsworth – TBC
Solle Michael, Clerkenwell
Mr Michaels, Fireguard, Stepney
Aaron Michaels, Shoreditch, WIA
David Michaels, Battersea
David Michaels, Whitechapel
Doris Michaels, Kingsland
Edith Michaels, Bethnal Green
Edward Solomon Michaels, Stoke Newington
Henry Michaels, B67
Henry P. Michaels ??
Ivy Michaels, Kingsland
Maurice Michaels, C32
Pizer Michaels, Millwall
Samuel Michaels, C22
Gerald Michaelson, A20
Isaac Michaelson, C39
Ronald Michaelson, West Hampstead
Sam F. Michaelson, A12, Deptford, later to RE
Section Officer Sidney Michaelson, West End Central/Manchester
    Square
Anthony Mifsud, Holloway
Lionel Milafsky, Shadwell
Bernard Milgrom, Cannon Street
Harold Milgrom, Knightsbridge
Golda Milgrome, B76

Morris Millanofsky aka Millan, Camden Town, a synagogue Beadle
Aaron Miller, C30
Abraham Miller, Euston
Abraham Miller, Brunswick Road
David Miller, Shadwell
Emmanuel Miller, Kentish Town
Golda Miller/Sorrin, Bishopsgate
Harris Miller, Westminster College
Harry Herman Miller, Brunswick Road
Isaac Miller, Millwall
Israel Miller, Euston
Jack Miller, Whitechapel
Jack Shier Miller, Clerkenwell
Lazarus Miller, Stoke Newington
Leslie Miller
Lewis Miller, Soho
Louis Miller, Whitechapel
Morris Miller, New Cross
Morris Miller, Cannon Street
Miss Phyllis Miller aka Peters, Barnet
Reuben Miller, Millwall
Sidney Miller, Homerton
Solomon Miller, Stoke Newington
Woolf Miller, Shadwell, WIA
Maurice Millet, Bishopsgate
Solomon Milner, Stoke Newington
Ruth Milstein, A20
Morris Minkin, Burdett Road
Ben Mintz, St 30
Hyman Miranda, C32
Firewoman Ms R. Mirman, Leeds
Zelda Miron, West Hampstead
Peter Mironoff, Wandsworth
Solly Misell, Stoke Newington
Austin Miskin, C28
Merton Mistovski, F1
Israel Mitelman, Shadwell
Heinrich Henry Mitlehmer, Kingsland, ARP
Philip Mitsmaker, Whitechapel
Ms S. Mitsmaker, C28
Harry Mitz aka Henry Mead, Millwall
Morris Mitzman, Bow
Harold Mizrah ??

Cyril Herbert Mocatta, St 8
Samuel Modelwich, North Kensington
Jack Modlin, Stoke Newimgton
Leslie Mohrman, West Hampstead
Emanuel Moizeck, Bow
Simon Molchansky aka Mole, Lambeth
Agnes Molen (sister of Evelyn)
David Molen, Whitechapel
Evelyn Molen, Firewatcher, Chelsea
Solomon Monharz, C38
Stanley Monitz, Soho
Myer Monkarz, Shooters Hill
Kleber Monod, HQ – TBC
Firewatcher Mary Monsby, Leeds
Frances Montagu-Pollock, Southwark – TBC
Max Montanjees aka Monty, Bethnal Green
David Monty, Burdett Road
Evelyn Moody/Cantor ??
Sydney Ben Moody, West Hampstead
Leading Fireman Louis Moont, Finchley, WIA
Cyril Moore, Sheffield
Leon Moore, Sheffield, brothers stationed at Division Street
Ben Moran, Leeds
Jimmy Moran, Leeds, brothers
Alfred Jacob Morris, Stoke Newington
Alec Morris, Clerkenwell
Bella Morris
Irene Morris, Whitechapel
Joseph Morris, Stoke Newington
Joseph Morris, Homerton
Lionel Morris, C28
Louis Morris, Whitechapel
Mark Morris, B75
Nat Morris, Bishopsgate, WIA twice
Nathan Morris, B67
Nathan Morris, Blackfriars
Nathaniel Morris, Soho
Phil Morris, Manchester
Samuel Morris, Firewatcher, London
Abraham Moscovitch, CTC
Alfred Moscovitch, Burdett Road
Barnett Moscovitch, Whitefriars
Barnett Moscovitch, Whitechapel

Abraham Moskovitz, Brunswick Road
Jack Moscow, C35
Joseph Moscow, Clerkenwell
Lewis Moscow, C34
Morris Moses aka Davis, CTC
Nancy Moses, A20
Barrington Nessim Moss, Soho
David Moss, Stoke Newington
Horace Moss, Bethnal Green
Jack Moss, C30
Leonard Moss, Lambeth
Michael Moss, Homerton
Sidney Moss, Bethnal Green
Sydney Moss ??
Leslie Mound, Firewatcher, Edgware, to RAF
Sub Officer Leah Mullem, Shoreditch
Hans Erich Muller, A11
Selina Munnickendam, Shoreditch
Inge Munro, Firewatcher, Empire Court, Wembley Park, German Refugee
Emmanuel Musaphia, Brunswick Road
Jeannette Musaphia, C23
Joseph Musaphia, Burdett Road
Jack Jospeh Mydat, Whitechapel
Alan Myers, Liverpool
Alfred Emmanuel Myers, Shadwell
Bessy Myers, Knightsbridge
David Myers, A12
Ella Myers, West Hampstead
H. Myers, Leeds – TBC
Hilda Myers, Kensington
Irene Myers, Euston
Isidore Myers, A20
Jack Myers aka Bentley, C38
Jessie Myers, Islington
Mr M. Myers, AFS Leeds – TBC
Manny Myers, Deptford
Marcus Myers, West Hampstead
Mark Myers, Lewisham
Millie Myers, Whitchapel
Muriel Myers, Manchester Square
Miss Ruth Myers
Sidney Simon Myers, West Hampstead

Solomon Myers, Stoke Newington
'Harry' Harris Myerson, Leeds – also served Hull, Liverpool and Swansea

Asst. St Officer Naal, St Dunstans, Golders Green (given by Eric Kauffman)
Felix J.N. Nabarro, Hendon, Company Officer
Andrew Nunes Nabarro, GM, Portsmouth (*JC* 2/5/41; *LG* 25/4/42 – see testimonies for citation)
Ben Nathan Nachemson, Belsize
Manuel Naddell, Glasgow
David Nadell, Shoreditch
Joseph Naden, Normand Road
Edward Naftali/Natali
Henry Nagelblatt, Camden Town
Michael Nagle, A12
Ernest Nagorsky, Euston
Lillian Nash/Goldstein, B72
Alfred Abraham Nathan, Red Lion Yard, WIA several times; invalided to clerical work 1945
Anita Nathan, Manchester Square
Annie Nathan, A20
Benjamin Nathan, Whitechapel
Edward Nathan, Shoreditch
Esta Nathan, C39
Ferolah Nathan, Kentish Town
Geoffrey Nathan, Lewisham
George Nathan, C28
Hannah Nathan, C22
Column Officer Harold Napier aka Hyman Nathan, Streatham
Henry Nathan, Stoke Newington
Jack Nathan, Whitechapel
Jacob Nathan, Stoke Newington
John Lewis Nathan, B66
Joseph Nathan, Kingsland
Kenneth Nathan, A20
Miss M.D. Nathan, Sub Officer, A2
Marcus Nathan, Burdett Road
Sub Officer Mary Nathan, Manchester Square
Millie Nathan, Edgware Road
Morris Nathan, C28
Nathan Nathan, Bethnal Green
Philip Nathan, Stoke Newington

Ronald Nathan, Lee Green
Sub Officer William Nathanson, Kensington, A8
David Nathoo, Shadwell – TBC
Andrew Nastri, Southwark – TBC
Mr I Nayman, Middlesborough NFS
Isaac Necklevitch, Homerton
Samuel Needle, Brusnwick Road
Ben Needleman, West Hampstead
Nathan Negin, B72, died in service
Ferdinand Daniel Nehmer aka Lloyd, Euston
Nathan Neidus, C28
Charles Neiman, Millwall
Morris Nemko, Bethnal Green
Bessie 'Betty' Nerden, formerly Cohen, Stratford and Canning Town
Sub Officer Stuart Neugass, A20
Maurice Joseph Newham, Dockhead
Arthur Newman, Kingsland
Harold Newman, Liverpool
Lionel Newman, A20
Cyril Newmark, Woolwich
Edward Newmark, Belsize
Leonard Newmark, B72
Israel Nicklesberg, Kingsland
Ernest Nickson, Liverpool
Nathan Nicolski aka Nicholas Nicholls, Millwall, WIA
Abraham Nieman, C28
Alfred Nieman, Wandsworth
William Nieman, 1HQ
Winston Nieman, HQ
Allan Niemeyer, Liverpool
Fay Nirenberg, Homerton
Isidore Nirenberg, Bethnal Green
Miss Norma Nissenthall, later Sanders, Firewatcher, East Ham and Gants Hill
Clare Noah, C22
Israel Meyer 'Math' Noble, West Kensington and Hampstead Garden Suburb, WIA
Sigmund Noble, Blackfriars
Ronald Nordhoff, Eltham
Alfred Abraham Nordman, Soho
Mick Nortman, Kingsland
Hyman Nossek, C28
Harold Nossick, Old Kent Road

Morris Novack, Shadwell
Nanette Novak, Finchley
Abraham Noverselsky, Kenninghall Road
Nathan Novitsky, Redcross Street
Nathan Novitsky, Stoke Newington
Fanny Novgorod, TC
Golda Novgorod, TC
Nathan Novgorod aka Harris ??
Alvin Nowack, Westminster – TBC
Andrew Nowack, Euston – TBC
Henry Nuhrenberg, Cherry Gardens – TBC
Michael Nunes, Bow
Eddie Nussbaum, Firewatcher at an engineering factory, London, whilst studying at university. Born in Hamburg he was on the Kindertransport to Britain and deported to Australia on the 'Dunera', returning in 1941 to Britain, to serve and study (Wiener Library).
Geoffrey Nuzum, Blackfriars – TBC
A.Nybaer, Belsize
Nathan Nykerk, Kingsland
John Nyman, Burdett Road
Lewis Nyman, Whitechapel
Manuel Nyman, C38
Morris Nyman, Bow
Miss Muriel Nyman, Lambeth, driver
Sam Nyman, Edgware Road
Sidney Nyman, Bow
Solomon Nyman, Bethnal Green

Simon Ososky/Osbourne, NFS 181864, City/St Paul's/River Fireboats, also a Union Rep; testified to intense anti-Jewish feeling among regular Firemen, especially as Jews began to get promotion
William Odenbreit, Old Kent Road – TBC
Albert Oehlrich, Cannon Street – TBC
Alfred Ohrenstein, Redcross Street
Willkiam Ohrenstein, Redcross Street
Isaac Okin, A20
Asher Oldschool, B63
Rosalie Oleska, Stoke Newington
Jack Oliver, Cricklewood and Docks, WIA
Harry Olman, Whitechapel
Leonard Olrich, Shadwell
Reuben Olsburgh, Ldg Fireman, Chapeltown Station, Leeds

Barney Ben Opas, Manchester Square, WIA
Samuel Opas, Clerkenwell
Ralph Opos, Shadwell
Georg Oppenheim, Firewatcher
Charles Oscar Oppenheimer, B73
Rebecca Oppenheimer, Manchester Square
William Opperman, Deptford
Sonia Oppos, C34
Harry Orchover, C22
David Orinsky, C28
Lewis Orinsky/Ormsby, St 28
Sub Officer Herbert Orlick/Orlisk, B68
Abraham Ornstein aka Horenstein, Shadwell
Mick Ornstein – Fratres newsletter
Sub Officer E.P. Ortweiler, B68
Eleanor Ortweiler, Kensington
Lewis Osler, Tooting
Barnett Ososky aka Bernard Alex Martin, Enfield
Leonard Oster, Bow
George Osterman, C34
Leonard Osterman, Stoke Newington
Charles Ostermeyer, Millwall
Harry Osterweil, Streatham
Jacob Ostrin, Liverpool
Raphael Ostrovsky, Burdett Road
Morris Otelsberg, Burdett Road
Solomon Ottolangui, Brunswick Road
Maurice Ouvronssoff, St 12
Kenneth Michael Overman aka Kurt Oppenheimer, Firewatcher trained by AFS, at North Kensington St Mark's Hostel, 1940–43, later Tank Corps, came over on Kindertransport. He says there were many Jewish refugees with him at the Hostel working as Firewatchers.
Lenn Ozin, Shadwell

Max Pacter, Southwark
Adolph Pallats, E85
Eric Palmer, Hull, Fire Engine driver
Harry Panther, Bow – TBC
Lucette Papier, Holloway
Michael Papier, Brunswick Road
Louis Paratsky/Paretsky aka Parry/Perry, Tyson Street, Manchester
Sidney Paratsky/Perry, post war Army Fire Service, son of Louis above

Joseph Park, Whitefriars
Lazarus Park, Whitechapel
Benjamin Lewis Parker, Whitechapel
E.J. Parker, Shadwell
Judah Parris, West Hampstead
Oscar Paschill, Beckenham – TBC
Hannah Pask, HQ – TBC
Harry Paskin, North Kensington
Dorothy Passow, Streatham
Ethel Passow, Streatham
Freda Passow, Streatham
Ashley Pater, Hendon
Louis Nathan Pater, Hendon/Stoke Newington
Sam Pater, Hendon, three brothers
Sidney Pather, Homerton
Alfred Joseph Pearl, D54
Miss Hazel Fay Pearl, Cricklewood, Moon's Garage, also in Red Cross
Marjorie Pearl, Firewatcher
Reuben Pearl, C30
Ruth Pearl, Firewatcher, sister of Marjorie
Sam Pearson, Sheffield
Rudolf Peierls, AFS Birmingham, German refugee
Peltz, Wood Green
Frederick Pennamacoor, Euston
Norman Penstone, Homerton – TBC
Leonard Penstone, Stoke Newington – TBC
Myer Pentol, Shadwell
Philip Pentol, Shadwell
Reiben Pentol, Homerton
Joseph Pepperberg, Kingsland
Michel Peretz, pharmacist, Firewatcher in West End before becoming
    Major in Royal Marines, and awarded MBE military in 1944
Woolf Perkof(f), Cannon Street
Arthur Perle, B75
Roy Perllman, Streatham
Samuel Perlman, Kingsland
Arnold Perlmutter, later Phillips, Firewatcher, served in Palmach in
    Israel 1930s and UK Army after Fire Service
May Perovich, Peckham
George Frederick Perschky, C38
Philip Pershke, Lewisham
Samuel Persoff, C34
Myer Pessell, New Cross

Joseph Petruckevitch, C22
Jack Peston, Firewatcher, Dalston
Harry Lewis Peterman, Kingsland
Aaron David Peters, Blackfriars
Harold Peters, Kingsland
Leslie Peters, served 1937–47 London Road, and Queens Road Manchester, also Station 4 Cheetham, Liverpool, Coventry, Birmingham, London, Glasgow, Plymouth
Samuel Peters, Stoke Newington
Annie Petrukevitch, C35
Joseph Petruckevitch, Burdett Road
Louis Pezaro, Stoke Newington
Charles Pfeiffer aka Robins, Clerkenwell – TBC
Abraham Phillips, Brunswick Road
Abraham Phillips, HQ
Alfred Phillips, Shadwell
Alfred Lewis Phillips, A20
Betty Bella Phillips, Ealing
Emmanuel Joseph Phillips, Shadwell
Sub-Officer Esther Estella Phillips, Shoreditch
Hyman Phillips, Whitechapel
Hyman Lazarus Phillips, Stoke Newington
Isidore Phillips, Old Kent Road
Leonard Isaac Phillips, West Hampstead
Leslie Sidney Phillips ??
Lewis Phillips, Islington – TBC
Marks Phillips, Bethnal Green
Max Phillips, Whitechapel
Morris Phillips, Soho
Nathan Phillips, Peckham Road
Nathan Phillips, C28
Philip Phillips, Chief Fire Warden, South Hackney
Philip Phillips, Shadwell
Raphael Phillips, Westminster College
Firewoman Rose Phillips, switchboard operator, Ash St., Manchester
Sadie Ruth Phillips, West Hampstead
Sidney Isaac Phillips, West Hampstead
Stanley Julius Phillips, West Hampstead
Woolf Phillips, C28
Stanley Phillipson, Eltham
Barnet Pikus, Whitechapel
Benjamin Pincus, C23
Irving Pincus, C22

Hyman Pinier, Stoke Newington
Henry Pinkov, Kingsland
Aaron Pinkus, Detmold Road
Aaron aka Harold Pinkus, Shoreditch
Barnett Pinkus/Pikus, C28
Benjamin Pinkus, Homerton
David/Davis Pickles Pinkus, Instructor, Cannon Street, C36, WIA
David/Davis Pinkus, A12
Morris Pinkus/Pinkervitch, Kingsland
Alexander 'Sunny' Pinner, pump operator/driver, East London, WIA twice
Joseph Pins, Firewatcher, East London
Algernon Isaac Pinsker, Firewatcher, Bristol
Simon Pinsker, Firewatcher, Bristol, brother of Algernon
Harry 'Hyam' Pittal, Firewatcher, Stepney then to Army D Day
Israel Pittenberg, Whitechapel
Angel Pizer, C39
Beryl Pizer, C22
David Pizer aka Lewis, Whitechapel
Esther Pizer, B1
Mary Pizer/Shine, C22
Israel Placks, Whitechapel
Sidney Placks, Whitechapel
Reuben 'Dick' Plagerson, Firewatcher, Bishop's Road, Manchester
Samuel Jack Platnauer, West Hampstead
Alfred Platt aka Abraham Plots, Bow
David Platter, Millwall
Henry Platz, B74
Manfred Plaut, Belsize
George Plosky, Whitechapel
George Leopold Plosky, Bow
David Plotkin, Southwark
Norman Plotzker, Shadwell
Sidney Pockler, Stoke Newington
Aubrey Podeschwa, Edgware Road
Lewis Podeshawa, Brompton
Joseph H. Podesta, Eltham
Harry Podguzer, Whitechapel
Solly Podguzer, Clerkenwell
Louis Podolsky, Bishopsgate
Francis Polak, HQ
James Polak, A13
Francis Poland, Cannon Street

Alec Polatchik, Stoke Newington
Israel Polatchik C39
Lewis Polatchik ??
Samuel Polinsky, Shadwell
Pearl Polishack
Joseph Politi, West Hampstead
Hilda Politz, Islington
Hyman Pollack, Firewatcher, Petticoat Lane, friend of Engelsman
Samuel Pollewader, Camden Town – TBC
Harold Pollins, Firewatcher, Cambridge, later Army, son of Percy
Jack Pollins, Bow
Myer Pollins, C24
Percy Pollins, Firewatcher, Leytonstone
Myer Pollock, Manchester
Moses Poluck, E85
Isaac Polus, Shoreditch
Sub Officer Isaac Jack Pomson, Whitechapel
Joseph Poolber, Whitechapel – TBC
Leonard Poppmacher, Streatham
Marion Portner-Ogus, Clerkenwell
Rebecca Posener, Stoke Newington
Harry Posnack, Whitefriars
Moses Posner, Brunswick Road
Selina Posner, Whitechapel
Charles Poulsen aka Kopel Polsky, served Kingsland/Haggerston, Watford, East Anglia RAF bases and also served in NFS abroad in France and Germany, following behind troops to extinguish fires in towns and air crash sites, attached US Army; poet, writer and taxi driver and Fire Brigade Union Official.
Clara Van Praag ??
Peter Prager, Firewatcher, Primrose Hill, German refugee
Sydney Prager, A2
Alexander Prensenz/Presence, Southwark – TBC
Henry Presky, Shadwell
Ms A.J. Press, C28
Jack Press, 199939, Hackney, injured and discharged October 1942
Morris Press, A12
Victor Press, Whitechapel
Hyman Pressinger, Burdett Road
Gordon Pressman, Whitechapel
Leslie Isaac Preston, Shoreditch
Sidney Samuel Price, Bethnal Green
Sub Officer Harry Isadore Proops, HQ D56

Lawrence Louis Pruim, Shadwell
Morris Pshedetsky, Greenwich
Alfred Pyzer, Bethnal Green

Samuel Quyatofski, Bethnal Green – TBC

Leo Rabbin, Brixton
Alfred Rabbinowitz/Rabin, Burdett Road
Henry Rabbinowitz/Rabinovitch, Millwall
Jacob Rabbinowitz/John Robins, B62
Mary Rabib, C30
Albert Rabin, C39
Benjamin Rabin, Redcross Street
David Rabin, C24
Joel Rabin, Bow
Louis Rabin, Millwall
Mark Nigel Rabin, A20
David Rabinovitch, C28
James Samuel Rabinovitch, C23
Lewis Rabinovitch, C39
Morris Rabinovitch
Ms Rae Rabinovitch, Shoreditch
Samuel Rabinovitch, C28, WIA
Syd Rabinovitch, C36
Sam Rabinovitz
Manuel Rabinowitz, C22, died on active service
'Ginger' Rabinowitz, Stock Exchange station
De Lisle Radice, Manchester Square
Victor Joseph Radstone, A2
Joseph Radstone, Soho
Samuel Marks Raingold, Clapton
Montague Rams, Kingsland
Sub Officer Asher Raphael, St 56/B66
Israel Raphael, Hendon
Michael Raphael, HQ
Sidney Raphael, Euston
Harry Bernard Rapoport, B67
Barney Rappaport, Whitechapel
Emmanuel Rappaport, C38
Frank Rappaport, Shadwell
Hyman Rappaport, Whitechapel
Mark Joseph Rappoport, C32
Ms Yetta Rappaport, Shoreditch

Solomon Rashefsky, Shadwell
Joseph Rasser, C28
Doris Rath, later Moritz, Trumpington, Cambridge, German refugee
Sub Officer R. Ratman, E86
Nathaniel Ratoff, Liverpool
Zusman Ratzker, Shoreditch
Charles Rauch, Lee Green
Philip Rauckwerk, Burdett Road
Hannah Ravech, West Hampstead
Maurice Ravech, A20
Ms B. Ravinsky, C28
Henry Rawinsky, Islington
Samuel Ray, Mobile, Manchester
Betty Rayner, Whitechapel
Edith Rayner, Bow
Eva Rayner OBE, Clapham, First World War Ambulance Driver
Eva Alexina Rayner, Streatham
Leslie Alfred Rayner, D57
Lili Rayner, Whitechapel
Sydney Rayner, C38
George Isidore Ravok, C39
Simon (Sid) Rebeck, Chief Firewatcher, Hackney
Ms Letty Redman, Stoke Newington
Louis Redom, Bow
Marky/Mark Redstone, Manchester
Aaron Philip Rees, Firewatcher, London
Abraham Reiner, Clerkenwell
Alan Reiner, Stoke Newington
Harry Reiners, Burdett Road
Henry Reiners, Millwall
Isidore Reinschreiber, Sheffield
George Reis, Brunswick Road
Julius Reisman, Shadwell
Sophie Reiss, Bethnal Green
Montague L. Reiter, Tooting; in the book, *Under Fire*, published by the London Fire and Civil Defence Authority (LFCDA), Reiter is quoted saying, 'Having damped down (i.e. hosed smouldering fires) all night, I found when it got light I had been standing over an unexploded bomb' (p.23).
A. Reuben, AFS Leeds
Harold Reuben, Firewatcher, Brondesbury, awarded Fire Service Medal
Hyman Reuben, Manchester Square
Israel Reuben, Islington

Joseph Reuben, Millwall
Lilly Leah Reuben, 'TC'
Sidney Reuben, C30
Ms Jean Reusser, Hammersmith
Andrew Reyersbach, Kensington
Julie Ribiekow, Stoke Newington
Emmanuel Ricardo, Stoke Newington
Joy Richer, Lee Green
Samuel Richman, C28
Sidney Richman, A12
Sydney Henry Richman, E89
Edward Richter, Millwall
Peter Richter, later Russell, Firewatcher, Golders Green, 1943 to RAF
Albert Abraham Richtiger ??
Barnett Rickman, C28
Israel Rickman, C34
Marcel Riebstein, Stoke Newington
Sub Officer Aaron Riffchin, C38 – lost both legs in action, Dalston station, WW1 veteran
Ms Lily Riffchin, AFS, wife
Millie Riseman, Shoreditch
Nathan Rishover, Stoke Newington
Isaac Rits/Ritske, Bethnal Green
Norman I. Ritterband, of 3 Augusta Road Moseley, Birmingham; awarded Letter of Commendation from his Regional Fire Commissioner for bravery on the night of 24/10/40 for staying at his post at the head of the turntable for many hours under dangerous conditions (letter in JMM archives)
Joel Ritz, Brunswick Road, WIA
Bennie Robins, Kingsland
Carl Raymond Robinson, Clapham
Edwin Robinson, Clerkenwell
Frederick Robinson, Islington
George Robinson, Islington
John Henry Robinson, Knightsbridge
Judah Robinson, 'C'
Ralph Robinson, Clerkenwell
Harry Rochlin, Bishopsgate
Samuel Rocklin, Stoke Newington
Lew Hyman Rockman, C34
Joseph Roden, Bishopsgate – TBC
Gabriel Rodriques, Whitechapel
Esther Rofe, Kensington
Joseph Rogansky, Liverpool

Godfrey Rogers, Bethnal Green
Joseph Rogers, Burdett Road
Moss Rogers, Burdett Road
Sidney Rogers, Bow
Cyril Rohleder, Burdett Road – TBC
John Rohleder, Whitechapel – TBC
John Charles Rohleder, Clerkenwell – TBC
William Rohleder, Pageant's Wharf – TBC
Isaac Roiter, Ilford
Annie Rolfe, B75
Rachel Rolfe, Shoreditch
David Rollnik, Brixton
Harold Rollo, North Kensington – TBC
James Rollo, Dulwich – TBC
Frank Rombach, Norwood – TBC
Barnett Rome, Shoreditch
Pearl Rome, A9
Ms V. Ronsen, Islington – TBC
Alfred Rose aka Rosenberg, Burdett Road
David Rose, Bishopsgate
Elias Rose aka Rosenberg, Homerton
Emanuel Rose, Kentish Town
Gerald Joseph Rose, Islington
Herbert Rose, Brunswick Road
Hilda Rose, A13
Jack Rose, Woodford
Jack Rose, West Hampstead
Jeffrey Rose, pump operator, Guys dental student, posted to Tunbridge
    Wells AFS, then Finchley, then 1947 to RAF
Joyce Rose, C30
Julia Rose, Shoreditch
Julian Rose, North Kensington
Leslie Rose, Stoke Newington
Louis Rose, served Coventry and Hampstead, WIA
Louis Rose, Belsize
Manny Rose, Shadwell
Mark Rose, 57Z
Maurice Rose, Clerkenwell
Michael Rose aka Mordecai Rosenberg, Whitefriars
Sidney Rose, Lewisham
Hyman Roseman, Southwark
Carl Rosen, Kentish Town
Carl A. Rosen, B75

David Rosen, Stoke Newington
Ms Dina Rosen aka Marcus, C28
Mordecai Rosen aka Rosenowicz, Greenwich and East London
Hyman Rosen, Whitechapel (i)
Hyman Rosen, Whitechapel (ii)
Louis Rosen, Soho
Mordechai Rosen, Greenwich
Morris Rosen, Whitechapel
Sarah Rosen, West Ham
Sarah B. Rosen, Kingsland
Sarah Rebecca Rosen, later Bloomfield, Haggerston and Gants Hill
Sidney Rosen, Soho
Solomon Rosen, Kingsland
Cecil Rosenband, Bishopsgate
Marks Rosenbaum, Peckham
Mr A. Rosenberg, AFS Leeds
Albert Stanley Rosenberg, A2
Alfred Rosenberg, Whitechapel
Barnett Rosenberg, Whitechapel (i)
Barnett Rosenberg, Whitechapel (ii)
Charles Matthew Rosenberg, E90
Ms E. Rosenberg, C28
Isaac Rosenberg, Whitechapel
Isaac Rosenberg, St 23
Jean Rosenberg/Ross/Genshaw, C30
Ms L. Rosenberg, Firewoman, AFS Leeds
Marcus Rosenberg aka Rowe, Liverpool
Mark Rosenberg, Brunswick Road
Morris Rosenberg, C22
Ralph Rosenberg, Detmold Road
Mr S.G. Rosenberg, AFS Leeds
Simon Rosenberg, Kingsland
William Howard H. Rosenberg, A13
Wolfe Rosenberg, Shoreditch
Nathan Rosenblatt, North Kensington
Aaron Rosenbloom, Burdett Road
Daniel Rosenbloom, Stoke Newington
Henry Rosenbloom, Euston
J. Rosenbloom, Whitechapel
Mr L. Rosenbloom, Leeds
Firewoman Ms L. Rosenbloom, Leeds
Mark Rosenbloom, Stoke Newington

Joseph Rosencovitch, Bishopsgate, WIA
Leslie Rosenfeld, Whitechapel
David Rosenfield, Plumstead
Jack Rosenfield, Battersea
Benjamin Rosenquit, Woolwich
Fireman Rosenthal, starred in firefighting film *The Bells Go Down* with Tommy Trinder
Bernard Rosenthal, Wolverley Street
Edward Rosenthal, Kentish Town
Coy. Off. Ernest Rosenthal DCM, served FB 1920–45, Greenwich, etc., First World War Sgt in West Ridings
Harry Rosenthal, West Ham
Harry Rosenthal, Liverpool
Joseph Rosenthal aka Ross, Deptford, WIA twice, when blown into Thames by explosions in Docks
Lawrence Rosenthal, Liverpool
Lily Rosenthal, West Hampstead
Max Rosenthal, Millwall
Phillip Rosenthal, C28
Solomon Rosenthal, Southwark
Sydney Rosenthal, Liverpool
Morris Rosenthall, Northwold Road, Stoke Newington/Wapping
Maurice Rosenway, A11
Helen Rosepka, Bethnal Green
Woolfe Rosinsky aka Rogers, Holloway
Maurice Harold Rosner, C28
Albert Ross ??
Albert Ross, Islington
Louisa Ross, Belsize
Phillip Ross, Stoke Newington
Rosemary Ross, Belsize
Sidney Ross, Shoreditch
Solomon Ross, Liverpool
John Roth, Manchester Square
Guenther Rothenberg, A11
Sarah Rothenberg, A1
Hyman Rothman, C28
Jack Rothman, F61
Samuel Rothman aka Rockman, Clerkenwell
Samuel Rothman, C23
Sidney Rothman, C30
Alfred Rothstein, C30

Isaac Rothstein, Whitechapel
Montague Rothstein, London, who had served in Jewish Legion in the
    First World War
Abraham Rotman, C38
Joseph Rotman, C38
Joseph Rotman, C37
Rudolf Rottensteiner, Liverpool
Leah Garcia Rovira, 'TC' – TBC
Geoffrey Harold Rowson, West Hampstead
Samuel Rowson, Kingsland
Marks Rozen, Millwall
Maurice Rozepka, HQ
Abraham Ruben, Liverpool
Hyman Ruben, Shadwell
Leonard Ruben, Fulham
Reginald Ruben, Kingsland
Isidore Rubens, Euston
William Rubens, B73
Harry Rubenstein, Homerton
**Jack Rubinstein, Central Liverpool, a shopkeeper, Commendation for
    control of incendiary bomb which saved a building and records
    from destruction, awarded with Fireman Kirwan**
Morris Rubenstein, 'C'
Nathan Rubenstein, Bow
Solomon Rubenstein, Bethnal Green
Benjamin Rubin, Lauriston Road, C30; at his wedding to Phyllis Kline
    in October 1939, his comrades formed a Guard of Honour outside
    the East London Synagogue in Stepney, with their axes (*ELA*
    14/10/39).
Israel 'Eddie' Rubin, invalided from Army to Firewatcher 1943
Lewis Rubin, St 46
Wolf Rubin, Shadwell
Wolfe Rubin, Stoke Newington
Miss Betty 'Betsy' Rubins, 875417, Blackburn and Portsmouth (later
    wife of Solomon Fine above)
Lazarus Rubins, Liverpool
Henry Ruckoff, Kenninghall Road
Jack Ruddick, Millwall
Joseph Joshua Ruddick, Stoke Newington
Ernest Rudiger, Shoreditch – TBC
Edward Rudkin, Whitechapel
Alfred Rudman, Burdett Road
Henry Rudman, Shadwell

Arthur Rudnick, Liverpool
Ms D. Rudstein, Ldg. Firewoman, Leeds
Stanley Rushowski, Bishopsgate
Alexander Russell, Shooters Hill – TBC
Alexander Kenneth Russell, Manchester Square
Samuel Russell, Bethnal Green
NB – there are many with Russell surname who are probably Jewish but it has not been possible to confirm
Charles Rustin, Westminster

Alfred Sabin, Belsize
Nathan Sabitsky, Whitechapel
George Sach, HQ 1939–48
Joseph Sach, Shoreditch
Joseph Alfred Sachs, B67
George Alfred Sack, 1HQ
Joseph Sack, Stepney, WIA
Sydney Sack ??
Firewoman Mrs Sacker, Stratford
David Sacklin, Bethnal Green, WIA – TBC
Abraham Sacksilver, Whitechapel
Emmanuel Sadler, Stoke Newington
Ernest Sadler, Kentish Town – TBC
Phyllis Safer, Aylesbury
Emmanuel Saffer, Kingsland
Israel Saffer, Bow
Company Officer Mr A. Sagar, Leeds
Harold Sagar, Cherry Garden River Service
Gustav H. Sail, Manchester Square – TBC
Miss Lynda Sait, despatch rider, Stepney
Claire Elizabeth Salaman née Rozelaar, Lancing (Sussex) and Crickhowell (Wales)
Euston David Salaman, Lambeth
Mr L. Salinsky, AFS Leeds
Martin Nathaniel Salman aka Solomon, Peckham Road
Montague Samuel Salmen, North Kensington
Michael Salmon, C38 – TBC
Myer Salmon, C28
Edward Salmons, Kentish Town
Joseph Salnow, C36 – TBC
Jerrold Maurice Salomon, C39
K. Sophie Salomon, A20
Martin Salomon, E84

Bertram Salomons, Walthamstow
Philip Saltman, Bethnal Green
George Saltzman, Shadwell
Walter Herman Samler, served 1920–46, Westminster etc – TBC
Alexander Sampson, Euston
Alfred Sampson, East Greenwich
Charles Sampson, Dulwich
Donald Sampson, Soho
Frank Sampson, Camden Town
Frederick Sampson, New Cross
Frederick W. Sampson, Bethnal Green
Henry Sampson, 'C'
Henry Sampson, New Cross
Henry Sampson, Clapham
Henry Joseph Sampson, Camden Town
James Sampson, Pageant's Wharf
John Sampson, Whitechapel
John G. Sampson, New Cross
Joseph F. Sampson, Blackfriars
Leonard Samuel Sampson, Dulwich
Michael Sampson, Shadwell;
Richard Sampson, Hammersmith
Sydney Sampson, Walthamstow
Cecil Samson, Finchley – TBC
Albert Basil Samuel, West Hampstead
Barbara Samuel, Belsize
David Samuel, Southwark
E. Samuel, 'F'
Ethel Samuel, West Hampstead
Howard Samuel, West Hampstead
Bert Walter Samuels, F60
David Samuels, Edgware Road
Ernest Samuels, Knightsbridge
Frederick Samuels, Islington
George Samuels, Shoreditch – TBC
Gerald Samuels, North Kensington
Herbert Samuels, Pageant's Wharf – TBC
Isidore Samuels, Detmold Road
Jack Samuels, Grimsby/Cleethorpes
Louis Samuels, Firewatcher, Grimsby
Louis Samuels, E84 LFB
Morris Samuels, Stoke Newington
Norman Samuels, Swansea

Ms Raie Samuels, Cannon Street
Simon Samuels, Whitechapel
Solomon Samuel, S. Wales
William Samuels, B76
Arthur Samuelson, Greenwich
Sylvia Sandberg/Thompson ??
Bat. Sgt Maj. Lawrence W. Sander RA, joined 1919–40, died 2/10/40
Albert Sidney Sanders, Millwall
George Leonard Sanders, Red Lion Square
Harry Sanders, Clerkenwell
Joseph Sanders, West Norwood
Ms L. Sandler, C36
Louis Sandler, Shadwell
Saul Sandler, Bethnal Green
Hyman Sandovitch, East Greenwich
Anne Sandpearl, Stoke Newington
Jack Sandpearl, Kensington
Harry Santaub, Whitechapel
Ms D. Saper, C30
Lazarus Saperstein, Stoke Newington
Harold Saunders, C23 –TBC
Leslie Saunders, Orpington –TBC
Rose Saunders, Shoreditch
William Saunders, Kingsland – TBC
Maurice Saunders, C30 – TBC
Woolf Saunders, 'C'
Joyce Savill-Cohen, Manchester Square
Morris Saville, Middlesborough NFS
Eva Savine, A9 – TBC
Max Sax, Shadwell
Friedrich Saxl, E47
Barnett Sayevitch, B21575, Bow, WIA twice, once as shock, at Wellington Garage
Michael Schaapwol, Burdett Road
Louis Schad, Clapham
Co. Off. Henry Schadenberg, formerly Sgt Queens Reg served 1920–46 Redcross Street, etc. – TBC
Julia Schaefer, Bethnal Green
Irene Schaffer, Fulham
Judah Schaffer, Burdett Road
Nathan Schaffer, Stoke Newington
Abraham Schafron, C28
Leonard Schapiro, Lambeth

Charles Schaverein, C28
Amelia Schaverien, Burdett Road
Section Officer Solomon Schaverin, St 34, to LFB 11/40
Leon Schechter aka Sheeter, Kingsland
Jack Scheinbroom, C28
Aleck Scheinholtz, Shadwell
Samuel Scheinman, C38
Issac Schenker, Stoke Newington
George Scheu, Islington
Sub Officer Albert J. Scheurer/Scheuer C23 (William Alfred?), Homerton station, Commended for Brave Conduct, Woolwich (*LG* 27/6/41), later died
Hyman Schiff, C28
James Schiffer, A9
John Schiltz, Edgware Road
Maurice Schiman, Bethnal Green
Theodore Schindler, Firewatcher, Lyttleton Road, N2, b. Berlin 1884
Harry Schissler, C38
Wilfred Schlachtaub, Shadwell
Daniel Schleich, Blackfriars – TBC
Ernest Schleich, Dulwich – TBC
Gerald Schlesinger, Manchester Square
Israel Schless, C30
Ms I.G. Schlimper, E85
Frederick Schluter, Streatham
Percy Schmedlin, Euston – TBC
Dorothy Collier/Schmid(t), Manchester Square – TBC
Erwin Schmidt, Whitechapel
Reuben Jacob Schmidt, Clapham
William Schmidt aka Smith, Westminster, WIA
Leonard Schnabel, Fulham
Irene Schneglberger, Streatham
Alf Schneider, Shoreditch
Alf Schneider, Shadwell
Barnett Schneider, Bishopsgate
David Schneider, Bishopsgate, WIA
Emmanuel Schneider aka Taylor, Fulham
Ernest Adam Schneider, B62
G. Schneider
Goodman Schneider, Firewatcher, Stepney, First World War veteran
Israel Schneider, Wolverley Street
Maurice Schneider, B76
Nathan Schneider, Shadwell

Samuel Schneider, Westminster College
Solomon Morris Schneider, C39
Sydney Schneider, C28, WIA
Max Schneiderman aka Summers, B72
Philip Schneiderma,n C28
Nathan Schneiders, Bishopsgate
Kathleen Schnellmann, Southwark – TBC
Frank Alex Schnitzler, A20
Frank Schnitzler, West Hampstead
Frank Schock, Deptford
Henry Schoenfeld, 'A'
Henry Scholar, Stoke Newington
Michael Schonhaut, Kingsland
John Hyman Schotness, C30
Sub Officer Joshua Schotness, Bethnal Green
Harry Schramek, A3
Doris Schreiber, C39
Norman Schreiner, Peckham Road
Samuel Schriber, Whitechapel
Frank Schubert, B1
George Schuelke, West Hampstead
Theodore Max Schuller, Soho
Sub Officer Albert J. Schultz, Greenwich
Harry Schultz, C28
Ethel Schulz, B73
William Schumann, Fulham
Sidney Schunmann, Islington
Morris Schuster, Kingsland
Barnett Schwable, C28
Agnes Schwartz/Windsor, Clapham
Albert Schwarz aka Smith, Euston
Betty Schwartz, TC
David Schwartz, Stratford/East Greenwich?
Lily Schwartz, Euston
Isi (Israel) Schwarzbart, aka Michael Sherwood, Firewatcher, later
    served Military Intelligence at D Day and after, German refugee
Israel (Isi) Schwartzberg/bart ??, C22 – WIA
Gertie Schwartzman, C30
Louis Schwartzman, Shadwell
Edward Schween, Holloway – TBC
Gordon Schwendtbauer, Brompton – TBC
Beatrice Schwodler, Streatham – TBC
L.C. Schwodler, 'TC' – TBC

Sub Officer Joseph Schworer, Brunswick Road
Section Officer Nathan Sclare, Whitechapel
Harry Scoble, C38
Reuben Scolnick ??
Neville Scorah, North Kensington
Louis Scott, Manchester Square – TBC
Edward Scott, Stoke Newington – TBC
Joan Scrivner/Barnett ??
Bernard Sears, Bethnal Green
Emmanuel Sears, Shoreditch
Cecilia Secker, Greenwich
Frederick Secker, Soho
Bernard Seelig, Norwood
Harry Sefton, Stoke Newington
Bertram Segal, London
Miss Beulah Segal, later WAAF
Edward Segal, St 55
Harry Segal, Soho
Harry/Hyams Segal, Whitechapel
Jack Segal, Shadwell
John Segal, Southwark
Louis Segal/Sigall, Southwark
Robin (Bob) Segal, later Army (brother of Edward and Harry [Soho], above)
Rosa Segal, Millwall
Hyman Segalowitz, Stoke Newington
Charles Segar, Bow – TBC
Sidney Segenfield, North Kensington
Mr G. Seidman, River Service, AFS Leeds
Max Seifert, Shadwell
Joseph Seigar, Kensington, WIA twice
Rita Seigel, B68
Jack Seigler, C30
Hugh Seligman, Kensington
Paul Seligman, A11
Abraham Selwyn, Kentish Town
Sub Officer Alfred Senett, Greenwich
Coy. Off. Sydney Senior, C32, served 1938–48
Rose Sennett, Homerton
Leading Fireman Sepel, Heckford Street Fire Station, Stepney
Morris Seratsky, Bethnal Green
Caplin Serkovitch/Sicovitch, Shadwell
Phillip Serkovitch/Sicovitch, Shadwell

Louis Serota, Kingsland
Alfred Setterich, Shoreditch –TBC
Jack Shaberman, Shoreditch
Cyril Joseph Shackson, A11 – TBC
B. Shadlofsky, after being invalided out of RF at Dunkirk
Alexander Shaer, Kingsland
Barnett Shaer, Detmold Road
Bernard Shaer, Shadwell
Morris Shaer, Stoke Nerwington
Fay Shabner, Willesden
Gershon Shaffer, Shadwell
Harry Shaffer, C30
Millie Shaffer, Whitechapel
Simon Shafran aka Sydney Shaffron, Burdett Road
Alfred Shakel, Dockhead – TBC
Lewis Shalet, Millwall
Mark Shalet, Stoke Newington
Moss Shalet, Bethnal Green
Phillip Shalet/Schalet, C39, Docks; a family story tells how a bomb landed in a river near the fire station and killed hundreds of fish. Quite a few were gathered up by the firemen and Phillip's share soon became gefilte fish at home! He also related how during a huge warehouse fire, one colleague suggested his team hold back momentarily; they did but several others who ignored the warning continued approaching the blaze and were killed before his eyes by a collapsing wall.
Leon Shalit, Belsize
Station Officer David Shank, 1938–45, served Dalston, Station Officer Hayes, Middx
Donald Shanks, Brompton – TBC
Harry Shapero, Liverpool
Solomon Shapira, Islington
Abraham Shapiro, Burdett Road
Alf Shapiro
Gerald Shapiro, Bishopsgate
Harry Shapiro, Burdett Road
Harry Shapiro, Kingsland
Isaac Shapiro, East Greenwich
Julius Shapiro, C28, Burdett Road E1 (b-in-law of H. Feldman, killed)
Lewis Shapiro, Edgware Road
Sender Shapiro, C30
Alfred Share, Homerton
Arthur Charles Sharman, Camden Town – TBC

James Sharman, Dalgleish Road School, E14 (*ELA* 11/39) –TBC??
Gerald Sharp, Burdett Road
Harold Sharp, Homerton
Lelsie Victor Sharp, West Hampstead
Jack Shatkovsky aka Jackson, ARP and Fireman, Defoe Road, Stoke Newington, WIA
Harry Shaw, Shadwell
Jack Shaw, Bethnal Green
Maurice Shaw, West Hampstead
Mark Shear, C34
Morris Shear ??
Miss Z. Shear
Israel Shecter, Liverpool
Jack Sheinbroom, Whitechapel
David Sheker, Stoke Newington
Myer Shell, Wandsworth
Morris Shenkman, Stoke Newington
Leonard Sher, Dockhead
Isaac Sheratsky, Greenwich
Mosche Sheratsky, aka Sherrick, Shadwell/Jubilee Street School station
Jack Sherick, Stoke Newington
Geoffrey Sherman, Holloway
Harry Sherman, Stoke Newington
Hyman Sherman, 'C'
John Sherman, Burdett Road
Laab/Louis Sherman, Clapton
Lou (later Sir Louis) Sherman, C28, WIA, cab driver. Veteran of the Spanish Civil War, he fell through the roof of a burning building in an Oxford Street store and was severely injured. He was invalided out of the NFS and later went into politics.
Morris Sherman, C28
Eva Charlotte Shernheim later Stenham, 8999919, Soho
Samuel Sherwin, Liverpool
Stanley Sherwin, Wandsworth
Ms E. Shiers, A2
Edwin Shiers, Dulwich
Israel Shilling, Stoke Newimgton
Jacob Joseph (Jack) Shiman, Harrow-on-the-Hill
Judah Shimansky, Epsom
Henry Shinasky, Bow
Horace Shine, Edgware Road
John Shine, A30
Leon Shine, Stoke Newington

Miss Lily Shine later Landau, Brick Lane
Nathan Shine, Bishopsgate
Nathan Shine, Homerton
Norman Shine, A11
Samuel David Shine, C28
William Joseph Shine, Islington, formerly RN served 1912–41?
S. Shinebaum, Firewatcher
Victor Shiner, North Kensington
Solomon Shinerock, C34
Doris Shinman, Edgware Road
Myer 'Gerry' Shinman, River Fire Service, Cherry Garden
Herbert Shinnick, New Cross
Ldg Aux Fireman Nathan Shipeck, C38
Jeffrey Shire, Edgware Road
Abraham Shlackman, Kensington
Leslie Shocket, Whitechapel
Reinhold Sholl, Dulwich
George Bernard Sholl, Brompton, WIA
Sam Shonberg later Shaw, Firewatcher, North London
Henry Shonfield, Lambeth
Bernard Shongold aka Stern, Homerton
Myer Shooliefer, Stoke Newington
Firewoman S. Shooman, Leeds
Mr J. Shooman, AFS Leeds
Harry Shoot, Firewatcher, Charterhouse Square
Simon Ian Shoot, West Hampstead
Semour Shore C38 – TBC
Samuel Shorn, West Hampstead
Leon Short, Shadwell
Jack Shrensky aka John Henry Stanton
Ms Renee Shriberman, Commercial Road station control room
Hyman Shuckmesser aka Sugarman, Camden Town
John Jacob Shulman, C24
Lionel Shulman, C30
Ben Israel Shulton, Shoreditch
George Shurman, Dockhead
Cyril Shutze, Sidcup – TBC
John Sichel, Blackfriars
Cecil Sichel, Clerkenwell
Gerald Siddler, Blackfriars
Lionel Sidlin, Stoke Newington
Morris Sidlin, C30
Samuel Sidlin, B72

Alick Siegel, 'B'
Harry Siegenberg, Euston
Louis Siegermister, Bishopsgate
Louis Sigall (Segal), Southwark
Louis Sigaloff, E1, Turney Road?
Alfred Siger, Peckham
Harry Siger, Soho
Israel Siger, B76
Charles Silber, Westminster
Mr S. Silberg, 121415, AFS Leeds
Solly Silberg, 121413, River Service, AFS Leeds
Zalig Silberman, Homerton
Ashar Silberston, Redcross Street, WIA
Clara Silk, Bethnal Green
Henry Charles Silk, Stoke Newington
Leslie Silk, Kingsland
Samuel Silkman, Shadwell
Miss Leila G. Sillman aka Marklings, Perry Vale
Abraham Silver, C28
Daniel Silver, Stoke Newington, died in service 4/5/40
David Silver, Islington, brother of Jack (below)
Davis Silver, Millwall
Miss Gladys Silver, Sheffield
Harry Silver, Shadwell
Ian Silver, D46
J. Silver, AFS Leeds
Jack Silver, Cannon Street, specialist high speed driver, later served in Coventry, Leeds, Hull (see Ascher Latner above KIA)
Jacob Silver, Cannon Street
Len Silver, Bethnal Green
Murray Silver, C38
Sam Silver, Whitechapel
Samuel Silver, Liverpool, First World War veteran
Stanley Silver, C30
Jack Silverberg, Cannon Street
Anne Silverman, C22
B. Silverman, AFS Leeds
Barnet Silverman, Bethnal Green
Dore Silverman, Firewatcher and journalist (Ministry of Information)
Gedalia Silverman, Homerton
Harry Silverman, Fire Warden, Bristol
Jack Silverman, St C28
Jacob Silverman, Whitechapel

Jacob Israel Silverman aka Selby, A36
Leonard Silverman, East London
Leonard Isaac Silverman, A36
Millie Silverman, Bishopsgate
Norma Silverman, Stock Exchange station
Mr P. Silverman, Leeds
Ms R. Silverman, C28
Rita Silverman, Pound Lane, Willesden
Samuel Silverman, Cannon Street
Victor Silverman, Manchester Square
Benjamin Silverstein aka Stanton, Clerkenwell
David Silverstein, Bethnal Green
David Silverstein/Silverstone?, C28
Harry Silverstein, C28
Israel Silverstein, Shoreditch
Louis Silverstein, Whitechapel
Simon Silverstein, C38
Hyman Silverston, C36
John Silverston, Euston
David Silverstone, Whitechapel
H. Silverstone, Homerton
Harry Silverstone, Kingsland
Jack Silverstone, Kingsland
Joseph Silverstone, Whitechapel
Myer Silverstone, Kingsland
Joseph Silvertand, B73 – TBC
Arthur Silverton, Knightsbridge
David B. Silverton, Kingsland
Jack Simberg, C39
Morris Simkin, Shadwell
Pinkas Simkin, F65
Thomas Harry Simkin, North Kensington
Sidney Simmonds WWI veteran, fire engine driver, South Norwood
Hattie Simmons, B72
Issy Simmons, Whitefriars
Jack Simmons, Shadwell
Station Officer Malcolm Simmons, West Hampstead
Norman (Noah) Simmons, Shadwell
Ms Raie Simmons, Belsize
Robert Louis Nathaniel Simmons, A11
Alexander Samuel Simms, Stoke Newington
Harry Simms aka Symons ??
Anne Simon, Camden Town

Harry Simon, Glasgow
Israel Joseph Simon, London Road Station, Manchester, also served
    Plymouth
Mr J. Simon, AFS Leeds, River Service
Michael Simon, B66
Sydney Simon, Stoke Newington, WIA
Vera Simon, C39
Barnett Simons, East Greenwich
Beatrice Simons, C37
Cecilia Simons, Holloway
David Simons, Bishopsgate
Isaac Simons, Cannon Street, WIA
Isiah Simons, Shadwell, WIA
John Simons, West Hampstead
Lawrence Simons, Holloway
Ronald Simons, Blackfriars
Samuel Simons, C37
Sidney Simons, C38
William Simons, Southwark – TBC
David Simonson, Islington
Sidney Simper, C28 – TBC
Simon Sinasky, Millwall, WIA
Jill Sinauer, Kensington
Maurice Moss Sinclair, Peckham Road
Benjamin Singer, Shadwell
Bernard Singer, St 28
Betty Singer ??
David Singer, Shadwell
Edward Singer, Burdett Road
Emmanuel Singer, Islington
Gertrude Singer, Whitechapel
Louis Singer, Westminster
Morris Singer, C35
Peter Singer, Fireman, Earls Court
Ronald Singer, Marlow Fire Service
Albert J. Sinstadt, C34, 1930–48 – TBC
Richard W. Sinstadt – TBC but KIA 19/4/41 Bishopsgate
Alfred Lewis Sirotkin, C28
Bernard Sirotkin, Bethnal Green
Michael Skulnick, Clerkenwell/Edgware Road
Jack Skuzer, 'C', boxer – TBC
Alma Wanda Slade aka Freeman – TBC
Rose Slater, Shadwell – TBC

Mr Slater, Firewatcher, Glasgow
Issy Slefkin ???
Mr Elia Sless, Glasgow
Rose Slesser, Manchester Square
Nathan Slipman, C28, brother of Alec, Firewatcher who was killed 17/4/41 (see Roll of Honour)
Harry Slobotkin, Stoke Newington
Morris Slonsky, C28
Abraham Slotsky, Shadwell, WIA
Mrs L. Sluys, Firewatcher at Greaves and Thomas in Hackney
Jaell Smith, Burdett Road
Solomon Smith, C22
Abraham Smoolovitch, C39
Arthur Morlines Snowman, later RA
Sadie Sober, C32
Ben Sochachewsky, C23
Albert Sockl, Streatham, TBC
Anne Soester, A13
Abraham Softness, West Hampstead
Michael Softness, Homerton
Joseph Sohl, Brixton – TBC
Hyman Sokolsky, Whitechapel
Rachel Solanovitch, F1
Frederick Solari/Solario, Bow
Peter Solari, Euston – TBC
Constance Sollender, A11
Jenny Sollender, B63
Cecil Soller, Bishopsgate
Morris Soller, Bishopsgate
Harry Sollinger, Shadwell
Mr I. Soloman, AFS Leeds
Douglas Solomon, D57
Edward Solomon, Euston
Frank Solomon, Shoreditch
Mr H. Solomon/Solomen, AFS Leeds
Henry Solomon, B74
Jack Solomon, Whitechapel
Joseph Solomon, Burdett Road
Joseph Solomon, Bow
Judah Solomon, Firewatcher, Stoke Newington, First World War MGC Veteran
Judah Solomon, Kentish Town
Louis Solomon, Whitefriars

Company Officer M. Solomon, Middlesborough
Maurice Solomon, Battersea
Morris Frederick Solomon, E89
Michael Nathaniel Solomon aka Salmon, Peckham Road
Phil Solomon aka Akivah/'Keevah' Patronovski, Firewatcher, Grimsby.
  b. 1906 in Poland
William H. Solomon, Brunswick Road/C24
Alderman Woolf 'Pat' Solomon, Cleethorpes and Grimsby, BEM 1946 for Services to the Fire Service as Fire Guard Training Officer, and Civil Defence
Abraham Solomons, Cherry Garden River Boat
Alex Solomons, C36
Alfred Solomons, Whitechapel
Miss B. Solomons, B30
Godfrey Solomons, Homerton
Henry Solomons, Whitefriars
Jack Solomons, 'E', TC
Leonard Solomons aka Selwyn, Eltham
Lewis Solomons, C36
Louis Solomons, C34
Michael Solomons, Hammersmith
Phillip Solomons, Stoke Newington
Samuel Solomons, Whitechapel
Sidney Solomons, C30
Israel Solonch, Burdett Road
Aaron Solsberg, Stoke Newington
Gerald Soltz, LFB St 13, Belsize
Edward Somers, Peckham Road
Station Officer John Harold Somers, Blackfriars
Ronald Somers, Wandsworth
Walter Somers, Lewisham
Reginald Sonn, Whitechapel
Myer W. Sopel, C34
Max Sorkin, Stoke Newington
Golda Sorrin aka Miller ??
Aaron Soskin aka Soskie, Stoke Newington
Jack Alexander Sossick, E89 – TBC
Barnet Souber, Edgware Road
Leslie Souber, A2
Stanley Souhamy, Peckham Road
Leonard Spain, Bow
Gisela Spanglet aka Eisner, Fire Guard, Nottingham
Philip Jack Spanjer, Belsize

Miss Shandrel Sparger, Manchester Square
Jesse Sparling, Millwall
Isaac Speck, Edgware/Docks
Isaac Specter, Shadwell
Joseph Spector ??
Philip Spector, Stoke Newington
Solomon Speigler, Northwold Road
Albert Spelman, Bethnal Green
Jack Spellman, Kingsland
Basil Spencer, Finchley
Bernard Spencer, 'A', TC
Cyril Spencer, Wandsworth – TBC
Harry Spencer, Stoke Newington
Harry Spencer, Lee Green – TBC
Stephen Spender, poet and writer
Doris Spevack, Clerkenwell
Marie Speyer, Belsize
Miss Sylvia Spicker, Wakefield, Yorks
Joseph Spiegel, Kingsland
Alec Spiegelman, Manchester Square
Benjamin Spiegelman, A2
Pinchas Spielman, Fireguard, Mile End/Whitechapel
Hans Spier, NFS 524662
Arthur Spiers, Shoreditch
Frank Spiers, Wandsworth
George Spiers, Shoreditch
Harvey Spiers, Kentish Town
Myer Spiezer, Bishopsgate, WIA
Benjamin Spillman, Whitechapel
Ernest Spillman ??
Miss Esther/Stella Spiro, later Black, Sub Officer C38, Brick Lane
Leon Spivack, Glasgow
Harry Hyman Spray, West Norwood
Herbert Spray, Peckham
Leslie Spray, Brixton
Louis Spray, Kingsland
Luois Sprengers, Shoreditch
Frederick Spreyer, Bishopsgate
John Spreyer, Bishopsgate
Nathan Spring, Whitechapel
Jack Springer, Stoke Newington
John Springer, Manchester Square
Frederick Spurling, Lewisham

William Spurling, A7
Joseph Staal, Shadwell
A.J. Staerck, Bow – TBC
Clifford Staerck, Bow – TBC
Arthur Stahl, Brixton
Frank Stahl, Brixton
Victor Stahl, Blackfriars
Cedric Stainer, Edgware Road – TBC
Eve Stamberg, A5
Edward Stanger, Euston
Jacob Stanger, Camden Town
Harry Stanger, Homerton
Montague Stanley, Whitechapel
Mark Stargatt, Shadwell
Alfred Stark, Lewisham – TBC
Alfred S. Stark, Pageants Wharf –TBC
Ernest Stark, Streatham – TBC
Frederick Stark, Deptford – TBC
George Stark, Peckham – TBC
Jack Starkie, Whitefriars – TBC
Solomon Starkman, Shadwell
Alfred Starks, Merton – TBC
Leonard Starr, Kingsland
Leslie Starr, Kingsland
Maurice Starr, Clerkenwell
Maurice Cohen Starr, Westminster College and Finchley (attached) Fire stations, George Medal as an ARP, wholesaler of 41 Leather Lane, husband of Lily, b. 4/6/10
Sidney Starr, C30
Herbert Stechmann, Whitechapel
Joseph Samuel Steele, Kingsland
Alexander Stefanski, Shadwell – TBC
Hilan Stefonovitch, Ethelburgh Road
Ethel Steib, Perry Vale
H. Steigman, C23
Henry Samuel Stein, C37
Lewis Stein, Camden Town
Marks Stein, Whitechapel
Rose Stein, C28
Osvald Stein, Watford, refugee from Prague
Gershon Steinberg, Holloway
Hyman Steinberg, Redcross Street

Morris Steinberg, East Greenwich
Column Officer Frank Nathaniel Steiner, A13, WIA
Teddy Steinman, Sheffield
P. Steitz, Invicta Road
Alice Stern, Kentish Town
Beatrice Stern, Whitechapel
Bernard Stern aka Shongold, Homerton
Harry Stern, Firewatcher, Citation for saving colleagues from carbon monoxide poisoning at Lamerton's Store, Ealing
Jack Stern, Kingsland
Jack Stanley Stern, Lambeth River Boat
Joseph Stern, Shadwell
Lawrence Stern, West Norwood
Lionel Stern, Bishopsgate
Louis Benjamin Stern, C36
Reuben Stern, Stoke Newington
Robert C. Stern, A13
Rosa Stern, Camden Town
Sam Stern, Whitechapel/Minories/Leyton
Sidney Stern, C28
Sydney Stern, Manchester Square
Sydney L. Stern, West Norwood
Betty Sternberg/Zagger, C36
Lottie Sternberg aka Goldsmith ??
Sven Michael Sternfeldt, A13 – TBC
Cyril Stevens, Stoke Newington – TBC
Lesley Joseph Stevens, Kingsland
Sidney Stevens, Brunswick Road
Richard Stiebel, West Hampstead
Charles Stieber, Stoke Newington
Frederick Stieber, Stoke Newington
Ms May Stieber
Abraham Stock, Shadwell
Davis Stock, Millwall – WIA
Israel Stock, Shadwell
Joseph Stock, C30
Joseph Stock, Cannon Street
Saul Stock, Shadwell
John Joseph Stockman, Cannon Street
Michael Stockman, Dockhead
Sydney Stockman, Lewisham, WIA
Isaac Stodel, Homerton
Louis Stodel, E85, Brixton

Morris Stodel, Stoke Newington, later POW Greece
Harry 'Harris' Stolerman, Shadwell
Alfred Stone, Bethnal Green
Annie Stone, C34
Benjamin Stone, Liverpool
Harry Stone, Stoke Newington
Harry Stone, Brunswick Road
Joseph Stone, Knightsbridge
Phillip Maurice Stone, Shadwell
Phillip Maurice Stone, Station 34, C District, C34, Docks, WIA twice
Reuben Stone, Eltham
Sabina Stone aka Lawson, Cannon Street
Jack Stonefield, Mobile, Manchester
Irene Stracstone, Clapham
Jack Stracstone, Stoke Newington
Maurice Stracstone, Bolingbrooke Grove, E2
Lawrence Strangman, Westminster – TBC
Grace Strasser, Barnet Urban
Catherine Strauss, Clapham
H. Strauss, Camden Street
Ronald Strauss, B75
John Strohman, Homerton –TBC
Carl Stromberg, Kensington –TBC
Frank Stromberg, Millwall –TBC
Cecil Stronach, 'B' – TBC
Michael Struber, Redcross Street
Felix Sturm, Firewatcher, aged 18, at Golders Green crematorium, German/Polish refugee
Max Stutz, Cherry Garden River Boat
Arthur Stygle, Brompton – TBC
Morris Sudic, Bow
Alfred Sugar, Plumstead
Betty Sugar, C34
Dora Sugar, C28
Fay Sugar, C34
Joseph Hyman Sugar, C30
Nathan Sugar, Bow
Section Officer Samuel Sugar, Bethnal Green
Joan Sugarhood, Homerton
Sub Officer Joseph Sugarhood, Soho, B72, 7/38 to 7/40
Fireman B. Sugarman, Bournemouth (Ted Hughes, *Bournemouth Firemen at War* [Dorset: Dorset Publishing Company, 1991])
Benjamin Phillip Sugarman, Kingsland

David Sugarman, Edgware Road
David Sugarman, Whitechapel
Miss Lily Sugarman later Smith, London
Norman Sugarman, Stoke Newington, WIA
Samuel Sugarman, C22
Julius Sulkin, Bow
Stewart Sulkin, Kensington
Harry Summers aka Hartog Zomerplaag, Stoke Newington, Dynevor Road
Leonard Summers, West Hampstead – TBC
Mark Summers aka Schneiderman, Soho
Saville Summers, Shoreditch – TBC
Sydney Summers, Camden Town – TBC
Firewoman Ms Z. Sumroy, AFS Leeds
Myer Sunderland, Millwall
Norman Sunderland, Redcross Street
Pizer Sunderland, Cannon Street
Sidney Sunkin, Soho
Firewoman Ms S. Supperstein, Leeds
Donald Zangwill Surfas, Stoke Newington
Phillip Surfas, Stoke Newington
Louis Susman, C38
Louis Susman, Kingsland
Charles W. Sutton, Stoke Newington – TBC
Frank Sutton, Whitechapel – TBC
James Joseph Sutton, Kingsland – TBC
Harry Sweden, Redcross Street
Louis Sweden, Shadwell
D. Swerdlow, Liverpool
Matthew Swerdlow, Liverpool
Harold Swift, Liverpool, TBC
George Swirsky, West Hampstead
1082 George Edward Switzer, Station Officer, Stepney, Whitechapel C28, aged 33 years, lived at 34 Lordsmead Road, Tottenham (*LG* 8/8/41), formerly Royal Navy, joined service 1920. 'During an air raid, on 19 March 1941, George Switzer was dealing with fires at St Katherine's Dock, when he received a message at 2135 about some premises, part of which was used as a stable, which had been set on fire by incendiaries nearby. They belonged to Carters, Henry Vile and Company. Officer Switzer went to the premises with two appliances and saw a two storey building with the upper floor and roof well alight. The stable, in which 39 horses were tethered, was filled with smoke and in complete darkness. The wooden roof and

the forage (hay, straw and oats) were very combustible and alight. Switzer first detailed a crew to deal with the spreading fire and then organized a party (two firewatchers, the horse keeper, two policemen and two firemen) and led them into the stable area to rescue the animals. He led the way into the building and succeeded in bringing out the frightened animals, eighty yards to the side of St Katherine's Dock. It was necessary to make several journeys taking over 20 minutes, while high explosive bombs were being dropped nearby. Station Officer Switzer's promptitude and leadership resulted in the rescue of all the animals and prevented the complete destruction of the building. Awarded the BEM, invested 24/2/42 and also the Silver Bravery Medal and Merit Certificate from the National Horse Association of Great Britain.'
TBC if Jewish.
Muriel Switzer, Eltham
Henry Symon, Islington
Maurice Symonds, Holloway, WIA – TBC
?? Symons, Whitechapel
Harry Symons/Simmons, Kings Avenue 'C'

Solomon Tabakman, Whitechapel
John Taber, Homerton –TBC
John Tabor, HQ
Alfred Tabram, Whitechapel – TBC
David Talisman, Area Commander, Glasgow/Clydebank
Harry Tannenbaum, Greenwich, WIA
Hilda Tannenbaum, TC
Toby Tannenbaum, Bethnal Green
Wolf Lieb Tapper, Shoreditch
Harry Aaron Tartes, Shadwell
Joseph Tasker, Whitechapel/Manchester Square, WIA
Sidney Taub/Schlactaub, C24
Woolf Taubler, St 2
Martin Hugo Taubman, B12
Emmanmuel Taylor/Schneider ??
Joseph Taylor, Stoke Newington
Nathan Taylor, Redcross Street
Neil Taylor, Redcross Street
Jack Teacher, C38
Philip Teacher, Kingsland
Louis Teiman, Euston
Jack Teller, Belsize
Norman Temkin, Burdett Road

Charles Temple, Edgware Road
Donald Temple, Stoke Newington
Edwin Temple, Fulham, WIA twice
Emmanuel Temple aka Fishberg, Stoke Newington, WIA
Eric Temple, Homerton –TBC
Frank Temple, Holloway – TBC
George Temple, West Hampstead
Jack Temple, C37
Jack Temple, Whitechapel
John Temple, Edgware Road – TBC
S. Temple (see photo with Jack Pollins)
Sidney Temple, C37
Louis Tencor, Whitechapel
Ms R. Tendler, C28
Sidney Tendler, C28
Jack Tennenbaum, Stoke Newington
Jack Tennenbaum, Mobile, Manchester
John Tenner, Whitechapel
Henry Tenser, Liverpool
Morris Tenser, Dulwich
Solomon Tenser, C28
Alexander Termehr, Cherry Garden River Service –TBC
Harry Ternofsky, Whitechapel
Joseph Ternofsky, Plumstead
Bernard Sydney Terry, A2
Marcel Terry/Langeveld, Lewisham – TBC
Edward Theil, Dulwich
Joseph Thomas, River Service – TBC
Betty Thurman, Belsize –TBC
Marguerita Thuroff, Streatham – TBC
Jack Tiktin, Stoke Newington
Simon Tiktin, Brunswick Road
Issac Tiller, Stoke Newington
Samuel Tiller, Shadwell
Samuel Tisch, Bethnal Green
Emmanuel Tishberg, C39
Albert Israel Tisman, Millwall – WIA
Miss Renee Titton aka Malin, Lambeth HQ
Alec Tobe, Whitestone Pond Station, Hampstead
Gerald Tobert, West Hampstead
Assistant Force Commander Cyril Gordon Tobias, No.34 (London) and Whitechapel, 1924–48, BEM (*LG* 22/8/41), formerly MGC in First World War. 'When high explosive and incendiary bombs

caused several fires in his area, District Officer Tobias took charge of the operations. The water supply failed, but with initiative and skill he organised a relaying service which prevented the fires from spreading. It was necessary for him frequently to visit the water relaying units and the journeys, which had to be made on foot, were extremely dangerous owing to falling debris. Tobias remained continuously at work for nineteen hours and he showed great coolness, efficiency and exceptional qualities of leadership.' Later Assist. Chief Officer Essex Fire Brigade and MBE 10/6/54.

David Emmanuel Tobias, West Hampstead
Joseph Ellis Tobias, Manchester
Section Leader Louis Clifford Tobias, C28
Percy Tobias, Lee Green
Samson Tobias, C23
Woolf Tobias, Shadwell
David Tobin, Shadwell
Horace Tobin, Bow –TBC
Leonard Tobin, Redcross Street
Rhoda Tobin, Holloway
Richard Tobin, Bethnal Green – TBC
Michael Tobovitch, Whitechapel
Sidney Tobovitch, Shadwell
Keith Tocher, HQ –TBC
Aaron Todrin, Cannon Street –TBC
Richard Toft, Kingsland –TBC
Jeremiah Tolansky, Stoke Newington
Max Tonchin, Manchester Square – TBC
Samuel Tondosky, Homerton
Abraham Topperman, C30
Gerald Torgel/Turgel, C34
Nathan Torgowitz, Shadwell
George Torobzoff, Shadwell – TBC
Murray Toubkin, West hampstead
Alfred Touchinsky, Shadwell
Marks Trager, Northwold Road
Harry Trainis, Clapton
Rudolf Traub, Edgware Road
Alfred Travers, Hendon
Jacob Israel Tree A20
Norah Treichler/Cox ??
Miss Frances Tribich, Islington
Charles Triebner, Kensington
Amelia Trilsbach, B66 –TBC

Josephine Tritschler, Plumstead
Samuel Trohsky, Bow
Myer Tropp, Bow
Student Rabbi Morris Turetsky, Manchester Firewatcher (see Louis Jacobs above)
Barrell Turner, Sheffield
Benjamin Turner, AFS Newcastle and Falkirk
Charles Turner, Shadwell – TBC
Joseph Turner, Bow – TBC
Harry Tutleman, Whitechapel
Max Tynas, Mobile, Manchester
Ethel Tzen, C36
Nathan Tzwirin aka Leslie, Hackford Road, Oval, WIA/part blinded

Anne Valeska Uhlig, A2
Lewis Ulansky, C28
Philip Ullinger, Dockhead
Clifford Ullman, West Hampstead
Otto Underfer, Kentish Town – TBC
Joseph Unermanm, Stoke Newington
Marcus Unger, E84
Bernard/Ben Urding, Liverpool
David Usiskin, St Paul's crypt/A2
Sydney Usiskin, St 2
Edward Uzielli, Hammersmith

Abraham Valensky, St 39
Alfred Valentine, Shadwell
Benjamin Valentine, Stoke Newington
Lily Vallin, Stoke Newington
Max Vallin, Kingsland
Samuel Vanbrook, Whitechapel
Isaac Sydney Vancliff, Burdett Road
Clive Van den Bergh, Belsize
Basil Van Leeuwen, Westminster
Clara Van Praag, Burdett Road
David Van Vlymen, West Hampstead
Morris Vandecar, Bow
Arthur Vandenbergh, Clerkenwell
Lambert Vandermolen, Camden Street
Samuel Joseph Vandersluis, Bow
Henry Vandersteen, Islington – TBC
Marie Vanderzee, Kensington

Stanley Vanhinsbergh, Hammersmith – TBC
Albert Vann, Bethnal Green
Harry Vanner, Shoreditch
Ivon Vant, C28
Montague Vanton, Bethnal Green
Emmanuel Vaschelfsky, Whitechapel
Joseph Vegoda, A20
George Veit, North Kensington
Abraham Velensky, Stratford/Kingsland
Henry Vellerman, Stoke Newington
Ralph Vellerman, Shadwell
Abraham Ascher Vestlar, Homerton
Albert Max Vetterlein, despatch rider, Commendation for Brave Conduct (*LG* 35104 14/3/41, pp.1506–7). He served at Station 35 (West Ferry Road, Millwall) and came from 37 Selby Road, Leytonstone, a milk roundsman by occupation. The citation from the Fire Brigade Archives (LMA FB/WAR/1/203) says, 'Without thought of his personal safety, Vetterlein maintained communication between the local station and the sub stations (on his motorbike) whilst the area was subjected to severe bombing on the night of 7 September 1940, when numerous fires were in progress and all telephone communications were out of order, thus ensuring the attendance of appliances. His courage was no doubt the means of several buildings being saved.'
Joseph Victor
Ms Rosalind Victor
Solomon Vidofsky, C30
Hetty Vine, Belsize
Nathaniel Vine, Soho, WIA – TBC
Leslie Ellis Viner, Camden Street
Sidney David Viner, Whitechapel
Samuel Vinter, Millwall
Maurice Visokli aka West, Stratford
Albert Vogel, Camden
Albert James Vogel, C37
Arthur Vogel, Dockhead
Charles Vogel, Old Kent Road
Henry August Vogel, 1HQ
Pierre Paul Vogel, A11
Harry Volckman, Brunswick Road – TBC
Lewis Volinsky, C28 – WIA
Simon Volkovitch, Euston
William Vose, Liverpool

Winifred Vugler, TC

Firewoman Ms S. Wachsberger, Leeds
Isaac Wagenfelt, Brunswick Road
Samuel Wager, C37 – TBC
Alfred Wagerman, Street Fire Patrol (SFP), Stamford Hill
Harry Wagman, Millwall
Samuel Wagman, C28
Arthur Wagner, Whitechapel – TBC
Frederick Wagner, Stoke Newington – TBC
Gyuri Wagner, Waterloo Road – TBC
Henry Wagner, Stoke Newington – TBC
Company Officer William Wagner, Streatham – TBC
Oscar Simon Wailer, East Greenwich
Louis Wainberg, Streatham
Harris Wainer, Stoke Newington
Hyman Wainer, Whitechapel
Mr J. Wainman, Bournemouth AFS – TBC
Sub Officer Jonah Waldman, C20, sadly lost his son in RAF in Second World War
Samuel Waldman, C28
Sydney Solomon Waldman, West Hampstead
Cecil Solomon Walker, Homerton – TBC
Charles Wallace, C37
Cecil Waller, Eltham – TBC
E. Wallhauser, Camden Street
Louis Wallis, Eltham
Louis Walman, Bethnal Green
Oscar Walser, Islington
Barnett Walters, C34
Leonard Walters, Bishopsgate
Louis Walters, Euston
Solomon Walters, Shadwell – WIA
Amelia Walvisch, Shoreditch
Mendel Wander, Tyson Street, served Trafford Park area, Manchester 1939–45
Morris Wander, C39
Walter Ward, Kensington
Solomon Warshawski, Eltham
Isaac Warshofsky, Millwall
E. Wartenberg, Bishopsgate
Launcelot Cyril Wartski aka Lewis, Shadwell
Bernard Wasmuth, Islington – TBC

Maurice Wasserman, C28
Maurice M. Wassey, Belsize – TBC
Florence Abigail Waterfield, Kingsland – TBC
Sarah Ann Waterfield, Kingsland – TBC
Archibald Waterman, Homerton
Dennis Waterman, Lambeth
Dora Waterman, Stoke Newington
Gershon Waterman, Firewatcher, Clapton
Israel Mark Waterman, St 30
Morris Waterman, Firewatcher, Clapton
Morris Isaac Waterman, Whitechapel
Stanley Waterman, E47
Miss E.G. Watermeyer, F60
Reuben Waters, Lewisham
Gerald Wauters, Shadwell – TBC
Monty Waxler, Stoke Newington
Abraham (Alfred) Waxman, B73
Mo Waxman, Queens Road, Manchester
Reuben Waxman, East End/Stratford
Jack Wayneberg/Wineberg, brother of Sybil Antrich above
Benjamin Weber, Belsize
Stanley Joseph Weber, East Greenwich
Wenzel Jospeh Weber, Clerkenwell
Sidney Wechsler, Whitechapel
Franz Wehden, Stoke Newington – TBC
Dora Weichman, Whitefriars
Gershon Weichman, A11
Joseph Peter Weidenbach, C24/C38
David Weidenbaum, C30
Jack Weidman, Bow
Gerhard Weiler, AFS Oxford, scientsist, German refugee, b. Berlin
Michael Weinbaum, East Greenwich
Anthony Paul Weinberg, C32, WIA
Betty Weinberg, Kingsland
Harold David Weinberg, B66
Harris Weinberg, Stoke Newington, WIA
Firewoman J.C. Weinberg, Leeds
Kopel Weinberg, Whitechapel
Louis Weinberg, C38
Louis Weinberg, Holloway
L. Weiner, Shadwell
Maurice Weiner, Whitefriars
Miss A.J. Weinfass, C28

Hyman Weinfulk, A12
Morris Harry Weinfulk, A12
Albert Weinling, Holloway
Jack Weinrabe, Bethnal Green
J. Weinstein, Wolverley Street
Julius Weinstein, Bromley
Morris Weinstein, Homerton
Miss N. Weinstein, C28
Samuel Weinstein, Belsize
Harry Weinstock, Cannon Street/St Paul's
Harry Weinthrop ??
Etta Weintraub, C30
Dora Weiss, Edgware Road
Harold Weiss, A36 – TBC
Harvey Weiss, Soho
John Donald Weiss, Peckham – TBC
William Weiss, Peckham – TBC
Miss D. Weissbloom, C22
Emmanuel Weissbloom, Burdett Road
Leslie Wellman, Clapham, WIA
Hanus Weisl, student and Firewatcher, Manchester
Esther Weissland, Kensington
Weissmann, served with Stephen Spender and Herzberg
Lewis Wencker, North Kensington
Morris Wenger, transferred to Army Fire Service – JC 1945 – and awarded MBE
Morris Wengrower, Bethnal Green – TBC
Carl Wentorf, Edgware Road – TBC
Isaac Werchowsky aka Irving Wilson, Shoreditch
Miss O.M. Werner, North Kensington
Harry D. Wernick, Firewatcher, Dagenham
Hyman Wernick, Kenninghall Road
Lillian Westerman, A20
Rebecca Westerman, B68
Solly Westnovote, Whitechapel
Kenneth Wexler, Shoreditch
Charles Weyman, Clerkenwell
David Weyman, Old Kent Road
Henry Weyman, New Cross
John Weyman, Westminster
Wilfred Wolf Whitby, Firewatcher, London
Henry Hart White, Kentish Town
Lou/Lewis White, WiA Holborn
Myer White, Soho

Lawrence Wiberg, Southwark
Hyman Levy Wicksman, A11
Ezekiel Joseph Wiener, Bethnal Green
Albert Wiesen, 'C'
Joseph Wild, Bishopsgate
Louis Wild, Dockhead
Alec Wilder, Bishopsgate/Shoreditch
Joseph Wilder, Bishopsgate
Ralph Wilder, Stock Exchange station, 36Y
Isaac Willenstein/Wallenstein, Burdett Road
Rudolf Friedrich Willer, Soho
David Joshua Williams, Whitechapel, WIA – TBC?
Reuben Wilner, Julian Street and London Road, Manchester
Fireman Irving Wilson, London Docks, Trade Union representative, brother of Leslie
Fireman Leslie Wilson, London Docks, WIA blown into Thames; station orchestra
Doris Windscheffel, Camden Town
Harry Winecor, Whitechapel
Joseph Winecor, Whitechapel
Solly Winegard, B73
Morris Winestein, Manchester
Nat Winestein aka Black, Manchester, brother of Morris
Arnold Aaron Winkler, A9
Philip Winner, West Hampstead
Louis Winnick, Shadwell
Percy Winnick, Belsize
Dr Helmutt Winsley-Stolz aka German Jewish refugee Henry Windschauer, MB, attached to AFS as medical officer to West Hampstead Fire Station 1944–45 (JMM files letter of 1986) and recalled the falling of a V2 on a housing estate near where he lived in West End Lane with 'the road littered with civilian casualties like a battlefield'.
Clive Winston, Firewatcher, Muswell Hill, 1943–44, later Grenadier Guards
David Winston, Leeds
Gerald Winston, Sheffield
David Winter, Bow
Reuben Winter, Kingsland
Allan Winterhalder, Homerton – TBC
Nicolas Winton, Firewatcher, commander in Hampstead before joining RAF in 1941, famous rescuer of Jewish children from Prague in 1939

Alan de Graf Wise, Westminster
Firewoman Ms A. Wiseberg, AFS Leeds
Louis Wiseberg, Burdett Road
Alfred Wiseman, Whitchapel
Barnet Wiseman, A12
Daniel Colman Wiseman, Whitechapel
Edgar Wiseman, Liverpool
Hyman Wiseman, Bishopsgate
Isaac Wiseman, Homerton
Jacob Wiseman, Middlesborough NFS
Joseph Wiseman, Burdett Road
Leslie Wiseman, Bow
Lily Wiseman, Finchley
Maurice Wiseman, Liverpool
Morris Wiseman, C39
Moss Wiseman, C34
Pinkus Wiseman, Bishopsgate
Samuel Wiseman, Homerton
Victor Emmanuel Wiseman, Redcross Street
John Witkowsky, Deptford
Samuel Witriol, Southwark
David Witt, C23
Sidney Witzenfeld, 'F'
Walter Wohlgemuth, Cannon Street – TBC
Adolf Wohlman, Shadwell
James Wohlman, Wolverley Street
Charles Wolbrom, Stoke Newington – TBC
Margaret Wolf, B67 –TBC
Elizabeth Wolfe, Brompton
Rachelle Wolff, later Ellis, Firewatcher at hostel in London and remembers putting out incendiaries with sand buckets, b. Cologne, Kindertransport refugee
Walter Wolff, Firewatcher, London
Mrs Wolff, Firewatcher, London, mother of above
Joseph Wolfshaut, Bow – TBC
Abraham Wolfson, Liverpool
Sub Officer Maurice Wolinski, HQ B62
Samuel Wolitsky, A30
M. Wolkovitch, Firewatcher, Whitechapel
Alfons Wollstein, Winstanley Road
Israel Wolosen, C34
Michael Woloshin, B62
Arnold Woolf, West Hampstead

Arthur Woolf, Edgware Road
Benjamin Isaac Woolf, Millwall
Cyril Woolf, Belsize, B22863??, WIA face and hands at Silvertown, Poplar
D. Woolf, Fire Guard, Hughes Mansions
David Woolf, East Finchley and Harrow
Dennis Woolf, Wolverley Street
Gertrude Woolf, Whitechapel
Company Officer Isaac Solomon Woolf, Stepney
Isaac Solomon Woolf, Kingsland
Joseph Woolf, Bethnal Green
Joseph Woolf, Tooting
Laurence Morris Woolf, Stoke Newimgton
Leonard Woolf, E86
Lewis Woolf, Bethnal Green
Marks Woolf, Stoke Newington
Max Woolf, Blackheath
Reverend Meyer Woolf, West Ham and District Synagogue, i/c Firewatchers of community
Milly Woolf née Silverman, Blackheath, wife of Max
Trudy Woolf, City of London
Sol Woolfe, Wolverley Street
Woolfs, Stratford
Thomas Worth aka Warschauer, Firewatcher, Brighton, later to Army and GP in Hackney post war
Betty Wosnitzer ??
Philip Wouters, Whitechapel
Berthold Boaz Hermann Wreschner, Firewatcher; also synagogue minister; German refugee
Clive Wunderlich, E88
Hyman Wyner, Edgware Road
Harry Wyner, West Hampstead
Benjamin Wynschenk, Whitechapel

Nathaniel Yaffee, Liverpool
Zalman Yaffee, Manchester
Alf Yale, Firewatcher, Grimsby
Hyman Yank, HQ
Harry Yanover, F61
Isaac Jacob Yantin, Stoke Newington
Karl Yauch, Clerkenwell – TBC
Bert Yelin, A11 – TBC
Barnett Yeloff, 'C'

Jack Yentis, Homerton
Alfred Yenush, Kenninghall Road
Esther Yeselevsky/Leslie, Burdett Road
Barnett Yesolofsky, Bethnal Green
Joseph Yoselovitch, Whitechapel
Herbert Charles 'Chonky' Young, Leeds and Coventry
Louis Young, Bow, WIA twice

Gertrude Zacher, Cannon Street
Alf Zackheim, Penge
H. Zagerman, S Wales
Hyman Zagerman, Whitechapel
Reuben Zagger, C36
Amy Zahl, Bethnal Green
Hyman Zahl, Bishopsgate
L Zangel/Zargel, Firewatcher, Stepney
Henry Zarach, Westminster
Edward Zausmer, Stoke Newington
Hyman Zausmer, Whitechapel
Harry Zealander, C30
Julia Zealander, Ilford
Philip Zeeman, C34
Jack Zeff, Bethnal Green
Morris Zeffman, Bethnal Green
Solomon Zeiderman, C28
Mr Elsley Zeitlyn, West Hampstead
Philip Zelin, C28
Sidney Zelkin, Camden Street
S. Zeltser, Liverpool
Miss Margot Zernick; Firewatcher and also a nurse, German refugee, later wife of Wreschner
Reginald Zettel, Perry Vale
Michael Zetter, West Ham, also AFS PT Instructor
Morris Ziants, Stoke Newington
Morris Ziedenberg, C30
Mr M. Ziedman, Leeds
Mr W.A. Ziegler, AFS Leeds, also PT instructor
Louis Mark Zigman, A9, WIA
Savile Zigman, Glasgow
Isaac Zilesnick, Bishopsgate
Adolf Zimbler, 'E'
Alfred Zimmer, Whitechapel
Charles George Zimmerman, E88

Derek David Zimmerman, B63, Cannon Street, met Churchill and
    played rugby for the LFB
Isaac Zimmerman, C24
Sub Officer Israel J. Zimmerman, HQ C37, 7/38 to 10/38
Jack Zimmerman, despatch rider/extra in film *The Bells Go Down*
Jacob Zimmerman, Whitechapel
Laab Zimmerman, Blackfriars
Leonora Zimmerman, Manchester Square
Louis Zimmerman, Bishopsgate/Stock Exchange fire stations, C36, WIA
Mr M. Zimmerman, Leeds
William A. Zimmerman, E47
Michael Zipson, Whitefriars
David Zissman, Birmingham
Stanley Zobel, Peckham
Harry Zobin, Shadwell
Marks Zobin, Burdett Road
Rose Zolas
Mis G. Nina Zoller, D46
John Zorn, Clapham – TBC
Maurice Zucker, Kingsland
Grace Zugg – TBC
Ronald Zugg, 1938–48 – TBC
Louis Zugzie aka Harris, Blackfriars
Gunther Zunz, Firewatcher, Oxford
Gottfried Zurbrugg, A9 – TBC
Henry Zuschlag, Shadwell
Jacob Zusman, Shadwell
Morris/Morrie Zweig, Clerkenwell

Important Miscellany

Military Fire Service
Graham Bravo, Army Firefighter, National Service and TA, son of
    Gilbert Bravo WW2 AFS
Leonard Clements, Army FS
Sgt Goodman 'Tony' Copitch (Manchester), Army FS
Adolphus 'Alf' Kay, RAF Glos. FS
Philip Rosenthal, Army FS
Stanley Rosenthal, RAF FS
Lt Sam Tiller, Army FS, India 1940–45

Currently Serving or Post War
John Arrenberg, Soho, 1970s – TBC
Jack Boas, Nottinghamshire, 2001 to present

Walter Clayton aka Kohn, 1952–63, German refugee
Michelle Kent, Essex Brigade, grandaughter of Joseph Sack, Second World War
Erhard W.W. Saar aka Edward Lees, formerly SOE, Chief Fire Officer for Neath Fire Brigade, German refugee (from Peter Leighton-Langer, *The King's Own Loyal Enemy Aliens*)
Jerrard Wilson, 1957–69
John Zaktrager, Station Officer, Kingsland Fire St., Hackney 1960s, seconded to Zambia as adviser

Believed to be Jewish, Died in Service before Second World War
Henry Berg, died 7/12/1882 at Alhambra Theatre, Leicester Square, b. Highgate cemetery at 'Firemens Corner'
Harry Joshua Green, born 1/11/89, previously RA, served FB 1913–17 and 1919–20, KIA Oliver's Wharf, Wapping 1/11/20
Joseph Schubert, served 1920–28, killed on duty 11/4/28 when he fell from a ladder on a training tower; b. at Walthamstow cemetery; record shows was a church service but TBC (LMA/FBA/STA/1/40)
Robert Schultz, died 3/7/1895, coachman, thrown from appliance
Edward Woolf, 1914–18, drowned accidentally

Served before First and Second World Wars
Isaac Bravo, born 20/2/84, joined 1907–08, Camden Town
Capt. Henry Edward Davis, a former Mayor of Gravesend who founded the local fire service in the 1870s in South-East Kent
James Goldsmith, whaler by profession, 1888–1924 in Fire service, London (see his son James above)
Station Officer Alfred Hiseman, formerly RMLI, served 1905–33 – TBC
Franz Joseph Huebner, joined 1903, later to RN – TBC
Sidney Isaac, 1909–14, later to RN
James Isaacson, previously Mercantile Marine, served 1922–23 and died
Arthur Itzinger, previously Army Reserve, served 1908–18
Stanley Victor Koch, previously RN, served FB 1920–35, then died
Frederick Krombach, served 1911 – TBC
Arthur Lander, previously RN, served 1904–23
Julius Lechner, served 1911–13 – TBC
Elisha Leoey (is this Loewy?), army 1914–18, Redcross Street FB, 1919
Barnet Levi, served 1907
Nathan Lewis, formerly RA, 1908–13, from North End Road, NW – TBC
George Marks, 1903–08, Edgware Road, etc.

Richard Marks 1901–19, Bishopsgate, Hackney, etc.
Simon Marks, served 1906, Bishopsgate
Richard J. Sinstadt, served 1890–1918, Bishopsgate area – TBC
Stanley Wolfe, 1906–29 – TBC
Edward Wulff, 1883–1911 – TBC
Walter Zappert, 1903–13 – TBC
George Zugg, 1906–30, died on duty – TBC

(Author's note – An interesting Jewish early link with the London Fire Brigade appears to be a song called, 'A Cheer for the Fire Brigade', written in the 1850s by one S. Rosenthal. The cover of the sheet music page, published by a company at 2 Red Lion Square, is at the LMA, reference SC/GL/PR/Dew 781.98)

Fire Service Artists
Enid Abrahams, daughter of George and Julia, born Hampstead
    10/5/06, lived 43 Arkwright Road, NW3. Royal Academy, 1939,
    AFS driver in Hampstead and Bethnal Green. She also did charity
    work at the Bernhard Baron Settlement in Stepney with bombed-
    out people, and drove a mobile canteen. Exhibited at the Royal
    Academy. Married Charles Dreyfus 11/2/47, one daughter. Died
    19/5/72, London.
Section Leader Balchin, No.36 Fire Area, Stepney/Poplar
Julia Halle Lowenthal, of 45 Marlborough Mansions, Cannon Hill,
    NW3; served West Hampstead station
Fireguard Samson Schames, exhibited at the Civil Defence Artist
    Exhibition in October 1941 at the Cooling Galleries, New Bond
    Street, W1 (LMA FB/WA/1/68)
Aux. Fmn Artists A. Silberston B23115 and J. Steinberg B19032 are
    also named in LMA FB/WAR/1/69
Fireman John H. Zorn exhibited at the Royal Academy Exhibition in
    August 1941 (LMA FB/WAR/1/71)

Overseas Miscellany

Abraham Hort, one of the early Jewish settlers in New Zealand, set up the Wellington City fire brigade in the 1840s.

In 1898, 90 per cent of the Fire Brigade in Bialystock, Poland was Jewish and most Jewish settlements in the Pale, of Eastern Europe, in the eighteenth and nineteenth centuries, had all Jewish fire brigades.

In Nachod, North East Bohemia, at the Decin Synagogue Museum, are two preserved leather water skins from 1781, bearing a Hebrew inscription, 'Kehilla Kedosha Nachod' (the Holy Community of Nachod), and were used by the Jewish Fire Brigade of the ghetto. The many studies of the history of East and Central European Jewry, show that among the first communal organisations established in the ghettos and villages was a Fire Brigade. The community well knew the huge potential danger of fire in the narrow streets of wooden buildings of the shtetls, not to mention the fact that frequent racist riots against Jews (pogroms) often led to attempts to burn down the houses of Jewish inhabitants – and a Fire Brigade was an essential part of self-defence (I am grateful to Wally Fields of Liverpool for pointing this out to me).

In Sofia, Bulgaria, in the 1870s the Jews founded their own Fire Brigade.

The Jewish Free School (JFS) in Bell Lane, Middlesex Street, was an NFS Fire Station throughout the war after the school had been evacuated to Ely. The school closed in 1945 and later relocated to Camden Town in the 1950s.

In South Central Santiago, Chile, the 'Bomba Israel' is an all Jewish Fire Brigade station since 1954, and flies the Israeli flag on its engines.

May 2008, Jewish Firefighter of Barrie and Creemore, Ontario, Edward van Severen, rescued a baby from a car that had driven into a river, by diving into the river, as reported in the Creemore Echo newspaper. Ed also led a team that refurbished a WW2 RAF Fire Engine for the local museum, back in the 1990's. Ed's mother Esther nee Thompson and grandmother (Helena nee Sugarman, from Whitechapel and who was a Canadian war bride in 1946) were Jewish. Ed was born in 1975 and is married with 4 children. He was awarded 2 medals for bravery from the Fire Service and Police.

On 9/11 in New York, the following Jewish Firemen were killed:
Steve Belson
Alec Feinberg
David Weiss
Paul Tauber survived and the Jewish Chaplain to the NYFD is Fireman Rabbi Joseph Potashnik. In approximately 2000, there were 400 Jewish Firemen in New York City and in the 1950s there was a Jewish Fireman club in New York.

The Parliamentary Documents

In 1942, the authorities at the Palace of Westminster asked the LFB if experienced men discharged through illness and injury from the Brigade, could be sought out and asked to serve as 'security cleared' Firewatchers at the Houses of Parliament. Many Jewish Firemen were contacted and served. The following letters were found at the

> FW/4
>
> 2. Bishops Rd.
> Hayes Middx.
> 3.4.43.
>
> Dear Sir,
>
> Recieved your letter dated 31st March. I am already in employment of national importance near my home. So I am unable to take the post you kindly offered me.
>
> I wish to thank you for your kind offer.
>
> yours truly
> C. Zimmerman

> 12 Oldhill St
> Stamford Hill
> N.16
> 1.9.44
>
> Dear Sir,
>
> I am in receipt of your letter of the 28th inst. I regret that I shall not be able to accept your vacancy on the Fire Prevention Dept. yet awhile, as at the present time I am having treatment for a Duedenol Ulcer, when I am fit to resume any employment I shall get in touch with you for an interview. I remain
>
> Yours faithfully
> Mr. M. Cohen

Parliamentary Archives (HL/PO/2/1 and passim) as examples of men who were unable to take up these posts after being interviewed and cleared – W. Perkoff of 32 Jessam Avenue, Clapton, E5; C. Zimmerman of 2 Bishops Road, Hayes; and M. Cohen of 12 Oldhill Street, Stamford Hill, N16. Among about fifty Jewish Firemen asked to re-join, one at least served (Mr I. Rothstein of 51 Woodville Road, Golders Green), as later records showed.

FW/4 (31)

32, Jessam Avenue, E. 5.
31st August 1942.

A.R.P. Officer,
Houses of Parliament.

Dear Sir,

Thank you for your letter of the 27th instant. I am afraid I am unable to take advantage of your offer as I in bad health generally and could not stand up to the long hours you mention.
Further, it would be acting contrary to my Medical Officer's advice if I undertook to perform duties which compelled me to day and night shifts.
Again, many thanks.

Yours truly,

W. Perkoff

The following is the list of Jewish Firemen, discharged because they were injured or sick, who were contacted to re-join the LFB in 1942 to serve as Firewatchers at the Palace of Westminster (from the Parliamentary Archives papers); ? means possibly Jewish.

F. Abdela, Grove Hall Court, NW8
Belofsky (more not known)
J. Baum, Poynders Gardens, SW4
C.S. Bloom, Imperial Avenue, N16
A. Bronstein, Christian Street, E1
B. Citron, Brent Road, Brent
W. Cogan, Bradley Street, SE9
D. Cohen, Leyton Park Road, E10
E. Cohen, Brookside Road, Golders Green
M. Cohen, Oldhill Street, E5
G. Danovitch, Cecilia Road, E8
J. Epstine, Aldridge Road, W11
H.D. Finkel, 3 Brenthouse Road, E9
M. Friedberg, Overton Road, E3
B. Glass, Nelson Street, E1
M. Goldberg, Cecilia Road, E8
M. Goolnik, St James Street, Hereford

A. Gopstein, Colveston Crescent, E8
A. Greenberg, Navarino Mansions, E8
G.W. Hyams, Carysfort Road, N16
R.S. Isaacs, 10 South Block, Stoney Lane, E1
S. Karminsky, Grove Lane, SE5
D. Kauffman, Geary Road, NW10
H. Kirsch, Florence Road, Northampton
P. Kiverstein, Elgin Avenue, W9
I. Kosky, Bolton Road, NW10
P. Kransky, Atherton Road, E7
H.D. Landrofsky, Hearnville Road, SW12
H. Levi, Fordwych Road, NW2
H. Levy, Hillside Road, N15
N. Levy, Station Road, Chingford
D. Liptz, Green Lanes, N16
J. Loubell, Ellesmore Road, NW10 (?)
I.J. Marks, Greenhurst Road, Willesden
P. Mendelson, Ruskin Road, Southall
D.V Meyer, Angell Road, SW9
T.W Meyer, Petherton Road, Highbury
M. Nagle, Acklam Road, W10
Peltz, Wood Green (more not known)
W. Perkoff, Jessam Avenue, E5
D. Pinkus, Minerva Road, E4
L. Pizer, 10 Hartland Court, Friern Barnet, N11
M. Pollins, Peoples Stores, Dartford (?)
H. Proops, Turnham Road, SE4 (?)
I. Rothstein, 51 Woodville Road, Golders Green
A. Sachs, Bunns Lane, NW7
F.A. Schnitzler, Hemstal Road, NW6
A.J. Schultz, Spencer Avenue, Hayes
J. Springer, Selwyn Court, Wembley
S. Tisch, Waverley Road, St Albans
W. Tobias, Reighton Road, E5
H. Zagerman, Cecil Close, Middx
C.G. Zimmerman, Bishops Road, Hayes

Some of those who Served

85. Frederick Abdela, standing second row from front, third from right; served on Massey Shaw Fireboat (note the NFS River Thames Formation Training Centre sign on right) and Battersea. Later served in the Royal Navy Reserve at sea.

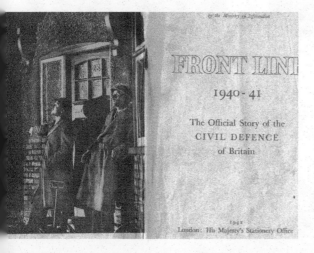

86. Firewatcher Richard Abraham, standing left, appears in this real time 'action photo', on duty outside 28 Kathleen Avenue, Wembley, which was on the inside front page *Front Line 1940–41: The Official Story of the Civil Defence of Britain* (London: HMSO, 1942). Stirrup pump, hose and bucket stand ready as they stare up at the approaching German bombers overhead.

326 *Jewish Participation in the Fire Service in the Second World War*

87. Leonard Eliezer Abrahams, second row, third from left in civilian clothes next to fireman with crossed belt. Probably taken at Station 39Y, Albion Road, Stoke Newington.

88. Max Abrahams, taken 11 November 1940.

89. Fireman David Adams of Leeds.

90. Alfred Adler served as a Medical Officer in the German Army in the First World War (photo taken in 1916).

91. Alfred Adler came as a refugee to the UK where he became a firewatcher in the Second World War (photo taken in 1938).

92. Harold (Harry) Barnett, AFS Kingsland, Hackney, First Aid Specialist.

93. Hyman Benstock, left, at Whitechapel Station.

94. Charles Berg, middle row, second from right, probably taken at Commercial Road Station. On his right is Jewish Fireman Lewis Orinsky aka Ormsby.

328   *Jewish Participation in the Fire Service in the Second World War*

95. Nathan Bernard Berg, far right at back.

96. Firewatcher Dr Walter Berlin, German Jewish refugee, served Manchester Square, London, 1941–45.

97. Woolf Bernstein, first left.

98. Woolf Bernstein by his fire engine.

99. Leon Blumenkehl, London.

THE FIRE BRIGADES UNION
(EX-AUXILIARY SECTION)

General Secretary: JOHN HORNER

Assistant Secretary:
HARRY SHORT

National Officer:
PETER PAIN

---o---

TO ALL MEMBERS

Attend all Branch Meetings and assist in the transaction of Branch business.

Retain your Contribution Card and produce it for the Collector to initial when payments are made. This Card is your receipt.

Adult Men, 4d. per week; Boys aged 18-20, 2d. per week; Boys under 18, 1d. per week; Adult Women, 3d. per week; Girls under 20, 2d. per week; Part-timers, 3d. per week.
Benefit Fund, 3d. per week.   Political Fund, 1/- per quarter.

THE FIRE BRIGADES UNION
(EX-AUXILIARY SECTION)   Regd. No. 1695T

Affiliated to the

TRADES UNION CONGRESS.

SCOTTISH TRADES UNION CONGRESS.

THE LABOUR PARTY.

LONDON LABOUR PARTY.

LONDON AND LOCAL TRADES COUNCILS AND LOCAL LABOUR PARTIES.

MEMBER'S CONTRIBUTION CARD

Name L. BLUMENKEHL   Register No. 25014

Region 5   Area 34   Division e

Sub-Division 3   Station Y

ONE PENNY

Walthamstow Press (T.U.), Forest Rd., E.17

100. Leon Blumenkehl's Fire Brigade Union Card (original at the JMM).

330 Jewish Participation in the Fire Service in the Second World War

NATIONAL FIRE SERVICE
CERTIFICATE OF SERVICE

Name (in full) .... Leon BLUMENKEHL ....
National Fire Service No. 463937 .... Date of discharge 19th August 1945
Rank on discharge .... Fireman ....
Cause of discharge .... Reduction in establishment ....

	WITH LOCAL AUTHORITY FIRE BRIGADE	WITH NATIONAL FIRE SERVICE
WHOLE-TIME SERVICE	from ____	from ____
	to ____	to ____
PART-TIME SERVICE	from ____	from 25.5.43
	to ____	to 19.8.45

19th August 19 45 .... F.P.P.(Bruckes) .... for Fire Force Commander.

101. Leon Blumenkehl's Certificate of Service with the NFS (original at the JMM).

102. Nathan Borenstein aka Renn, Hackney Firewatcher.

103. Firewoman Doris Bluston in the AFS before joining the Army ATS.

COMMENDED FOR GALLANTRY

Mr. Solomon Bogush, of Blackstock Road, London, N.4, a member of the Auxiliary Fire Service, has been commended, and his name duly published in the LONDON GAZETTE, for his gallant conduct in an air raid on a night early in the year. As a member of a fire brigade crew he helped to fight fires for four hours and prevented the flames from reaching a large unexploded bomb.

Mr. Bogush gave up a lucrative business career to serve his country.

At a civic function held recently in Lambeth during "Red Cross Week," with Admiral Evans as the guest of honour, the first thousand pennies were presented by the Brixton Synagogue in the Mile of Pennies launched by the Mayor.

JC article – Solomon Bogush 'For gallantry'

104. *JC* article describing Fireman Solomon Bogush's Commendation for Gallantry.

105. Arnold Brewer, Sunderland NFS, second left as Deputy Chief Fire Officer.

106. Firewatcher Irmgard Broniatowski, née Fruchtzweig, served London and Merseyside.

107. Gustav Bunzl on the Dewsbury Fire Boat sitting centre left.

Some of those who Served

108. Gustav Bunzl standing back row second left.

Borough of Cheltenham
FIRE DEPARTMENT.

Central Fire Station
Cheltenham,

J. R. JONES
CHIEF OFFICER

TELEPHONE NO. 2222

RJO/B.   June 4th., 1940.

G.G. Bunzl, Esq.,
Parkward Mansions,
Shurdington Road,
Cheltenham.

Sir,
        Aliens in the Auxiliary Fire Service.

    I very much regret to have to inform you that the Council have decided to suspend all enemy aliens from the services of the A.F.S.

    I therefore have no alternative but to ask you to hand in your resignation and return all equipment supplied to you.

    On behalf of my chairman and myself I wish to express our appreciation of the manner in which you have carried out your duties since you enrolled on April 3rd., 1939.

    I can assure you that this is not our wish that these steps are being taken but as you will see we are acting under orders.

    If at any time you should need a reference of any description I shall be only too pleased to supply you with same, and in conclusion wish to thank you for all you have done for the A.F.S.

                            Yours faithfully,

                            ACTING CHIEF OFFICER.

109. Rare copy of an apologetic letter to Gustav Bunzl from his Acting Station Officer in Cheltenham, informing him of the decision to sack all 'enemy aliens' from the service during the invasion scare of 1940; submitted by his daughter Liz.

110. Jack Clifford aka Jacob Cohen, Walthamstow Fire Station, taken in 1945.

111. Fireman Harry Cohen on right, in action. Note his First World War medal ribbons on his tunic (he served in the Royal Fusiliers). The other fireman appears to be Jewish too but the donor family did not know his name.

112. Henry/Isidore Cohen, later Henry Coe, second from right, served in the Bishopsgate area and then on the Massey Shaw Fire Boat (later a Dunkirk 'Little Ship').

Some of those who Served

113. Henry/Isidore Cohen standing top, far left.

114. Henry/Isidore Cohen standing far right.

115. Fireman Henry/Isidore Cohen talking to Churchill during the Blitz in the film *1940; A Reminiscience*, made by the BBC in 1965.

336 *Jewish Participation in the Fire Service in the Second World War*

116. Fireman Lew Cohen.

117. Mendel Cohen, Belfast

118. Sgt Tony Copitch of Manchester standing far left in the Army Fire Service in the Second World War.

119. Jack Cramer standing to the left of pump 22V at water's edge, probably at the Serpentine in 1939.

120. Fireman Harry Denton.

121. Fireman Alec Deutch with his wife at their son's Bar Mitzvah post war. Both parents were in the Fire Brigade in the Second World War.

122. Firewoman Sylvia Dloogatz/ Douglas, later Kaye, Northampton AFS.

123. Sylvia Dooglatz, front row third from left.

124. Sylvia Dooglatz, first firewoman on left, front marching row.

125. Sylvia Dooglatz, fifth person from left, with her crew making toys for local children in Northampton.

126. Despatch Rider Firewoman Renee Donn aka Glambotsky, Homerton Fire Station, Hackney, on her motorbike training course.

127.

129. David Louis Ellis, Leeds Fire Brigade.

128. Renee Donn in action

Some of those who Served 341

130. David Ellis (front row, third left) with No.1 Crew, Leeds, 1941.

131. David Ellis (standing third from left on fire engine without helmet), at Quarry Hill flats, Leeds.

132. Sidney Enlander, Belfast Fire Brigade in 1942, standing back row, fifth from left.

342 *Jewish Participation in the Fire Service in the Second World War*

133. Philip Evans aka Even, Glasgow, 1941, before joining the Royal Artillery in August.

Metropolitan Borough of St. Pancras.

AIR RAID PRECAUTIONS DEPARTMENT.

№ 12991

..............10-7..1942

𝔗𝔥𝔦𝔰 𝔦𝔰 𝔱𝔬 ℭ𝔢𝔯𝔱𝔦𝔣𝔶 𝔱𝔥𝔞𝔱

(Name) .....Miss S. Fabian.............................

(Address) ......16ᶜ North Villas...........................
is a member of a Fire-fighting party organised by the ST. PANCRAS BOROUGH COUNCIL and possesses the powers of entry and taking of steps for extinguishing fire or for protecting property, or rescuing persons or property, from fire, which are conferred by the Fire Precautions (Access to Premises) (No. 2) Order, 1941.

(Signed) ....

Chief Warden and A.R.P.O.

134. Steffi Fabian's Firewatcher ID card (later Mrs Elias).

Some of those who Served

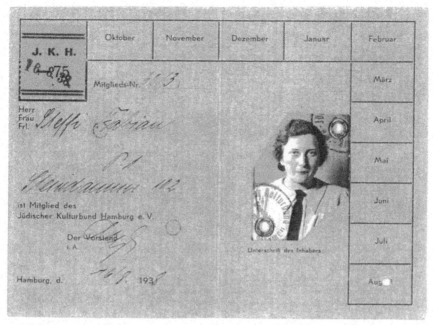

135. Steffi Fabian's German membership card of the Hamburg Jewish Cultural Society, before fleeing to the UK.

137. Firewatcher Hans Nathan Feld.

136. The Kindertransport identity document for refugee and later Firewatcher, Daniel Falkson, courtesy of his son Howard.

344 *Jewish Participation in the Fire Service in the Second World War*

138. Rae and Larry Feldman, husband and wife in AFS in London in 1941 (unnamed/undated postwar magazine).

139. Firewoman Betty/Betsy Fine aka Rubens.

140. Fireman Max Fox, far left and his five serving brothers.

141. Fireman Clarence Colman 'Frank' Franklin.

142. Louis Franks, AFS. Based in London he was injured several times while fighting fires in the London docks, once falling through several floors of a warehouse when he was on the roof and the building collapsed.

Some of those who Served 345

143. Firewoman Libby Frumkin/Sacks, mother of Emeritus Chief Rabbi, Lord Jonathan Sacks.

144. Firewoman Zelda Gatoff, Newcastle.

145. Barnett 'Benny' Glass, seated second from right, at the London Officers Training School (LOTS); served in Whitechapel and in Exeter.

146. Alfred Bernard Gold.

147. Samuel Goldberg, back row, third from left, Swansea.

148. Barnett 'Barney' Grant, standing extreme right, St Katharine's Dock.

346 *Jewish Participation in the Fire Service in the Second World War*

149. Firewoman Gertie 'Gerry' Grant, back row extreme right, Leeds; later married Max Abrahams.

150. Fireman Philip Grossman.

151. Lawrence Isaac Halon, fourth row from front, sixth from left, Manchester.

152. *JC* article about the double BEM awards to Harry Harris and Cyril Davis in early 1941

153. Section Officer Fireman Harry Harris BEM, Second World War, and First World War veteran, on an AJEX Parade in Hull in the 1930s in light overcoat.

154. Firewoman H. Harris, London, from the files of Jack Lennard.

155. Section Leader Oscar Edward Harris, Brixton 1938–45. Seated far right.

156. Mick 'Michael Isaac' Hart. Third row from front, far left.

157. Henry 'Harry' Hart. Standing back row, third from left.

348 Jewish Participation in the Fire Service in the Second World War

158. Firewatcher Georg Heim, refugee from Vienna, with grandson John Francken.

159. William Heiser/Hayes, centre with arm on pump.

160. Philip Jacobs AFS, later Sqdn Ldr RAF in Bomber Command and POW for three years.

161. Fireman Arthur Wolfe Joseph, Birmingham, photo taken in 1960.

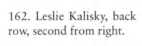

162. Leslie Kalisky, back row, second from right.

Some of those who Served

163. Izzy 'George' Kaufman, father of Harry Kaufman, Bomber Command National Serviceman.

164. Nathaniel Kaufman, AFS and later Pioneer corps.

165. Adolphus 'Alf' Kay who served at RAF bases in Wiltshire and Gloucestershire.

166. Joe Kerbel on right.

350 *Jewish Participation in the Fire Service in the Second World War*

167. Eva Evans in back row, second from left.

168. Eva Evans later Klopstock.

169. Jack Jacob Korn.

170. Fireman Phillip 'Philli' Kruyer, served Millwall and Bristol, second cousin to the author.

171. Firewoman and telephonist Nita Krotosky/Greene, of Cardiff.

352 *Jewish Participation in the Fire Service in the Second World War*

172. Benjamin Lakumsky-Isaac, later Lakum.

173. Samuel Lang in Hull, fourth row back with glasses at centre of group.

Some of those who Served

174. Samuel Lang, centre with glasses, holding hose.

175. Fireman Myer 'Mick' Levy.

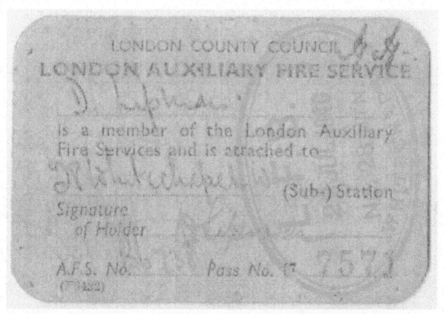

176. Fireman David Lipman's various Fire Brigade documents.

176. Fireman David Lipman's various Fire Brigade documents. (cont.)

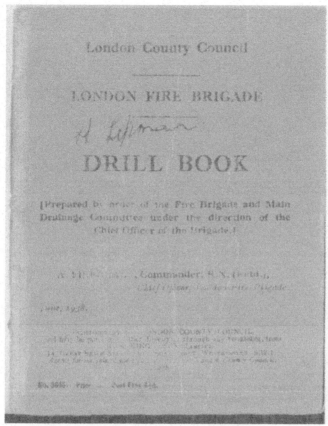

176. Fireman David Lipman's various Fire Brigade documents.

177. Barney and David Lipman.

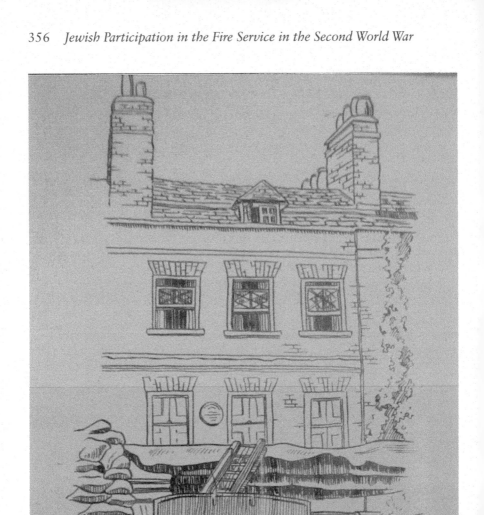

178. Sketch of West Hampstead Fire Sub-Station by Jewish Firewoman artist, Julia Lowenthal (courtesy of the LFB Museum).

179. Fireman Joshua Manches.

180. Fireman A. Marks, second left, New Cross Station, London.

181. Judith Marks aka Shaw, telephonist, Holdenhurst Road Fire Station, Bournemouth.

182. Fireman Solomon Marks, probably far right, but not confirmed on this unidentified photo.

183. Fireman Bernard Martin.

184. Fireman Leslie Martin.

185. Fireman Leslie Miller, right.

186. Fireman Louis Moont, Finchley, with wife Joyce (Civil Defence).

187. Louis Moont at the Fire Station communications centre.

188. Louis Moont sitting far right.

189. Manuel Nadell, Glasgow.

190. Edward Natali.

191. The Nissenthal family 1942–43, left to right Jack Nissenthal, RAF; Lewis Harris, Fireman (uncle); Michael Nissenthal, RAF.

192. Lewis Nyman, Whitechapel.

193. Jack Oliver, Cricklewood.

194. Simon Ososky/Osbourne, standing centre, in action.

195. Eric Palmer, Hull, second from right.

196. Phyllis Peters, (Epping).

197. Firewoman Hazel Pearl.

198. Alexander 'Sunny' Pinner.

199. Manfred Plaut.

200. Jack Pollins, third from left.

Some of those who Served

201/202. Three identified Jewish Firemen at No 26 Fire Fighters Instructors Course, 1943: Jack Pollins, third row from front, third from right; Hyman Benstock, second row from front, second from right; S. Temple, second row from front, fourth from right. Below is signed back of photograph. Burchell sitting centre on floor.

203. Myer Pollins (in the van) loading toys made by firemen, for children in hospital.

364 *Jewish Participation in the Fire Service in the Second World War*

204. Myer Pollins, front row far right; Michael Kay (his brother in law) back row second from right with moustache.

205. Firewatcher Peter Prager, taken in 2002.

206. Jack Press with fire 1941, at back on far left. Je Fireman Murray Medway a photo but unidentified.

207. Barney Prever aka Brifor, standing far left.

208. Barney Prever with his Bow Station crew, sitting sixth from left.

NATIONAL FIRE SERVICE - FIRE AREA NO. 36.

To: Fireman J. Press
Via: Assistant Fire Force Commander.
From: Fire Force Commander, No. 36 Area.
E/AWW/

    I regret that I have to give you notice of the termination of your services on medical grounds. For the purpose of this notice, your last day of service will be 8.10.42.

    I take this opportunity of thanking you for your work in the London Fire Forces, and trust that before long you will find yourself well enough to take up some other work of national importance.

    By direction of the Fire Force Commander.

Area Establishments Officer.

No. 199939   Fire   J. Press,

36 A.1.A. Station.

30.9.42.

209. Discharge through injury/illness certificate of 199939 Driver/Fireman Jack Press aka Meyer Isaac Prachzker, dated 8 October 1942. Formerly of Stoke Newington, he served in Ilford and Ruislip, lived 1909–70.

210. Jewish refugee Doris Rath later Moritz, AFS Firewoman in Cambridge, taken in 1949.

211. Driver/Fireman Morris Rosenberg, front row, third left, East India Dock Fire Station.

212. Jewish Firefighter Michelle Kent (Loughton 2006) and her grandfather, Second World War Fireman Joseph Sack.

368 Jewish Participation in the Fire Service in the Second World War

213. Firewoman Clare Elizabeth Salaman.

214. Fireman Michael Sampson with brother Julius, who was in the Army.

215. Solomon Samuel, n row, third from left, in Sw

216. Siblings left to righ Segal AFS, Beulah Segal A then WAAF; and Robin Segal AFS to Army. All enl the AFS in 1939.

217. Louis Serota, secon right, London.

218. Philip Shalet, first left in back row.

219. David Shank, Downham Road Station, Dalston and later Hayes.

220. First World War medals of Moshe Shertasky aka Sherrick, 38th Bat. Royal Fusiliers (Jewish Legion) and Second World War Fireman.

370 *Jewish Participation in the Fire Service in the Second World War*

221. Jack (Jacob) Joseph Shiman, one row from back, 10th from left, with the Stepney Stretcher Party in December 1941; he later joined the Fire Brigade. Note the many wearing First World War ribbons.

222. Jack Silver, who served at Canon Street with David Latner (who was killed).

223. Reuben Sloan, New Cross Fire Station.

224. Noah (Norman) Simmons, back row, second from right.

Some of those who Served

225. Esther Spiro, later Black, far right, with the Brick Lane crew 1941–43.

226. Esther Spiro with her full crew, second row from front, third from right.

227. Fire Guard Phil Solomon aka Akivah 'Keeva' Patronovski, in Grimsby with his son Leo.

228. City Alderman and Fire Guard organizer Woolf Solomon BEM, Grimsby.

230. Isaac Speck, third from left.

229. Sylvia Spicker, Wakefield.

232. Philip Maurice Stone with his wife.

231. Firewoman Eva Charlotte Sternheim aka Sternham, Jewish refugee, London.

233. Philip Maurice Stone with his crew, standing centre.

234. Fireman Albert Tisman.

Some of those who Served

235. Reuben Waxman with his Street Patrol (note SP on helmets), standing third from left.

236. London Fireman Reuben Waxman in AFS uniform (portrait).

237. Michael Visokle aka West, who served at Stratford, London.

374 *Jewish Participation in the Fire Service in the Second World War*

238. Fireman brothers Nathan (left) and Morris Weinstein.

239. Fireman Leslie Wilson, middle row, third from left.

240. David Winston, Leeds Fireman

241. Moses 'Michael' Zetter, Physical Training Instructor at West Ham station; back row, 2nd from right.

242. Derrick David Zimmerman standing left under the number '63'

243. Moses 'Michael' Zetter, Physical Training Instructor at West Ham station; 2nd row from front, 2nd from right.

The Manchester Album

244. Fireguards (FG), many Jewish, at the factory of David Matz in Manchester, makers of waterproof coats, taken in 1940.

245. Tyson Street station, Manchester: Solly Lieberman, front row, third from left; Mendel Wander, third row from front, far right; Louis Parretsky aka Parry back row, seventh from left.

378 *Jewish Participation in the Fire Service in the Second World War*

246. Morris Goldstone standing top left and Arthur Geller sitting second from left, Manchester.

247. Morris Goldstone.

248. Sonny Goodman, Manchester, standing back right with glasses.

249. Judd Goldberg.

250. Queen's Road sub-station, Manchester: Leslie Peters sitting centre on car bumper; Moe Waxman, third from right standing with moustache; Solly Guise, standing far right.

251. Judd Goldberg with his original fireman's axe, taken in the 1990s.

252. Queen's Road sub-station 1940: Leslie Peters centre standing; Solly Guise, third from right.

253. Harold Basil Glaskie, Manchester.

Miscellany: Last Voices

254. Whitechapel Fire Station Commercial Rd, E1, probably taken 9 September 1941, two days after a Blitz raid on the night of 7/8 September, when a bomb fell nearby, fracturing a gas main and causing a huge fire, a hundred feet high, according to eyewitnesses. The blast blew out windows and doors and two firemen were killed. The vast majority of the firemen here were Jewish.

255. This unique photograph shows the Jewish Fire Brigade at the Fohrenwald DP (Displaced Persons) camp Germany 1945–46. This UNRRA camp became the last to close (1957). Although this photo does not technically fit into the remit of this book, it is possible some of the men would have gone to the UK to live, but it is of interest in itself on the subject of Jewish Fire Brigade personnel. Courtesy of the Wiener library, London.

256. Jewish members of the various Civil Defence branches at the Great Synagogue Duke Street (before it was bombed) remembering a fellow synagogue member, Myer Cash, killed in an air raid. The men are mostly Air Raid Wardens and Street Patrol/Stretcher Party personnel. Courtesy of the Imperial War Museum.

257. Hendon Fire station with Phyllis Miller, second row from front, second from right; Enid Harris/Perez, third row from front, second right; Olga Charnie, second row from front, first left; Dianne Leapman, third row from front, second left.

258. Firewoman Enid Harris said this Fireman at Hendon station was Jewish but could not recall his name.

259. A reunion of Jewish Firewomen at Sinclair House in Redbridge, on 13 January 2008, partly organised by the author Martin Sugarman, and Stephanie Maltman; back row of women left to right: Enid Harris/Perez, Doris Nayman, Fay Sennit/Nyrenberg, Benna Lessing/Greenberg, Gertrude/Trudy Woolf/Joseph (?), and not known; front row of women left to right: Sarah Rosen, Betty Cohen/Nerden, Ruth Crosbie, Sylvia Dorff/Beer, Lily Landau/Shine, Sylvia Kaye.

386 *Jewish Participation in the Fire Service in the Second World War*

260. Sylvia Dorff/Beer as a young Firewoman.

261. *Ilford Recorder* article, 17 January 2008, about the reunion of Firewomen, with additional visitor and former Firewatcher, Norma Sanders/Nissenthal, top right.

Appendix 1

A Note on Other Fire Units
Stephanie Maltman

'Street Fire Patrols' (SFP) were set up in areas where there was thought to be high industrial or other risk (dense housing for instance); these were volunteer fire parties, groups of men and women who were part of the community living on the same street or round the corner from each other who would have access to a simpler version of a trailer pump, hand-operated, located somewhere convenient nearby. For instance, the Bruce Road pump, in Poplar, was kept in the yard of the local pub. Street parties were often first on the scene at an incident and able to deal with it themselves; if not they would call on the Fire Brigade. Incendiaries in themselves were not particularly difficult to deal with but they fell in their hundreds and that was very dangerous. Street fire parties were a sort of self-help organization that arose spontaneously almost from the community and were neither part of the Fire Service nor any other branch of ARP, though they were recognized as an important part of the anti-fire war effort. In the case of Alfred Wagerman, his son Peter remembers his father wore an official white painted helmet with SFP painted on it in large black letters.

There were also 'works brigades'. Large factories or other industrial installations (power-stations, gas works, oil refineries) had volunteer fire parties drawn from among their employees who functioned in more or less the same way as street fire parties but with responsibility for a particular industrial site. The initiative for these came from the management. It is important to note that both street fire parties and works brigades were given a certain amount of initial training by members of the Fire Service.

In some very large factories or plants in outer areas, such as Ford's, and in airports and the like, there existed even before the war an approximation of their own fire brigade. This was not war related but a permanent fixture and they would have had at least one motorized fire appliance. During the war they continued to function independently, although by that time they probably had their own firewatchers and so on, all drawn from employees who would leave their usual work and operate in a fire-fighting capacity in the event of an emergency. Again they were independent organizations and did not come under any branch of Civil Defence until the formation of the NFS to which they were eventually affiliated, and so joined the order of battle as it were.

Appendix 2

Aspects of Anti-Semitism

The following extracts are from an interview by Stephanie Maltman on 1 March 2006 with George Wheeler (not Jewish), who was a 14-year-old AFS messenger boy in Bow, stationed at Lush and Cooks cleaners near the River Lea.

> There was always a bit of ill-feeling in the East End between English people and Jews. The Blackshirts ... were very good at stirring up trouble. A lot of men ... liked going down the pub ... and when you've had a few drinks, if you had a few agitators ... it didn't take long to fan the flames. They said 'the Jewish boys didn't want to fight and went into the Fire Service to stay out of the army' ... I say to them, 'Were you there then?'. They fought fires just like anyone else. They were in the thick of it and when you're in the open, you've got no shelter, you're working at a fire, all the sky's lit up and there's bombs dropping down among you, they didn't run away, they fought the fires like the rest of us. This is the trouble ... I would support the Jewish boys all the way along the line ... we had a big complement of them, but they were the same as the rest of us. You're going out night after night, and if they were scared, we were all one way and another, but you don't show it ... certain people were trying to put the Jewish race in a very bad light. They didn't succeed. When the crunch came, when the Blitz started, the Jewish Firemen earned the respect of everyone. They were accepted like any other fireman.
>
> The driver (... most of them were Jewish because they were mostly taxi drivers ...) was also a pump-operator ... so the crew relied on them for the supply of water ... they stood there on their own, more vulnerable. A lot of us were brought up among Jews ... if anyone starts slating a Jew we'd be very quick to stand up for them

... when it came to the Sabbath you had to ignore it, it was war. They didn't observe it ... you're on duty for 48 hours. You have to ignore it ... we all had to stick together ... the Jewish people came out of it as good as any other British person. They did what was expected of them ... which upset the agitators quite a bit!

From Maurice Richardson, *London's Burning*

My temperamental namesake, who hated the instructor's guts – part of his hate was anti-Semitism; the instructor was unmistakably Jewish – said, 'Bunk, you're just as good as the rest of us. He's picking on you because e thinks you got money 'cos you speak educated. He's on the tap, see? If you slipped him one he'd never say another word. Them ____ Yids is all the same.'[1]

There was only one taint in the otherwise intensely amiable dispositions of these men; this was virulent anti-Semitism. Gizzie was so far gone that you couldn't argue with him about it. Johnny was nearly as bad. The old sub was another Jew hater. He refused to believe there were any poor Jews in England, all Yids were twisters, etc.; I used to shout at him till I was quite tired, but he only shook his head like an old dog and said, 'You can say what you like, mate, you're an educated man and you may know what you're talking about, but you'll never convince me that Yids ain't bastards. Mind you, I don't say there aren't exceptions, like young Solly here and Nat.'

Solly Greenbaum, one of the three or four Jews in the station, was a brisk, lively little man who had worked in the advertising business, so gay and friendly nobody could help liking him. Nat Marks was a huge, quiet, sardonic man with a brown face and curly hair like a spaniel's. He came from Jamaica and spoke in a deep slow growl. It was a good thing that these were so popular, for there was a great deal of anti-Semitism latent in the station, especially among the men who had had small, one-man businesses of their own and suffered competition from Jewish street-market traders.

In the boxing and burgling underworld of Gizzie and Johnny, with its sporadic gang or rather mob warfare, anti-Semitism flourished of course. The Yiddisher boys had their mob and you had yours. The genuine (economically) proletarians, like Joe Whigham, who was a building trades worker, had no racial prejudice whatever, and together with myself and George Fitt, an intelligent and educated little fair man, who'd been a photographer for a sports press agency and was a solid socialist, they used to reprove the anti-Semites. Several men came from Shoreditch, a lumpenish district where Mosley's propaganda had taken some root. One or two had very likely been Blackshirts for a time. Almost certainly Jack Connor had; he was one of the leading auxiliaries, an ex-army man, Guards, I think, and he had some of the fascist patter by heart. I found him pleasant enough but he wasn't very popular. The arch Jew-baiter, Massey, a cross-eyed, hard-faced, surly fellow, had also been in the army*. There was undoubtedly rather a savage, brooding strain in this man, and the pro-Semites among us were able to turn it to advantage. We referred to him as the Jew baiter, and the name stuck so that even the anti-Semites used it; 'like Massey and Jack Connor talk that way. This anti-Jew stuff is all bunk, and you know it', had remarkable propagandist effect. Gizzie, Johnny and even the old sub didn't need to be taken seriously. They could be dismissed as comics. Massey's chief victim was the third Jew, an ex-taxi driver called Tasker. He was a member of one of the little extreme left sectarian bodies of the SPGB, I think. Intelligent, but with something peculiarly irritating about his personality. He was the most tactless political propagandist imaginable. I once heard him say to someone: 'You've learnt quite a lot from me, you have; you wouldn't have spoken like that a week ago.' But he stood up to Massey all right and threatened to lay him out with a billiard cue if he didn't leave him alone.

    Much of the anti-Semitism failed to survive the first month of the Blitz. The few imbeciles who said things like 'I wouldn't save a ____ in' Yid's house from burning' learnt sense at the fires in Whitechapel. Correspondingly, one's own feelings towards them changed. Even if you had the strongest theoretical reasons for disliking somebody, it was impossible to feel bitter about him when you were on the job together with bombs dropping. The night came when I felt a wave of friendliness towards Massey.

    *I am not trying to disparage the Army in this connection. The point is that the peace-time private soldier tends to be a rather lumpen type, no fault of his own, and as such is liable to anti Semitism.[2]

After the start of the blitz the atmosphere became even more friendly. Anti-Semitism disappeared or was in abeyance. Political arguments lacked sting because the arguers were in agreement about so many immediately topical questions like shelters, evacuation etc.[3]

The driver was Nat Marks, a fat, dashing driver and an expert mechanic. He was supposed to be the best pump operator in the station. Unlike some pump operators, who were content to stand by the pump and keep as far away from the fire as possible, Nat was always thinking about the rest of the crew up on the branch. If you were in an awkward place with the hose caught on something, his huge form would suddenly come looming up in the glow and get you loose with a shove and a tug.[4]

From H.S. Ingham (ed.), *Fire and Water; an NFS Anthology*

Fireman Stephen Spender wrote, 'There were two Jewish Leading Firemen at this station [i.e. where Spender was posted], Weissmann and Herzberg. One of them was the son of a Rabbi, simple, devout, friendly and honest. The other was an ex-Communist. He resigned from the Party because one day he asked awkward questions of the local secretary about the balance sheet. The secretary replied that there were 'too many of these bloody Jews about'. No amount of explanation of this remark would satisfy Herzberg, and he left the Party. Both these men, slightly apart, and considerably concerned with discussing between themselves their chances of promotion, took a kindly and sympathetic interest in the other men. They had more authority than any other officers I have met in the Fire Service, and yet they were always quiet, patient and polite. There was no anti-Semitism at [this station].'[5]

NOTES

1. Maurice Richardson, *London's Burning* (London: Robert Hale, 1941), pp.33–4.
2. Ibid., pp.62–5.
3. Ibid., p.137.
4. Ibid., pp.166–7.
5. H.S. Ingham (ed.), *Fire and Water; an NFS Anthology* (London: Lindsay Drummond, 1942), p.182.

Appendix 3

Attitudes to Aliens

The London County Council War Diary, Volume 1, 24 August 1939 to 31 July 1940 (in a private collection) contains the following entries about Aliens in the Fire Service and illustrates what at first was their progressive deterioration in status in Britain. For Aliens, read Jews, who made up the bulk of this refugee group in Britain.

4 November 1939 – AFS Aliens – Home Office Circular ARP/297/1939 … for part-time service only.

24 May 1940 – Aliens – London regional circular 144 stating that no aliens of any nationality should in future be employed in key positions in any ARP (Air Raid Precaution) service. Details to be sent to DAC (Deputy Assistant Commissioner) CID Scotland Yard of all aliens in any service. Home Office circular FB 55/1940 instructing local authorities to review the position of any aliens in the AFS – *none to be employed in key positions* but consideration to be given to their transfer. [author's emphasis]

Council decided to terminate forthwith services of all German, Austrian and stateless aliens. Czechs and Poles *to be watched* and particulars of all aliens in the department to be forwarded to Clerk of the Council. Special watch to be kept on any officer or employee of British nationality whose loyalty is in any way doubtful. [author's emphasis]

Home Office circular FB 64/1940 stating that all aliens in AFS and casualty services should be suspended, but individuals might be reinstated if granted exemption from restrictions on movement imposed by the *Aliens Order* and subject to consultation with the police.

31 May 1940 – particulars of seven aliens in AFS forwarded to the Clerk of the Council.

4 June 1940 – Aliens – Home Office circular FB 71/1940 drawing attention of local authorities to the necessity of their satisfying themselves as to the reliability of individual members of the civil defence services.

5 June 1940 – Ten aliens in the AFS suspended and required to return all articles of uniform and equipment.

6 June 1940 – Particulars of three aliens in addition to the seven referred to on May 31st 1940, forwarded to the Clerk of the Council and Scotland Yard.

12 June 1940 – <u>Employment of Aliens</u> – Services of aliens in the Service already reported to be dispensed with at one week's notice on 20th June, but not to be allowed to resume duty. While individual aliens may be subsequently reinstated under certain conditions, none of the above mentioned should be reinstated except under authority from the Civil Defence and General Purposes Committee ...

13 June 1940 – <u>Aliens</u> – 10 aliens given one week's notice of termination of services on 20 June 1940.

4 July 1940 – <u>Aliens</u> – Chairman of Civil Defence and General Purposes Committee decided that aliens discharged on 21 June should not be reinstated and that aliens should not in future be employed in the fire services.

Addendum

ADDENDUM TO OVERSEAS MISCELLANY (Page 318)

In WW2 the Dutch Jews in Amsterdam formed their own 40 man fire brigade to protect the wooden superstructure of the Great Synagogue in the Jewish quarter, in case it should be bombed; they also added emergency water supply pipes and fire escapes and covered the attic floor with fire retarding blankets. When the men of the Jewish FB were deported to Auschwitz, the municipal FB promised to care for the building and it survived the Nazis and the war to this day.

ADDENDUM TO WW1 AND POST WAR SERVICE

Sabrina Cohen-Hatton – Chief Officer West Sussex 2019
Mike Hatton – husband of Sabrina – see JC Aug 3rd 2019
Sidney Gompertz Gamble, 2nd in charge London Fire Brigade during the bombings in WW1 and served from 1892; awarded a knighthood gazetted 9/2/17 in London Gazette page 1460. Grandson of Solomon (capmaker) and Jane Gompertz of Goulston Street in Whitechapel, and son of Moses Gompertz, an artist, and so of recent Jewish origin.

ADDENDUM TO RECORD OF HONOUR

Lily Alexander – Fratres newsletter
Miss Betty Baker (later Freeman) Firewatcher in Dodd Street E1 at Victor
    Value warehouse – personal interview Feb 2018 aged 97 years
Balcombe – Kingsland Station
John Berge, served RFC/RAF WW1 no. 59199 – BJBH p537 – was AFS in
    1939 census, wife Lily lived Bexley Heath, born Aldgate – WW1 medal
    in M Sugarman collection
Marion Bloom, Ealing – Filmed in 2010 by FBU
Joe Bostoff – Fratres newsletter

Morrel Bravo, Firewatcher brother of Gilbert Bravo AFS
Ralph Bricker 1939-40 – Wembley – to RAF 1940, won DFC
Charlie Brooker (relative of Harold Pollins, historian)
Firewatcher Moses Montefiore Canin, Birmingham (WW1 Veteran RAMC)
Aaron 'Acky' Cohen Glasgow Fire AFS WW2 – info/photos from son Prof Bernard Cohen
Mr and Mrs John E Cohen of Richmond, London, Firewatchers – Mr Cohen was a Boer War and WW1 veteran (JC, July 1941)
Lottie or Erika Cohn, later Jacobs – German Jewish refugee from Hamburg – switchboard operator, grandson Paul Jacobs has letters specifying Stations at Lambeth/Cable St/Shadwell/Camperdown House/Roseberry Avenue. Also Coastal watch in Dorset and PT instructor.
Anita Cowen, Fireguard – JC Feb-March 1943
Richard Dytch, Leeds AFS – later Dyson – info from son Robert
Betty Goldburg, of Cheltenham, JC 12/12/41
Joseph Goldstein, Fireguard – Jack Lennard archives/photo with armband
John Joseph Goodkind, Willesden and Leeds, b1907-d 1998
Ellwood 'Ted' Gould AFS Bethnal Green (JC obit 10/8/18)
Leslie Greenburgh, Manchester – from niece Ruth Harris of London
Harry Grossman Station 38 Kingsland – Thames Fireboat WiA – joined AFS Oct 1938. B. Glasgow, lived London, Hairdresser
Sam Gordon, of Hendon, from daughter Irene Leaman
Gudelovich is aka Gedalovitch – his wife Molly killed in Blitz 11/5/41
Eli Hackenbroch, Hampstead Firewatcher
Sam Kirkwood, Firewatcher (Fratres magazine Vol 27/1, June 1941)
Sid Kosky – Fratres newsletter
Israel Jack Lambert aka Lampert, b. Whitechapel of Russian Jewish immigrants, cabinet maker by profession, lived Enfield and served Brimsdown fire station and sent into London, and St Paul's on many occasions. Call from daughter Ruth Lincoln of Bedford
Wolf Lennard – Brook Rd substation, Clapton – Coronation Ave bombing rescue – see p61 'Just Like the end of the World' by Camilla Loewe, 2012
Victor Marco Levy, Didsbury, Manchester (submitted by nephew Louis Rapaport served Korea)
Nat Lutsky – Fratres newsletter
Jerry Markofsky – Fratres newsletter
Ginger H. Mazer – Fratres newsletter
Mick Ornstein – Fratres newsletter
Laura 'Leah' Philips, nee Victor, Firewatcher Cricklewood, later famous designer – info from daughter Sue Summers
Firewoman Phyllis Polack
Max/Mark Preska – Firewatcher, Hackney area – info daughter Ruth now Glassman

Firewoman Edna Presky
Jack/Jacob (Francis) Reuben – ARP Red Cross card, says transferred to AFS 1941, lived Constantine Road, Hampstead, born 1907, husband of Lily
Jack Reiderman, lived Old Castle Street E1 – Firewatcher – from daughter Sylvia Joseph
Philip Romain
Sassoon, Kingsland – seconded to Haifa, Israel 1945-46
Mrs Sax – Firewatcher – Fratres newsletter
Pamela Ruth Sholto later Pamela Eyre, actress; Firewatcher at RADA and wounded by bombs in May 1941. Obit JC 13/7/18
Oscar Sawn aka Isidore Swirsky – later joined RAF
LFW Sylvia Tucker, Ilford Federation Synagogue war memorial
Michael Vardy, Hackney from niece Ruth Harris
S. Wagenfield (of Gunton Rd, London E5)
George Warshawsky aka Darnell, served Massey Shaw Fireboat
Sidney Winston aka Weinstein, b 1899, hairdresser, lived ??? info Gina Marks TBC
Winch – Kingsland station

ADDENDUM TO THOSE SERVING BEFORE WW1

Before WW1 – Possibly Jewish – Joseph Jacobs, killed Wandsworth 1899?

New grave headstone for Firewatcher Philip Freeman/Friedman, killed in the Exeter Blitz, erected after his remains were lost and then identified in 2022. Erected by Jerry Klinger and Martin Sugarman of the Jewish American Society for Historic Preservation, UK branch and AJEX UK.

Selected Bibliography

Anon, *Front Line 1940–41: The Official Story of the Civil Defence of Britain* (London: HMSO, 1942).
Astor, John, *When Sirens Sounded: An Account of Air Raid Precautions in Printing House Square 1937 to 1945* (London: Office of the Times, 1949).
Bassie, Gavin, *Liverpool's Finest: The History of the City's Fire Brigade* (Liverpool: Trinity-Mirror-Media, 2008).
Black, Tom, *The Bells Go Down: The Diary of a London AFS Man* (London: Methuen, 1942).
Calder, Ritchie, *The Lesson of London* (London: Secker and Warburg, 1941).
Demarne, Cyril, *The London Blitz: A Fireman's Tale* (Essex: After the Battle, 1991).
Demarne, Cyril, *Our Girls* (Edinburgh: Pentland Press, 1995).
Fry, Helen, *The King's Most Loyal Enemy Aliens* (Stroud: Sutton Publishing, 2007).
Hollis, Barry, *The Forgotten Front Line* (Newport Pagnell: Enthusiast Publications, 1985).
Hollis, Barry, *37 Fire Forces: Fire and Rescue, S.E. London, 1941–46* (Newport Pagnell: Enthusiast Publications, 1988).
Holloway, Sally, *Courage High; a History of Firefighting in London* (London: HMSO, 1992).
Hughes, John, *Port in a Storm: Air Attacks on Liverpool and its Shipping in the Second World War* (Merseyside: Merseyside Port Folios, 1993).
Hughes, Ted, *Bournemouth Firemen at War* (Dorset: Dorset Publishing Company, 1991).
Ingham, H.S. (ed.), *Fire and Water; An NFS Anthology* (London: Lindsay Drummond, 1942).
Leighton-Langer, Peter, *The King's Own Loyal Enemy Aliens, 1939–45: German and Austrian Refugees in Britain's Armed Forces* (London and Portland, OR: Vallentine Mitchell, 2006).
Lewey, F., *Cockney Campaign* (London: Stanley Paul, 1946).
Lloyd-Elliott, Martin, *City Ablaze: Life with the World's Busiest Fire-fighters* (London: Bloomsbury Books, 1992).
Lockyear, Arthur, *Warriors in Fire Boots: A Tribute to the Valour of Firefighters* (Huddersfield: Jeremy Mills Publishing, 2011).
Longmate, Norman, *How We Lived Then* (London: Hutchinson, 1971).
Richardson, Maurice, *London's Burning* (London: Robert Hale, 1941).
Sandall, Alan G., *Are you 17? Vivid Real-life Stories of Every-day Men and Women who became the Fire-fighting Saviours of Britain from the World War Two Blitz* (Frome: Private Publication, 1993).

Simpson, A.W. Brian, *In the Highest Degree Odious: Detention Without Trial in Wartime Britain* (Oxford: Clarendon Press, 1992).

Sugarman, Martin, *Fighting Back: British Jewry's Military Contribution in the Second World War* (London and Portland, OR: Vallentine Mitchell, 2017 (2nd edition)).

Sweet, Matthew, *The West End Front; the Wartime Secrets of London's Grand Hotels* (London: Faber and Faber, 2011).

Under Fire (London: London Fire & Civil Defence Authority, n.d.).

Walker, Harold W., *More Memories: Waltham Abbey in War and Peace – A Fireman's Recollections* (London: Sewardstone, 1993).

Wallington, Neil, *Firemen at War: The Work of London's Firefighters in the Second World War* (London: David and Charles, 1981).

Wassey, Michael, *Ordeal by Fire* (London: Secker and Warburg, 1941).

Index

Please note that page numbers relating to Notes will have the letter 'n' following the page number. Page references to photographs and other non-textual matter that are not on the same page as the text are in italics. Only those regions of particular interest (such as suffering hits in the Second World War) are named.

Abdela, Frederick, 325
Abney Cemetery, Hackney, 119
Abraham, Richard, 325
Abrahams, George Isaac, 14
Abrahams, Leonard Eliezer (*later* Graham), 157, 326
Abrahams, Max, 151n, 326
acts of bravery, failure to adequately recognise, 8
Adam, David (aka Adaminsky), 157
Adams, David, 326
Addison, Sir Joseph, 10n
Adler, Alfred, 326, 327
AFS *see* Auxiliary Fire Service (AFS)
Air Raid Precautions (ARP), 2, 6
air raid shelters, 71, 91, 95, 139, 140, 141, 173
Air Raid Wardens, 176, 384
air raids *see* bombings and air raids
aircraft: crashed, 147; *see also* V1 and V2 aircraft
AJEX Jewish Chaplain cards, 185
AJEX Jewish Military Museum, 13, 40, 104
AJEX Jewish Parade, 65
Albert Embankment, London Fire Brigade HQ, 1
Aldgate, London, 2, 109; Aldgate Pump, 4, 149
Aliens: 'Aliens' scare (1940), 6; attitudes to, 393–4; Curfew for, 162; Enemy Aliens, 93, 161

Allied Services Overseas Fire Column (International Fire Column), Europe, 146
Altmann, Rabbi, 7
Amiel, Isaac, 14
Anson, Colin (aka Ascher), 9n
anti-aircraft guns, 120–1
anti-Semitism in Fire Service, 3, 4, 5–6, 7, 10n, 78, 79, 87, 138, 145, 389–92
Appleby, David/Davis, 14
archives, 17–18, 36; London Metropolitan Archives *see* London Metropolitan Archives (LMA); researching, 2–3; St Marylebone Civil Defence Records, Westminster Council Archives, 65; *see also* AJEX Jewish Military Museum; records/registers
Armed Forces, 6, 36, 141
Army Corps, Manchester, 153
'Army Pals' battalions, First World War, 3
Aronowsky/Aron, Eric, 15
Association of Jewish Refugees (AJR), 6–7
Astor, John, 13
Atheneum Club fire (1940), 50
Atomic Bomb project, USA, 136
Auxiliary Fire Service (AFS), 1, 2, 3, 4, 13, 14, 166, 167, 168–9, 171,

174, 175, 176, 387;
LFB/AFS/NFS boundaries, 141;
short stories, 158, 161, 162, 163, 164, 166, 168–9, 175;
testimonies, 47, 61, 63, 71, 78, 87, 89, 91, 93, 97, 102, 104, 110, 113, 116n, 117, 118, 125, 135, 141, 145, 153, 154–5; war work, film to celebrate, 7–8
awards, 14, 65, 79, 104, 129

Baedekker raids, 145
Balham, London, 34, 171
Bank Station bombing, 144–5
Barnard, Jim, 3, 4
Barnett, Harry (Harold) 'Barney,' 157–8, 327
Beaumont, A.R., 7
Belinsky, Solomon, 15, 16
The Bells Go Down: The Diary of a London AFS Man (Black), 4, 10n
Belsen concentration camp, 56
BEM, 22, 91, 104, 164, 190, 221, 226, 228, 232, 241, 251, 256, 298, 304, 305, 346
Benstock, Hyman, 32, 327
Berg, Charles, 327
Berg, Nathan Bernard, 327
Berger, Ron, 158
Berkon, Simon, 16
Berlin, Walter, 327
Bernstein, Woolf, 327
Bethnal Green Underground Station disaster (1943), 122
Bialystock, Poland: Fire Brigade, 318
Billiter Street fire, London (1941), 51
Billman, Karl (aka Bartlett), 9n
Black, Louis, 16
Black, Tom, 4, 10n
Blackshirts, 4, 6
Blackwall Tunnel, near Whitechapel, 117
Blitz *see* bombings and air raids; City of London bombings and raids; fires
Blitz (documentary), 54

'Blitz Spirit,' 94
Blumenkehl, Leon, 158, 327, 329
Blumson, George William, 16
Bluston, Doris, 330
Bogush, Solomon, 331
Bolshevism, 4
bombings and air raids, 2, 5, 7, 14, 204; Baedekker raids, 145; City of London *see* City of London bombings and raids; Exeter City Hospital, 20; Liverpool (1941), 69, 103; Nottingham (1941), 107, 160; Shanklin bombings *see* Shanklin bombings, Isle of Wight; short stories, 158, 160, 163, 164, 165, 170, 174; sirens, 48, 49, 50, 71, 84, 86, 87, 90, 117, 122, 144, 160; Spain, 117; testimonies, 48, 49, 50, 71, 79, 84, 86, 87, 90, 107, 117, 120, 121, 122, 141, 144, 145; *see also* fires
Borenstein, Nathan (aka Renn), 330
Bounds Green Underground Station bombing (1940), 8
Braach, Bergit (*later* Forchhammer), 45–6
Braham, Sidney Joseph, 158–9
Brainin, Norbert, 167
Breck, Alf, 5
Brewer, Arnold, 331
Brilleslyper, Louis, 17
Bristol Chevra Kadisha (Jewish burial society), 30
British Union of Fascists (BUF), 3–4
Broniatowski, Irmgard, 332
Brooke Road Fire Station, Stoke Newington, 71
Brunner, Walter, 159
Buerk's chemical factory, East Ham, 74–5
Bunzl, Gustav, 332, 333

Calder, Ritchie, 8, 11n
Canada Life Building, Charles II Street (Piccadilly), 74

Caplin, Rebecca, 159
Carason, Abraham, 17
Carlton House Terrace, fire at (1940), 50
Cash, Myer, *384*
Chambers Wharf grain warehouse, Rotherhithe, 46
Charing Cross Hospital, London, 168
Chauveau, Sam, 47–54
Churchill, Winston, 159, 178
City of London bombings and raids, 2, 3, 6, 8, 166, 169, 172, 178, 308; Bomb census accounts, 66n; and Roll of Honour, individuals listed in, 19, 20, 22, 24, 25, 36, 37; 'Second' Blitz (1944), 46, 85; short stories, 157, 158, 159, 165, 167, 169, 171, 172, 173, 177, 178; testimonies, 46, 49, 51, 53, 59, 62, 63, 65, 74–5, 77, 84, 86, 90, 91, 98, 99, 106, 109, 110, 111, 117, 118, 120, 121, 133, 134, 138, 139, 140, 141, 144–5; *see also* bombings and air raids; fires; London Fire Brigade (LFB); London Metropolitan Archives (LMA); *specific regions in London*
Civil Defence (CD), 7, 116, 118, 177, *384*; Jewish service, 2, 6
Civil Injuries Act, 63
'civilian' casualties of 'enemy action,' losses of Firemen and women regarded as, 8
Clements, Leonard, 55–6
Clifford, Jack (aka Jacob Cohen), *334*
Clydeside area (Scotland), 2, 27
Coe, Robert, 178n
Cohen, David, 17, *23*, 28, 160
Cohen, George Leslie, 17–18
Cohen, Harry, *334*
Cohen, Henry (Isidore), *later* Henry Coe, 159, *334, 335*
Cohen, Isaac, 18
Cohen, Lewis, 159–60, *336*

Cohen, Mendel, 160, *336*
Cohen, Monty, 18
Cohen, Simon, 18, 34
Commonwealth War Graves Commission (CWGC), website, 8, 13
Communist Party (CP), 137, 138, 150
comradeship, 122–3
conscientious objectors, 174
Cook, George, 162
Copitch, Goodman 'Tony,' 165, 166, *336*
Corby, Jacob Woolf(e), 18, *19*
Cornhill fire (London, 1941), 52
Coronation Flats/Imperial Avenue disaster (1940), 119
Coster, Albert Victor, 19
Coster, Harry, 19
Courage High; a History of Firefighting in London (Holloway), 10n
Cramer, Jack, *337*
Cricklewood Broadway, London, 97, 98
Crutched Friars (sub-station, East London), 133
Curfew for Aliens, 162
CWGC *see* Commonwealth War Graves Commission (CWGC)

D Day Landings (6 June 1944), 99, 111
Darke, Bob, 150
Davies, Howard, 66n
Davis, Cyril, *346*; BEM, *346*
Davis, Maurice, 25
Demarne, Cyril, 13, 41n
Dennis pumps, 74
Denton, Harry, *337*
Deutsch/Deutsch, Alec, *337*
Deutsch/Deutsch, Israel, 19, *20*, 39, 158
Dloogatz/Douglas, Sylvia, *338, 339*
Docks areas, 50, 53, 71, 74, 75, 79, 80, 83, 89, 90, 98, 104, 106, 111, 139, 140, 142, 164, 172,

178; Chambers Wharf, 46; East India Docks, East London, 150, 367; Hammett's Wharf, 142; King George V Docks, London, 120, 121; New Fresh Wharf, 53; Newport, 175; Rum Quay Dock, London, 110; St Katherine's Dock, London, 111, 118, 120, 139; Swansea, 175; Victoria Docks, London, 121; West India Docks, 25; Whisky Wharf, 75
Donn, Renee (aka Glambotsky), 4, *340*
'Doodlebug,' 86
Dorff/Beer, Sylvia, *386*
'Dunkirk Little Ships,' 106

East End, London, 3, 4, 47, 50, 79, 83, 98, 114, 117, 121, 122, 137, 142, 166, 173; Jewish people living in, 2, 5
East London Advertiser, 7
East London Rubber Company, Shoreditch, 49
Ehrengott, Solomon and Bella, 57
Eisner, Gisela (née Spanglet), 160
Electric Trailer pumps, 161
Elizabeth II, Queen, 151
Ellis, David Louis, 161, *340*, *341*
Emden, Miriam 'Dolly,' 20
'enemy action,' casualties caused by, 8, 19, 40
Enemy Aliens, 93, 161
Engelsman, Solomon, 161
Enlander, Sidney, *341*
enrolment in the Fire Service, by Jewish men and women, 3
Errington, Harry/Ehrengott, 40, 57–66; George Cross event (September, 1940), 62–3; George Cross, x, 40, 58, 60
Erskine, Rivie, 161
European Central Inland Transport Organisation (ECITO), 114
Evans, Eva, *350*
Evans, Philip (aka Even), *342*

Exeter, Devon, 26, 64, 174, *345*; bombing of, 20, *21*, 145
Exeter City Hospital bombing (1942), 20, *21*

Fabian, Steffi, *342*, *343*
factories/plants, 387–8
Fairclough Street (AFS substation), London, 2
Falkson, Daniel, *343*
families, serving together, 3
family narratives, 2, 9n, 13
Farago, Nicholas, 161
fascism, Britain, 3–4, 47
Feld, Hans Nathan, 162, *343*
Feldman, Hyman, 14, 20, 162
Feldman, Jack, 64
Feldman, Louis, 14, 20, 162
Feldman, Rae, *344*
Fieldman, Larry, 170–1
Fieldman, Rae (née Lubart), 170–1, *344*
Fine, Betty/Betsy (aka Rubens), *344*
Fine, Solomon, 162, 175
Fire and Water: an NFS Anthology (Ingham), 392
Fire Brigade, 1, 3, 4; discussion groups, 141–2; see also London Fire Brigade (LFB)
Fire Brigade Union (FBU), 141
Fire Guards, 1, 7, 160, 164, 377
Fire Officers, 71, 78, 89, 103, 125, 139; Chief/Deputy Chief, 25, 75, 95, 103, 133, *331*
Fire Service, 181, 182; anti-Semitism in, 3, 4, 5–6, 7, 10n, 78, 79, 87, 138, 145, 389–92; artists, 318; records, 2–3; see also London Fire Brigade (LFB)
Fire Services College, Moreton-in-the-Marsh, 65
Fireman Benevolent Society, 131
Firemen and women: leaving the AFS by 1940–41, 14; lists, 2–3; losses regarded as 'civilian'

casualties, 8; recruitment from the ranks of the Navy, 5
fires: short stories, 157, 159–60, 162, 165, 167, 173, 175; testimonies, 49–54, 55, 61, 62–3, 67–8, 69, 71, 78, 79, 85, 90, 94, 106, 109, 110, 111, 116, 117, 118, 119, 133, 135–6, 139–47, 150–1; *see also* bombings and air raids; City of London bombings and raids
Fires Were Started (film on Fire Service by Ministry of Information), 7–8
Firewatchers, 1, 2, 7, 9, 14, 241, 273, 304, 314, 321, 323, 390; short stories, 158, 161, 162, 166–7, 172–3, 173; testimonies, 121, 140
First World War, 1, 2, 3, 58, 77; *see also* Second World War
'Flying Columns,' 145
Fohrenwald Displaced Persons camp, Germany, 383
Forchhammer, Bergit (*previously* Braach), 45–6
Fox, Andrew, 31
Fox, Max, 344
Frank, Anne, 55
Franklin, Clarence Colman 'Frank,' 344
Franklin, Jack 'John,' 162–3
Franks, Louis, 344
Freeman, Philip, 20, 21
Friedberg, Michael, 163
Friedman, Daniel, 20
Frischler, Ernst/Frinton, 163–4
Frumkin, Louisa 'Libby,' 164, 345
Fry, H., 9n
furriers, 185

Gabriel, Sidney, 67–8
Gaidelman, Benjamin, 22
Gassman-Sherr, Rosalie, 164; BEM, 164, 221
Gatoff, Zelda, 345

Geller, Asher 'Arthur,' 165
George Cross, 40, 58, 65
George Medal, 129, 300
Gevelb, Morris, 22
Gevelb, Sydney, 22
Gibbens, Bryan, 166
Gilbert, Hyman, 22, 69
Gilbert, Joe, 71–2
Gilbert, Nellie (*previously* Silverstone), 69
Gilbert, Richard, 7
Glantzpe(i)gel, Harry F A (aka Lewis), 22, 23
Glaskie, Harold Basil, 382
Glass, Barnett 'Benny,' 345
Gold, Alfred Bernard, 164, 345
Gold, Dave, 79, 81n
Gold, Manny, 73–6
Goldberg, Carl, 39
Goldberg, John, 23
Goldberg, Julius 'Judd,' 35, 164–5, 380, 381
Goldberg, Samuel, 345
Golden, Herbert Benjamin Henry, 23–4, 165
Golders Green fire station, London, 2
Goldman, Sidney Solly, 123n
Goldschmidt, Erol, 24
Goldsmith, B., 24
Goldsmith, George Eric (aka Goldschmitt), 24
Goldsmith, Neil, 24
Goldstein, Morris, 24
Goldstone, Morris, 165–6, 378
Goodman, Edwin, 24
Goodman, Joshua, 24
Goodman, Samuel 'Benny,' 166
Goodman, Sonny, 379
Gordon/Cohen, Jack, 25
Gould, Tommy, 66n
Grant, Barnett 'Barney,' 345
Grant, Gertie 'Gerry,' 346
graves, locating, 8, 13–14, 30
Great Synagogue, Cheetham (Manchester), 7

Green, Isidore, 166
Greenbaum, Aubrey, 11n
Greenbaum, Solly, 390
Greenberg, Barnett 'Barney,' 25, 26
Greenberg, Harry, 26
Greenberg, Joseph, 8, 26, 151n
Greenberg, Nat, 26, 27
Grossman, Philip, 346
Guise, Solly, 380, 381
Gush, Emmanuel, 26
Guttenberg/Godfrey, Samuel, 77–81

Haggerston School sub-station, Queensbridge Road, 138, 145, 146
Hailstone, Bernard, 130
Haimovitch, Izik and Itke, 101
Halon, Lawrence Isaac, 346
Hammett's Wharf, London, 142
Harris, Enid, 385
Harris, Harry, 346; BEM, 232, 346
Harris, Henry, 26–7; BEM, 232, 346
Harris, Joel, 41
Harris, Oscar Edward, 347
Harrison, Myre/Moier, 27
Hart, Henry 'Harry,' 347
Hart, Mick 'Michael Isaac,' 347
Hart/Hartz, Sidney, 83–4
Hedwig Klopstock, Eva (later Evans), 168
Heim, Georg, 166–7, 348
Heiser, Aaron (Harry), 3, 14, 27
Heiser, Jacob, 3, 14, 27
Heiser/Hayes, William, 348
Hemel Hempstead, American Flying Fortress clash near, 145–6
Hichberger, Martin, 5, 85–6
Hitler, Adolf, 138
Hollingshead, John, 62
Hollis, Barry, 13, 41n
Holloway, Sally, 10n
Holmes, Richard, 54
Holocaust, 9, 61, 148, 160
Holton, Shirley, 178n
Home Guard, 6

Homelite pumps, 46
hook ladder test, 149
horseplay, 5
Hort, Abraham, 318
Howard, Ruth, 178n
Hurst, Renee (née Gordon), 87–8
Hutchinson Square Camp, Douglas, 159
Hyams, Mick, 167
Hydes, H., 134
hydrants, water, 49, 52, 67, 68, 75, 118, 139, 154, 169

I, Witness (History Channel film), 54
In the Highest Degree of Odious: Detention Without Trial in Wartime Britain (Simpson), 10n
incendiaries, 48, 167, 169, 175, 176, 196, 197, 303, 313, 388; short stories, 158, 160; testimonies, 50, 94, 121, 140, 150
Ingham, H.S., 148n, 392
Isaacs, Leslie Walter Joseph, 27–8
Isle of Wight, Shanklin bombings *see* Shanklin bombings, Isle of Wight

Jackson, William, 169
Jacobs, Leslie Alfred, 28
Jacobs, Margaret 'Peggy' Sara (née Joseph), 89–91; BEM, 241
Jacobs, Philip, 348
Jacobs lager factory, Tower Hill, 158
Jacobson, Fay (née Cohen), 178n
Jennings, Humphrey, 7–8
The Jewish Chronicle (JC), 1, 2, 6, 7, 13, 23
Jewish Free School (JFS), Bell Lane, 3, 319
Jewish Military Museum, 13
Jewish Refugee Council, 9
The Jewish Telegraph, 21
Jones, Goronwy, 175
Joseph, Arthur Wolfe, 348

Kaggervin, Belgium, 56

Kalisky, Leslie, *348*
Kaufman, Izzy 'George,' *349*
Kaufman, Nathaniel, *349*
Kaufmann, Eric Alexander, 93–4
Kay, Adolphus 'Alf,' *349*
Kay, Sylvia, 5, 95
Keep Smiling (song, by Ben Levinson), 108
Keiner, Chaim, 167
Kent, Michelle, *367*
Kerbel, Evelyn, 167
Kerbel, Joe, 167, *349*
Kindertransport, 85, 160, 173, *343*
Kings Cross fire, London, 139–40
The King's Most Loyal Enemy Aliens (Fry), 9n
klaxon, 86
Klopstock, Felix, 168
knots, tying, 115
Kol Nidre service (Yom Kippur), at Fire Station, 7
Korn, Jack Jacob, *351*
Krisman, Audrey, 97, 98
Krisman, Jack Noah, 97–9
Krotosky/Greene, Nita, *351*
Krugolski, Adelbert H., 10n
Kruyer, Phillip 'Philli,' *351*

ladders, ascending, 115
Lakumsky-Isaac, Benjamin (*later* Lakum), *352*
Lambeth, London, 158
Lancaster Bombers, 63
Landau, Noel, 22, 101–4; BEM, 22, 104, 251
Landau, Oscar and Debora, 101
landmines, 9, 98, 99, 121
Lang, Samuel, *352*, *353*
Lappin, John, 103
Lattner/Lettner, Ascher/Arthur (David) Davis, 28, 29
Lattner/Lettner, Erna Helen, 28
Lennick, Hyman Marks, 28
Lesser, Morris, 79
The Lesson of London (Calder), 8, 11n

Levenson, Albert, 29
Leveson, Leslie, 105–6
Levinson, Ben, 107–8
Levy, Abraham, 29
Levy, Albert 'Bert,' 8, 109–12
Levy, Alf, 168
Levy, Harold, 168
Levy, Myer 'Mick,' *353*
Levy, S. (Revd), 7
Levy, Samuel, 29–30
Lewin, Hetty, 30, *31*
Lewis, Abraham (aka Bookatz), 30, *31*, *32*, 123n, 168–9
Libbert, Samuel, 32, *33*, *34*, 169–70
Lieberman, Solly, *377*
Lipman, Barney, *355*
Lipman, David, *353*, *354*, *355*
Lipman, Hymie, 178n
Liverpool Blitz (1941), 69, 103
Liverpool Street Station fire (1941), 84
Lloyd-Elliott, Martin, 66n, 91n
Lockyear, Arthur, 66n
The London Blitz: A Fireman's Tale (Demarne), 13
London County Council War Diary, 393
London Fire Brigade (LFB), 1, 3, 113, 145; HQ (Southwark) *see* Southwark, LFB HQ at; LFB/AFS/NFS boundaries, 141; Members Association, 46n; records *see* records/registers
London Firefighter magazine, 28
London Gazette, 60, 66n
London Metropolitan Archives (LMA), 13, 30, 36, 40–1; LFB Registers, 10n; *see also* records/registers
London Stock Exchange (LSE), 48, 49, 50, 54
London's Burning (Richardson), 4, 10n, 390–2
Lowenthal, Julia, *356*
Lubart, Rae (*later* Fieldman), 170

Ludgate Hill, fire at Bravingtons jewellers, 119
Lustig, Morris Samuel, 7, 171

Malin, Renee (née Titton), 113–14
Maltman, Stephanie, 3, 4, 8, 28, *31*, 171, 389–92
Manches, Joshua, *357*
Manning, Joan, 123n
Marks, A., *357*
Marks, Ella, 178n
Marks, Judith, *357*
Marks, Leonard (Jonas), 115–16
Marks, Nat, 392
Marks, Solomon, *357*
Marlow Road (East Ham) Cemetery, 8, 14
Martin, Bernard, *358*
Martin, Leslie, *358*
Marylebone, London, 7
Massow, Jesse Thomas, 32
Matz, David, *377*
McDuell, Superintendent, 7
memoirs, 3
Mesnick, Hyman ('Hymie'), 117–23
Michaelson, Victor, 34, 171–2
Miller, Leslie, *358*
Miller, Phyllis, *384*
Millet, Morris, 34
Millet, Percy, 34
Mitcham cemetery, GWGC headstone at, 8
mobile pumps, 176
Moont, Louis, *359*
Morris, Harry, 34
Morris, Marie/Miriam (née Garcia), 125
Mosleyites, 139, 145
Mount Pleasant Sorting Office, Holborn, 171, 260
Munday, John, 162
Myers, Margaret, 35
Myers, Ruth (née Carne), 127

Nabarro, Andrew Nunes, 129–30; George Medal, xi, 129

Nachod, North East Bohemia, 319
Nadell, Manuel, *360*
Namur, Belgium, 147
Natali, Edward, *360*
Nathan, Abraham 'Alf,' 131
Nathan, Morris, 133–4
National Fire Service (NFS), 1, 80, 118; LFB/AFS/NFS boundaries, 141; short stories, 170, 174
'natural causes,' death by, 40
Newman, Frances, 178n
Nichols, Gerry, 29
9/11 terrorist attacks, death of Jewish Firemen in, 319
Nissenthal family, *360*
Norton Folgate fire (London, 1941), 51
Nottingham Blitz (1941), 107, 160
Nyman, Issac, 35
Nyman, Lewis, *361*
Nyman, Muriel, 172

'Occurrence Book,' 154
O'Connor, B., 165
Old Castle Street fire (London, 1941), 52
Oliver, Jack, 172, *361*
Ordeal by Fire (Wassey), 10n
Ososky/Osbourne, Simon, *361*
Osterer, Sarah, 35
Our Girls (Demarne), 13
Oxford Circus, London, 58–9
Oxford Street fire, John Lewis, 151

Palestine Mandate Auxiliary Fire Service, Second World War, 9
Palmer, Eric, *361*
Parker, Bob, 8, 11n
Parker, Henry, 8
parliamentary documents, 321–4
Patronovski, Akivah 'Keeva,' *371*
Paul, Alexander, 35
Pearl, Hazel, *362*
Pearl, Pizer, 36
Peierls, Rudolf, 135–6
Perlmann, Rev'd, 7

Perlmutter, Arnold (aka Philips), 172–3
Peter Street (near Piccadilly, London), 9
Peters, Leslie, *380*, *381*
Peters, Phyllis, *362*
'phoney war' (1939–40), 47, 61, 109, 117, 135, 149
Piccadilly, London, 9
Piccadilly, Manchester, 35, 165
Pinner, Alexander 'Sunny,' 173, *362*
pits, 147–8
Plaut, Manfred, 173, *362*
Pollack, Hyman, 161
Pollins, Jack, *362*, *363*
Pollins, Myer, *363*, *364*
Poplar, London, 25, 50
Portsmouth, Hampshire, 78–81
Portsmouth Evening News, 130
Post Traumatic Stress Syndrome (PTSD), 119
Poulsen/Paulsen, Charles (aka Kopel Polsky), 137–48, 181
Prachzker, Myer Isaac, *366*
Prager, Peter, 173, *364*
Press, Jack, *364*, *366*
Prever, Barney (aka Brifor), 174, *365*
Priestley, J.B., 178n
propaganda, British Fascist anti-Jewish, 3
pumps, 182; Bruce Road, Poplar, 387; Dennis, 74; Electric Trailer, 161; Homelite, 46; mobile, 176; short stories, 158, 160; stirrup, 161, 175; testimonies concerning, 46, 48, 50, 51, 53, 54, 61, 71, 74, 86, 93, 120, 133, 138, 139, 142, 144, 145, 150

Queen Mother (Elizabeth Angela Marguerite Bowes-Lyon), 79–80

Rabinowitz, Eliezer (Rabbi), 36
Rabinowitz, Louis (Rabbi), 36
Rabinowitz, Manuel (Mendel), aka Rabinowsky, 36

racial stereotypes, breaking down, 5
radios, lack of, 167
Randal, Max, 36
Raphael, Jack, 36
Rath, Doris (*later* Moritz), 174, *366*
records/registers, 10n, 13; Record of Honour 185–319; Registration Cards, 2, 25, 148n, 185; St Marylebone Civil Defence Records, Westminster Council Archives, 65; *see also* archives
Red Cross, 8, 9
Ree, Harry Alfred, 174–5
refugees, Jewish, 6–7, 9
Remembrance Day, 123
research techniques, 2–3
Richardson, Maurice, 4, 5–6, 10n, 390–2
RMMV *Athlone Castle*, 80
Robinson, Captain William Leefe, 81n
Roll of Honour, 13–41; details of individuals, 14–41; graves, details of, 13–14; Jewish casualties, 14; sources, 13
roof spotters, 48–9
Rose, Maurice Sydney, 36–7
Roseman, Hyman, 37
Rosen, Rabbi Kopel, 170
Rosenberg, Morris, *367*
Rosenthal, S., 318
The Roundthreads (newsletter of retired LFB Members Association), 46n
Royal Air Force (RAF), 78, 118, 145, 158, 161, 170
Royal Fusiliers (Jewish Legion), 175, *369*
Rubins, Betsy, 175

Sacks, Lord Jonathan, 164
Salaman, Claire Elizabeth, 175, *368*
Salkeld, Frederick Charles, 37
Salvation Army, 140
Sampson, Michael, *368*
Samuel, Stuart, 104n

Savile Row, London, 59
Schneider, Ernest Adam, 37–8
'Schonfeld' kinder, 159
Schooler, Alexander, 38
Schwartzberg, Israel, 38
'Second' Blitz (1944), 46, 85
Second World War, 1, 40, 46, 47, 181; Palestine Mandate Auxiliary Fire Service, 9; 'phoney war' (1939–40), 47, 61, 109, 117, 135, 149; *see also* bombings and air raids; City of London bombings and raids; fires; First World War; Hitler, Adolf; testimonies
Segal, Bert, 368
Segal, Beulah, 368
Segal, Robin, 368
Serota, Louis, 368
Shalet, Philip, 369
Shank, David, 369
Shanklin bombings, Isle of Wight, 7, 17, 22, 171; war memorials, 23, 28
Share, Morris/Maurice, 38
Shaw, Henry E., 134
Sheffield firemen, naming on synagogue memorial, 13
Sheldon, Benjamin Joseph/John, 38–9
Shellhaven, London, 110
Sheratsky, Morris/Moshe (aka Sherrick), 175–6, 369
Sherman, Lou, 120, 149–51
Shiman, Jack (Jacob), 370
Shoreditch, London, 49, 161, 163
Shorters Court, Drapers Hall (London), 48, 54n
Sifrei Torah (Scrolls of the Law), 162
Silver, Jack, 28, 370
Silverstone, Nellie (*later* Gilbert), 69
Simmons, Noah (Norman), 370
Simon, Harry, 39
Simons, Robert Stanley, 41
Simpson, A.W. Brian, 10n

Sinclair House, Redbridge, 385
Singer, Ronald, 176
sirens, air raid, 48, 49, 50, 71, 84, 86, 87, 90, 117, 122, 144, 160
Six Day War (1967), 54
Slipman, Alec, 39
'Slippery Sam' (gambling game), 115, 116
Sloan, Reuben, 370
Smith, Alexander, 19, 39
SOE (Special Operations Executive), 174, 179n
Sofia, Bulgaria, 319
Soho Fire Station, London, 58
Soho Ghetto, 71
Solomon, Phil, 371
Solomon, Samuel, 368
Solomon, Woolf, 371; BEM, 298
Southwark, LFB HQ at, 10n, 13, 28; Museum, 45, 48, 54, 65
Spanish Civil War, 4, 10n
Special Operations Executive (SOE), 174, 179n
Speck, Isaac, 176, 372
Spender, Stephen, 6, 10n, 97, 392
Spicker, Sylvia, 372
Spira, M. (Revd), 2
Spiro, Esther, 371
Sprague, James, 21
SS *Malakand* (ship), 69, 103
St Katherine's Dock, London, 111, 118, 120, 139
St Marylebone Civil Defence Records, Westminster Council Archives, 65
St Paul's Cathedral, London, 98, 177
Stamford Hill, London, 161
Steinman, Teddy, 176
Stepney, London, 7, 19, 20, 22, 26, 34, 37, 67, 122, 137
Stern, Harry, 177
Sternheim/Stenham, Charlotte ('Lottie') Eva (née Kohn), 8–9, 11n, 372
stirrup pumps, 161, 175

Stock, Joseph Simon, 177
Stock Exchange *see* London Stock Exchange (LSE)
Stoke Newington, Kingsland fire station, 110
Stone, Philip Maurice, 372
Strange, Alfred, 151n
Street Fire Patrols (SFPs), 1, 387
Sussman, Helen, 39

tailoring, 59, 73, 76, 172
Tasho, Harold Alan, 40
taxi drivers, London, 3, 137–8, 148n, 149, 151; Jewish, 10n, 158, 163, 391
Terry, John, 61, 62–3, 64
testimonies: Braach, Bergit, 45–6; Chauveau, Sam, 47–54; Clements, Leonard, 55–6; Errington, Harry/Ehrengott, 57–66; Gabriel, Sidney, 67–8; Gilbert, Hyman, 69; Gilbert, Joe, 71–2; Gold, Manny, 73–6; Guttenberg/Godfrey, Samuel, 77–81; Hart/Hartz, Sidney, 83–4; Hichberger, Martin, 85–6; Hurst, Renee (née Gordon), 87–8; Jacobs, Margaret 'Peggy' Sara (née Joseph), 89–91; Kaufmann, Eric Alexander, 93–4; Kay, Sylvia, 95; Krisman, Jack Noah, 97–9; Landau, Noel, 101–4; Leveson, Leslie, 105–6; Levinson, Ben, 107–8; Malin, Renee (née Titton), 113–14; Marks, Leonard (Jonas), 115–16; Mesnick, Hyman ('Hymie'), 117–23; Morris, Marie/Miriam (née Garcia), 125; Myers, Ruth (née Carne), 127; Nabarro, Andrew Nunes, 129–30; Nathan, Abraham 'Alf,' 131; Nathan, Morris, 133–4; Peierls, Rudolf, 135–6; Poulsen/Paulsen, Charles, 137–48; Sherman, Lou, 149–51; Wilner, Reuben, 153–5

Thames River, 51, 71, 106, 120, 142, 150, 178; low water levels, 120, 123n, 150
Thameshaven oil refinery, near Chatham, 118, 150, 204
37 Fire Forces: Fire and Rescue, S.E. London, 1941–46, 13
Tisman, Albert, 372
Tobias, Alan, 30
Tokenhouse Yard fire, near Bank of England (1940), 50–1
Tooting cemetery, GWGC headstone at, 8
Tottenham Court Road, London, 36, 71, 91
Tower Hamlets, London, 77
Tower of London, 150, 158; Tower Bridge, 49, 51; Tower Hill, 51, 118, 119, 123n, 158, 169, 193, 216
Trinity House Trust, 169
Tyson Street station, 377

Under Fire (Sam Chauveau), 53–4
United Synagogue graves website, 14
Upper Thames Street fire, 1941, 52
Usiskin, David, 177

Van Severen, Ed 319
V1 and V2 aircraft, 9; short stories, 161, 168, 172; testimonies, 46, 53, 76, 80, 86, 111, 114, 122
Venturi principle, 161
Viener, David, 40
Viktoriaschule (now Bettinaschule) High School, Frankfurt, 45
Visokle, Michael (aka West), 373
Vogler, Hilary, 178n
volunteering of Jews for Fire Service, 6

WAFS Training offices, Highbury, 1
Wagerman, Alfred, 387
Wallington, Neil, 66n
Wand, Myer, 40, 62
Wander, Mendel, 178, 377

Wapping Lane, London, 49
The War Illustrated magazine, 130
Wassey, Michael, 5, 10n
Watkins, Bert, 121
Waxman, Reuben, *373*
Weinstein, Morris, *374*
Weinstein, Nathan, *374*
Wellclose Square (AFS substation), London, 2, 8, 110
Wellington Bombers, 173
West Central Jewish Youth Club, 61
West End Jewish community, 59
West Hampstead fire station, London, 2, *356*
West Hill Fire Station, Wandsworth, 27-8
Westminster Council Archives, St Marylebone Civil Defence Records, 65
Wheeler, George, 4-5, 389-92
When Sirens Sounded (Astor), 13
When the Bells Go Down (film), 111
Whisky Wharf explosion, 1940, 75
Whitchapel, London, 2, 3, 4, 6, 7, 158; Fire Station, Commercial Road, 22, 133, 149, 150, 170, *327*, *383*
Willesden Jewish Civil Defence workers, 2
Wilner, Reuben, 153-5
Wilson, Leslie, 178, *374*
Winston, David, *375*
Wolff, Herbert Thomas, 40
Wolkoff, Anna, 4, 10n
women, in Auxiliary Fire Service, 1
Woolworths fire, Roman Road (Bow, London, 1941), 52
working-class Jews, 4
works brigades, 387
World Within World (Spender), 10n
Wormwood Street (near Liverpool Street), London, 109

Zage(a)rman, Phillip, 40
Zeppelins, 59, 77
Zetter, Moses 'Michael,' *375*
Zimmerman, Derrick David, 178, *376*